PLAYERS'
SCEPTERS

THE TRAGICK-COMEDY

OF

TITUS OATES,

Who sometime went under the Notion of The Salamanca Doctor;

Who being Convicted of PERJURY

And several other Crimes, at the *Kings-Bench Bar*, *Westminster*, May 16; 1685, had his Sentence to
Stand in the *Pillory*, to be VVhip'd at the *Carts Arse*, and to be sent back to Prison.

When all your Wits, and Antidote your Eyes,
Before you hazard here to play this Prize,
Or gaze (like Eagles) on a Show so rare,
No time brought forth an Object yet so fair;
Lo! here's the Bug Bear-Rampant of the PLOT,
Which *Whig* on *Tory* (in a Shamm) Begot;
Here A-la-mode the Guardian of the Land
In a New-fashion'd Pulpit now doth stand;
The Tub's o're-whelm'd, and all the Hoops are flung,
And Deput-*Jack* he peeps out through the *Bung*.
Barensheb's here, the Star of *Englands* Sky,
Deciphet'd now *The Son of PERJURY*;
Th'*Ægyptean-Cow*, the Oaten-blasted Blade,
Which hath (these several Years) eat up our Trade;
The *States* Anat-mist, th' *Church* Confusion,
Who Dream'd a *Plot*, and Swore it was a *Vision*;
A Doctor who Degree did ne'r Commence,
A Rhetoritian that spoke never Sence;
Like *Proteus* he still changeth to the time,
His Pulse and Temper suits with any Clime;
His Birth's equivocal, by Generation
Seditions By-Blow, Loyaltys privation;
A Linsey-Woolsey *Emp'rick* of the State,
That hugs the Church, and knocks it o're the Pate.
He stands in state, and well becomes his station,
Using a Truckling-Stool for Recreation;
Now should he, in contempt of *Peter's* Chair,
Leap from the Pillory to the Three-leg'd Mare,
And with *Empedocles* desire to be
But Canoniz'd an Oaten-Deity,
He would spring up (but that he is a Sot)
A Mandrake, to conceive another PLOT.

His Crime no *Alas* can ballance with a Curse,
For still the *Hydra* doth deserve a worse;
Then let him live a *Minotaur* of Men,
Like *Hora-Corvus* Couchant in his Den;
The Monument of Mischief, and of Sin,
To spread no farther than the Sooterkin
Of old Sedition, set before our Eyes,
As Buoy and Beacon unto Loyalty;
Yet at the Wheels of Fortune let him Dance
A Jigg of Penance that can make him Prance;
Relenting all his Errors (though in vain)
With fruitless wishes calling Time again;
His Face is Brass, his Breech is made of Steel,
And who knows but his Back is made of Stool;
His Soul is proof, perhaps his Body may
Be made of Mettle harder than the Clay;
Then put him to the touch, make *Titus* rore,
The Chase is turn'd, now he's *Son of a W——*
Then conjure him with Eggs and Kennel-Dirt,
And Contradictions that his Mouth did squirt;
To tell his Name, we'l Christian him once yet,
And mold and *Agnum* which can with him sit;
He is no *Doctor*, for by horrid Lies
He cures Sedition, only Tinker-wise.
He is no *Papist*, for he ne'r had Merit,
Nor yet a *Quaker*, for he hath no Spirit.
To keep him from a falsifying face.
He is no *Turk*, for always (like a Swine)
He lov'd to wallow in a Tub of Wine.
No name can fit him, therefore let him bee
The grumbling Ghost of Old Presbitery.

London, Printed by *J. M.* and Published by *Randal Taylor*, MDCLXXXV.

A broadside of 1685 prompted by Titus Oates's perjury conviction illustrates the intermingling of politics, law, and drama in the Restoration. Oates's real troubles are perceived in the fictional form of tragicomedy, though the hostile inventor of this broadside would hardly have appreciated the further comedy provided by Oates's release from prison after the Glorious Revolution and his being awarded a pension of £5 a week by William III.

PLAYERS' SCEPTERS

Fictions of Authority in the Restoration

Susan Staves

University of Nebraska Press
Lincoln and London

*The publication of this book was assisted by a
grant from The Andrew W. Mellon Foundation.*

Library of Congress Cataloging in Publication Data

Staves, Susan, 1942–
  Players' scepters.

  Includes bibliographical references and index.
  1. English drama—Restoration, 1660–1700—History
and criticism.   2. Authority in literature.   3. Great
Britain—Intellectual life—17th century.   I. Title.
PR698.A98S8   822'.4'09   78–24346
ISBN 0–8032–4102–X

Manufactured in the United States of America

CONTENTS

FREQUENTLY CITED WORKS

In order to avoid unnecessary notes to works cited frequently, especially to works cited in more than one chapter, short references are given in parentheses in the text and further bibliographical information is provided here. Law reports are cited from *English Reports*. Particular reports may be found by consulting the *Chart of Reports*, which gives the standard abbreviations and the volume of *English Reports* in which a particular report is reprinted. Statutes are cited from *The Statutes at Large*, ed. Danby Pickering (Cambridge, 1792). Play dates given in the text are dates of first performance, according to *The London Stage, 1660–1800*, 5 vols. in 11, ed. William Van Lennep, et al. (Carbondale, Ill.: Southern Illinois University Press, 1960–68); dates for plays not performed are dates of the first edition. Unless otherwise noted, references in my text to plays and prose works in the editions noted below are to volume and page. Abbreviations used in my text are given in the left margin here.

> Beaumont, Francis and Fletcher, John. *The Works of Beaumont and Fletcher.* 14 vols. Edited by Henry Weber. Edinburgh, 1812.
>
> Behn, Aphra. *The Works of Aphra Behn.* 6 vols. Edited by Montague Summers. London: Heinemann, 1915.
>
> Blackstone, Sir William. *Commentaries on the Laws of England.* 4 vols. 10th ed. London, 1787. References are to book, chapter, and page.

Boyle, Roger. *The Dramatic Works of Roger Boyle.* 2 vols. Edited by William Smith Clark, II. Cambridge, Mass.: Harvard University Press, 1937.

Crowne, John. *The Dramatic Works.* 4 vols. Edited by J. Maidment and W. H. Logan. Edinburgh, 1873–77.

Dryden, John. *The Works of John Dryden.* 18 vols. Edited by Sir Walter Scott and George Saintsbury. Edinburgh, 1882–93.

HPC   Hale, Matthew. *Historia Placitorum Coronae: The History of the Pleas of the Crown.* 2 vols. Published from MSS by Sollom Emlyn. Edited by George Wilson. London, 1778. References are to part, chapter, and page.

Hobbes, Thomas. *Leviathan, or the Matter, Forme and Power of a Commonwealth Ecclesiastical and Civil.* Edited by Michael Oakeshott. Oxford: Blackwell, 1960. References are to part, chapter, and page.

Lee, Nathaniel. *The Works of Nathaniel Lee.* 2 vols. Edited by B. Stroup and Arthur L. Cooke. New Brunswick, N.J.: Scarecrow Press, 1954–55.

Locke, John. *The Works of John Locke.* 10 vols. 1823. Reprint ed. Darmstadt, Scientia Verlag, 1963.

Locke, John. *Two Treatises of Government.* Edited by Peter Laslett. Cambridge: Cambridge University Press, 1967. References are to treatise and paragraph number.

Otway, Thomas. *The Works of Thomas Otway.* 2 vols. Edited by J. C. Ghosh. 1932. Reprint ed. Oxford: Clarendon Press, 1968.

Parl. Hist.   *The Parliamentary or Constitutional History of En-*
(Before   *gland* [720–1660]. 10 vols. London, 1751–61.
1660)

Parl. Hist.   *The Parliamentary History of England from the*
(After   *Earliest Period to the Year 1803.* 36 vols. Edited by
1659)   William Cobbett. London, 1806–20.

POAS   *Poems on Affairs of State: Augustan Satirical Verse, 1660–1714.* 7 vols. Edited by George de Forest Lord, et al. New Haven, Conn.: Yale University Press, 1963–75.

Shadwell, Thomas. *The Complete Works of Thomas Shadwell.* 5 vols. Edited by Montague Summers. 1927. Reprint ed. New York: B. Blom, 1968.

Southerne, Thomas. *The Works of Mr. Thomas Southerne.* 2 vols. London, 1721.

S.T.   *A Complete Collection of State Trials.* 21 vols. Compiled by T. B. Howell. London, 1816.

Stephen, Sir James Fitzjames. *A History of the Criminal Law of England.* 3 vols. London, 1883.

Wycherley, William. *The Complete Plays of William Wycherley.* Edited by Gerald Weales. New York University Press, 1967.

INTRODUCTION

Authority is the power to command obedience or assent and the power to create obligation. Authority decrees what must be done or believed. In a prephilosophical culture the only real authority is custom. Rites must be performed in a certain way because they have been performed that way before; we know which spirit controls the rain because our people have known his name for a long time. In the Middle Ages, the source of all authority was thought to be God. It was God who elected popes and kings, his vice-regents, and gave them their authority on earth, God who inspired Scripture and gave it its authority. Now, though we find such phrases as "political authority" or "the authority of the facts" intelligible, it is more difficult to identify an ultimate source of authority or even to agree that such a source exists.

The idea of authority changed in two related ways in the early modern period: it was detached from the hierarchical structure of feudal society and it was secularized. Authority no longer came down from above, from God to king, from priest to people. It was understood, instead, to originate in the people or in the needs and ends of individuals.

The protestant Reformation attacked hierarchy within the church, abolishing pope and bishops and stressing instead the priesthood of all believers. Radical protestant sects declared there should be no separate caste of priests. Some congregations proceeded to elect their own ministers; others preferred to make no formal distinction between preacher and people. Radical protestantism also attacked ordinary social hierarchy. The House of Lords was abolished in England during the interregnum; a number of radical sects allowed women to preach.

Locke justified revolution by ascribing political sovereignty to the people. At the end of his *Two Treatises of Government* he says that the people may delegate political power, but that such power "by the Miscarriages of those in Authority" may be forfeited, and then, "upon the Forfeiture of their Rulers, or at the Determination of the Time set, *it reverts to the Society,* and the People have a Right to act as Supreme, and continue the Legislative in themselves, or erect a new Form, or under the old form place it in new hands, as they think good" (2, 243).

In the early modern period the idea of authority was dissociated from the idea of God. Traditional natural law theory as articulated by Aquinas gave way to a new moral philosophy independent of the will of God and revealed religion. The church fathers had considered man's reason clouded or imperfect because of the Fall and maintained that without the supernatural light of revelation man could not discern the moral imperatives of the law of nature. Such supernatural light, however, appeared less and less necessary. Around the middle of the seventeenth century the Cambridge Platonists emphasized the power of reason to discover natural law and to differentiate between true and false religion. Benjamin Whichcote, one of the Platonists, declared, "The Reason of a man's Mind *must* be satisfied; no man *can* think against it."[1] Reason became the rule of interpreting Scripture instead of Scripture the rule of reason. In 1662 the Bishop of Exeter was confident "nothing is by *Scripture* imposed upon us to be believed which is flatly *contradictive* to *right Reason* and the suffrage of all our *senses.*"[2] By 1699 the third Earl of Shaftesbury said explicitly that moral ideas like justice and goodness are known prior to and independently of the idea of God and articulated his doctrine of the moral sense within each man. The order that obliged men turned out to be immanent rather than transcendent.

One of the clearest manifestations of the dissociation of the idea of God from the idea of authority in the early modern period is the transfer of powers from ecclesiastical courts to temporal courts.

Courts enforce law, but there is always a question of what law or whose law they enforce. Ecclesiastical courts are intended to enforce God's law, temporal courts to enforce the laws of the secular state. Much of the loss of jurisdiction by the ecclesiastical courts in the seventeenth century came about because they were perceived as less concerned with the rights of subjects than the common law courts and because they were attacked by protestants as remnants of popish domination. The protestant reformers, of course, had no desire to secularize the legal system. What they favored was the kind of Christian state embodied in the theocratic governments of Geneva and a few New England settlements. Nevertheless, their attacks on the English ecclesiastical courts did contribute substantially to the transfer of power to the temporal courts.

This transfer is most evident in the treatment of a class of crimes that may be called crimes against order. Many common crimes are crimes against persons or crimes against property, but behavior that does not necessarily injure persons or property may also be stigmatized as criminal in a particular society because it threatens the order of that society. To this class of crimes belong treason, sedition, blasphemy, heresy, perjury, bribery, fornication, sodomy, and other so-called crimes against nature. If we study the history of these crimes in the seventeenth century we see changes in their treatment that reflect the secularization of authority and its detachment from hierarchical principles. After the Glorious Revolution the doctrine of treason was altered to acknowledge the right of resistance against a tyrannical sovereign. Also, behavior that earlier would have been construed as treasonous began to be prosecuted under the categories of lesser offenses like seditious libel or riot. The rights of defendants in treason trials were protected by legislation. Almost from the beginning of the protestant Reformation in England parliament began to pass statutes against crimes like sodomy and bigamy that previously—and perhaps more logically—had been within the exclusive jurisdiction of the ecclesiastical courts. In the Restoration the temporal courts declared themselves guardians of the morality of the king's subjects and proceeded to punish various sorts of profanity like indecent exposure, obscenity, and blasphemy, not yet even the subjects of statutory prohibition. The order of society was to be defined and defended by the state, not by the church.

Players' Scepters studies the changing fictions of authority in late seventeenth-century England and shows how secular democratic myths of authority replaced religious and feudal myths. Chapter 1 begins by looking briefly at the experiences of the interregnum, not only because the revolution itself attacked earlier beliefs about authority, but also because the experiences of the interregnum continued to affect Englishmen profoundly in the generations that followed. Chapters 2 and 3 consider authority relationships between persons: sovereign and subject in chapter 2; father and child, husband and wife in chapter 3. The relationship between sovereign and subject changed with the Glorious Revolution and the triumph of Whig ideology. When that relationship changed, other authority relationships between persons that had been perceived as analogous were also affected. The old analogies between public authority and domestic authority had to be sacrificed or else new accounts of these domestic relationships had to be invented.

The fourth chapter deals with oaths and vows as signs that obligation to authority is recognized. Older feelings of the religious significance of oaths—indeed, of their magical potency— give way to a modern understanding of oaths as nothing more than emphatic affirmations, mere words. As Samuel Butler wrote, prompted by the experience of the Civil War:

> Oaths are but words, and words but wind,
> Too feeble impliments to bind,
> And hold with deeds proportion, so
> As shadows to a substance do.[3]

The changing understanding of authority is linked to a changing understanding of reality in which the transcendent "realities" words point toward are perceived as less real than the objects of sense perception. This increased nominalism of early modern culture is frequently discussed by historians of philosophy, but it appears with exceptional vividness in the Restoration treatment of perjury and in its attitudes toward evidence in trials where the authority of words confronts the authority of facts. A final chapter examines the demise of God's natural law as an ultimate source of

authority from a more strictly philosophical point of view, tracing
the rise of a secular moral philosophy theoretically independent of
revealed religion.

The method of *Players' Scepters*—if it may be dignified by that
name—requires some indulgence from the reader both because it is
odd and because it is somewhat arbitrary. I began by trying to
understand Restoration drama, trying, for instance, to appreciate
what interest its more peculiar manifestations like heroic plays and
pathetic she-tragedy could have had for their original audiences.
Several recent writers have argued that our view of Restoration
drama has been seriously distorted by too much focus on the
famous comedies of Etherege, Wycherley, and Congreve, and not
enough attention to the wide variety of plays by other writers. A.
H. Scouten, for example, has complained, "modern critics and
commentators . . . give the impression in their criticism that they
have never read any other Restoration plays but those of . . . three
dramatists."[4] Robert Hume has also cautioned, "when we think of
'Restoration comedy' we generally have in mind only a tiny and
atypical part of the whole, and . . . the usual categories (manners,
humours, etc.) and evolutionary assumptions are extremely
misleading."[5] I agree entirely with this position. Articles and
chapters proliferate on *The Man of Mode* while almost everyone
remains mute on Sedley's *Mulberry Garden*, Howard's *Duke of
Lerma*, Crowne's *Ambitious Statesman*, and even Dryden's *Sir
Martin Mar-all*. Literary history is distorted, a few strong plays are
treated to increasingly ingenious overinterpretation, and weak
plays of a few dramatists receive undue attention while strong
plays of others are ignored.

However, although I agree we should read more widely in
Restoration drama, I do not agree with the antiintellectualism also
recently expressed by John Harold Wilson in *A Preface to
Restoration Drama* (1965), James Sutherland in *English Literature
of the Late Seventeenth Century* (1969), and Robert Hume in *The
Development of English Drama in the Late Seventeenth Century*
(1976)—a reaction against what they perceive as the overinterpretation of certain Restoration plays. All three stress the importance of the plays as entertainment and deprecate thoughts of
their profundity. Hume, for example, notes that "some recent

critics have tried to rescue" Restoration drama "by making claims
for profundity and high seriousness" and then separates himself
from this trend by announcing, "the plays are often acute, pointed,
pathetic, or satiric—but very seldom do they probe character
deeply or present ideas which are essentially more than com-
monplaces."[6] Later criticizing Anne Barbeau's *Intellectual Design
of John Dryden's Heroic Plays* (1970), he remarks, "One may ask if
viable stage plays are the place for profound and original
philosophy."[7] Such remarks, it seems to me, set up straw men. Of
course comedies and tragedies are not the place for careful
development of original philosophical arguments. But it is a long
way from saying that to saying they cannot reflect perceptions of
philosophical interest. If "profound and original philosophy" is
going to have a broad impact on a culture it is not going to do so in
the form of Newton's *Principia* or Kant's *Critique of Pure Reason.*
Furthermore, and more important, works of "profound and
original philosophy" are not created in vacuums of pure
ratiocination: the best of them are likely to respond in some way to
the experience of the philosopher in his culture and to attempt to
answer questions raised by that experience. This is particularly
true of political philosophy and moral philosophy.

Players' Scepters tries to understand how changes in ideas about
authority were shaped by common cultural experiences shared by
late seventeenth-century English philosophers, dramatists, lawyers,
M.P.'s, and the less distinguished ladies and gentlemen who were
their audience and clients. From this shared experience, particularly, in this period, political experience, come some common
problems responded to by philosophers and dramatists alike.
Though we are used to influence studies and to books on "intellectual background" and though my book may at times appear
to resemble such books, I do not really see the other cultural
evidence as influence or background to Restoration literature. It
seems perverse to think of Locke or Sir Matthew Hále as
background for Edward Ravenscroft. Some readers, especially
those principally interested in drama, may be tempted to see the
philosophical, legal, or historical material as "theoretical"
material that is then given a "practical application" in the interpretation of the play texts. I do not, however, consider that this

book depends upon such a duality. Indeed, legal ideas do not seem to me in any way more "theoretical" than the ideas expressed in drama; if anything, the law represents a considerably more "practical application" of ideas than tragedy does. Throughout I am trying to discuss changing *fictions* of authority as they are constructed in various areas of thought—in politics, in law, in drama, and so on. My interest is in analyzing what seem to be parallel changes within several different spheres of thought, not in asserting the primacy of one particular sphere and certainly not in implying anything about causality.

The selection of cultural evidence is to some extent arbitrary, influenced partly by my original interest in drama, but not without some common-sense justification. If we want to know what a culture thought about authority, then politics, philosophy, drama, and the law seem more obvious and likely places to look than, say, agriculture or music. Although I indulge in occasional literary excursions outside the drama, since tragedy deals directly with sovereigns and subjects in conflict and comedy with parents and children, husbands and wives, there is more of immediate relevance to say about drama than about lyric poetry. Drama is also a public medium. The legal material is likely to seem least familiar, particularly to readers whose primary concerns are literary. It is, however, exceptionally valuable for the kind of argument about change I am trying to conduct. Poets and philosophers are under no binding obligation to be aware of the state of the art or the state of the question when they produce new work. A poet can write a tragedy that defies all the conventions of tragedy in his period and a philosopher can try to open up an entirely new field of inquiry if he is imaginative enough. Such poets and philosophers, though they may not be well understood by many of their contemporaries, are likely to be praised by posterity for their originality. Judges and lawyers, on the other hand, especially British judges of the seventeenth century, are responsible for knowing what the state of the law is at a particular time and are sensitive to departures from precedent. Though their attachment to precedent can obscure change—since while they are changing they may try to deny they are doing so—it also provides clearer evidence of change when it occurs. Furthermore, the essential conservatism of the law tends to highlight change by keeping it to a relative minimum and—at least over periods of a century or two—by according innovations some stability. For example, verse tragedy may come and go in and out of literary history, but once the temporal courts decide the credibility of prosecution witnesses may be challenged and their sworn testimony discounted, such challenges continue to be allowed. The legal material generally has been too little used by historians.

Players' Scepters invites multitudinous lines of attack. I have tried to do as much reading in contemporary sources and modern scholarship as practicable short of engaging in an infinite regress where writing can never begin, but there is much I have not read. Almost all the areas touched on are subjects of debate in modern scholarship, of revisionist views and counterrevisionist views. Historians have by no means agreed on the significance of the Glorious Revolution; philosophers offer a range of interpretations of Hobbes presenting him as anything from the first genuinely secular political philosopher to a pious Christian squarely in the medieval tradition. It would be impossible to defend my position on all these issues in the course of making another argument; so, though I have tried to profit from the debates, I have usually simply adopted a stance and passed over the debates in silence. The nature of the subject encourages speculation, and I can only hope that the insights to be gained from an unconventionally inclusive look at the culture will earn me a little indulgence for claims that should be expressed more tentatively or documented more fully. In general, I tend to give considerable weight to seventeenth-century opinion and to think that, as contemporaries said, Roman Catholicism did represent a threat to the freedoms of protestant Englishmen, Hobbes was not a pious Christian, and Restoration cuckolding comedies were not morally uplifting. I am probably too inclined here to a Whig view of history, but this may be a useful corrective to the revisionist Tory views expressed in so much modern Restoration and eighteenth-century literary criticism. The case for the piety of various Restoration authors has perhaps already been adequately made.

PLAYERS'
SCEPTERS

united in their detestation of those hypocritical parricides, who, by
sanctified pretences, had so long disguised their treasons.[2]

In the 1640s especially there was much instability and
dislocation. Most obviously, many people simply left the homes
their families had lived in for generations. Soldiers who had never
in their lives been further than the nearest market town went
trecking over the country under officers who were sometimes
forced to dismiss their troops after they had led them hundreds of
miles from home. Soldiers deserting or disbanded because there
was no more money to pay them or soldiers escaping with their
lives after a battle wandered over the countryside trying to get
back to their homes. Wage laborers, no longer under restrictive
laws keeping them to their own parishes, traveled about more or
less freely looking for work. When the tide of battle ebbed and
flowed, parliamentary sympathizers and royalists in turn found
their property being confiscated and their estates occupied by
troops. As the defeat of the king appeared increasingly inevitable,
more and more of the royalist gentry and aristocracy fled the
country. Not only were many of their estates sequestered and sold
in their absence, but physical damage was done as well. Occupied
or abandoned estates were plundered. The Duke of Newcastle
returned in 1660 to find most of the deer gone from his parks and
timber cut to the value of £45,000. The Duchess reported, "As for
pewter, brass, bedding, linen, and other household stuff, there was
nothing else left but some few old feather-beds, and those all
spoiled, and fit for no use."[3] At a less exalted level of society,
Richard Baxter told of royalist soldiers in Shropshire plundering
his father "and all his neighbors that were noted for praying and
hearing sermons . . . so that some of them had almost nothing but
lumber left in their houses."[4]

The story of Charles II's narrow escape after the battle of
Worcester in 1651 had a strong hold on people's imaginations.
After fighting bravely, he fled on horseback, got rid of his en-
tourage, and started for London on foot. The twenty-one-year-old
king, over six feet tall, attempted to disguise himself by putting on
"a pair of grey cloth breeches, a leather doublet and a green
jerkin." He had his long hair cut and wore "a greasy gray soft hat

without ribbon or lining."[5] This tale of the true prince in humble disguise, for seven weeks forced from one hiding place to another by his enemies, has a mythic quality and became a historical analogue of all the true kings in disguise who are restored to their rightful thrones in the fifth acts of Restoration heroic drama. Practically, the effect of these adventures on Charles II's later policy was to inspire him to great efforts to avoid going on his travels again. More generally, the fate of Charles I and the miseries of Charles II left the English with a vivid sense that at any moment the center might not hold. People who had expected God's wrath to destroy a nation of regicides were soon confronted by the spectacle of most men living peaceably under the usurpers while a victorious Cromwell made England more powerful than before. Then Cromwell, the mighty cynosure of Europe, had in his turn been hurled from the wheel of fortune.

Since the Restoration itself was a successful counterrevolution, people afterward generally were apt to disown the revolution: to dissociate themselves from the regicides and "parricides," as Hume significantly called them, to try to show how they had suffered under the usurpers, and to characterize the revolutionaries as a small group with whose mad ideas they themselves had had not the slightest sympathy. Like the twentieth-century Frenchmen Marcel Ophuls interviewed in *The Sorrow and the Pity*, late seventeenth-century Englishmen liked to think they had been in the resistance and hardly anyone felt like a collaborator. As Baxter complained in his own justificatory papers published after his death and after the Glorious Revolution:

> The prodigious lies which have been published in this age in matters of fact, with unblushing confidence, even where thousands or multitudes of eye- and ear-witnesses knew all to be false, doth call men to take heed what history they believe, especially when power and violence af-fordeth that privilege to the reporter, that no man dares answer him or detect his fraud, or if they do their writings are all suppressed.[6]

The triumph of winner's history in the Restoration distorts our perception in three ways. First, the winners were able to characterize their enemies as intrinsically less worthy than themselves, as stupid rabble, hostile to all authority and order, mercenary, and so on. The canon of Restoration and eighteenth-century literature is dominated by writers like Dryden, Butler, Swift, and Pope so there are many more Hudibras-like characters than there are characters like Bunyan's Lord Hategood who persecutes Christian and Faithful in Vanity Fair. Second, anybody who shared some common ground with the losers was under great pressure to differentiate his views from theirs, not simply out of narrow self-interest, but in order to get a hearing for those views. Latitudinarian clergymen in the Restoration, for example, were constantly trying to prove they had nothing in common with "Puritans," "Presbyterians," or other rebels. This tendency has the effect of obscuring such important connections. Third, transitory groupings of people around particular issues very rapidly got reified into fixed parties. Propaganda postulated the immiscibility of puritans and cavaliers, parliamentarians and royalists, dissenters and Anglicans, when, in fact, alliances shifted as issues and circumstances changed. It is not even that there was a con-tinuum of opinion ranging from most radical to most conservative, but rather that given individuals might be to the left or to the right of each other depending on particular issues and particular cir-cumstances. John Gauden, after the Restoration Bishop of Exeter, before the war was an enthusiast for Laudian liturgy, but could not reconcile his conscience to infant baptism; Baxter, after the war a dissenter, had more orthodox notions of baptism and, had the Savoy Conference gone differently, might have been a bishop himself. If Hume's preachers shed their "unsuborned tears" for Charles, they did so because hardly any of them had wished for his death; a few years later they were content to cooperate with Cromwell in so far as he tried to further the reforms they had originally demanded from the king.

Because its influence was so critical and yet so liable to distortion, the interregnum experience needs to be explored. Though this chapter is not the place for a conventional history of the interregnum, it will be necessary to sketch the range of Englishmen's responses to the revolution. First, the more radical and sectarian protestant enthusiasts for reform, important after the Restoration not only as the forerunners of the dissenters, but also as representing a radical protestant antinomianism from which less radical Restoration protestants struggled to dissociate themselves. Second, the more moderate protestants sympathetic to many so-called puritan reforms in church and state, but reluctant to attack fundamental established institutions, especially monarchy. A large number of gentlemen fell into this class and it is crucial to recognize how their positions shifted with events. Third, there were, of course, those royalists hostile to virtually all the aims of the reformers who considered loyalty to the Stuarts the only principled course even after the execution of Charles I. Of special importance to my later argument is the behavior during the interregnum of those gentlemen who were paid to think about authority: the lawyers and judges, the university dons, the clergy, and, in a way, the poets. Many of these men would fall into my second class of moderate protestants; some would not.

To begin with the dramatic, the usurpation of power by those forces that succeeded in driving one king to the scaffold and another into exile was undoubtedly the most frightening aspect of the revolution. Genuine radicals were always in a minority and rarely controlled events, but radical and sectarian enthusiasts for reform made themselves heard, sometimes in the form of mobs petitioning parliament. Men were unleashed into public life who previously had had no voice and no power. Parliament's suppression of the Court of the Star Chamber set the press free and allowed the "people" to express themselves. A note of menace in some of the ballad writers was unmistakable as early as 1641:

> Though Wentworths beheaded,
> Should any Repyne,
> Thers others may come
> To the Blocke beside he:
> Keep thy head on thy Shoulders
> And I will keep mine;
> For what is all this to thee or to mee?
> *Then merrily and cheerily*
> *Lets drink off our Beere,*
> *Let who as will run for it*
> *Wee will stay here.*[7]

By June 1643 Commons had passed its own ordinance on licensing the press, but in August 1644 this was sufficiently ineffective that they directed another ordinance to be prepared and a search to be conducted for the authors and printers of Milton's pamphlets on divorce. To more conservative members of the propertied classes, the New Jerusalem of Milton looked like the anarchy of hell. Another ballad gives their sense of the new republic:

> Come clownes and boyes, come hoberdehoys,
> Come Females of each degree,
> Stretch your throats, bring in your Votes,
> And make good the Anarchy. . . .
> We're fourscore Religions strong
> Then take your choice, the major voice
> Shall carry it right or wrong; . . .
> Then let's ha' King Charles, sayes George
> Nay we'll have his son, sayes Hugh
> Nay then let's ha' none says jabbering Joan,
> Nay lets be all Kings, sayes Prue.[8]

The threat of anarchy during the interregnum is well captured in the *Journal* (1694) of George Fox, itself a classic of Restoration autobiography. There were wilder movements than Quakerism during the middle of the seventeenth century—the Fifth Monarchy Men, for instance, who considered the end of the world to be imminent—but Fox's *Journal* shows clearly both the eschatological excitement of many of these sectarian movements and the social challenge they represented. In September 1643, at the age of nineteen, and about the time of the first battle of Newberry, Fox left his home and began to wander about the countryside as a religious seeker. He returned home briefly in 1644 to have some of his relations propose that he marry and others tell him to enlist as a soldier. Both of these alternatives he rejected to continue his search for spiritual truth. Gradually he felt God "opening" his truth, showing by direct revelation that "being bred at Oxford or Cambridge was not enough to fit and qualify men to be ministers of Christ" and that "God, who made the world, did not dwell in temples made with hands."[9] In his wandering he encounters not only the better-known sectarians like Baptists and Ranters, but also some who hold that women have no souls and others who rely for direction on dreams. In 1648 he goes to a meeting in a church at Leicester where Presbyterians, Independents, and Episcopalians are all gathered in dispute. A woman rises to ask what it means to be born again, only to be rebuked by the clergyman, who announces, "I permit not a woman to speak in the church" (p. 92). The priest is in his turn rebuked by Fox, whereupon the meeting breaks up in confusion and adjourns to the local inn.

Fundamentally Fox's religion goes back to the eschatological excitement of the gospels: normal life is suspended and little attention is given to the problems of the world. Fox simply travels about declaring the day of the Lord. Christ is not going to come eventually or even in 1666, as some of the Fifth Monarchists expected, he has come already: "He was now come to teach the people Himself, and His heavenly day was springing from on High." Until his death in 1691 Fox preached that the kingdom had already come and that the grace of God had come to all men, not only to a few of the elect. Speaking with authority like the apostles themselves, Fox the weaver's son did not hesitate to offer his counsel either to Cromwell, whom he warned against persecuting the saints and against accepting kingship, or to Charles II, to whom he wrote in 1660, admonishing him "to restrain the profaneness and looseness that was risen up in the nation upon his return" (pp. 214–15, 319–22, 354).

Both Fox and John Bunyan, in his autobiography, *Grace Abounding to the Chief of Sinners* (1666), reveal how they shared the eschatological excitement of first-century Christianity by identifying with Paul. Like Paul on the road to Damascus, both report hearing the voice of God address them directly. Fox stresses how he knows God experientially and tells of hearing a voice saying, "There is one, even Christ Jesus, that can speak to thy condition" (p. 82). Though Fox will support his positions with reference to Scripture, the crucial saving truths come to him by direct revelations, in what he calls "the pure openings of the light" (p. 102). The people do not know Scripture aright because they are not "in the same Light, power, and Spirit which those were who gave forth the Scriptures" (p. 149). Fox brings that light. Less comfortably, Bunyan reports, "a voice did suddenly dart from Heaven into my Soul, which said, *Wilt thou leave thy sins, and go to Heaven? or have thy sins, and go to Hell?*"[10] To Fox, his attack on ceremonies is continuous with Paul's campaign against Judaizing in the early church. Churches are merely steeple houses and tithes

paid to a beneficed clergy inappropriate because Christ is come,
"who ended both the temple and its worship, and the priests and
their tithes" (p. 156). Bunyan early finds the Pauline epistles
especially "sweet and pleasant." When he undergoes his own
travail in a spiritual Valley of the Shadow of Death, consolation
comes in the form of a badly worn copy of Luther's commentary
on Galatians. Throughout *Pilgrim's Progress*, with its emphasis on
the Pauline rejection of old law righteousness, references to
Hebrews, Galatians, Romans, and Corinthians are frequent. In
Hebrews, which of course Bunyan regarded as a genuine Pauline
epistle, he found not only a clear statement of the differences
between the old covenant and the new, but also the vivid image of
Mount Sinai blazing with fire that terrifies Christian on his way to
Mr. Legality's house. Such revelations of the freedoms of the new
law were weapons not only against the law of the Old Testament,
but also against those laws of the seventeenth-century magistrate
not in accord with the consciences of the saints.

Given confidence by feelings of direct experience with God and
secure in the knowledge that the new freedom of Christ had
replaced the old law, both Fox and Bunyan found their experiences
of worldly persecution given meaning by their obvious parallel
with Paul's persecution. When the scholars of Cambridge jostle
Fox and unhorse one of his companions, he explains their hostility
as caused by the scholars' fear of having their future livelihoods
vanish: "They knew I was so against the trade of preaching, which
they were there as apprentices to learn, that they raged as greatly
as ever Diana's craftsmen did against Paul" (p. 228). Kept close
prisoner in Scarborough Castle and allowed no visits from his
friends, Fox tells his captors they treat him worse than the heathen
treated Paul. Bunyan affirms it is his intention to live peaceably
under the new government in 1661, but refuses to stop preaching at
public meetings. The magistrate argues he must obey because *"the
powers that are, are ordained of God,"* and Bunyan antagonizes
him by observing: *"Paul* did own the powers that were in his day,
as to be of God; and yet he was often in prison under them for all
that. And also, though *Jesus Christ* told *Pilate,* that he had no
power against him, but of God, yet he died under the same *Pilate;*
and yet, . . . I hope you will not say that either *Paul,* or Christ was

such as did deny magistracy, and so sinned against God in slighting the ordinance."[11]

The eschatological sense was productive of uncontrollable enthusiasm and potentially hostile to every social institution. Some of Fox's followers were moved to go about naked in the streets as a sign to the hypocrites that God would strip them naked too. In 1656 James Nayler, a Quaker Fox had to disown, entered Bristol on horseback and was thought to be proclaiming himself Christ returned in the flesh. Women walked through mud and rain to follow him, strewing garments before him, and singing "Holy, holy!" He was interrogated by members of parliament who debated his fate for ten days and finally convicted him of blasphemy.[12] Quakers generally were sufficiently suspect that in 1659 royalists thought it a good idea to spread rumors of an impending Quaker uprising and armed themselves on the pretext of needing to defend their families.

Fox, of course, regarded as unreasonable the more or less constant persecution he met with at the hands of the civil authorities. Yet his contempt for outward forms and ceremonies was unlikely to appeal to any organized church or government and the authority of the inner light resisted institutionalization. Fox denounced tithes, proclaimed that paid clergy were simply hirelings and false prophets, and insisted that there was no need for baptism or for any formal marriage ceremonies. Quakers refused to take their hats off before civil authorities, persisted in addressing their social superiors as "thee" and "thou," and refused to swear oaths. Quaker autobiographies of the period relate endless conflicts between individuals and their social or domestic superiors over these points. Thomas Ellwood, for instance, was torn between his inner conviction that the Quakers were right and his apparent duty to obey a father who told him angrily, "Sirrah, if ever I hear you say *thou* or *thee* to me again, I'll strike your teeth down your throat!" Ellwood at last decided to disobey his father, considering "the extent of paternal power, which I found was not wholly arbitrary and unlimited, but had bounds set unto it; so that, as in civil matters it was restrained to things lawful, so in spiritual and religious cases it had not a compulsory power over conscience, which ought to be subject to the Heavenly Father."[13] It was the refusal of Quaker soldiers to swear oaths of allegiance that led to their being mustered out of Cromwell's army, and Fox's refusal to swear an oath of allegiance to Charles II that earned him his last jail term. Though Fox always professed to be against violence and even wrote a pamphlet, *Fear God, and Honour the King*, he was also clearly against compromising with the demands of civil authority and was therefore constantly and correctly accused of political and social subversion. He himself describes how he went among Cromwell's soldiers preaching that they should do no violence. Twice after provoking disturbances he was jailed for blasphemy. Fox makes much of confounding the magistrates by pointing out that there is no scriptural warrant for the removal of hats, indeed, that there is not even an English law that commands a prisoner to take off his hat before a magistrate (p. 246). He is obviously aware of how irritating his behavior is and seems to derive pleasure from describing the fits of rage he provokes. Using informal forms of address is meant as "a sore cut to proud flesh"; denying the marks of deference to class superiors will teach them that their status is an "honour which God would lay in the dust, though they make much ado about it" (pp. 381, 248). The Quakers and other religious enthusiasts were persecuted not only for their religious opinions but also for the social consequences of those opinions. Quakers were jailed by parliament during the forties, by Cromwell's regime during the fifties, and by the king's government during the sixties. The inner light was a challenge to any other form of authority. How to reject such radical protestant antinomianism and its social consequences without at the same time falling back into Roman Catholic doctrines of authority was a central problem for the Cambridge Platonists and also for their Restoration heirs, especially the Latitudinarian divines and Locke.

Although such radical and sectarian enthusiasts may have been the most colorful Englishmen of the mid-seventeenth century, more moderate protestants sympathetic to reform were more numerous and, in the long run, more directly influential. Many protestants who repudiated what they considered the errors of the Quakers or various other radical sectarians nevertheless were conscientiously concerned with religious issues. The Presbyterian Samuel Rutherford, for instance, defended resistance to Charles I in the name of religious conscience, insisting aggressively, "Christ, the Prophets, and Apostles of our Lord went to heaven with the note of traitors, seditious men, and such as turned the world upside down. . . . Truth to Christ cannot be treason to Caesar, and for his choice he judgeth truth to have a nearer relation to Christ Jesus than the transcendent and boundless power of a mortal prince."[14] Protestants less radical than Fox or Bunyan were also in some cases prepared to attack established social and religious institutions. During the 1640s and fifties the gentlemen in parliament attacked the hierarchy of the Church of England and succeeded in stripping it of power. In 1642 the archbishops and bishops were denied voice and vote in the House of Lords; later they were deprived of their lands and titles. The Court of High Commission, a sort of ecclesiastical supreme court, was abolished in 1641 and the ecclesiastical courts generally were stripped of their powers. These attacks were prompted by a concatenation of religious and political motives. Baxter described parliament in the early forties as consisting of two sorts of men, one most concerned with arbitrary government and the vulnerability of property, the other,

> the more religious men, . . . more sensible of the interest of religion; and these most inveighed against the innovations in the Church, the bowing to altars, . . . the casting out of ministers [presumably those defying Laudian directives], the troubling of the people by the High Commission Court, the pillorying and cutting off men's ears . . . for speaking against the bishops, with such other things which they thought of greater weight than ship-money. But because these latter agreed with the former in the vindication of the people's propriety and liberties, the former did the easilier concur with them against the proceedings of the bishops and the High Commission Court.[15]

The bishops were attacked on the grounds that their powers had no warrant in Scripture or the practice of the early church, that their worldly power and luxury elicited contempt rather than respect from serious Christians, and that they were too dependent on the king for office to sit in parliament as free men. Ambitious bishops, Nathanael Finnes told his fellow M.P.'s in 1640, "Fat" and living "at their Ease," persecute "other Godly Ministers, that live more according to the simplicity of the Gospel, and the Example of Christ."[16] Viscount Falkland, who later died fighting for the royalist cause, complained that bishops were trying to bring in an English Popery: "I mean not only the *outside*, and *dress* of it, but equally absolute, a blind dependence of the People upon the Clergy, and of the Clergy upon themselves."[17] Lord Saye and Sele, particularly jealous of the bishops as augmentors of the king's party in the House of Lords, dismissed arguments for their continued sitting in parliament on the ground of custom and precedent by saying flatly, "Antiquity is no good Plea."[18]

Both bishops and ecclesiastical courts were vulnerable as relics of papacy. Ronald A. Marchant has compared the attitudes of seventeenth-century Englishmen toward the ecclesiastical courts to the attitudes of twentieth-century African nationalists toward British colonialism. The Church of England, as Marchant says, "not only had an unreformed judicial and administrative system, papal in origin, but it was using a law which was foreign to the country."[19] Civil law, the foundation of English ecclesiastical law, understood the king as the source of law and tended to reflect political absolutism; common law, on the other hand, was explicitly concerned with the rights of citizens and could be appealed to by those who wanted to discover not the king alone but the king-in-parliament as the source of law. The presence of two legal systems based on fundamentally different premises in itself inevitably produced confusion. For example, according to the canon law children born after simple spousals were legitimate, according to common law they were neither legitimate nor capable of being legitimized by later matrimony.[20] Critics of the ecclesiastical courts particularly objected to their jurisdiction over anything affecting property rights, including their jurisdiction over wills and marriage. Christopher Hill has also argued that the ecclesiastical courts were attacked because they interfered with the free working of the market and were out of touch with the commercial spirit of the age, but this argument does not seem entirely convincing to me, partly because much of the complaining about fees, delays, lack of adaptation to commerce, and so on might as well have been directed at the secular administration of justice.[21]

Most of those who voted to abolish episcopacy and church courts did so not to annihilate discipline but to make the state the instrument of discipline. That state was to be a Christian state, properly one of God's agents, not a secular state in the modern sense. As Emil Friedberg acutely observed, the Reformation "released the state from its shell of 'worldliness,' ascribed to it ethical tendencies, and made it the bearer of morality. Formerly the state was unholy, because it belonged to the world; now the world became ethical, because it fell within the sphere of the state, for the state itself was moral."[22] Once parliament had gotten rid of the bishops and the bishop's courts, it proceeded to create its own instruments to accomplish similar ends. A statute of May 1648 made various blasphemies and heretical opinions punishable as felonies if they were not abjured. Lesser heresies to be punished by imprisonment included, "That man by Nature hath free will to turn to God" and "that man is bound to believe no more than by his reason he can comprehend."[23] By 1650 the Independents had gained strength over the Presbyterians and succeeded in passing a milder ordinance making certain "Blasphemous and Execrable Opinions" misdemeanors, the first offense punishable by six months in prison, the second by banishment. This ordinance also made it a misdemeanor for any person "not distempered with sickness, or distracted in brain . . . to affirm and maintain him or her self, or any other meer Creature, to be very God" or to affirm that "Uncleanness" is holy and not forbidden by God.[24] Another act in 1650 made incest a felony without benefit of clergy, adultery with a married woman a felony "for every person, as well the man as the woman," and fornication a misdemeanor punishable by three months imprisonment. Theoretically these sexual offences were not punishable in the temporal courts before 1650 or after 1660 when the legislation of the interregnum was overturned. However, justices of the peace were often not well-trained in the law and indulged in actions not strictly authorized; we also know that such offenders were occasionally indicted.[25] These parliamentary acts of the forties and fifties represent in part simply an intensification of a process that had been going on almost from the beginning of the Reformation when parliament had begun to pass legislation concerning behavior formerly punished only by the spiritual courts: sodomy, giving birth to an illegitimate child, bigamy, and so on.

Among the laws making the state the instrument of discipline

formerly the responsibility of the church was the important Civil
Marriage Act of 1653. This act reflected much of the spirit of the
draft *Reformatio Legum Ecclesiasticarum* of 1552, an attempt at
reforming the ecclesiastical laws nulified by the death of Edward
VI. It may be seen as the culmination of one hundred years of
protestant struggle against the Roman Catholic understanding of
marriage and against what protestants considered the abuses and
profiteering of the ecclesiastical courts. Milton praised the act,
observing that puritan divines had denied marriage to be a
sacrament, "yet retained the celebration, till prudently a late
parlament recovered the civil liberty of marriage from their in-
croachment; and transferred the ratifying and registering therof
from the cannonical shop to the proper cognizance of the civil
magistrates."[26] The act provided that marriages be celebrated by
justices of the peace and removed all litigation concerning
marriages from the ecclesiastical courts to the civil magistrates.
The words of the spousals stipulated in the act differed from the
forms used in the Book of Common Prayer. The phrase "till death
do us part" was eliminated from the words to be spoken by both
partners, the man simply promising to be "a Loving and Faithful
Husband," the woman "a Loving, Faithful, and Obedient Wife."[27]
Almost certainly the omission of "till death do us part" reflected
the puritan belief that divorce and remarriage were allowable
under certain circumstances. The *Reformatio Legum* permitted
divorce for adultery, desertion, deadly hostility, and even
prolonged ill-treatment.[28] At the third reading of the Civil
Marriage Act an amendment to allow justices of the peace to grant
divorces for adultery was considered but defeated.[29]

    Little of this more dramatic legislation survived the Restoration.
The bishops were restored and the various ordinances concerning
blasphemy, adultery, and civil marriage declared void. One
significant exception was that the Cavalier Parliament did endorse
an enfeebling of the ecclesiastical courts. In 1663, while announcing no wish to interfere with the "ordinary powers" of the
ecclesiastical judges, parliament ratified the abolition of the Court
of High Commission and the abolition of the ex officio oath.[30] The
subsequent history of these courts is of importance to my argument
about the secularization of authority and will be looked at in

various ways in subsequent chapters. Generally, after the Restoration their powers slowly withered away, partly because of specific prohibitions from the temporal courts, partly because of competing secular legislation, and partly, it seems, from sheer apathy. In theory eighteenth-century ecclesiastical courts retained the right to proceed against laymen for fornication and all sorts of other sins, but they gradually ceased to do so.[31] The sins of the upper classes had attracted the special attention of the Court of High Commission and that was abolished. As for jurisdiction over the lower classes, as Christopher Hill says, "the true residuary legatee" of discipline for them came to be the J.P.'s acting under the authority given them by parliamentary legislation.[32] In spite of the apparent demise of much of the interregnum legislation at the Restoration, that legislation generally is important in understanding the culture of the later seventeenth century. First, as I shall argue later, because it conditioned and contributed to the social experience of the generation surviving the war. Second, as I shall also try to show, because the ideas that animated the legislation were not necessarily repudiated when it was repealed.

The hard-core royalists, of course, were not pleased by such parliamentary interference with the established institutions of church and state. Some took arms against parliament and even after the cessation of open battle continued to resist through conspiracies.[33] Others went into exile abroad; still others retired into as much obscurity as they could find at home. And, at one point or another, many of those who had initially been hostile to the aims of the reformers ceased to hope for a counterrevolution and decided to cooperate with the new government.

The careers of two royalist poets, Davenant and Waller, illustrate the kinds of problems the royalists faced. William Davenant, successor to Ben Jonson as poet laureate, links the Elizabethan and Caroline theaters to the Restoration theater. He wrote plays for the public theater in the 1630s and masques for the court of Charles I and Henrietta Maria. After the Restoration he led the Duke of York's Company. Davenant had seen Joseph Taylor, Richard Burbage's successor, play Hamlet before the Civil War; in 1661 he coached Thomas Betterton in the part.[34] His life was tempestuous. In the Bishops' Wars he served as a paymaster

under the Earl of Newport. In May 1641 he was caught in an
unsuccessful plot to rescue Strafford from the Tower. His fellow
conspirators were Henry Jermyn (Abraham Cowley's patron),
Henry Percy, a Captain Billingsley, and another poet, Sir John
Suckling. Davenant alone failed to escape before he was apprehended and was reduced to trying to extricate himself from
prison with a "Humble Remonstrance . . . To the Honorable
Knights, Citizens, and Burgesses of the House of Commons
Assembled in Parliament" in which he claimed, "I have perhaps
committed errours, but never maliciously against Parliamentary
government." There was not much real evidence against the
laureate and he was not taken to be a very serious threat, so after a
short imprisonment he was released on £4,000 bail and escaped to
the Continent. Henrietta Maria soon got him a commission as
lieutenant general of ordinance under the Duke of Newcastle. Acting as the queen's agent in Holland, Davenant procured ships and
supplies for the army with such effectiveness that he was attainted
for high treason by the Long Parliament.

Next there was a royalist scheme to strengthen the loyalist colony
of Virginia by sending Davenant to reinforce it with skilled
craftsmen. After recruiting men from Paris prisons who at least
claimed to be craftsmen, Davenant outfitted a ship and sailed for
Jersey. There he received from the king an alternative commission
to be lieutenant governor of Maryland. In the king's words, "The
Lord Baltimore . . . doth visibly adhere to the Rebells of England,
and admit all Kinde of Schismatics, and Sectaries, and other ill-
affected persons unto the said Plantations of Maryland, so that We
have cause to apprehend very great prejudice to Our Service
thereby, and very great danger to Our Plantations in Virginia."
Before Lord Baltimore could be challenged, however, Davenant
was captured at sea and imprisoned on the Isle of Wight.

From this point on, Davenant began trying to accommodate
himself to the government. His situation was more serious than it
had been during his previous imprisonment for several reasons,
among them his service as lieutenant general of ordinance and the
fact that parliament was considering trying selected royalists for
their lives in retaliation for the assassination of several
parliamentary representatives and agents abroad by royalists in

exile. Davenant began by drawing up another petition, this time to Cromwell's Council of State, claiming that he had only been planning to emigrate to America in accordance with a resolution he had made not to oppose the English government, that he had certainly done no more than others who had been allowed to compound, and asking for bail. Others supported his request, including, apparently, Milton. These appeals were successful, but after the poet's release, he was first arrested again as a debtor and then his Maryland commission fell into government hands. At this juncture he appealed directly to Cromwell and in April 1654 received a pardon.

Once free, Davenant set out to revive the English theater. Always a rhetorician willing to consider his opponent's point of view, he began with a memo to Secretary John Thurloe arguing that to revive the theater would be good for trade ("pleasant assemblies" would bring the upper classes back to London to spend their money) and that diversions would combat the melancholy that bred sedition.[35] He also offered a flattering panegyric on the occasion of Cromwell's daughter's marriage and two other poems to children of Henry Lawrence, Lord President of Cromwell's council. Deciding he had softened governmental resistance sufficiently with such arguments and conciliatory gestures, Davenant produced *The Siege of Rhodes*, an opera or musical entertainment, not a play, and therefore not quite so offensive to puritan sentiment. Then, having gotten away with that, he followed with a patriotic play, *The Cruelty of the Spaniards in Peru*, and the English theater was back in business. Davenant was imprisoned once more for a short period for reasons that are not known, but was free in 1660 to welcome Charles back to his throne with a panegyric.

Edmund Waller's attempt to get through the Civil War was a notorious debacle.[36] Born into a substantial country family, after short stays at Eton and Cambridge and while still a teenager, Waller began his first term as a member of the House of Commons. That third parliament of Charles I was dissolved in 1629, no others being called until in 1640 the king was desperate for money. Waller began by attacking Charles for exceeding the limits of prerogative but ended by defending him against the demands of the more radical parliamentarians. While Charles was at Oxford, Waller remained in parliament as one of his agents. In March 1642 he volunteered to act as a go-between for members of parliament sympathetic to the king and citizens involved with a commission of array trying to recruit royalist troops in London. By May 1643 Charles had authorized Richard Chaloner, a linen draper, to begin collecting money for the scheme. Waller tried to persuade members of parliament to join in what was by this time crystallizing into a plan for a *coup d'état.* The conspirators formed a secret association to assess the strength of the king's party in and around London and to plan a military take over of the City. One night when they were in a majority, royalist guards in the trained bands were to seize ammunition stores and strategic military positions. The Lord Mayor of London, his chief supporters, and at least six leaders of parliament were to be captured while they slept. Agents within the City were also to open its gates to royalist troops waiting outside. Successful counterintelligence enabled John Pym to expose to parliament what became known as "Waller's plot" and indignation strengthened resistance against the king. By 12 June, "abject in his terror," Waller was publicly denouncing his coconspirators—the one act of his life that was never forgotten. Six coconspirators, not including Waller, were court-martialed; of these, two were executed, one died in prison, and the other three were allowed to live. Because Waller himself was still an M.P., he could not legally be court-martialed without the consent of the House of Commons. Like Davenant a good rhetorician, Waller appeared before the House to do penance and to remind them that they might create a precedent they themselves would be reluctant to live with were they to hand him over to the army for trial. This appeal was so successful that he was simply imprisoned for one year, then fined £10,000 and allowed to go into exile. Two other conspirators who were members of the House of Lords were tried by their own peers and released on bail after spending seven weeks in jail.

Waller then joined the royalist exiles in Paris. Davenant turned up in 1646, hard at work on his epic, *Gondibert.* The principles upon which modern epics should be composed were much debated, particularly by Davenant, Cowley, and Hobbes. Cowley had earlier published several books of his own biblical epic, *Davideis*, which was to be an important model (and antimodel) for *Paradise Lost*. When Davenant set off for America, Cowley contributed a graceful poem, "To Sir William Davenant, Upon His first two Books of Gondibert, Finished Before his Voyage to America," and Waller offered another on the same subject.

By 1651, though, Cromwell, who was never particularly bloody-minded, was sufficiently secure in his power to allow Waller to return. The poet celebrated this event with one of his best poems, "A Panegyric to My Lord Protector: Of the Present Greatness, and Joint Interest of His Highness, and this Nation." Congratulating Cromwell on the restoration of domestic peace, on his ambitious attempts to make England a major European power, and on his clemency toward defeated enemies, Waller presents a picture of England under the Protector as a demi-Eden:

> Our little world, the image of the great,
> Like that, amidst the boundless ocean set,
> Of her own growth has all that Nature craves;
> And all that's rare, as tribute from the waves.
>
> As Egypt does not on the clouds rely,
> But to her Nile owes more than to the sky;
> So what our earth, and what our heaven, denies,
> Our ever constant friend, the sea, supplies.
>
> The taste of hot Arabia's spice we know,
> Free from the scorching sun that makes it grow;
> Without the worm, in Persian silks we shine;
> And, without planting, drink of every vine.
>
> To dig for wealth we weary not our limbs;
> Gold, though the heaviest metal, hither swims;
> Ours is the harvest where the Indians mow;
> We plough the deep, and reap what others sow.[37]

Such euphoria was shared by many Englishmen. It is also reflected in Milton's *Second Defence of the People of England* (1654) and Andrew Marvell's "First anniversary of the government under O. C." (1655); elements of it persist in the young Dryden's "Heroique Stanzas" on Cromwell's death.

Like a number of other royalists of their generation, Davenant and Waller each had protracted experience of political chaos and each was wrenched out of what would have been his career in more normal times to live the uprooted life of an exile. Each of them also had close contact with the unreal court life of the deposed Stuarts. At one point or another, each had bowed to superior force and, at least in words, had betrayed his sovereign. Each had also finally accepted the inevitability of Cromwell's rule and returned to England to accommodate himself to the new government. Some of the conclusions participation in such events prompted in the minds of English gentlemen are nicely indicated in another interregnum ballad:

> Lay by your pleading, law lies a bleeding
> Burn all your studies down, and throw away your reading;
> Small power the word has, and can afford us
> Not half so many privileges as the sword has;
> It ventures, it entres, it circles, it centres,
> And makes a prentice free in spite of his indentures,
> This takes off tall things and sets up small things;
> This masters money, though money masters all things;
> 'Tis not in season to talk of reason
> Or call it legal when the sword will have it treason?[38]

"Small power the word has, and can afford us"—an interesting idea for a generation of writers to confront. And this difference between words—now perhaps for the first time often thought of as "mere words"—and things—cash or the sword—remained for writers, lawyers, and philosophers a critical issue left to the later seventeenth century as a legacy from the Civil War.

After the Restoration, the fiction developed of the parliamentary side as a small fanatical revolutionary clique who had somehow seized power and forced the overwhelming majority of right-thinking royalists into two decades of starvation and political suspended animation. The fact was that the country could not have been run for eighteen years by such a small band of fanatics. Normal life was suspended to some extent during the interregnum, but it was not suspended nearly as much as the post-Restoration royalists liked to pretend. The issues were not so clear in the early forties as the later myths presented them, nor was resistance to parliamentary government anywhere so universal among gentlemen or so die-hard as it was alleged to have been. The very categories I have been using up until this point—radical protestant, moderate protestant, and royalist—though of some use in discussion are themselves misleading because they imply more disjunctive and more static divisions than actually existed.

At the beginning of the fighting in 1642 the royalists were in the majority. Not surprisingly, though, many supporters of the king were fairly passive, failing to rush to his standard or to sacrifice very much of their treasure for his support. Paul Hardacre concludes from his study of the royalist party during the revolution, ''The single tendency most apparent throughout the early years of the civil wars is the general inclination toward neutrality, and there can be little doubt that the vast majority of Englishmen would have been content to remain impartial in the quarrel between king and parliament.''[39] Many gentlemen were reluctant to go to war for perfectly principled reasons: they saw some justice on both sides and they dreaded the real horrors of civil war. Colonel John Birch wrote:

> I am not so senseless (though it were almost to be wished I were) that there are two armies, the one the king's, the other the parliament's, each seeking to destroy [the] other, and I by oath bound to preserve both, each challenging the Protestant religion for their standard, yet the one takes the papists, the other the schismatics for their adherents, and (for my part) my conscience tells me they both intend the Protestant religion. What reason have I therefore to fall out with either?[40]

John Locke told his father that he considered taking up arms, but could not decide on which side to fight. Clarendon describes the king's sending a handwritten appeal for a loan of five or ten thousand pounds to one wealthy lord near Nottingham. The lord claimed to be broke and would only volunteer to tell where his unpopular aristocratic neighbor had a trunkful of money hidden. Later he also refused to give anything to the victorious parliamentary government and had his estate sequestered. Clarendon comments with some justice, ''it may be seen, that the unthrifty retention of their money, which possessed the spirits of those, who did really wish the King all the success he wished for himself, was one of the unhappy causes of all his misfortunes."[41]

Some Englishmen actually did manage to keep their personal involvement in the war and interregnum politics to a minimum either by living in social or rural obscurity or by protracted foreign residence. The poets Samuel Butler and Charles Cotton, for example, elected obscurity. Butler, as the son of a yeoman farmer, was undoubtedly under less pressure than the son of a gentleman would have been to make his position clear. His life during the interregnum is not well documented, but it is clear that he never fought, that he published nothing, and that he worked as a secretary to various men in the country and in London.[42] *Hudibras* shows the influence of the war ballads and Butler was certainly writing it during the fifties, but had it not been for the Restoration the poem would have remained "for the drawer" like much modern Soviet literature. Cotton, the most important nature poet of the Restoration, was only twelve in 1642 and therefore too young to go off to the wars. He remained at home at Beresford Hall on the borders of Staffordshire and Derbyshire throughout most of the interregnum, apparently even staying away from the universities and the inns of court. He did spend a few months on the Continent in 1655 and it should be noted that he had to acknowledge the existence of the government to obtain a license for this excursion. Manuscript poems were circulated, but none published. One of Cotton's early compositions is an invective against Waller, "To the Poet E. W.," apparently prompted by Waller's "Panegyric to my Lord Protector" and written in the fifties though not published until 1689:

> From whence, vile Poet, did'st Thou gleane the witt
> And words for such a vicious Poem fit? . . .
> What servile Divell tempted thee to bee
> A Flatterer of thine owne Slavery?
> To kisse thy Bondage, and extall the deed,
> Att once that made thy Prince and Cuntry bleed?[43]

There is, I think, something gratuitous in attacks like these from the noncombatants, who, after all, had themselves run no risks, not even the risk of being compromised.

Individuals caught up in the turmoil of these decades inevitably lacked perspective. The man deciding what to do in 1643 had no means of knowing the king's forces were going to be defeated. The man trying to decide what to do about his estates in 1655, at the height of Cromwell's successes, had no way of knowing that in five short years Charles would be restored. The longer the interregnum lasted, the more pointless it seemed to resist. For the governing classes especially, a continued refusal to participate in national life could seem not only futilely self-destructive, but also an abrogation of responsibility for what was, after all, one's country. Parliament for its part made provision for receiving the royalists, offering its pardon as early as January 1644, from which time a long series of gentlemen proceeded to compound for their sequestered estates. There was another act of general pardon and oblivion in 1652. The royalist John Evelyn spent the years between 1643 and 1652 abroad. In 1652, however, he called a halt to his travels and obtained the king's permission to compound for the estate of his wife's family, his wife's father being Richard Browne, Charles's ambassador in Paris, commenting, "I made preparation for my settlement, no more intending to go out of England, but endeavor a settled life . . . there being now so little appearance of any change for the better, all being intirely in the rebells hands, and this particular habitation & the Estate contiguous to it . . . very much suffering, for want of some friend."[44] Even as late as Michaelmas term 1659, according to John Aubrey's recollection of his attendance at meetings of Harrington's Rota, one of the political ideas being discussed seemed "very taking, and the more because, as to human foresight, there was no possibility of the king's returne."[45]

Abraham Cowley, conventionally remembered as the royalist poet par excellence and cited by C. V. Wedgewood as an example of one who remained faithful to Charles throughout, went into exile and assisted Queen Henrietta Maria but returned to London in 1654.[46] In 1655, amidst rumors of plots for royalist uprising against Cromwell, Cowley was arrested, questioned personally by Cromwell and Secretary Thurloe, and committed to prison pending further investigation. While in prison he wrote three poems that seem designed to invite favor from Cromwell's government.

An ode on "Destinie" urges the acceptance of the usurper and criticizes those who were defeated:

> Here I'm amaz'ed at th'actions of a *Knight*,
>   That does bold wonders in the fight.
>   Here I the losing party blame
>   For those false *Moves* that break the *Game*,
>   That to their *Grave* the *Bag*, the conquered *Pieces* bring,
>   And above all, th'*ill Conduct* of the *Mated King*.[47]

In another ode Brutus, the hero of the classical republicans throughout the seventeenth and eighteenth centuries, represents Cromwell in a parallel history equating Charles I with the "tyrant" Caesar. "To Mr. Hobs" also has political overtones, since at this point the parliamentary side had decided *Leviathan* supported Cromwell. While still in jail, Cowley wrote in the preface to the first edition of his collected works:

> Now though in all *Civil Dissentions*, when they break into open hostilities, the *War* of the *Pen* is allowed to accompany that of the *Sword*, . . . yet when the event of the battel and the unaccountable *Will* of *God* has determined the controversie, and that we have submitted to the conditions of the *Conqueror*, we must lay down our *Pens* as well as *Arms*, we must *march* out of our *Cause* itself, and *dismantle* that, as well as our *Towns* and *Castles*, of all the *Works* and *Fortifications* of *Wit* and *Reason* by which we defended it. . . . The enmities of *Fellow Citizens* should be, like that of *Lovers*, the *Redintegration* of their *Amity*. The Names of *Party* and *Titles* of *Division*, which are sometimes in effect the whole quarrel, should be extinguished.[48]

After these peace offerings from Cowley and £1,000 bail from his friend Dr. Charles Scarborough, the government released him. Cowley's apparent capitulation was later criticized, but as Arthur Nethercot points out, had Charles's restoration never occurred, the words of Cowley's preface would probably seem like common sense from a graceful loser who was unwilling to engage in useless, die-hard resistance.

Events lessened resistance to the interregnum government and the government also exerted itself to win the allegiance of as many Englishmen as possible, using tactics ranging from force to reasoned appeals to shared ideals. One of its tactics important to my later argument was the repeated imposition of oaths on citizens. In part, these oaths were the instruments of purges, designed to rid important institutions like parliament, the army, the church, and the universities of subversives. The oaths were also intended to create loyalty by invoking religious sanctions on disloyalty. Later counterrevolutionary myths aside, most gentlemen subscribed to one or the other of these oaths, at least abjuring resistance. Immediately after learning that Charles I had established communication with the Irish rebels, members of parliament bound themselves by a covenant to support parliament's forces against the king, "so long as the Papists not in open war against the Parliament shall by force of arms be protected from the justice thereof." Of greater importance was the Solemn League and Covenant sealing the alliance between the Scotch and the English parliament in 1643. Subscribers undertook a variety of obligations, including "the reformation of religion in the kingdoms of England and Ireland in doctrine, worship, discipline and government, according to the Word of God and the example of the best reformed churches."[49] Considerable political maneuvering had been needed initially to produce texts satisfactory to both the Scotch Presbyterians and the English Independents.[50] Although the Covenant contained a pledge to preserve the person and authority of the king, since parliament was already in arms against Charles, common sense seemed to indicate that anyone who had taken the oath of allegiance and supremacy to Charles I would be perjuring himself if he were to take the Solemn League and Covenant. Considerable casuistry was required to reconcile consciences to this oath, including the consciences of some parliamentary enthusiasts. A cornerstone of the arguments defending the covenant, and probably the one that most rankled the cavaliers, was the claim that parliament was fighting on the side of the king in an attempt to rescue him from his evil counselors. Distinctions were made between the king's royal authority and his personal will, covenanters claiming they still regarded the first as sacred. The author of *The Plain-Meaning Protestant. Or, An Honest Defence of the Taking the Covenant* maintained, "we are so farre from crossing our former Oaths made to the King, that this Covenant more firmly binds us and strongly

contradictions between this engagement and earlier oaths in particular. William Prynne contributed his *Summary Reasons against the new Oath and Engagement* (1649), later adding *Concordia Discours, or the Dissonant Harmony of Sacred Publicke Oaths.* Criticism was so intense that the penalties against nonengagers were first suspended in February 1650 and then repealed in 1654. Cromwell disliked forcing men's consciences with unnecessary oaths and repealed the act itself in 1654.

A great many sober and well-educated gentlemen who were shocked at the execution of Charles I and who would not themselves have instigated revolutionary change nevertheless eventually swore submission to parliament and were prepared to cooperate in the administration of the country. In spite of the exiles and in spite of the purges, if we look at the institutions whose personnel were paid to think about authority and obligation—the church, the universities, and the law courts—we see more collaboration than later royalist myth acknowledged. Such collaboration was not necessarily motivated by self-interested clinging to places. Many were prompted by genuine sympathy with the aims of the reformers, by what may be called public spirit, and—since no seventeenth-century government could exert anything like the control of a modern totalitarian state—by a reasonable hope of moderating the effects of the rule of the saints. Cromwell himself wanted to have competent people in positions of public trust and there were shortages of qualified candidates.

Although the bishops suffered considerably during the interregnum, almost three-quarters of the clergy episcopally ordained before the war either held on to their livings or accepted new preferment before 1660. So radical a person as William Prynne urged the reinstatement of one Anglican clergyman who had taken the Covenant and Negative Oath because "in times of scarcity of ministers there is necessity of admitting such, though they have been against us, rather than people should want ministers to instruct them, and so fall into atheism, profaneness, schisms, or heresies, for want of preachers to instruct them."[55] In a significant essay, Claire Cross has recently discussed "The Church in England 1646–1660," not as a collection of different sectarian churches but as a Commonwealth Church, Cromwell's state church, continuous with the Church of England before and after, though broader in its accommodation of various sorts of protestants and with more toleration for those peaceable Christians who scrupled to join. She offers the sentiments of one Thomas Fuller as representative of many moderate episcopalians who were willing to work within a protestant church supported by the state:

> I know that religion and learning hath flourished under the Presbyterian government in France, Germany, and the Low Countries. I know many worthy champions of the truth, bred and brought up under the same. . . . If . . . denied my first desire to live under that Church government I best affected, I will contentedly conform to the Presbyterian government, and endeavour to deport myself quietly and comfortably under the same.[56]

Even a Laudian clergyman like John Cosin who went into exile as Queen Henrietta Maria's chaplain, wrote polemics against the French Catholics who thought to convert him, fraternized happily with the Huguenots, and tried for a reconciliation with the Presbyterians at the Savoy Conference after the Restoration.

The universities were subjected to even more effective purges, yet retained a very considerable number of learned fellows. With the exception of those who were in exile abroad or kept at home on royalist principle, a generation of Restoration writers and thinkers was educated at universities subjected to successive purges designed to produce fellows in some sympathy with parliament and religious reformation. Thomas Shadwell, Nathaniel Lee, and Dryden were at Cambridge; Locke, Sedley, and John Holt, later Chief Justice of King's Bench, were at Oxford. Crowne was a student at that ultimate seminary of sedition, Harvard University. The political situation of the Cambridge Platonists in particular has often not been properly appreciated. The student of literature especially is apt to get the idea that the Platonists were quite apolitical, unworldly, mystical figures who tried to fight atheism and keep the spirit of poetry alive in a hostile world. Basil Willey, for instance, in his widely read *Seventeenth-Century Background*, says, "The Cambridge Platonists were contemplative, mystically-minded men to whom the realm of essence was more real than the material world."[57] Nevertheless, Cambridge fellows during the mid-seventeenth century were not secluded from the political fray. Far from it. By 1643 parliament was in control of Cambridge and soldiers were quartered in the colleges. Some members of the university left to join the king's forces; some moved to Oxford, which was then still in royalist hands; some retired to less exposed church livings or to the service of royalist families; some went into foreign exile. In February 1644 the Earl of Manchester appeared at the university, authorized by parliament to conduct a purge by administering the Solemn League and Covenant. Royalists appealed to the heads and fellows of the colleges to refuse the oath: "The eyes of the whole land are now fixed upon you, . . . wee conjure you to make a timely and generall Declaration of your unanimous dissent from the taking of this Oath, so derogatory to the Honour of God, so destructive to the peace of the Church, and so prejudiciall, in the consequence, to His Majesties just rights and power."[58] Seven members of the university, including Isaac Barrow, collaborated on a pamphlet, *Certain Disquisitions . . . representing to the Conscience the unlawfulness of the Oath*, which, not very surprisingly, had to be printed secretly in London with an Oxford imprint.

The Cambridge Platonists ignored these appeals and collaborated with the representatives of parliament, generally retaining their own positions and sometimes acquiring those of colleagues who had fled or been ejected. While it is true that the Platonists were concerned to argue against certain Calvinist tenants and that they rejected the antinomianism of the radical sects, it is not true, as Simon Patrick felt compelled to assert in his *Account of the new Sect of Latitude-Men* (1662) "that they were always looked upon with an evil eye by the successive usurping powers."[59] If they had been inveterately hostile to the usurping powers, they would not have continued to be Cambridge fellows. Henry More later liked to remember himself as faithful to Charles, exclaiming in print in 1681, "as if I were either Presbyterian or Independent! When as my nearest relations were deep sufferers for the King, and my self exposed *(by constantly denying the Covenant)* to the loss of that little preferment I had before those times, as I never received any employment or preference in them."[60] Leslie Stephen in the *Dictionary of National Biography* describes him as "intensely loyal to the King, both during the civil war and after the Restoration." It is true that More, unlike most of the Platonists, did not accept a promotion during the interregnum, and, of course, he was opposed to Calvinism. Nevertheless, there is evidence that More, one of only four fellows who were not ejected from Christ's College by Manchester, did subscribe to the Covenant.[61] At Emmanuel, Nathanael Culverwel, Ralph Cudworth, and John Worthington presumably also complied, since they remained while others were ejected and while the Presbyterian Anthony Tuckney was brought in to replace the imprisoned Richard Holdsworth as master. When Samuel Collins was removed as Provost of King's College, Manchester summoned Whichcote from a church living in Somersetshire to replace him. Cudworth succeeded Thomas Paske as Master of Clare in 1645 and in 1647 was in sufficient favor to be invited to preach to parliament itself.

Further changes came after the execution of Charles I. Peter Sterry, who had been elected a fellow of Emmanuel in 1636, now was appointed preacher to the Council of State, his new duties including certifying the fitness of ministers and preaching before both Cromwell and parliament. A second round of purges was made possible by the Engagement and an order that all heads, fellows, graduates, and officers of the university, and all who were taking any degree declare their allegiance to the Commonwealth. Some members of the university who had subscribed to the Covenant now balked at the Engagement; those who supported it found various rewards. More was one of the first to submit at Christ's. Worthington moved from his fellowship at Emmanuel to replace Thomas Young as Master of Jesus. Whichcote continued as Provost of King's, presumably subscribing this time. Cudworth continued to prosper, in 1654 moving from Clare to become Master of Christ's and advancing the interests of his college and his protégés by correspondence with Secretary Thurloe. In 1657 he sent George Rust, the author of a *Discourse of Truth*, to Thurloe, recommending Rust himself and ten others as highly "qualified for civil employments."[62]

The judges and lawyers responded to the interregnum crisis of authority in ways ranging from enthusiastic support for the revolution, which after all was partially made in the name of the legal rights of subjects, to firm support for the king, who claimed to be exercising his own legal rights. The common lawyers generally were allied to parliament in its resistance to James I and Charles I, and G. E. Aylmer has argued that the bureaucracy of the courts, partially as a consequence, was less disturbed during the interregnum than the other state bureaucracies.[63] A few judges and lawyers, however, declined to acknowledge the interregnum governments. Justice Malet of the King's Bench, who was sitting in 1642, refused to recognize the legality of the Militia Bill, which the king had refused to sign and which was thus the first genuinely revolutionary act of parliament.[64] He was imprisoned in the Tower until 1644, then released and disabled from serving as a judge until after the Restoration. Justice Heath of the King's Bench fled Westminster to join the king at York; Charles I named him Chief Justice, but he never sat. John Kelyng, a judge after the Restoration, in 1642 tried to present a group of men drilling in accordance with the militia ordinance before the Hertfordshire quarter sessions. He was summoned to the House of Commons and imprisoned in Windsor Castle until the Restoration. Most of the lawyers and judges, though, did not offer such clear-cut resistance. After finding for the king in the ship money case in 1640, Justice Berkeley was arrested by parliament while sitting in open court, "to the great terror of the rest of his brethern, and of all his profession." He was impeached for high treason, but since by Michaelmas term of 1642 Malet was in the tower and Heath with the king, parliament put off his trial and asked him to continue acting as a judge, which he agreed to do. Justice Bacon was appointed by the king in 1642 and kept sitting until the king was executed. Bulstrode Whitelock reported that when the Solemn League and Covenant was administered to the lawyers and officers "so many came to take it, that they were fain to appoint another day for it."[65]

The attrition of judges in the various courts was severe enough that by 1644 parliament had to supply vacancies, but all the new judges were conventionally educated gentlemen who had been admitted to the bar before 1640. The king's parliament at Oxford declared these judges and the lawyers pleading before them guilty of high treason. Henry Rolle, already named a serjeant-at-law by Charles in 1640, was named a justice of the King's Bench by parliament in 1654 and Chief Justice in 1648. (After the execution of the king, King's Bench was often called the "Upper Bench," but its function did not change.) Rolle had been an M.P. who urged redress of grievances in the Long Parliament, pledged one hundred pounds for the support of parliament in 1642, and apparently took the Covenant out of conviction, but was one of the members ejected from parliament in Pride's Purge. After the execution of Charles, six sitting judges, including Rolle, agreed to continue to serve; six others refused. David Underdown cites Whitelock, one of the commissioners of the great seal and so analogous to the earlier Lord Keepers as a chancery judge, as at this juncture "no doubt sincere in his belief that in these revolutionary times there was an 'absolute necessity' of preserving what was left of the legal system." "My obedience," Whitelock told what was left of parliament, "is only due to you, and there is no other visible authority in being but yourselves." Rolle joined the new Council of State and Underdown notes his presence as evidence that the radicals "were anxious to enlist as many moderates as could reasonably be expected to accept the *fait accompli*."[66] Rolle eventually asked to be relieved of his duties in 1655 when confronted with *Cony's Case* in which a merchant refused to pay custom duties on silk in accordance with Cromwell's customs ordinance, arguing that tax ordinances not ratified by parliament were illegal. Rolle apparently retired rather than give a verdict. Cony was imprisoned, and the three lawyers defending him (Wadham Wyndham, John Maynard, and Thomas Twysden) were imprisoned until they retracted their argument. The three defense counsel all received preferment after the Restoration as opponents of Cromwell, but even they had obviously continued to practice when the Oxford Parliament had declared such practice treason. John Glyn, who replaced Rolle as Chief Justice of King's Bench in 1655, was a Welsh Presbyterian who as an M.P. had been active against Strafford and Archbishop William Laud, supported the Grand Remonstrance, and, like Rolle, contributed one hundred pounds to parliament in 1642. He apparently escaped rather than be arrested in Pride's Purge, but later was willing to be named a serjeant-at-law and to act as Chief Justice until the removal of Richard Cromwell. He was one of a number of moderates who urged Oliver Cromwell to allow himself to be named king, apparently in a speech later published as "Monarchy asserted to be the best, most ancient, and legal form of Government" (1660). Charles II raised no objection to having him included in the group of twenty named serjeants in 1660. Indeed, of the twelve King's Bench judges who served parliament during the interregnum, seven had died of natural causes by the Restoration, two who were members of the Rump Parliament received neither preferment nor punishment, and three were renamed serjeants, one of them also being made a judge in Common Pleas.

The most memorable account of a judge's behavior during the interregnum is Gilbert Burnet's *Life and Death of Sir Matthew Hale* (1682). Born in 1609, Hale had already distinguished himself as a lawyer before he defended Strafford and Laud in their impeachment trials; after the Restoration he became first Lord Chief Baron and later Chief Justice of the King's Bench. He was certainly the most significant writer on law of his period. When the fighting broke out in 1642, Hale continued to assist various royalist defendants. In 1653 Cromwell invited him to become a judge of Common Pleas. Burnet explains:

> He did deliberate . . . the Lawfulness of taking a Commission from Usurpers; but . . . he came to be of opinion, *that it being absolutely necessary, to have Justice and Property kept up at all times; It was no Sin to take a Commission from Usurpers, if he made no Declaration of his acknowledging their Authority,* which he never did: He was much urged to Accept of it by some Eminent Men of his own Profession, who were of the *Kings* Party, as Sir *Orlando Bridgeman,* and Sir *Geoffrey Palmer;* and was also satisfied concerning the lawfulness of it, by the resolution of some famous *Divines,* in particular Dr. *Sheldon,* and Dr. *Henchman,* who were afterwards promoted to the Sees of *Canterbury* and *London.*
>
> To these were added the importunities of all his Friends, who thought that in a time of so much Danger and Oppression, it might be no small Security to the Nation, to have a Man of his Integrity and Abilities on the *Bench;* and the Usurpers themselves held him in that Estimation, that they were glad to have him give a Countenance to their Courts.[67]

Burnet's attitude toward Hale is hagiographic, and both this attitude and his need to defend his own position make his claim that Hale made no acknowledgment of the usurpers suspect, even if the casuistry of a distinction between accepting an official post and swearing allegiance be accepted.[68] It is conceivable that Cromwell might have excused Hale from the Engagement in order to get him to be a Common Pleas judge, as he excused Sir Thomas Fairfax, but it seems most likely that Hale had had to take the Engagement if not the Covenant itself in order to act as an advocate. Hale was an extraordinarily serious and pious man who richly deserved the accolades bestowed on his character by almost all his contemporaries. His collaboration with Cromwell despite his earlier royalist allegiance is worth notice not because it reveals moral turpitude, but because it was prompted by the same mixture of motives that influenced many moderate clergy, dons, and lawyers, especially in the 1650s: genuine sympathy with some aims of the protestant reformers, despair that the "usurpers" would be defeated, civic responsibility, and the realistic hope of influencing the government with their own principles. Hale, in fact, not only served as a judge, but also accepted appointment as chairman of a parliamentary commission on law reform.[69]

There were, thus, a significant number of well-educated gentlemen prepared to help the interregnum governments administer the country. Many of the moderates would cooperate for a time and then resist—for example, in the wake of the execution of Charles or the death of Oliver Cromwell or over some particular issue like Cony's case. Though there was nothing necessarily discreditable about such collaboration, many tormented themselves with scruples at the time, and after the success of the counterrevolution there was a general attempt to bury the painful memories as deeply as possible.

What suggestions, then, can we make at this point about how the experience of the interregnum affected the culture of the Restoration? The effects of exile, voluntary or involuntary, are perhaps most obvious. Before the 1640s, of course, numbers of Englishmen had gone through the paces of the grand tour in the tradition of late humanism. Nevertheless, the travels and prolonged residence abroad of the exiles seem to have a slightly different character. The career of John Evelyn illustrates the increased contact with European culture, particularly French culture, that such exile could succeed in forcing. Evelyn was a royalist, though as the writer in the *Dictionary of National Biography* fairly comments, "It must be confessed that his zeal had been tempered by caution." For nine years he spent time at Paris, Naples, Rome, Venice, Padua, Verona, and Milan, dividing his attention between the fine arts and the sciences. Before the war mature travelers naturally would have had responsibilities at home to attend to and would not have had the same incentives to remain abroad for more than a year or two. Evelyn seems to have used his time to good purpose. At Padua, one of the most advanced centers of science in the mid-seventeenth century, he studied anatomy and botany. For a month he attended dissections of human cadavers, marveling at the "extraordinary apparatus" used and obtaining "rare Tables of *Veines & Nerves*, & . . . a third of *Lungs, liver, & Nervi sexti par:* with the *Gastric* vains . . . the first of that Kind had been ever seene in our Country."[70] In Paris he inspected hospitals, witnessed "an operation of Lithotomie," and viewed the natural curiosities of Pierre Morrin, who had an extraordinary collection of shells and insects. After the Restoration he used his knowledge as a member of commissions for attending to the care of sick and wounded seamen, for improving the streets, for regulating the mint, and as a member of the Council for Foreign Plantations. Also, of course, Evelyn was one of the original members of the Royal Society and made a number of practical contributions to their work. Contacts that Evelyn and men like him had established with foreign scientists were to become an important element in the development of English science.[71]

But Evelyn, whom George Parks calls "the first articulate amateur traveler of aesthetic interests," was far from being exclusively devoted to science.[72] His experiences on the Continent helped him to gain a reputation as an authority on art and architecture and after the Restoration he shared his learning with his countrymen in such works as *Sculptura; or the History and Art of Chalcography . . . to which is added a new manner of engraving in mezzotinto* (1662), *A Parallel of the Antient Architecture with the Modern, with Leon Baptista Alberti's Treatise of statues* (1664),

Lisideius, it is generally agreed, represents Sir Charles Sedley, who with his friend Charles Sackville (Eugenius, the defender of the moderns in Dryden's *Essay*) and others translated Corneille's *Le Mort de Pompée* for presentation on the English stage in 1663. Sackville's family had not sent him to the university during the interregnum, allowing him instead to travel through Italy and France, where he had ample opportunity to observe the progress of dramatic poetry. Neander, representing Dryden himself in the essay, ends by defending the merits of the English theater against the French. He nevertheless agrees, "The fury of a civil war, and power for twenty years together abandoned to a barbarous race of men, enemies of all good learning, had buried the Muses under the ruins of monarchy." (Dryden here also shows the progress of counterrevolutionary mythmaking well under way in the sixties—the "barbarous race of men, enemies of all good learning" did not interfere with the pious Cambridge dons who helped give Dryden his own excellent education.) Though Neander claims that since the Restoration there have been many plays "which yield not to those of any foreign nation" (1:88–89), his specific examples in defense of the English theater are drawn from Beaumont, Fletcher, Shakespeare, and, especially, Jonson. Dryden the author of the dialogue has enough respect for the merits of the French theater to make it a subject of protracted debate. Dryden the playwright, like many of his contemporaries, drew upon the French for both inspiration and plots.[75] Even before Dryden, Sackville, and Sedley made their contributions to the English stage, Davenant was applying the result of his own observations in Italy and France. Just as Dryden's work shows his awareness of both the native English tradition and foreign drama, so Davenant's important early opera, *The Siege of Rhodes*, reflects both the tradition of the Stuart masque and the poet's knowledge of the developing continental opera. As Arthur Nethercot has pointed out, while Davenant was in Paris alone he would have been able to see *La finta pazza* (1645), Francesco Cavalli's *Egisto* (1646), Luigi Rossi's *Orfeo* (1647), and Abbe Mailly's *Akebar* (1646).[76] His *Cruelty of the Spaniards in Peru* continues this development and is in its turn reflected in Dryden's earliest ventures into the theater of extravagance, *The Indian Queen* and *The Indian Emperor*, which were, incidently, also based in part on Davenant's source, Bartholomew de las Casas's *Tears of the Incas*, and on Davenant's work itself.

The enforced retirement from public affairs of royalists also appears to have had some interesting effects, even when the royalists stayed at home. A number of dispossessed clergy and other learned gentlemen devoted themselves to historical scholarship that was later to provide important ammunition in Restoration political and religious controversy. William Somner, for instance, who had been an official of the ecclesiastical courts, occupied himself with antiquities and succeeded in producing an important Anglo-Saxon dictionary by 1659. William Dugdale's zeal to record and publish documents, including the monastic charters in his *Monastican* and medieval ecclesiastical records generally, was stimulated by not unjustifiable fears that the revolutionaries might destroy such documents.[77]

As for poetry, Earl Miner has observed, "One of the lasting benefits of the Cavalier winter seems ... to be precisely the discovery, or rather the immortalizing, of the joys of English country life and its *convivialities* in the strictest sense."[78] On the one hand, what appears to be a genuinely new kind of nature poetry emerges, a poetry in which natural objects are considered for their own sake and for their benefit to men, not principally as emblematic of significances beyond themselves. Metaphysical poetry like Marvell's "Garden" gradually gives way to locodescriptive poetry like Cotton's "Wonders of the Peake." On the other hand, along with this new focus came also a practical interest in agriculture and a strong desire to develop a more scientific basis for farming. (The economic situation of the gentry was in itself an incentive to try to make estates more profitable; the ruins in which returning cavaliers sometimes found their property made radical measures seem necessary.)

In Cowley the longing after retirement as a direct result of feeling weary of the complexities of war is apparent, as is the development of a new interest in nature for its own sake and for its practical uses. When his friend Davenant was captured on his journey to Maryland, Cowley, still in Paris, remarked, "We are strangely persued in all things, and all places, by our evil fortune;

even our retreats to the other world (except by death) are cut off."[79]
Later, when he himself was imprisoned, he announced in the
preface to his works an intention to emigrate to America, "to
forsake this world for ever, with all the vanities and vexations of it,
and to bury myself in some retreat there (but not without the
consolation of letters and philosophy)." In England in the late
fifties Cowley studied medicine, an effort that culminated not in
the establishment of a practice, but in the publication of long
poems on plants and herb lore. The poems are a combination of
citations from classical natural history, of observation, of folk
superstition, and of contemporary science. Cowley's *Essays, In
Verse and Prose* is a characteristic formulation of the attractions of
the country life, complete with translations of appropriate passages
from Martial and Virgil and longer poems of Horace, including
"Beatus ille qui procul." A prose essay on agriculture criticizes the
landed gentry for being too proud or too ignorant to improve their
estates and offers the practical suggestion that agriculture be made
a university subject. "The Garden" section of this book consists of
a short prose epistle to John Evelyn, complimenting him on sharing
his art and knowledge, and a longer poem on the wisdom of
cultivating one's own garden. As a member of the Royal Society
Evelyn made his most important contributions in forestry and
agriculture. Cotton, perhaps the most advanced of the later seventeenth-century poets writing about nature, can find in rural retirement a simpler world where there is some chance of maintaining
one's integrity:

> Oh my beloved Nymph! fair Dove,
> Princess of rivers, how I love
> Upon thy flow'ry Banks to lie,
> And view thy Silver stream,
> When gilded by a Summer's Beam!
> And in it, all thy wanton Fry,
> Playing at liberty,
> And with my Angle upon them
> The All of Treachery
> I ever learn'd to practise and to try![80]

Yet however successful this solution to the crisis of the Civil War
and its aftermath might have been for an individual member of the

landed gentry, such privatism could hardly provide the answer for society as a whole.

The display and triumph of raw force against ancient right had an impact that could not be forgotten. The king had been judicially executed, the social order of bishops, lords, and even marriage suspended, and, contrary to the expectations of many, the heavens had not fallen. Men who had compromised their beliefs or betrayed them altogether when faced with Cromwell's sword had to live with their guilt long after Cromwell was dead. In their turn, idealistic supporters of reform who had seen their revolution defeated had to deal with their own feelings of impotence, or worse, with the spiritual temptation of interpreting the apparent defeat of the revolution as a sign of God's abandonment, a temptation faced by Milton in *Samson Agonistes* and by Bunyan in *Pilgrim's Progress*. The only truly successful way to escape disillusion during the civil wars was to get killed in them. With the exception of a few people who had spent eighteen years in jail, the survivors of 1660 were those who had compromised or at least given up active resistance to their enemies or those whose cause had been defeated. Of the surviving writers, many seem to have been left with a strong suspicion that there were no heroes, or at least that whatever heroes there might be were really only imperfect men. Yet there was naturally also considerable resistance to accepting such an idea.

The character of the hero consequently became one of the most problematic issues in Restoration literature. Cowley's *Cutter of Coleman–Street*, set in London in 1658 and produced shortly after the Restoration, was intended as a satire on the puritans, but was badly received by its first audiences, who accused Cowley of also satirizing the royalists. The poet protested that his sympathies were with the king's party, but that it would be unrealistic to present perfect characters: "It is hard for any Party to be so Ill as that no Good, Impossible to be so Good as that no Ill should be found among them." Particular exception was taken to Colonel Jolly:

> Some others sought out a subtiler hint to traduce me upon the same score, and were angry that the person whom I made a true Gentleman, and one both of considerable Quality and Sufferings in the Royal party, should not have a fair and noble Character throughout, but should

submit in his great extremities to wrong his Niece for his own Relief. . . . The truth is, I did not intend the Character of a *Hero*, one of exemplary virtue, and as *Homer* often terms such men, Unblameable, but an ordinary jovial Gentlemen, commonly called a Good Fellow, one not so conscientious as to sterve rather than do the least Injury, . . . for if his true Metal be but equal to his Allay, it will not indeed render him one of the Finest sorts of men, but it will make him Current, for ought I know, in any party that ever yet was in the World.[81]

In *The Old Troop* (1664?, 1668) the actor and playwright John Lacy, who served as a royalist lieutenant in the war, satirizes the hypocrisy of the puritans but also shows undisciplined royalist soldiers guilty of plundering. Such relative realism, however, was very rare after the Restoration, royalists generally being represented uncritically in a series of plays including Sir Robert Howard's *Committee*, Sedley's *Mulberry Garden*, and Aphra Behn's *Round-heads; or the Good Old Cause*. Even in Lacy a virtuous royalist Captain in the fifth act cashiers the errant plunderers who so abuse "the King's honour and interest" and gives back "wealth" some country gentlemen tried to save by entrusting it to the parliamentary forces, remarking, "Although the wealth that's here be great, and the King's wants require it, yet, to show that he had rather have his subject's hearts than money, he has commissioned me to return every man his own again."[82]

The significant effects of the interregnum are not evident in propagandistic representations of life before 1660, but rather in the general collapse of older ideals and the older genres that embodied them. The Restoration was the great age of the failed epic. Davenant found himself unable to finish *Gondibert*, Cowley could not complete *Davideis*, and Waller struggled with his peculiar *Battle of the Summer Islands*. The one great epic that was completed, *Paradise Lost*, has as a central problem the absence of a conventional hero. The epic itself was finally annihilated and replaced by the mock-epic, the most successful poems of the period being satires like *Hudibras*, "McFlecknoe," and *Absalom and Achitophel*. The most famous Restoration comedy, beginning as early as 1663 with Dryden's *Wild Gallant*, has as its heroes men whose morality, loyalty, and truthfulness are highly questionable. The serious drama shows similar symptoms. The heroes of the best

Restoration tragedies, Dryden's *All for Love* and Thomas Otway's *Venice Preserved*, are so far from exemplifying heroic virtue that Anthony is open to accusations of cowardice and Jaffeir is involved in treason; both are strangely passive, reacting rather than acting. In a series of spectacular plays including Lee's *Nero* and Elkanah Settle's *Empress of Morocco* protagonists seem to struggle to outdo one another in criminality. Dryden, in "Of Heroic Poetry," the important essay prefaced to *The Conquest of Granada*, makes explicit his intention to depart from the French models and to use instead heroes who are *not* "patterns of perfect virtue." There is an odd ambivalence in the audience that both admires and laughs at the extravagance of the heroic protagonists. Panegyric and parody generally become dangerously close. Waller's panegyric "Instructions to a Painter" almost immediately provokes a long series of satiric replies, including Marvell's brilliant "The Last Instructions to a Painter." And the closest Dryden could ever get to his dream of writing the great English epic was that wildly inventive cross between opera and panto, *King Arthur*.[83]

The early years of the Restoration, as we shall see, witnessed numerous attempts to bury the embarrassing realities of the interregnum past and to revive and strengthen prewar ideals. Ultimately, however, the hierarchical ideals had been too seriously weakened, the sympathy with some of the aims of the reformers too powerful, and the disillusionment of the interregnum too great. The 1670s and 1680s saw a revival of many of the issues raised but not resolved in the civil wars and franker acknowledgment of the confusion of values left in the wake of the fighting. Finally, toward the end of the century, new orthodoxies began to be erected—supposedly on ground cleared by skepticism—but the new orthodoxies were accepted in large part by a new generation that had not personally endured the trauma of the civil wars.

2
AUTHORITY AND OBLIGATION IN THE STATE:
"Let Majesty no more be held Divine"

I

The issues which erupted into the civil war were not solved by that war but remained for Englishmen to struggle with until nearly the end of the seventeenth century. In particular, the revolution failed to define the limits of the king's authority over his subjects. It merely weakened the executive in certain specific areas—there was no longer a Star Chamber, for instance—and postponed the fundamental problem. The nature of the subject's obligation to the powers set over him was perhaps even less clear. Henry Neville was essentially correct when he wrote in 1681, "we are to this day tugging with the same difficulties, managing the same debates in parliament ... which our ancestors did before the year 1640; whilst the king has been forced to apply the same remedy of dissolution to his first two parliaments, that his father used to his four first and King James to his three last."[1]

Nor did violence go out of political life at the Restoration. Armed conflict still broke out sporadically. Venner's Rebellion was followed by Monmouth's Rebellion, by William's invasion, and by Jacobite uprisings against William.[2] Plots and suspicions of plots for rebellion and assassination continued to flourish. The Popish Plot, the Meal Tub Plot, the Rye House Plot, the Lancashire Plot, and the Montgomery Plot are only a few of the more famous. To participate in public life still meant to run the risk of impeachment, indictment for treason, and attainder. Sometimes prosecutions and even convictions were secured by political enemies on the flimsiest evidence or on nothing but perjured testimony. Not only great ministers and magnates like Clarendon, Buckingham, Shaftesbury, and Danby had cause to fear allegations of treason. A faithful and humble servant of the crown like Samuel Pepys could be terrorized by parliament and the courts. When Pepys signed a warrant for the sale of anchors to the French he worried that he might be committing treason; during the agitations over the Popish Plot he was actually accused of being a Roman Catholic and of committing treason. In 1663 one John Twyn was convicted of treason for printing a book called *A Treatise of the Execution of Justice*. Conviction of treason still meant hanging, drawing, and quartering for men and burning for women. Alice Lisle, the last woman in England judicially sentenced to burning for treason, was convicted when she was alleged to have hidden a participant in Monmouth's Rebellion. The surgeon James Yonge noted in his journal that shortly after Monmouth's Rebellion he rode from Exeter to Exminster, "where we dined, and here we began to meet heads and quarters in all the little towns, crossways, and bridges, being of such as were executed for the late Rebellion."[3]

Toward the beginning of the period, Tory ideology—pretending unhistorically to be simply a reflection of ancient practice—attempted to promote a doctrine of divine right kingship. According to this doctrine, the subject had virtually no rights as over against his sovereign; what in the sixteenth century had already been called the rights of the subject or the rights of parliament now were said to be merely privileges granted by the sovereign and revocable by him at any time. Also, according to divine right doctrine, the identity of the sovereign was determined by indefeasible hereditary right; neither the fortune of battle nor the will of parliament could create a legitimate king. Kings *de facto* were simply usurpers. By the end of the seventeenth century, on the contrary, Whig ideology—pretending equally unhistorically to be simply a reflection of ancient practice—had institutionalized its version of the correct relationship between sovereign and subject. The rights of the subject against his sovereign had been practically increased and the legitimist distinction between kings *de jure* and kings *de facto* had been substantially abolished in favor of kings *de facto* declared to be kings *de jure* by parliament. This victory of Whig ideology over Tory demanded the replacement of old fictions of authority with new ones and a general transvaluation of values in the culture. The new understanding of the right relationship between sovereign and subject had to be reflected not only in political theory, but also in statutes, in criminal law—particularly in the law of treason, the law of seditious libel, and in the conduct of treason trials—and in the poems and plays that undertook to represent sovereigns and their subjects.

Although John Loftis has a chapter on "The Political Themes of Restoration Drama" in his *Politics of Drama in Augustan England* and both Anne Barbeau and Geoffrey Marshall have more recently asserted the political relevance of at least some heroic plays and tragedies, it has been usual to understand Restoration heroic drama and tragedy as fundamentally apolitical and unconcerned with contemporary political problems.[4] Bonamy Dobrée claimed the most striking thing about Restoration tragedy was its "unreality." Louis Teeter concluded his thorough and valuable "Political Themes in Restoration Tragedy" by lamenting that Elizabethan plays "are more organically connected with actual political thought and problems than are those of the Restoration, which are romantic in the worst sense of that ambiguous word." D. W. Jefferson has praised the exuberant wit and rhetoric of Dryden's heroic plays, but simultaneously argued, "It is because the heroic plays are completely unreal that it was possible for Dryden to play with his material in this way. . . . The theme is so far removed from reality, his version of heroism so cut off from serious values and ideals, that it was possible for him to exploit his material in whatever way suited his fancy." Still more recently, Eric Rothstein has also asserted, "political allusions in Restoration tragedy almost never do more than add spice or set norms in an otherwise conventional and apolitical plot." Finally, Anne Righter pronounces heroic tragedy a hollow retreat "to a land of rhetorical make-believe": "the tragedies produced between 1660 and the formal end of the Restoration in 1685 were essentially frivolous."[5]

At the same time the plays are generally found to be unreal, the individual playwrights are dubbed political turncoats and

timeservers. Everyone is familiar with the charges leveled at
Dryden for changing his politics from support of Cromwell to
support of Charles and for changing his religion from Anglicanism
to Roman Catholicism. A major writer like Dryden has found
defenders willing to explain his conversions as carefully thought-
out progressions, not matters of expediency.[6] Lesser writers of the
period, equally given to conversions, have received less sympathy.
Nathaniel Lee is said to have changed from Whig to Tory and back
to Whig again. Frances Barbour notes Whiggish tendencies in Lee's
first five plays, not only in the notorious *Lucius Junius Brutus*
(1680), then observes of Lee's collaboration with Dryden on the
Tory *Duke of Guise* (1682), "whether the desertion of the Whig
cause by Lee was due to Dryden's influence or to his own
realization that a playwright would do well to be prudent in his
political utterance, *Constantine the Great*, written in the same year
as the *Duke of Guise*, glorifies the theory of divine right. It is
possible that Lee was conscious that his powers were failing, and
was striving frantically to get his plays before the public even at a
sacrifice of his political principles." Of Lee's last published plays,
especially the prologue and dedication to *The Princess of Cleve* and
The Massacre of Paris, Thomas B. Stroup and Arthur L. Cooke
note Williamite sympathies and remark, "Like his father before
him, he had very little objection to setting his sails to a changed
wind."[7] Elkanah Settle enthusiastically supported the Whig side
during the Exclusion crisis not only with anti-Catholic pope-
burning pageants and the rather exciting *Female Prelate* (1680),
but also with a prose *Character of a Popish Successor and What
England may expect from such a One* (1680) and poems like
Absalom Senior, a Whig version of Dryden's *Absolom and
Achitophel*. After Shaftesbury went into exile, however, Settle's
biographer Frank Brown tells us, "The Tory cause had triumphed,
and Settle, having lost his friend and patron, who had been, it
seems, chiefly instrumental in rewarding the poet for his work in
support of the Whigs, . . . renounced his Whig allegiance." Settle's
Narrative attacks the Popish Plot as a fiction, stresses the contradictions in the testimony of Titus Oates and other witnesses, and
says that the Whigs who claimed to believe in the plot were either
fools or "Incendiaries" attempting to impose on those of weaker

understanding. Then, at the advent of the Glorious Revolution, Settle's biographer continues, "Defeated, but apparently not greatly discouraged by the change of party control, the poet allowed party to shape his allegiance a third time, and celebrated the occasion by writing A *View of the Times. With Britan's Address to the Prince of Orange*" (1689).[8] John Crowne's numerous tragedies of the seventies indulge in high flights of divine right rhetoric. After the revolution, though, he dedicated *Caligula* to Henry Sidney as "an eminent instrument in this revolution, which has been so happy to England, and the greatest part of Europe" (4:348). The play itself, as Crowne says, sets "tyranny before the eyes of the world, and the dreadful consequences of lawless and boundless power" (4:349). Adolphus Ward consequently belittles Crowne: "He seems to have had no hesitation in changing his political colors in deference to the times, becoming in turn an ardent servant of the Stuart Court and an upholder of the Protestant principles of the Revolution." After 1689, according to John Loftis in *Politics of Drama in Augustan England*, both Crowne and Thomas D'Urfey "now wrote Williamite satire as they had earlier written royalist." Finally, Thomas Southerne, in Clifford Leach's opinion, belonged to "that large company of writers who have changed their political opinions for the sake of personal gain."[9] The evidence for Southerne's alleged disloyalty consists partly of his having offered to provide evidence against papists in the pay of the French and partly of his having supported James II in *The Loyal Brother* (1682) and later helping John Dennis with the Whiggish *Liberty Asserted* (1704).

Both the claim that Restoration heroic drama and tragedy are essentially not concerned with politics and the repetitive claims that individual writers were politically disloyal seem to me misguided. (Though these claims are not necessarily logically inconsistent. One might argue, for instance, that political positions were so unimportant to the playwrights that they changed them freely whenever convenience seemed to dictate.) I would like to argue, on the contrary, that the plays are often intensely political and that much of their interest lies in their concern with the problems of political authority and obligation. Many plays explore the dilemmas of subjects who have to determine the legitimacy of rival rulers and the limits of their own obedience. In these plays we can trace the gradual assimilation of the political experience of the Civil War and, finally, see the emergence of new political myths to correspond to the new secular and utilitarian ideology of Locke and his eighteenth-century followers. It is no accident that accusations of bad faith multiply around writers who lived through the Exclusion crisis or the Glorious Revolution in roughly the same way they multiplied around the many poets who wrote successive panegyrics to Cromwell and Charles. During this period parties were much more fluid than the labels or our inheritance from the Whig and Tory mythmakers would have us believe. Those who are so freely accused of disloyalty and timeserving for the most part had little to be loyal to. Furthermore, what has appeared to many later readers the frivolity and preposterousness of the political ideas and situations represented in the drama, I think, reflects not so much the dissociation of Restoration drama from politics as the extravagance and preposterousness of Restoration political experience itself: civil war and revolution followed by an unexpected counterrevolution and then another revolution all within fifty years.

Apart from the plays themselves, there are several extrinsic reasons for regarding suspiciously claims that Restoration drama is essentially unreal and apolitical. Many dramatists were personally involved with politics and administration. Roger Boyle, Buckingham, and Sir Kenelm Digby sat in the House of Lords; Sedley, Sir John Denham, Sir William Killigrew, and Sir Robert Howard were in Commons. Howard exerted himself to defend Boyle when the Duke of Ormonde tried to have Boyle impeached. Buckingham was a member of the Cabal. John Wilson was impeached as recorder in Ireland. John Caryll was committed to the Tower on suspicion of being involved in the Popish Plot, later appointed James II's agent at the court of Rome, and finally in William's reign attainted for high treason. Henry Nevil Payne was accused of being an architect of the Meal Tub Plot and later tortured (unsuccessfully, and in Scotland where torture was legal) to force a confession of his involvement in the Montgomery Plot.[10] Colley Cibber joined his father in arms for William in 1688. Nicholas Rowe served as Secretary of State for Scotland.

Many dramatists also wrote directly about politics. Dryden's satirical poems are most familiar, but Dryden also wrote *His Majesties Declaration Defended* (1681) and *A Defence of the papers written by the late King* (1686). Nahum Tate collaborated with Dryden on the second part of *Absalom and Achitophel*; Settle and Shadwell each responded with Whig verions of the Absalom story. D'Urfey wrote at least seven satires against Shaftesbury and William Sherlock. Sir William Killigrew was the author of *A Proposal showing how the Nation may be vast Gainers by all the Sums of Money given to the Crown without lessening the Prerogative* (1663). Sir Robert Howard wrote histories of the reigns of several English kings that reflected on contemporary political issues, attacks on Danby, a defense of the Whig propagandist Samuel Johnson, and a vindication of William's title to the throne, *A Free Discourse Wherein the Doctrines which make for Tyranny are Displayed . . . And the mischievous Tendency of the odious distinction of a King de Facto, and de Jure, discovered* (1697). John Dennis was also a defender of the Glorious Revolution, secured a government appointment through Marlborough, and wrote several political tracts, including *The Danger of Priestcraft to Religion and Government, with some Political Reasons for Toleration* (1702). John Wilson, on the other hand, offered *A Discourse of Monarchy . . . with a close . . . as it relates to the succession of his Royal Highness, James, Duke of York* (1684) and *Jus Regnum Coronae, or, the King's Supreme Power in dispensing with the Penal Statutes* (1688). The political tracts and treatises written by playwrights show not so much that playwrights were especially interested in politics—as a class the Anglican clergy probably produced more political tracts than did playwrights and poets put together—as that political issues during the Restoration, especially the issues of sovereignty and the limits of the sovereign's authority over his subjects, were sufficiently urgent and interesting to engage the attention of literate men generally. That some of this writing was undoubtedly done with an eye to preferment says nothing special about playwrights in the days of the Pension Parliament. Even Samuel Johnson, a clergyman prominent among the Whig theoreticians, supported himself as chaplain to the great Whig Lord Russel.

We know, moreover, that the government took the political implications of plays seriously enough to censor and to prohibit quite a number of them. At one time or another many Restoration writers had difficulty with the politics of a play they had written, either because their intention had been to touch upon a dangerous issue or to satirize a prominent political figure or because the censors had seen fit to discover a dangerous implication or parallel history. Buckingham and Sir Robert Howard were never allowed to produce *The Country Gentleman* (1669). Dryden had trouble with *Mr. Limberham, The Spanish Friar, The Duke of Guise,* and *Cleomenes;* Lee with *Lucius Junius Brutus* and *The Massacre of Paris;* Crowne with *Henry VI, Part I* and *City Politiques;* John Banks with *The Island Queens* and *The Innocent Usurper;* Tate with *The Sicilian Usurper;* and Cibber with *Richard III.* Several playwrights who were consciously supporting the government got themselves into trouble merely by representing the opposition and allowing antigovernment arguments to be articulated, even in a context that made it clear they were to be rejected. The best documented cases of such loyalist plays are probably John Wilson's *Cheats* and Thomas Southerne's *Spartan Dame.* In *The Cheats* (1663) Wilson obviously intends to ridicule the subversive, nonconformist parson, Scruple. Yet when Scruple urges his followers not to despair in their days of trial after the Restoration, not to give up the good old cause "lest the Malignants reioyce," the censor cut those lines.[11] In most cases, of course, we simply do not know about deletions forced by the censors, and, unless the author happens to complain later in print or to be able to bring out his play in more sympathetic times, we do not know about plays that were forbidden altogether. Southerne must have thought *The Spartan Dame*, begun in 1684, would be acceptable because it supports James II's position so thoroughly, but the censor apparently considered that the arguments of the revolutionaries were articulated too fully. Over four hundred lines were cut, enough to make the play incomprehensible and to persuade Southerne to withdraw it until 1714. A citizen's speech in the first act is typical of the passages cut: "The old king Leonideas is fled to the Temple of Juno; the Ephori have cited him to answer some Misdeameanors; but he not appearing, has forfeited his Recognizance to the People so they have depos'd him according to law, and proclaim'd Cleombrotis King in his Roome" (2:355). Restoration governments, at least, did not consider these plays notably unreal.

The best evidence for the claim that Restoration heroic plays and tragedies have genuine political interest, however, cannot be such extrinsic evidence as censorship or the careers of the writers provide. The evidence must come from the plays themselves. For my purposes, it is convenient to discern three rough stages in the development of the Restoration political play: first, the heroic romance; second, the political tragedy; third, the democratic romance. These stages are dictated not simply by aesthetic or dramaturgical principles but by the massive changes in political ideology between the Restoration and the establishment of the Glorious Revolution. The heroic romance mirrors the counterrevolutionary politics of the Restoration, the political tragedy reflects the break down of the new Tory myths, and the democratic romance attempts to establish the new Whig myths of the Glorious Revolution.

II

Heroic romances dominate the sixties and early seventies. They include plays like Boyle's *Generall* (1664), Edward Howard's *Change of Crowns* (1667), Dryden's *Conquest of Granada* (1670–71), and Crowne's *Juliana, or the Princess of Poland* (1671). These plays customarily present civil wars, revolutions or counterrevolutions, serious confusions about the title to the throne, and deposed or otherwise legitimate claimants who are miraculously restored. Much concern is lavished upon noble-minded subjects who wish to preserve their honor intact under such difficult conditions. In one common version of this romance, an apparently rebellious subject is discovered to be a true king who has been unaware of his own claim to the throne. These heroic romances are the most obvious candidates for labels like "frivolous" and "preposterous" and are wonderfully burlesqued in Buckingham's *Rehearsal*.

Nevertheless, frivolous as they may appear, the heroic romances do constitute one stage of the culture's gradual assimilation of the civil war experience. The heroic drama indulges in a fantasy of pure honor while simultaneously acknowledging such honor to be impossible. Its early protagonists are the creatures of wish-fulfillment dreams. They always behave well and always preserve honor intact under kaleidoscopically shifting circumstances—and are thus quite unlike the vast majority of real royalists who endured the Civil War, compounding for their estates when given a chance in the forties, deserting the cause by taking the Covenant and Negative Oath, and accepting the inevitability of Cromwell's rule in the fifties. Characters like Boyle's Mustapha behave as their creators and their audiences would like to have behaved, but, for the most part, did not.[12] The preposterous complexity and wild exaggeration of the circumstances in which the heroic protagonist finds himself reflect an awareness of the heroic ideal as impossible. There is a dream logic: the political crises of the war had seemed as wild and as impossible; so if the situations in which one found oneself were indeed absurd, then not having coped with them very well must be excusable. At first the political crises people had lived through were both unassimilated and unassimilatable. That the audiences' reaction to the heroic protagonists mingled admiration and amusement reflected both their lingering respect for the ideal and their awareness that it was unrealistic. As Mrs. Evelyn said after seeing *The Conquest of Granada*, it is "a play so full of ideas that the most refined romance I ever read is not to compare with it: love is made so pure, and valour so nice, that one would imagine it designed for an Utopia rather than our stage. I do not quarrel with the poet, but admire one born in the decline of morality should be able to feign such exact virtue."[13]

The relation between the protagonists of heroic drama and real life is particularly clear in the case of Roger Boyle, often considered the creator of the genre. Boyle, a son of the Earl of Cork, not unnaturally had strong royalist sentiments in the 1640s. After the execution of Charles I he "vowed to devote the rest of his life to revenge for the king's death; 'to bear with all sorts of men for this purpose'; and to impose a curse on his sons if they should slaken in that duty."[14] But in 1649, even as Boyle was in London preparing to join Charles II on the Continent, Cromwell visited him, said that his treasonable intentions were known, produced incriminating letters, and offered him a choice of punishment or of serving the protestant cause in Cromwell's war against the native Irish. A protestant himself, Boyle chose to fight in Ireland and later held several high administrative posts under Cromwell. Later when Richard Cromwell succeeded, Boyle at first advised him, and then intrigued for Charles's Restoration. As Kathleen Lynch says, Boyle's heroic plays mirror his own life "in their recurring images of formidable usurper, restored warrior king, and king-restoring general."[15] In *The Generall* (1664) the other characters are repeatedly struck with admiration for the scrupulous behavior of Clorimun in affairs of love and valor. The subject and general of a usurper, Clorimun is in the middle of the play asked why he does not take advantage of his control over the army to restore the true king, Melizer. He replies:

> Justice herself wou'd blush, shou'd shee receive
> A right which treachery does to her give,
> And virtuous *Melizer* wou'd never owne
> From falsehood the possession of the Throne.
> Disgrace I feare lesse than to be unjust.
> 'Tis such to take and then betray a trust.
>   [1:135]

However the virtuous Melizer might feel, it would be unreal to suppose that Charles II would have been loath to owe his throne to an act of treachery. The ethical and political dilemmas Clorimun faces are real though, and so is Boyle's desire for self-justification.

Boyle's very popular *Tragedy of Mustapha, Son of Solyman the Magnificent* (1665) is less obviously autobiographical. Mustapha is a general whose popularity with his soldiers arouses the jealousy of his father, who is attempting to usurp the throne of Hungary. The play presents a phantasmagorical political world where policy is constantly at odds with nature. The givens of Turkish politics place an enormous strain on the characters: the Sultan may marry anyone but the mothers of his sons; he must exile his oldest son to rule over an outlying province until his own death; and, hardest of all, when the eldest son does succeed to the throne he must kill his younger brothers. The Sultan Solyman has found this harsh political tradition too difficult to accept and has already married Roxolana, Zanger's mother, and failed to send Mustapha, his oldest son, into exile. Mustapha is even more critical and decides to value his friendship with Zanger over tradition and power:

> How can that wisdom in our Sultans be,
> Which of it self is fear and cruelty? . . .
> And who would not a Monarchy refuse,
> When, to gain power, he must his nature lose?
> The vertue of that man was never strong,
> Who fear'd not more to do than suffer wrong.
>
> [1:235]

Mustapha and Zanger therefore exchange vows, Mustapha pledging not to kill Zanger, Zanger pledging to kill himself should Mustapha die. Boyle seems attracted to the spectacle of Turkish polity because it presents such an impossible set of givens. Solyman and Mustapha cannot bring themselves to conform to it, but their efforts to escape also lead to disaster. Boyle's sense of the impossibility of his own political choices—loyalty to Charles entailed indictment for treason and desertion of the protestant cause in Ireland, loyalty to the protestant cause in Ireland and the preservation of his country as he knew it entailed betrayal of his rightful sovereign—finds an objective correlative in Turkish politics.

Unlike Boyle, however, Mustapha and several other characters manage to preserve honor intact. Romance complications develop when first Zanger and then Mustapha fall in love with the captured and newly widowed Queen of Hungary. Rustram also seeks to find favor with Roxolana by inciting Solyman's jealousy against Mustapha and manages to have Mustapha banished. The several characters are thus confronted by the impossible choices typical of the heroic drama and articulate their predicaments in set speeches. Roxolana is tempted to have Mustapha killed as the only way of protecting her own son. Mustapha reflects:

> Fortune did never in one day design
> For any heart, four torments great as mine;
> I to my Friend and Brother rival am;
> She, who did kindle, would put out my flame;
> I from my Fathers anger must remove,
> And that does banish me from her I love. . . .
>
> [1:155]

Like Mustapha, the Queen of Hungary throughout defends strict virtue against policy. When Hungary has just been conquered at the opening of the play, she refuses to yield her crown and shows contempt for death. She refuses also to purchase safety by surrendering the infant king and scorns her subjects who advise such a course. Later the Cardinal urges her to abandon loyalty to the dead king and to submit to her new suitors:

> Be taught by Nature; she forsakes the Dead;
> Your precious tears you but on ashes shed. . . .
> [1:266]

Cynically, he at last tells her to pretend to love both Mustapha and Zanger and to wait to see which one triumphs. Rejecting this advice, the queen decides to flee. Then Roxolana, who earlier has interceded on behalf of the infant prince, enters to suggest the queen pretend to love Mustapha. Again the queen rejects pretense and compromise. Her speech to Roxolana poignantly expresses Boyle's sense of the value of that strict honor he had found impossible to preserve:

> But Honour, Madam, quickly will forget
> And lose it self whilst it does counterfeit;
> As men a little us'd to speak untrue,
> The just remembrance lose of what they knew,
> Till their first shapes grow to themselves unknown.
> [1:271]

Mustapha also contrasts the aristocracy's honor morality with the mob's morality of self-preservation. The Turkish and Hungarian mobs bear a suspicious resemblance to the English. Solyman heaps contempt on the religious leaders of his people:

> *Divans* like Common-wealths regard not fame,
> Disdaining honour they can feel no shame;
> Each does, for what they publick safety call,
> Venture his Vertue in behalf of all,
> Doing by pow'r what Nature does forbid,
> Each hoping, amongst all, that he is hid. . . .
> [1:231]

"Publick safety" recalls the language of the parliamentary party during the war and the reference to commonwealths comes oddly from a Turkish sultan, though not from Boyle.

Yet Boyle knew very well that it was not only the mob that thought of present safety, and, more seriously, *Mustapha* also contrasts honor with nature, ultimately suggesting that honor may be the feebler force. Roxolana and the queen debate in verse as pointed as that of Dryden's early heroic plays:

> *Queen.* I ever was without dissembling bred,
>   And in my open Brow my thoughts were read:
>   None but the guilty keep them selves unknown.
> *Rox.* No wonder we so soon subdu'd your Throne.
>   [1:272]

Duty and loyalty are opposed to power and desire for power; ties of friendship are opposed to ties of blood. Roxolana, Solyman, and the Cardinal are the most frequent spokesmen for force and for the more primitive passions: pride, desire for dominion, self-preservation, and a mother's love for her child. Expressing his suspicion of Mustapha, Solyman says:

> Pride is more natural than duty is;
> Duty is only taught by care and Art,
> Pride is by nature planted in the heart.
>   [1:259–60]

When Solyman perceives his son as a threat to his power, he sacrifices him. Roxolana, torn between her duty to her husband and her love for her son, sacrifices duty (1:283).

On the other hand, the Hungarian queen, Mustapha, and Zanger set themselves against what they understand to be the cruelty and bad faith of natural savagery and win limited victories. Very early Mustapha proclaims, "Friendship's a stronger tye than that of blood" (1:235). Roxolana, by contrast, later says, "Friendship, to Love and Pow'r, seems but a name" (1:270). Absolutely alone, deserted by her people and given bad counsel by her spiritual advisor, the queen rejects the lies that could apparently save her son and herself. Warned that Solyman is setting a trap for him, Mustapha insists on confronting his father: "Rather than duty lose,

I'le lose my life" (1:286). Mustapha is killed; the queen is awarded the Hungarian crown but determines to fly from power and retire to a cloister. Though tempted by the possibility of becoming king himself and tortured by jealous love, Zanger remains true to his vow and his friend, finally stabbing himself. Thus Boyle's "patterns of perfect virtue" preserve honor in the face of incredible odds and serve as a powerful wish-fulfillment fantasy for the audience of the sixties—even though they have no impact on the public world and even though Boyle's own experience does not permit him to save Mustapha in the tragicomic denouement more usual in heroic romances.

Boyle's other plays differ from *Mustapha* in being more concerned with the rights of the reigning sovereign to the throne. Also, since the action of these other plays usually replaces an illegitimate *de facto* sovereign with a powerful legitimate sovereign, the most virtuous characters are left alive at the end. *The History of Henry V* (1664), for instance, begins with Henry at Agincourt about to assert his claims to Anjou, Normandy, and Aquitaine; depicts Henry's struggle against the French queen, the Dauphin, and various French nobles; and concludes (unhistorically) with representatives of the French people recognizing the legitimacy of Henry's claim. Characters debate the strength of claims based on force or possession, the confusions of title left in the wake of Lancastrian and Yorkist civil war in England, and the French invocation of the Salic law to bar Edward III's claims.

In *Tryphon* (1668) the central issue is whether the murder of a successful usurper can be justified. As someone who had good opportunities to murder both Oliver and Richard Cromwell, but failed to take advantage of them, Boyle had every reason to be personally interested in this question. As in *The Generall*, the simple fact that Tryphon's usurpation has been successful appears to be one reason for not resisting his power. Demetrius argues at the beginning of the play:

> What ever sins to gain a Crown are done,
> The Gods do pardon when they put it on.
> We ought, when Heav'ns Vicegerent does a Crime,
> To leave to Heav'n the right to punish him.
>
> [1:380]

The wise and elderly Nicanor later concurs:

> He whom the Gods into the Throne do call,
> Should therefore only by their Justice fall.
> [1:401]

Their logic is the same as that of Marvell's " 'Tis madness to resist or blame / The force of angry heaven's flame." Unlike Cromwell, though, Tryphon has apparently complicated the woes of the legitimists by murdering not only the real king, but also everyone else who has any title to the throne. This twist makes the predicament of the virtuous subjects more difficult and so increases our sympathy for their reluctance to act. Demetrius, serving the usurper, argues that he is thus at least able to moderate his excesses and also asks:

> Were *Tryphon* kill'd, who should the Scepter sway?
> All the Ambitious for the throne wou'd fight,
> For where none has the Title, all have Right.
> [1:379]

Tryphon himself justifies his usurpation by pointing out that the old king gave him too much power and then jealously plotted to kill him. He killed the king in self-defense:

> But Natures Dictates which no man can wave
> Obliges everyone his life to save.

Nicanor retorts with passive resistance:

> Nature whose Dictates in defence you bring,
> Ties Subjects by their Deaths to save their King.
> [1:382]

As the characters argue their way from act to act, the spectator is not sure whether a counterrevolution would be justified. Finally, however, Tryphon tries to force Stratonice to marry him by threatening to kill her father unless she consents. He also agrees to let Aretus and Demetrius, who he has discovered is his rival for Stratonice, be killed as traitors. Aretus, who has from the beginning been the chief advocate of overthrowing the usurper, now pronounces his doom: "This Crime for Heavens Revenge makes *Tryphon* ripe" (1:425). Demetrius at last consents:

> But since to this vile way he hath recourse,
> 'Tis just to end such Tyranny by Force.
> [1:425]

Love here provides escape from political impasse, as it often does in Boyle. Romance complications are used to incite the heroes to actions that cannot otherwise be justified, and that, indeed, are often wildly irresponsible from a political or military point of view. In *The Generall* Clorimun cannot decide whether to lead the revolution against the usurper or to accept heaven's apparent judgment setting him on the throne until the usurper threatens to rape the woman he loves. In *Henry V* Henry goes in disguise to the French court to press his suit to Princess Katherine, provoking Warwick to comment:

> Would Love had led the King a safer way.
> Kings, in whose chances Nations fall or rise,
> Hazard too much in private Gallantries. . . .
> [1:198]

The plays as a whole, though, invite us to respect the heroes both for their valor and their dedication to love, not to condemn them as reckless or insufficiently concerned with public issues. Rape and threats of rape or forcible marriage are consistently used by Boyle and in Restoration serious drama generally as the ultimate signs of absolutist tyranny; sympathetic male characters are regularly provoked to revolt by threats against their women. Especially since rape and forcible marriage were felt to be as much if not more property crimes against the man whose woman was attacked than they were crimes of violence against the woman, they make convenient stand-ins for the confiscations and trespasses against property rights that in reality helped provoke Englishmen to revolution. At the same time threats of rape are easier to assimilate into an essentially romantic drama than tax increases or arbitrary ejections from revenue-producing offices would be. Rape, also, was finally to become a favorite political metaphor for the abuses of arbitrary power, as in Burnet's complaint that James II's standing army if unchecked would soon proceed to "a rape upon all our Liberties, and a Destruction of the Nation."[16]

When the counterrevolution succeeds in *Tryphon*, Nicanor

abruptly reveals that Aretus is the son of the dead king. Such revelations are also used by Dryden in *The Conquest of Granada* and in the upper plot of *Marriage à la Mode*. A character, apparently only a private citizen, who has throughout the play shown contempt for an illegitimate monarch and maintained that his tyranny ought to be resisted turns out in the end to be the legitimate monarch himself. We are left puzzled as to whether his arguments are supposed to be universally applicable or whether they are only valid for legitimate monarchs. Boyle seems to adopt this strategy because he himself is not certain. On the one hand, he sees something in the claim that heaven has revealed its will by installing a particular person on the throne and he appreciates the chaos likely to ensue if private citizens take it upon themselves individually to settle the problems of succession. On the other hand, he cannot imagine passively submitting to tyrannical threats to murder or rape his friends and relations. In this play, since his heroes unite their resistance to Tryphon's tyranny with the resistance of a true prince who had undoubted right they are understood to be blameless. The problems in Boyle's heroic drama are genuine enough and clearly articulated, though the solutions depend upon romance. Boyle had no realistic solutions, and in the sixties neither did anybody else.

That Boyle's exploration of the relationships of subjects and illegitimate sovereigns confronts problems the culture found genuinely difficult is evident in the law of treason in this period. In the years immediately following the Restoration jurists were forced to create legal fictions rivaling those of the heroic drama in extravagance. For centuries in England the fount of most treason prosecutions was the Treason Act of 1351, 25 Edw. 3, stat. 5, c. 2. One part of this statute made it treason to compass or imagine the death of the king and another made it treason to levy war against the king. In its preface the statute declared that Edward's subjects had recently suffered from the vagueness with which treason had been defined and that the statute intended to remedy this grievance by limiting and defining the crime. As Sir James Stephen pointed out, this statute was drawn up in relatively tranquil times and, perhaps consequently, does not deal with several sorts of political behavior apt to be troublesome in less quiet times: imprisoning or deposing the king, challenging the king's title or right to rule, conspiring to levy war against the king, sedition, and so on (2:250). Not surprisingly, therefore, 25 Edw. 3, stat. 5, c. 2. was later embellished with various constructive treasons—judicial declarations that acts not obviously compassing the death of the king or levying war against him nevertheless amounted to the same thing—and with further statutes adapted to particular political circumstances, several of which remained in force only during the life of one sovereign. After the Reformation several Tudor statutes made it treason to maintain the supremacy of the pope, to deny the validity of Henry VIII's various divorces, or to deny the right of parliament to establish the succession.[17]

Ordinarily the question of who is king has an obvious answer. When the line of succession is broken, however, the question of who is king within the terms of the Treason Act becomes more interesting. Under Henry VII, the first of the Tudors, an act was passed providing that "hensforth no manner of persone ne persones whatsoever he or they be, that attend upon the king and sovereign lord of this lande for the tyme being" shall be attainted of treason. This act was still in force during the Restoration and was generally thought to protect supporters of *de facto* kings, including successful usurpers, from later prosecution for treason by a *de jure* king who managed a successful counterrevolution.[18] Since Cromwell refused the title of king—a bad mistake in this context—it became necessary for the interregnum parliament to remodel the Treason Act to suit his title, which was accordingly done in 1654. The *State Trials*, of course, relate the cases of a number of royalists executed for treason during the interregnum. In 1649 parliament had already passed an "Act declaring what offences shall be adjudged treason." J. T. Tanner calls this act "a wide departure from the older conceptions of treason as mainly consisting of an overt act proving the traitorous imagination of compassing the king's death or levying war against the king" because it included such offenses as writing, printing, or openly declaring that the Commonwealth is unlawful or that Commons are not the supreme authority of the nation, yet the language of the act seems patterned on the Tudor statutes making it treason to deny the sovereign's title, to declare him a heretic, or to support papal claims.[19] One of the arguments advanced to Cromwell to persuade him to accept the title of king was that his doing so would, under 11 Hen. 7, c. 1, protect his supporters from later treason prosecutions.

At the Restoration the interregnum legislation fell into the oblivion sometimes created for memories of the past by modern totalitarian regimes. Restoration and eighteenth-century writers all regard the question of who is king under the Treason Act as an important one, but all also ignore the interregnum acts—which were also not printed in the statute books. A few key acts were publicly burned by the hangman.[20] Justice Kelyng explains in his law reports that in 1660 the judges decided to proceed against the regicides under 25 Edw. 3, stat. 5, c. 2, using the murder of Charles I "as one of the overt acts to prove the compassing of his death." When Sir Henry Vane was tried in 1662 for compassing the death of Charles II during the fifties, Kelyng says, "he justified that what he did was by the authority of Parliament, and that the king was then out of possession of the kingdom; and the Parliament was the only power regnant; and therefore, no treason could be committed against the King." To this theoretically plausible but practically hopeless argument the court replied: "It was resolved, that tho' King Charles the 2d was *de facto* kept out of the exercise of the kingly office by traitors and rebels; yet he was King both *de facto* & *de jure*. And all the *acts* which were done to the keeping him out were high-treason."[21] Had Cromwell taken Boyle's advice to have himself declared king (Boyle also advised him to marry his daughter Frances to Charles), Justice Kelyng might have found this argument to Vane harder to make. As it is, to declare Charles II king *de facto* throughout the fifties seems a high flight of legal fancy.

The greatest of the Restoration jurists, Sir Matthew Hale, entangles himself when he tries to discuss treason in *Historia Placitorum Coronae*. Hale ignores Cromwell but discusses usurpers at some length, citing Henry IV, Henry V, Henry VI, Richard III, and Henry VII as examples. Though he says that usurpers may be considered kings within the statute, he is close enough to believing in a divine right theory of indefeasible hereditary succession that he cannot bring himself to neglect the claims of kings *de jure* not in possession. He maintains that attempts to compass the death of a usurper "have been punished as treason, unless they were attempts made in the right of the rightful prince, or in aid or assistance of him" (*HPC*, 1, 10, 60–61). Later he claims that acts of hostility against a usurper "in assistance of the rightful heir of the crown, which afterwards obtained," were not treason, but that acts in aid of a usurping *de facto* king have later been punished as treason (*HPC*, 1, 13, 102). Hale here wants to forge a union between legitimist theory and historical practice, a union that does not exist. (Wilson's notes complain about Hale's misuse of cases here.) Whether attempts against a usurper are made in the name of a rightful prince is irrelevant to whether they will be punished as treason or not; the usurper will punish them no matter in whose name they are made; the prince in whose behalf they are made will not punish them if they are successful, whether or not he is a "rightful prince." Hale is too close to Cromwell to admit that the idea of a *de jure* king who is not also king *de facto* can have no force in law. The law may declare past kings usurpers, but no present king can possibly be a usurper in law. There may be governments in exile and popes in Avignon, but the law proclaims whoever is king "for the tyme being" king in law as well as in fact.

Hale, Kelyng, and Boyle all share similar quandries, find themselves in similar impasses, and experiment with similar fictions. In spite of the traditional insistence that subjects are not proper judges of the legitimacy of a sovereign's title, all three are sufficiently influenced by events and by divine right theory that they are unwilling to think of acts against a "usurper" in the name of a "rightful prince" as treason. Hale's acquiescence in this principle is really more surprising than Boyle's.

But legitimacy was not the only political issue of the 1660s. Another heroic romance of this decade, Sir Robert Howard's *Duke of Lerma* (1668), is less concerned with reliving the Civil War traumas and more interested in the post-Restoration struggle between an admittedly legitimate monarch and his subjects. Howard's play is both a propaganda piece against favorites and

evil counselors and another exploration of the problems of subjects
confronted with wrong rule. Since Howard as an M.P. had recently
been in the forefront of the fight to have Clarendon impeached, this
topic had immediate relevance for him. Clarendon's downfall had
many causes, chief among them Charles's own impatience with his
moralistic and dominating advisor and Clarendon's opponents'
desire to get places for themselves. Nevertheless, the overt attack on
Clarendon was based on the premise that he was an evil counselor.
One genuine ideological grievance against him was that he desired
to make the king too independent of other advisors, especially
parliament. Clarendon, for example, had complained that a bill
permitting parliamentary audit of money spent in the Dutch War
was an encroachment on the king's rights. Warning Charles that
the Cavalier Parliament was behaving too much like its
revolutionary predecessors, he recommended dissolution in both
1666 and 1667. His opponents charged he had advised Charles to
do without parliament altogether. Howard intends no point for
point correspondence between Clarendon and Lerma, simply an
exploration of the problems raised by bad counselors.

As the play opens, King Philip of Spain has just died and the
Duke of Lerma, who has been the king's favorite, fears his enemies
will now succeed in banishing or even killing him. Prompted by his
confessor, Lerma determines to use his beautiful daughter Maria to
capture the favor of the new king, young Philip. Maria is appalled
at the idea of prostituting herself, but promises obedience when
Lerma says that otherwise he may have to kill the young king in
self-defense. Philip does fall in love with Maria and promptly
restores her father to favor. Lerma's brother, the Duke of Medina,
speaks out forcefully against favorites, "lawful" traitors "by
permission," who usurp power kings ought to exercise personally.
(Charles in the sixties was, in fact, inclined to allow parliament
more leeway than Clarendon thought wise.) Medina's rebukes
endanger him, but he considers it his duty to speak out:

> I think it is no Treason
> To snatch a King from falling down a precipice. . . .[22]

The dialogue between King Philip and Medina might well be
dialogue between Charles and any member of parliament who was

attacking one of the ministers he had chosen, Clarendon in the sixties or later the Duke of Lauderdale or the Earl of Danby, whom he persisted longer in wanting to retain:

> *King.* 'Tis boldness, and not duty, to question
>   Princes favours.
> *Med.* But not to beg 'em Sir, no more than 'tis
>   To pray, That Heav'n wou'd turne a vengeance from us,
>   Threatening in *Lerma's* power. . . .
>   Turne, mighty Sir, your lookes the other way,
>   And see your widow'd People want their King,
>   Drooping like dayes unlook'd on by the Sun.
>   Your Councel wither'd more with care then Age,
>   Grown as much strangers to your great Affaires
>   As unto *Lerma's* pleasure. . . .
> *King.* Must Princes favours then be limited,
>   Or Judg'd by common Breaths?
>   'Tis restless Envy, that urges Mutinies
>   Shelter'd under Duty.   [*Exit*]
> *Med.* So the lesson is learn't perfect.
>   Oh Impudence! to make the Majesty of Kings
>   The pawn of all their villanies.
>
>   [Pp. 31–32]

Restoration parliaments avoided attacking the king directly, proclaiming enthusiastically "the king can do no wrong," but interpreting that old maxim to mean that whatever wrong was done was the responsibility of the king's ministers. Howard writes from the point of view of those who sought to control the king's policies by exerting parliament's power to impeach his ministers, sometimes to impeach them for high treason.

The Duke of Lerma is an exceptionally focused and lucid play that succeeds in capturing the spectator's interest not only in the daring Lerma, but also in the plight of his intelligent daughter Maria. Like any decent Cavalier heroine, Maria is prepared to protect her father's life, no matter how villainous he may be. On the other hand, she is a virtuous and public-spirited girl not prepared to become either a whore or a traitor. She therefore invents a ruse to teach the king a lesson. Ordered by Lerma to have Philip sign warrants that will send two of his faithful counselors to distant posts, Maria urges upon the king all the arguments for his absolute power and persuades him to disregard the need to consult his advisors on such an important matter. Having got Philip's signature, she then shows him how he has betrayed his better judgment, gets his promise to spare her chastity and her father's life, and warns the good counselors of the plot against them. The moral of the play is simple enough, but carefully articulated: in the relations between sovereigns and subjects, parents and children, the inferior cannot abandon his own moral sense. As Maria tells Philip when he points out that Lerma has obviously intended him to enjoy her:

> Yet his Commands makes not my Guilt less,
> For Heaven allows no pious wickedness.
>
> [P. 21]

Obedience may entail eschewing active rebellion, but it cannot entail blind conformity to the superior's will. The good inferior tries to change the will of his superior if it is wrong and will not cooperate in evil. In Stuart days of paeans to absolutism and passive obedience and of angry rebukes to Commons when it tried to advise about church policy, foreign policy, or the governance of the militia, this lesson seems to have been less than obvious.

Dryden's *Conquest of Granada* (1669–70) provides a final illustration of how political arguments about authority and obligation function in heroic romance.[23] At the conclusion of *The Conquest of Granada* and in Dryden's similar heroic romances we are offered the same formula Boyle relied on: the possessor of the best legal title to the throne is identical to the mythical natural law sovereign who best dispenses justice, who listens sympathetically to the genuine grievances of his subjects, and who never forces them to choose between their obedience to him and their own integrity. Like Boyle too, though, Dryden constructs problematic political situations and allows his characters to argue their way through them. Granada, like several of the countries in Dryden's heroic plays, is being torn apart by civil war between hard-to-distinguish rival factions and by what soon turn out to be rival kings, Boabdelin and the Duke of Arcos representing King Ferdinand of Spain. "The last king of Granada," Boabdelin is weak and decadent. Granada itself, expiring in the supercivilization of "soft peace," is obviously in need of an infusion of raw power and new blood, an infusion Almanzor is able to provide. Even Ozmyn, one of the most attractive and virtuous of Boabdelin's courtiers, is effete in comparison to Almanzor. Like the bull he fights in the first act, Almanzor is a natural monarch. His right to rule is based on his own superiority (and on his as-yet-undiscovered birth) and not on a corrupt social order.

Almanzor begins by denying the supposed sovereignty of Boabdelin. When Almanzor draws his sword in the monarch's presence and kills a man, Zulema points out:

> Outrage unpunished, when a prince is by,
> Forfeits to scorn the rights of majesty.
> [4:43]

But Almanzor's outrage remains unpunished and the king's majesty is successfully scorned. Almanzor himself explains:

> I saw the oppressed, and thought it did belong
> To a king's office to redress the wrong:
> I brought that succour, which thou ought'st to bring,
> And so, in nature, am thy subjects' king.
> [4:43]

He then proceeds to give Boabdelin a cameo political science lecture on the folly of letting factions grow in a kingdom. Later when the Abencerragos and Zegrys threaten civil conflict again, Boabdelin pleads with them in vain, but a word from Almanzor commands instant obedience.

We then learn that not only does Boabdelin fail to protect his subjects or to make them feel his authority, but that his claim to the throne is itself a weak one. Boabdelin and the Duke of Arcos debate the title to Granada's throne. Boabdelin asserts his right rests on the "long possession of eight hundred years." Arcos replies that the Spaniards were there first and that Boabdelin's claim comes only from force. The king retorts:

> 'Tis true from force the noblest title springs:
> I therefore hold from that, which first made kings.
> [4:47]

But we also learn that Ferdinand has earlier conquered Boabdelin, receiving from him a "contract" pledging that Boabdelin would remain a tribute-paying vassal for his life and then "lay aside all marks of royalty" when his father dies. Boabdelin now declares, "the force used on me made that contract void"—apparently disagreeing with Hobbes's dictum that covenants entered into by fear are obligatory, but vindicating Hobbes's warning that "before the time of civil society, or in the interruption thereof by war, there is nothing can strengthen a covenant of peace agreed on, against the temptations of avarice, ambition, lust, or other strong desire, but the fear of that invisible power, which they every one worship as God" (1, 15, 93). Thus, the most ancient claim to Granada does not belong to Boabdelin, and whatever title he might have had has already been given to Ferdinand. To add to Boabdelin's other failings, he is not a Christian.

Part of the exposure of Boabdelin as not exemplifying the mythical natural law sovereign suggests a second way in which the problem of the sovereign's legitimacy is explored: what may loosely be called Hobbist arguments are offered and attacked. The idea that Dryden was himself a political Hobbist has been advanced, but it is now generally recognized that though Dryden was obviously interested in Hobbes's ideas, those ideas are usually expressed by his villains and attacked by his heroes. I would, though, seriously disagree with Louis Teeter's claim that both in Dryden and in Restoration drama generally the use of Hobbist ideas was essentially decorative and that the ideas were primarily "valuable to the dramatists who wished to have their political villains up to date." Like some more recent critics, Teeter also resents the messiness with which Hobbist ideas are used and the general lack of coherent and correct explication of particular philosophical points, commenting, for example, on one passage: "The passage illustrates to perfection the clever way in which Dryden made use of any handy theory for dramatic effect. It is a weird mosaic of contradictory conceptions and unwarranted applications of ideas." It is, I think, unreasonable to expect dramatists who were interested in Hobbist ideas to provide technically correct accounts of them. Teeter's analysis also rests on the assumption, now successfully challenged by Quentin Skinner, that Hobbes's political ideas were notorious but unique.[24]

In *The Conquest of Granada* Boabdelin and Lyndaraxa, both

clearly undesirables, are the main proponents of Hobbist ideas.
With the utmost cynicism imaginable, Lyndaraxa attempts
throughout to seduce the successor to the throne as a husband.
Unfortunately for her, the tempestuous fluctuations of Granada's
political climate leave the identity of that successor in constant
doubt. After five acts, she is provoked into spurning Abdalla with
this *Realpolitik* definition of a king:

> A king is he, whom nothing can withstand;
> Who men and money can with ease command.
> A king is he, whom fortune still does bless;
> He is a king, who does a crown possess.
>
> [4:99]

Lyndaraxa herself is like man as Hobbes envisioned him in a
state of nature; in fact, she may be seen as an alternate version of
the noble savage and therefore as an antithesis to Almanzor.
Almanzor, at least until the revelations at the end of the play, and
Lyndaraxa, throughout, refuse to acknowledge the rules or
covenants of society and so live outside it. Almanzor exemplifies
the noble savage of soft primitivism, while Lyndaraxa exclaims:

> Yes! I avow the ambition of my soul,
> To be that one to live without control!
> And that's another happiness to me,
> To be so happy as but one can be.
>
> [4:54]

Engaged in "the war of every man, against everyman," she
discovers that "there is no way for any man to secure himself, so
reasonable, as anticipation; that is, by force, or wiles, to master the
persons of men . . . till he sees no other power great enough to
endanger him" (1, 13, 83, 81).

Dryden, typically, does not seem to perceive any contradiction in
the coexistence of two such characters as Almanzor and Lyndaraxa
in the same play. That is, he does not seem to feel Almanzor and
Lyndaraxa are two mutually exclusive answers to the question,
"What is the nature of man: is he essentially generous and peaceful
or essentially greedy, vicious, brutal, and power-crazed?" Lyndaraxa's way is clearly rejected; her view of the world leads to

catastrophe. Nevertheless, because she exists and because her view is fully expressed, the play is an agon where the view ultimately rejected is sufficiently interesting and persuasive to be considered.

The political dilemmas Dryden, Howard, and Boyle treat seriously, if abstractly, are brilliantly burlesqued by Buckingham and his collaborators in the extraordinarily popular *Rehearsal* (1671). Many heroic romances present legitimate or illegitimate sovereigns who are challenged by rebellion, but perhaps the Restoration anxieties over political authority and obligation are nowhere better reflected in the theater than in *The Rehearsal*, usually thought of as a purely literary satire of the absurdities of heroic romance. A given of Buckingham's play within a play is that there are two kings of the same place. Bayes explains:

> Now the people having the same relations to 'em both, the same af-fections, the same duty, the same obedience, and all that; are divided among themselves in point of devoir and interest, how to behave themselves equally between 'em; these kings differing sometimes in particular; though, in the main, they agree.[25]

(Note the mordant balancing of "in point of devoir," with its belittling court French, and "interest," the plain English word unconvincingly relegated to second place.) As S. Briscoe very early observed in his *Key to the Rehearsal*, there were two kings in Henry Howard's *United Kingdom* (now a lost play) and "Mr. Dryden has, in most of his serious plays, two contending kings of the same place." So does Boyle. With baroque exuberance, Edward Howard's *Change of Crowns* (1667) has not only two contending kings of Lombardy, but two contending queens of Naples. A cheerful chiasmus occurs in the ending when the true king of Lombardy can marry the false queen of Naples and the true queen of Naples can marry the false king of Lombardy, thus providing thrones for all. And Howard here only doubles the suggestion Boyle seriously made in 1657 that Cromwell's daughter should marry Charles, an idea that crops up again in *The Generall* when the usurper tries to marry his son to the princess Rosocleere. Banks later preferred to draw from authentic British history to produce two queens of the same place: Elizabeth and Mary, Queen of Scots, in *The Island Queens* and Lady Jane Grey and Mary Tudor in *The Innocent Usurper.*

Buckingham proceeds to develop what is, after all, not only the germ of countless heroic plays and Restoration tragedies, but also the problem of Cromwell and Charles, James and William. The burlesque reduces the issue to farce by making the two kings quite indistinguishable. They enter hand in hand and they do not have separate names, being called simply "1st King" and "2nd King." Further absurdity is introduced by baroque doubling: there are not only two kings, but two usurpers. This is the same joke Gilbert and Sullivan use with the chorus of twenty love-sick maidens in *Patience.* One love-sick maiden might be pathetic enough, but a massed phalanx of twenty love-sick maidens is ludicrous. One rightful king and one usurper might be taken seriously, but two indistinguishable kings and two usurpers is absurd.

The doubling is also like a dream fantasy. Minds wearied with the serious problems of divided loyalties see them as resistant to solution and excuse themselves from responsibility or guilt by reducing them to impossibility: "Claimants to my loyalty have multiplied uncontrollably—they seem merely doubles of one another—certainly it's not my fault if I can't choose among them or if I make the wrong choice." Just as the kings are indistinguishable, the motives of the usurpers are rendered unintelligible. All the conspirators' reasons are offered in whispers the audience cannot hear. Challenged on his use of whispering, Bayes defends this dramatic practice with wonderfully misapplied logic: "Why, Sir (beside that it is new, as I told you before), because they are supposed to be politicians; and matters of state ought not to be divulged" (p. 47). When the usurpation itself comes in *The Rehearsal* there are no soldiers, no rioting mobs, and no bloodshed. The two usurpers are talking quietly in the throne room and suddenly decide to sit down on the throne:

> And, since occasion now seems debonair,
> I'll seize on this, and you shall take that chair.

Bayes comments with self-approbation: "There's now an odd surprise; the whole state's turn'd quite topsy-turvy, without any puther or stir in the world, I gad" (p. 52). The joke is very funny, though exactly why it should be is perhaps not immediately obvious. Partly, Buckingham simply parodies the frequent suddenness of revolution and counterrevolution in heroic romance. Yet there is a deeper comedy of baffled expectation. After the initial traumas of the civil war, anxiety itself is mocked. The absurdity is taken one step further in the fifth act when, instead of using the position they have seized to offer fierce resistance to the rightful sovereigns, the two usurpers merely slink away at the apparition described by Prince Pretty-Man:

> Behold, with wonder, yonder comes from far
> A god-like cloud, and a triumphant car;
> In which our two right kings sit one by one,
> With virgin vests, and laurel garlands on. . . .
> [*The two right Kings of Brentford descend in the clouds, singing in white garments; and three Fiddlers sitting before them, in green.*]
>
> [Pp. 77–78]

But then where was Richard Cromwell when Londoners were celebrating Charles's Restoration with even more elaborate pageants? Where, for that matter, was James II when William marched on London?[26]

During the earlier years of Charles II's reign the heroic romance dominated the serious theater. As unreal as these tales of hidden true kings miraculously restored may seem to us now, they had a certain relevance in the decade or two immediately following Charles's restoration. It was comforting, too, that so many of these restored kings were willing to overlook any deviations from the path of strictest loyalty of which their subjects might have been guilty. These theatrical kings not only tended to echo Charles's sentiments at Breda, but also are not infrequently reminded that whatever loyalty was displayed ought to be rewarded. At the end of Edward Howard's *Usurper* (1667), for instance, the true king proclaims:

> There shall be an Indemnity for those
> Whose frailty, and not malice, made 'em Act
> Under the Tyrannt.

Cleomenes, described in the dramatis personae as "a Faithful noble Person," reminds him:

> Mercy becomes a king, which as it flows
> Upon your Enemies, should have a free
> Stream to your Friends, whose Faith, Sir, has been try'd;
> You else would break their Honest hearts.[27]

III

In the later years of Charles's reign, however, the king's honest-hearted subjects were less impressed with the miraculousness of his restoration and more worried about what he was going to do with the kingly prerogatives that had been restored along with his person. The early years of the Restoration were shaky enough politically, but the period 1674–88 is rightly called by Clayton Roberts "the Crisis of Confidence."[28] By this time the Cabal had been destroyed. Shaftesbury and Buckingham had gone into opposition, and parliament, impatient with the Lords' unwillingness to impeach without evidence of criminal misconduct, had discovered that it could note addresses against unpopular ministers with the concurrence of the Lords and then enforce them by refusing to pass money bills until their grievances were redressed. When parliament met again in 1675 after an interval of fifteen months the tone of political debate became increasingly hysterical and violent. In February Shaftesbury and Buckingham were sent to the Tower for arguing that Charles had dissolved parliament in November 1675, not simply prorogued it. Danby was impeached for treason in 1678 and Commons refused to allow him to plead the king's pardon in bar to an impeachment. The Popish Plot led to a series of judicial murders. Finally, the series of bills in 1679, 1680, and 1681 to exclude James from the throne or at least to limit the prerogatives of a Roman Catholic successor became a major test of what authority remained to the monarchy. Charles had to take the precaution of summoning parliament to meet at Oxford far from the London mobs. The party labels *Whig* and *Tory* were heard for the first time. Both the Duke of Monmouth and Mary of Orange were considered as protestant rivals to James for the succession. It is even possible that Buckingham, who was brought up with Charles I's children, and who claimed descent from the Plantagenets, "thought himself as suitable a pretender as Monmouth."[29] By 1681 Charles had had enough of parliaments to summon no more for the rest of his reign.

It is crucial to understand that the opposition between the newly crystallizing Whig and Tory parties in this period was not simply an opposition between discontented place-seekers and defenders of the *status quo*. Since the greatest poet of this period, Dryden, happens to have been a Tory propagandist, students of literature are especially likely to come away with such erroneous impressions. In particular, the divine right of kings proclaimed by some Tories was not a venerable political theory inherited from antiquity. The germ of the doctrine was created largely for the defense of late medieval emperors against the pope and then further developed in the sixteenth and seventeenth centuries to strengthen Roman Catholic kings against rebellious protestant subjects and protestant kings against Roman Catholic subjects.[30] In so far as the Tudors had any theories about the divine rights of kings, they used them to assert their sovereignty over the English against popes, especially popes who thought a Tudor sovereign ought to be excommunicated, and to inculcate a duty to obey constituted authority in the interest of domestic tranquillity. According to J. W. Allen, "the theory of divine right of Kings must assert that God intended mankind to be governed by monarchs and himself established monarchies and monarchies only" and "the theory must assert that moral obligation to obey the monarch is the result of a divine grant of real authority. It must deny that such obligation could possibly be created by any human arrangements."[31] Given this definition, Allen concludes that in England divine right theory belongs to the seventeenth century, not the sixteenth. Because of the weakness of their own claims, the Tudors could not insist that sovereignty was indefeasible and depended on hereditary succession by primogeniture in the legitimate line. As I have said, an Elizabethan statute made it high treason to question parliament's right to alter the succession.

James I's claim to the throne, on the other hand, such as it was, rested on heredity alone; two acts of parliament had barred him from the succession. Not surprisingly, therefore, the Stuart propagandists were inclined to insist on hereditary right. As tensions grew between the king and parliament, supporters of the king tended to become increasingly vehement about the sanctity of law, tradition, and parliamentary rights. James I himself, while he still had to worry about his Scotch Calvinist subjects like George Buchanan, argued in his *True Law of Free Monarchy* that kings are accountable only to God, never to their subjects; that kings are the source of law, not its creations; and that all resistance to kings is sinful. The English parliament, however, later suspended one Mr. Barber, Recorder of Wells, when he said he knew his actions were illegal but that he feared to resist the king. Similarly, Sir Edmund Sawyer was expelled from parliament and imprisoned in the Tower in spite of his plea that he acted on the king's command and in spite of Charles I's confirmation of that plea. By the early years of Charles I's reign some of the Anglican clergy were insisting that subjects had a religious duty to obey the sovereign's commands even if they were illegal. Should the sovereign's commands be not merely against the laws of England but "against the lawes of 1 God, or of 2 Nature or 3 impossible," argued Robert Sybthorpe in a sermon preached in 1627, still *"subjects* are *bound to undergoe the punishment* without either *resistance,* or *railing* and *reviling,* And so yeield a *passive obedience,* where they cannot exhibit an *active one."* Roger Maynwaring insisted that there could be no rule of justice between kings and subjects because justice only pertains to relations between equals. The king's authority, he says in *Two Sermons* (1627), derives directly and solely from God: "not from any consent or allowance of men . . . not in any *Municipall Law,* or *Locall custome,* not in any law *Nationall,* nor yet in the law of *Nations,* which consent of men, and tract of time, hath made forcible." Parliaments exist not to challenge subsidies to the king but simply "for the more equall *Imposing,* and more easie *Exacting* of that which, unto *Kings* doth appertaine, by *Naturall* and *Originall Law,* and *Justice;* as their proper *Inheritance* annexed to their *Imperiall Crownes,* from their very births."[32] Far from expressing traditional and conventional sentiments, Maynwaring's position was extremist and shocking. Even Archbishop Laud did not want his sermons published; when they were published anyway, parliament responded by impeaching Maynwaring.[33]

The most thoroughgoing arguments for divine right before the Restoration were offered by Sir Robert Filmer. Filmer was a more serious political theorist than James or clergymen like Maynwaring and in his various works all the elements of divine right theory are articulated: (1) of all forms of government, monarchy alone is divinely ordained, (2) hereditary right is indefeasible, (3) kings are accountable to God alone, so mixed or limited monarchies are contradictions in terms, (4) law is created by the king's will, (5) nonresistance and passive obedience are enjoined by God. Filmer's *Free-holders Grand Inquest* must have made people like Prynne scream with rage. According to Filmer's researches into British history, the glorious rights conferred upon the British people by Magna Charta were nothing but a cheap deal offered by King John, who was an illegitimate usurper trying to flatter the people. Commons were not even summoned to parliament until the time of Henry I, who was also a usurper seeking to buy popular support. The king makes the laws, the Lords offer counsel, and the Commons are to consent. The so-called ancient and undoubted rights of parliament are no more than acts of grace that may be revoked at the king's pleasure.

Such a position could never have been endorsed by a majority of men in parliament or in public life generally at any time in the seventeenth century. Neither before nor after the Restoration were the claims of the divine right theoreticians calmly and generally accepted. After the Restoration, also, the most vehement advocates of divine right and passive obedience tended to be Anglican clergy, not M.P.'s. Especially during the seventies and eighties statements about divine right were more likely to be part of a heated political controversy than they were expressions of universally accepted sentiment. Samuel Parker, Bishop of Oxford, spoke for the king's prerogative in his *Discourse of Ecclesiastical Polity, wherein the authority of the civil magistrate over the consciences of subjects in matters of external religion is asserted* (1670) and was promptly answered by Andrew Marvell, M.P. for Hull, in the brilliant *Rehearsal Transpros'd* (1671). Lauderdale's personal chaplain, George Hickes, became a defender of Charles's position in *A Discourse of Sovereign Power* (1682), *Jovian* (1683), and *The Harmony of Divinity and Law* (1684). His chief opponent was Samuel Johnson, chaplain to William Lord Russel, the prominent Whig.

Furthermore, it cannot be stressed too often how frequently practical Whigs and practical Tories agreed on important issues, how ideology shifted with the new illuminations of new circumstances, and how fluid political alliances were throughout the Restoration. Most Whigs and most Tories protested their devotion to monarchy and to protestantism, abhorred the thought of another civil war, considered the law a relevant curb on policy, and claimed that a study of British history showed their position to rest on tradition and their opponents' position to be an innovation. Both sides tended to idealize a harmonious mixed monarchy in which parliament respected the king's prerogative and the king valued parliamentary counsel and respected parliamentary privilege. Division occurred when it was necessary to determine precisely what these prerogatives and privileges were.

Even when the terms *Whig* and *Tory* began to be used with some frequency during the Exclusion crisis, they certainly did not point to two neatly organized ideological camps. The ideological difference between the Tories and Whigs in this period was theoretically that the Tories held the king's authority to derive directly from God and not to be derived from the consent of the people, whereas the Whigs believed in a contract theory. Hickes, for instance, wrote in 1682:

> The opinion that I am speaking against is this, that the People are the fountain and foundation of all power and dominion, which is understood to be derived from them even upon those whom Custom calls sovereign Princes, who are but their *trustees*, or *fiduciary ministers*; with whom they have at least a *virtual* contract, and if they do not perform their trust by not using their power to the ends for which they received it, or abuse it to contrary ends, then they forfeit the power and authority with which they were entrusted by them, and ought to be answerable for their defaults.[34]

However, although the Whig position theoretically justified revolution, almost to a man, the Whigs were not prepared to revolt at the time of the Exclusion crisis.[35] A number of so-called Whigs in parliament were more interested in setting limits on a Catholic successor's prerogatives than they were in excluding James from the throne. Marvell's *Account of the Growth of Popery and Ar-*

bitrary Government, certainly written in support of Shaftesbury, and sufficiently dangerous to have been published anonymously and with a false imprint, nevertheless argues that the king's prerogative is limited by the law without emphasizing a right of resistance and without even discussing contract theory.[36]

The Tory position theoretically justified the king's confiscation of property, the quartering of soldiers on civilians, and any other measures the king declared to be necessary, but Tory M.P.'s were certainly not prepared to accept illegal acts of a sovereign without "reviling." Most Tories did not accept the more extreme ideas of Filmer or Hickes. As B. Behrens points out, "The bulk of Tory polemical writing clearly presupposes that the king is not in a position to override the law, except on certain specified occasions, such as a national emergency . . . they maintain that the law of the constitution imposes limits on royal power, and by implication, that the judges, whose duty it is to interpret the law, cannot enforce in the courts the king's decisions unless they are in accordance with the law."[37] Whatever impecunious Anglican clergymen might say, the Tories in parliament did not intend to surrender their right to criticize Charles's policies or their right to pass resolutions and laws infringing on what he, at least, claimed were his rightful prerogatives. During the seventies, for example, the Whigs were able to muster increasingly broad support for parliamentary controls over the military.[38] In the spring of 1678 parliament passed a militia bill that the king "might have no further use of an army"—a standing professional army, they meant. In November 1678 Commons resolved unanimously that all forces raised since 29 September 1677 and still abroad should be disbanded. After Charles finally dissolved this increasingly uncooperative Cavalier Parliament, the new House of Commons assembled in April 1679 promptly declared that a standing army was illegal and a grievance.

Not surprisingly, many of the plays written during this crisis of confidence which saw the emergence of political parties, especially those written during the Exclusion crisis itself, were more overtly political than the heroic romances had been. The most immediately topical plays have been studied and neatly divided into "Whig" plays and "Tory" plays.[39] Prominent among the so-called Whig plays are Lee's *Caesar Borgia* (1679) and *The Massacre of*

Paris (written about 1678, though not produced until 1689) and Settle's *The Female Prelate* (1680). Though Settle certainly was associated with Shaftesbury at this time and dedicated *The Female Prelate* to him, and though the Whigs were certainly interested in whipping up anti-Catholic feeling, it would be more to the point simply to call these anti-Catholic plays. They contain none of the abstract political theorizing that characterizes a genuine Whig play like Lee's *Lucius Junius Brutus* or Rowe's *Tamerlane*. Dryden, after all, wrote his *Spanish Friar* in 1680, in the same atmosphere of anti-Catholic hysteria. Unlike Dryden, both Lee and Settle remained faithful to protestantism throughout their careers. So-called Tory plays like Mrs. Behn's *Round-heads; or, the Good Old Cause* (1681) and D'Urfey's *Royalist* (1682) have little to say directly about the politics of the Exclusion crisis. They simply imitate earlier plays like Howard's *Committee* written shortly after the Restoration and are intended to revive memories of the interregnum and to insist on the myth of the bad parliamentarians and the good cavaliers, bad parliamentarians being the ancestors of bad Whigs.

With a few exceptions like *Lucius Junius Brutus*, the most politically interesting plays of this middle period are not the topical plays surrounding the Popish Plot, but the plays I would like to call political tragedies. These plays had less immediate use as political propaganda than *The Female Prelate* or *The Royalist*, yet they continue the exploration of the difficult problems of authority and obligation between sovereigns and subjects begun in the heroic romance. The political tragedies include plays like Crowne's *Ambitious Statesman* (1679), Otway's *Don Carlos* (1676) and *Venice Preserved* (1682), Lee's *Lucius Junius Brutus* (1680), Banks's *Innocent Usurper* (written about 1684 and prohibited), and Southerne's *Spartan Dame* (written about 1684, though not performed until 1719). As in the heroic romances, in these plays the political situation remains treacherous and confusing. Sympathetic protagonists struggle to preserve honor, but now can do so only at the cost of their own destruction or are unable to do so at all. The problem of whether or not a subject should obey a ruler who is corrupt or vicious or whose authority is otherwise questionable can no longer be dealt with painlessly. What begins to happen to the relations between sovereigns and subjects represented in these plays reflects the dissolution of older ideas of political authority. Authority—the power to create political obligation—was traditionally thought to come from "above": from God, from the king acting as God's regent, from peer to commoner, from master to man, from father to son. These plays, however, by focusing on situations where such traditional upper authorities are absent, by insisting on the failure of traditional sources of authority to create obligation, or by showing two upper sources of authority in hopeless conflict with each other (for example, king with father) prepare the way for the early modern idea of political authority, authority coming from below, authority as the voluntary creation of individual men for their own self-preservation and betterment.

Crowne's *Ambitious Statesman: or The Loyal Favourite* (1679), his seventh play and the one he called "the most vigorous of all my foolish labours," represents something of a transition between heroic romance and more realistic political tragedy (3:146). Its protagonist, Vendosme, deviates only slightly and momentarily from strictest honor, but all his courage and essential loyalty are quite powerless to keep him from destruction. Crowne himself, in earlier plays, was a practitioner of heroic romance. His second play, *The History of Charles the Eighth of France* (1671), out-aristocrats the aristocratic Boyle. In an episode frequently ridiculed, Charles VIII, about to invade Naples and conquer Ferdinand, learns rebellion has broken out within the city. Instead of taking advantage of this good fortune, Charles sends a general with an offer to Ferdinand to help put down the revolt. "Rebellion," he explains,

> is a monster would devour
> The Kingly dignity, and Sovereign power.
> A sort of atheism, that doth crowns blaspheme,
> And styles the sacred power of Kings a dream. . . .
> For though 'tis true I am their lawful Prince,
> To whom they all allegiance owe; yet since
> Titles of Kings are mysteries too high
> Above the reach of ev'ry vulgar eye,
> They must the present shrines of power adore.
>   [1:145]

Ferdinand refuses this magnanimous offer, but later avoids death at the hands of Charles's army by challenging his fellow monarch to single combat. Charles's troops are ultimately victorious. He is, however, so impressed with Ferdinand's gallantry that he awards him the crown of Naples anyway. The two kings complete their happiness by marrying sisters.

Such magnanimity and such triumph have no place in *The Ambitious Statesman: or the Loyal Favourite.* The Constable of France is the eponymous ambitious statesman; his son Vendosme the loyal subject. The Constable, a Machiavellian villain of deeper die than the Duke of Lerma, is the primary source of the treacheries that dominate the play. As in *The Duke of Lerma,* we are interested in whether or not the villain will be able to corrupt his child. Avoiding the simplicity of command, the Constable first tries to alienate Vendosme from the king by forging a letter from his son to Mme de Guise, to whom his son is secretly contracted, confessing inconstancy and asking for a mutual release of vows. Thus scorned, the haughty Mme de Guise secretly marries the Dauphin instead, allowing the Constable to blame the Dauphin for stealing her. When we first see Mme de Guise she is in a bedchamber with the Dauphin, weeping over what seems to be Vendosme's betrayal. The king rebukes his son for making a clandestine and impolitic marriage and contrasts him unfavorably with the heroic Vendosme returned triumphant from the wars. Vendosme, however, far from glorying in his successes, proves modest and philosophic, more a man of feeling than an Almanzor:

> Wars are good physic when the world is sick.
> But he who cuts the throats of men for glory,
> Is a vain savage fool; he strives to build
> Immortal honours upon man's mortality. . . .
> I hate these potent madmen, who keep all
> Mankind awake, whilst they by their great deeds
> Are drumming hard upon this hollow world,
> Only to make a sound to last for ages.
>
> [3:177]

The Constable continues trying to manipulate his son into disloyalty, telling him that the Dauphin has made Mme de Guise

his mistress, that the couple plot Vendosme's death, and that
Brisac, the Dauphin's favorite, has been charged with treason and
tortured because he opposed this scheme. Not one of these
allegations is true. Although the Constable provides evidence of his
charges, Vendosme, suspicious, sounds out his plot by pretending
to be prepared for rebellion.

Vendosme begins to long for an escape from the treacheries,
temptations, and hollowness of public life, and even for escape
from love itself. Like many melancholy heroes in the tragedy of the
later seventies and eighties, he longs for withdrawal:

> In some dark forest will I live, whose shades
> May guard my eyes securely from the moon,
> Because 'tis bright, and changing like a woman.
> [3:197]

When the Dauphin publicly celebrates his marriage, insults and
threatens Vendosme, and finally demands his commissions, Vendosme's only response is to soliloquize on how "a brave fool, that
had more blood than brains" would be tempted to revolt and
revenge, "though he pulled all the kingdom on his head." Vendosme and Mme de Guise have an interview in which the fact that
his letters were forgeries appears, but the two are seen by the
Dauphin, who draws his sword on Vendosme. Vendosme disarms
the Dauphin—a crime for which he later asks the king's pardon—
refuses to kill him, and is apprehended when his father calls the
king to witness the *lèse-majesté*. Though Vendosme proclaims his
father's various treacheries, his indictment backfires when the
Constable is able to produce Brisac unscathed; his mangled appearance earlier was another deception.

Vendosme's position rapidly deteriorates until in the fifth act he
is in prison about to be racked by his father. The prison setting, the
instruments of torture, and the pessimism of the dialogue between
father and son are all characteristic of these tragedies. Ethical
behavior in the public world seems futile:

> *Ven.* Who looks upon this world, and not beyond it,
>   To the abodes it leads to, must believe it
>   The bloody slaughter-house of some ill-power,
>   Rather than the contrivance of a good one. . . .
>   Those things that seem his friends are false to him:

> The air that gives him breath gives him infection. . . .
> *Const.* Whoever wou'd be virtuous, is a fool;
>   For he endeavours to plant virtue here
>   In a damn'd world, where it no more will grow
>   Than oranges in Lapland.
>
> [3:222–23]

After Vendosme has been racked, his troops seize the city. He commands them to throw themselves at the king's feet to ask pardon and insists, "my present sufferings / Are what appearances gave warrant for." Dying in a blaze of absolutist rhetoric, he declares, "Princes are sacred!":

> They who derive all power from the people,
> Do basely bastardize it with that buckler
> Which fell from heaven to protect innocence.
> They protect villany; no sacrilege
> Greater than when a rebel with his sword
> Dares cut the hand of Heaven from King's commissions,
> To hide the devil's mark upon his own.
> I lifted up my arm against the Dauphin,
> It ought to have died and rotted in the air.
>
> [3:238–39]

This time no ancient shepherd or sign from heaven appears to reveal that Vendosme is the true king. Appointed by heaven "to protect innocence," the true king has been woefully unable to see through the machinations of his constable or to protect his loyal subject from destruction. The Dauphin is clearly a less worthy successor to his father than Vendosme would be. The court is dominated by perjury, forgery, and tricks. Given such a world, Crowne's hero can delight only in death. At the end of the play he discovers the corpse of Mme de Guise and in a final access of Liebestod begs the Dauphin:

> May I have leave, sir—
> To sleep in death by her who was your Princess?
> But in the grave there's no propriety,
> In death's dark ruinous empire all lyes waste. . . .
> The grave's our bed, and death our bridal night,
> None will disturb, or envy our delight.
>
> [3:239]

Crowne's play tells a story at considerable distance from the facts of fifteenth-century French history and thus also seems transitional between the earlier heroic romances with their abstract or exotic settings and the increasingly realistic settings of political tragedies in the last years of Charles's reign. Three kinds of settings seem of particular significance. First, the use of fairly recent European history in plays like Lee's *Massacre of Paris* (1678) and Dryden and Lee's *Duke of Guise* (1682) not only offered some protection against the censors, but also made it natural to deal more realistically with more concrete political issues. Second, the rediscovery of British history itself as a subject tended to force playwrights away from abstract confrontations between tyrants and usurpers and into a realization that succession to the British crown itself had not proceeded strictly according to divine right principles. Subjects had conspired to deny legitimate heirs before; not only might they do so again, but the titles of later heirs were based on these illegitimate successions. Crowne's *The Misery of Civil–War* (1680, reprinted as *Henry the VI: The Second Part* [1681]) deals with Henry VI, Warwick, and Richard Plantagenet, and his *Henry the VI: The First Part* (1681) presents the murder of Humphrey, Duke of Gloucester. Tate's *Sicilian Usurper* (1680) is based on Shakespeare's *Richard II.* Banks offered *The Unhappy Favourite; or, the Earl of Essex* (1681), *Vertue Betray'd; or, Anna Bullen* (1682), and *The Island Queens; or, the Death of Mary, Queen of Scotland* (prohibited, but published 1684). Crowne, Tate, and Banks could not by the furthest stretch of the imagination be-called Whig dramatists at this time. Nevertheless, since these are history plays—however imperfectly faithful to the facts—usurpers successfully usurp and people with indefeasible hereditary claims are murdered. The Exclusion crisis had made British history, especially at moments when the succession had been disputed, a matter of great contemporary political interest. It is not surprising that all three of these playwrights had trouble with the censors. Try as Tate might to elevate the character of Richard II above Shakespeare's version of that unfortunate monarch, he could not eliminate the fact that Richard had been deposed and that fact itself was offensive to royalist sentiment. Banks avoids showing usurpers becoming British sovereigns, but chooses to exemplify legitimist principles by showing how Bloody Mary followed Edward VI and by lamenting the murder of Mary, Queen of Scots, for her involvement in Catholic plots against the life of Elizabeth—hardly a way of making legitimist principles attractive to protestant Englishmen in the 1680s.

A third setting for serious plays in the later years of Charles's reign escaped even more completely from romance by selecting a locale where there were no kings and queens at all, only senates, assemblies, councils, and executive officers of various kinds. To set a tragedy in republican Rome or in a Venetian city was to transform utterly all the issues of political allegiance. If there were no monarch, there could be no loyalty to pure divine right theory. Louis Teeter remarked of *Venice Preserved*, pertinently if inaccurately, "the fact that there is no king, no duke, in the play, allowed [Otway] to do what had never been done on the Restoration stage before, to arouse sympathy for a rebel who does not turn out to be the real heir to the throne."[40] For many reasons, divine right theory is not very congenial to drama. Too extreme a reverence for kings is likely to make dramatists represent them as faultless and to offer no plots except static harmony or rebellion from motiveless malignity. The heroic drama escaped stasis principally by hiding the true king and letting rebels and usurpers generate the action until he was discovered in the fifth act. In the later tragedies, however, the characters of true kings are allowed to degenerate substantially, and rulers who are neither true kings nor usurpers are allowed to be guilty of definite abuses. The romances distinguish between true kings and usurpers by their behavior; the tragedies, more realistically, show legitimate rulers who are nevertheless unjust, sometimes tyrannical, sometimes even guilty of atrocities. Rebels in these tragedies have definite grievances and their revolts are accorded some sympathy. More importantly, the focus of the political tragedies is on the subject, not on the king, as was usual in Renaissance tragedy. John Bancroft—*pace* Teeter—makes a hero out of Sertorius (1679), the exiled Roman general who was champion of the democratic party after Sulla's victory. Though some of the professed lovers of liberty are corrupt, Sertorius and his friend Berbricius are sincere and genuinely appalled by Sulla's proscriptions. Berbricius greets Sertorius:

> Hail noble Patriot of a happy State,
> . . . When *Sylla's* bloody hands,
> Embru'd in Slaughter, threatned Death and Fate:
> When all the terrors froze us up with fear:
> Thou sav'dst our Country, and dispers'd the Foe.[41]

The conspirators in *Venice Preserved* have a number of legitimate grievances against the senate, grievances that increase sympathy for Jaffeir's joining the rebellion. Lee's Brutus has to contend with the archtypal tyrant, Tarquin.

In the romances, loyalty to the state becomes impossible for many characters, but the guilt of their rebellion is dissolved by the discovery that the sympathetic rebels are themselves the legitimate rulers. In these later tragedies, on the other hand, subjects are likely to be forced into rebellion by the intolerable behavior of their rulers or faced with a choice between accepting the guilt of disobedience to a father or a husband or the guilt of treason. The paradoxes of conflicting loyalty so dear to the heroic romances remain, but they are now destructive paradoxes. Conflict between fathers and children frequently leads to the children's deaths. In Lee's *Mithridates, King of Pontus* (1678), for example, Mithridates rapes Semandra, the woman his son Ziphares has asked to marry. In darkness and in the confusion of a revolution fomented by Mithridates's other son, Ziphares accidentally stabs Semandra and then poisons himself. In Banks's *Innocent Usurper*, Lady Jane Grey adamantly refuses to declare herself queen until Northumberland and her mother point out that Mary Tudor is in the field and that Lady Jane's parents and husband have already gone so far in rebellion that they will be executed as traitors unless she accepts the crown. Left to herself, Jane relapses into loyalty and wants to fling herself at Mary's feet:

> How wretch'd is my State! I either must
> My Virtue lose, or Duty to my Parents.[42]

But her submission to Mary is prevented by the news that she has been deposed and by her capture. In Otway's *Don Carlos* (1676) King Philip has married a woman who first loved the prince and

exchanged vows with him. The king's jealousy and suspicion and
the intrigues of corrupt courtiers drive the prince into planning to
join the rebellion in the Spanish Netherlands:

> *Don Carlos. Father!* and *King!* both names bear mighty sence:
>   Yet sure there's something too in *Son*, and *Prince*. . . .
>   To *Flanders Posa*, strait my Letters send,
>   Tell 'em the injur'd *Carlos* is their Friend.
>   And that to head their Forces I design,
>   So vindicate their Cause, if they dare mine.
> *Posa.* To th' Rebels!—
> *Don Carlos.* No, th'are Friends, their Cause is just,
>   Or when I make it mine, at least it must.
>
> [1:211–12]

(There is later a suggestion that Carlos meant to subdue the rebels,
but in any case his unauthorized secret negotiations with them
amount to treason.) King Philip discovers his son's dispatches and
also thinks he has evidence that Don Carlos is the queen's lover.
Enraged, he kills the queen with a slow and tormenting poison;
Don Carlos kills himself. At the beginning of the play Don Carlos
perceives his predicament and exclaims:

> Curse! What's obedience? a false Notion made
> By Priests, who when they found old Cheats decay'd,
> By such new Arts kept up declining Trade.
>
> [1:177]

Louis Teeter observed very justly that though the sentiments Don
Carlos utters here were common enough on the lips of
Machiavellian villains, Otway departs from tradition both by
ascribing them to a relatively sympathetic character and by
changing that character's attitude toward his own perceptions:
"The Machiavellian had always expressed his recognition of the
artificiality of moral sanctions in a tone of boasting superiority.
He, at least, saw through the trick and knew what to do about it."
Don Carlos's "Curse!," on the other hand, "is the despairing cry of
a man who is faced with a problem he cannot solve, and even falls
back temporarily into a cynicism foreign to his nature."[43]

The destruction of protagonists like Lady Jane, Don Carlos,
Jaffeir, or Titus in these tragedies reflects a dissolution of the older
myths justifying constituted authority and the absence of any

satisfying and generally acceptable new myths. Legitimist theory, which had supported the romance, was subjected to too much pressure from the realities of the Exclusion crisis to remain tenable. Protestant adherents of passive obedience could only regard the succession of James II with apprehension. Contract theory was still too suspect and still too tainted by its association with the parliamentary party during the Civil War. Even in the best of these political tragedies, *Venice Preserved* and *Lucius Junius Brutus*, sympathetic protagonists are apt to appear stupid, without ideas. Unlike the clever heroes of heroic romance who can speak so pointedly about the intricacies of succession or debate so wittily the relative weight to be given to possession and to legal title, characters like Jaffeir and Titus are reduced to sighs and ex-clamations of distress. They have no satisfactory political ideas because there were no satisfactory political ideas in 1680; they demonstrate what sensitivity and intelligence they possess by realizing this ideological vacuum. Legitimist theory is irrelevant to their situations and no new theory has arisen to replace it. Bancroft's Sertorius and Lee's Brutus go furthest in articulating a new democratic faith, but Sertorius is killed by his allies and Brutus is forced to murder his own sons—just as the tyrants he hates so often have ended by murdering their own children.

IV

In November 1682 the enfeebled King's Company gave up its rivalry with a stronger Duke's Company and the two merged into a single United Company. From 1682 until 1695 there was only one company acting in London. The number of new plays produced declined considerably. During the three years of James II's reign only one new tragedy seems to have been produced, Crowne's *Darius, King of Persia* (1688).[44] Dryden himself did not write a single new play during James's reign.

James's reign, however, while it was a kind of theatrical in-terregnum, succeeded in changing political opinion and prepared the way for the democratic romances that dominated the stage during the reign of William and Mary. In his attempt to reestablish Catholicism, James tested the limits of the king's prerogative beyond anything his brother had attempted. There has been much debate over how realistic James's policies were, but there is no doubt that they provoked another period of protracted crisis. J. R. Jones has argued that James's policies could only have been wrecked by William's invasion "and that Englishmen generally were alarmed enough to believe that only such an invasion could insure their failure."[45] James tried to suspend the penal laws against the Roman Catholics and dissenters and to allow both freedom of public worship by royal declaration. When parliament proved uncooperative, the king resorted to suspending the charters of corporations and boroughs. Such attempts to pack parliament and attempts to secure the cooperation of the country administration by political purges of deputy-lieutenants and justices of the peace significantly increased opposition to the court.

James also set about using his dispensing power to Catholicize the Privy Council, the army, and the universities. At Magdalen College, for example, the fellows defied the king's mandamus ordering them to elect as their president a man not statutorily qualified for the office.[46] They elected their own candidate instead and after further conflict James issued another mandamus for the admission of Marvell's old antagonist, Samuel Parker, Bishop of Oxford, as president. James himself appeared before the still recalcitrant fellows, obviously disappointed with their understanding of the favorite Oxford doctrine of passive obedience, admonishing and threatening them "with much greater appearance of anger" than at least one observer had seen in him before. When the fellows continued to resist, commissioners were appointed and shortly appeared in Oxford accompanied by three troops of horse. The Bishop of Chester came to scoff at the fellows' claim that to obey the king would be to violate the oaths they had taken to become fellows and so to commit perjury. He addressed them in harsh terms, insisting, "Never a true son of the Church of England was, or will be, disobedient to his Prince. The loyalty which she has taught us is absolute and unconditional." Finally James had no recourse but to expel the resisting fellows and to appoint more sympathetic men in their places. Parker himself died after a convulsive fit apparently brought on by another mandamus from James demanding that he admit nine more Roman Catholic

In "The Clerical Cabal" the bishops are accused of wanting a liberty for themselves that they refuse to others:

> For if conscience be thought a sufficient pretense,
> Why should it not salve the Dissenters' offense,
> When refusing to bow to their Common Pray'r idol,
> They were forc'd to take quarters in Newgate & Bridewell.
>
> [POAS, 4:220–21]

James responded to the petition of the seven bishops by arresting them for seditious libel. On the day they were acquitted an invitation was sent to William of Orange asking him to come to the defense of the liberties of Englishmen.

People shifted their allegiances from Whig to Tory during the Popish Plot or in reaction to Whig enthusiasm during the Exclusion crisis or from Tory to Whig at the time of the Glorious Revolution not simply because they were unprincipled. Sides were less fixed than the words seem to indicate. Some of the so-called shifts from country to court or Whig to Tory or vice versa were caused by individual judgments of what principles and interests were at stake in a given cause. D. T. Whitcombe's recent *Charles II and the Cavalier House of Commons, 1663–1674* illustrates this very nicely for the earlier part of the period.[48] Sides became more distinct during the Exclusion crisis, but numbers of moderates and trimmers tried their best to avoid conflict over fundamental issues and to devise pragmatic solutions to immediate problems. Halifax, for instance, in 1681 proposed that the crown should descend to James but that William III should be appointed regent.[49] Many shifts occurred when religious issues cut across court and country issues. Protestant fears of Catholicism were pervasive and strong enough to determine much political behavior in the seventies and eighties. In January 1679 ladies were buying daggers with Godfrey's name on them to protect themselves against a Papist uprising.[50] Titus Oates's story of a Popish Plot was supported not only by the murder of Sir Edmund Bury Godfrey, but also by the revelation of the correspondence between Father Coleman, James's secretary, and Louis XIV's confessor.

James II seems to have expected that removal of the penalties against Roman Catholics and giving them some share in preferment would soon reveal the weakness of the Anglican church. He seriously underestimated not only the zeal with which Englishmen would defend their property rights and their prerogatives as free men, but also their attachment to protestantism. Some who were willing to tolerate a Catholic king in his fifties in hopes of a protestant successor ceased to be tolerant when a Catholic heir was born. It is worth noting that of the many writers charged with turncoatism, only Dryden converted to Rome during James's reign. Several of the so-called Whig plays of the Exclusion crisis are simply anti-Catholic plays, and several of the so-called Williamite plays are also basically anti-Catholic plays. Crowne's *English Friar* (1690), for instance, exposes the Roman Catholic Father Finical as owing allegiance only to "the holy Roman Ecclesiastical nation of priests" and as conspiring to subvert fundamental English law (4:116). "But say we have no law on our side," Father Finical is made to concede after he has been made a bishop, "we have lawyers." The fear of how successfully purges of the universities, the church, the army, and the courts could change the nation—a fear given force both by the experiences of the interregnum and by those of James's reign—is clear enough in Finical's next words: "Laws are but rusty cannons kept for show, men are the mounted guns to do execution, and we can turn their muzzles any way; we have men of our side, gown-men, and sword men, and you have laws, that is, letters, A's and B's" (4:91). The alleged disloyalty of playwrights like Southerne and Crowne might better be called consistent protestantism coupled with the abandonment of divine right theory in the face of events.

Just as they had done during the interregnum, people shifted their allegiances during the Restoration. And they often did so because—fortunately—they allowed events and realities to influence their judgments. In the end, James's use of his prerogative alienated his subjects and resulted in the transfer of sovereignty from the crown to parliament. As J. H. Plumb says, in 1688, "Parliament, it seemed, was free to harry monarchs, topple ministers, cut supplies, refuse taxation, concern itself with peace and war, formulate those constitutional changes that it felt necessary for its protection, and generally ride rough-shod over the administration."[51]

Political doctrine that had been tainted by association with the parliamentary side during the Civil War became respectable at the Glorious Revolution. Many of the Anglican clergy who tried to cling to divine right theory modified that theory in the light of the revolution. The idea that conquest, rather than heredity alone, might be God's way of declaring the monarch he favored, anathema to Tory legitimists during Charles's reign, now was accepted by many clergymen. According to William Sherlock, there was no conflict between a legal entail derived by hereditary right and possession derived by conquest: "It is all but Providence still."[52] More importantly, contract theory was on its way to becoming political orthodoxy. The Reverend Samuel Johnson, who had first written *Julian's Arts to Undermine and Extirpate Christianity* to promote Exclusion and been jailed for refusing to produce copies, and then been jailed and defrocked for distributing a broadside to James's protestant soldiers arguing "that Resistance may be us'd, in case our Religion and Rights shou'd be Invaded," now found his conviction declared illegal, his degradation from the priesthood void, and himself the recipient of a generous sum of money from William.[53]

Locke returned from the self-imposed exile into which fear had driven him at Shaftesbury's downfall to publish the *Two Treatises of Government* he had written during the Exclusion crisis. The *First Treatise* attacks Filmer's version of divine right theory, arguing that modern kings could not possibly have inherited an indefeasible hereditary right to rule from Adam. The *Second Treatise* maintains that though normally men are obliged to obey governments, there are circumstances under which the people are entitled to resist and even to replace the "executive":

> If they have set Limits to the Duration of their Legislative, and made this Supreme Power in any Person, or Assembly, only temporary; Or else when by the Miscarriages of those in Authority, it is forfeited; upon the Forfeiture of their Rulers, or at the Determination of the Time set, *it reverts to the Society*, and the People have a Right to act as Supreme, and continue the Legislative in themselves, or erect a new Form, or under the old form place it in new hands, as they think good. [2, 243]

Locke uses his considerable rhetorical skill to strip the idea of kingship of its sanctity. Sometimes he uses the word *king*, but kings are simply one sort of executive and he often uses the less resonant *executive*. To the complaint that acknowledging any right of resistance must necessarily lead to the anarchy of frequent rebellion, he replies that rebellions occur anyway: "For when the *People* are made *miserable*, and find themselves *exposed to the ill usage of Arbitrary Power*, cry up their Governours, as much as you will for sons of *Jupiter*, let them be Sacred and Divine, descended or authoriz'd from Heaven; give them out for whom or what you please, the same will happen" (2, 224). Divine right theory is here ripped from its Christian moorings and cast adrift into a pagan sea, exposed to the same ridicule all right-thinking moderns would bestow on any superstition invented by the cleverer pagans for the control of their stupider brethren. *Rebellion*, indeed, turns out in Locke's vocabulary to be a word more properly applied to tyrannical executives who break the laws than to their right-thinking subjects who get rid of them: "For Rebellion being an Opposition, not to Persons, but Authority, which is founded only in the Constitutions and Laws of the Government; those, whoever they be, who by force break through, and by force justifie their violation of them, are truly and properly *Rebels*" (2, 226). Furthermore, Locke even manages to find a biblical example showing God's approbation of revolt against a king who rules by force, not right: "*And the Lord was with Hezekiah, and he prospered; wherefore he went forth, and he rebelled against the King of Assyria, and served him not*" (2, 196).

That the idea of kingship was being gradually secularized—the king being turned into an executive whose authority only belonged to him through a "fiduciary trust" conferred by the people—and that sovereignty was being transferred from king to people is evident even in that most conservative of institutions, the law. Though changes in law and legal procedure are apt not to be as dramatic or rapid as changes in pure theory, we can say generally that the Restoration law of treason changes in ways parallel to the shift from divine right theory to contract theory.

Most obviously, after the Glorious Revolution the doctrine of treason was modified to acknowledge the right of resistance against a tyrannical sovereign and to insist that kings *de jure*, like James II, had no rights as over against kings *de facto*, like William III, who now was declared by parliament to be both king *de facto* and king *de jure*. The nonresistance oath was taken out of the Corporation Act shortly after the beginning of William's reign. One overt act of treason charged against Algernon Sydney had been justifying resistance in his unpublished *Discourses on Government*, but after 1688 the right to resist became so politically orthodox that Blackstone in discussing levying war remarks blandly, "in cases of national oppression the nation has very justifiably risen as one man, to vindicate the contract subsisting between the king and his people" (4, 6, 82). In answering the question who is king under the Treason Act, William Hawkins (1716–21) abandons the concessions to kings *de jure* that Hale had made and announces flatly: "First, that every king for the time being has a right of the people's allegiance. . . . Secondly, That one out of possession is so far from having any right to our allegiance by virtue of any other titles, which he may set up against the king in being, that we are bound by our duty of allegiance to resist him."[54] At a little more distance from the immediate needs of the Glorious Revolution and the threat of Stuart pretenders, Blackstone finds this last claim, based obviously on 11 Hen. 7, c. 1, rather paradoxical, observing, "the consequence would be, that when Cromwell had murdered the elder Charles, and usurped the power (though not the name) of king, the people were bound in duty to hinder the son's restoration: and were the king of Poland or Morocco to invade this kingdom, and by any means to get possession of the crown . . . the subject would be bound by his allegiance to fight for his natural prince to-day, and by the same duty of allegiance to fight against him to-morrow" (4, 6, 77).

Less obviously, there was some reduction in constructive treasons. Acts that in the sixties would have been liable to prosecution as high treason tended by the ninties to become lesser crimes like sedition or riot. From a modern point of view, of course, words criticizing the executive—including calling him a "bloody tyrant"—ought to be protected as free speech necessary to political discussion. As Stephen points out in discussing seditious libel, from this point of view, there can be no such thing as seditious libel. If the ruler is the servant of the people, "every member of the public who censures the ruler for the time being exercises in his own person the right which belongs to the whole of which he forms a part" (2:299). To prosecute such words as seditious libel is certainly not fully modern, but represents progress over prosecuting them as high treason. Since anyone could be the object of libel but only the sovereign the object of treason, this redefinition treated the king less as a quasi-divine figure and more as an ordinary person. It also dramatically reduced the penalties, seditious libel being only a misdemeanor. The progress from prosecuting words as treason to prosecuting them as seditious libel was slow, not unilinear, but real nonetheless.

Shortly after the Restoration parliament passed "an act for safety and preservation of his Majesty's person" making conspiracy to levy war high treason if expressed by printing, writing, preaching, or malicious and advised speaking. This statute, 13 Car. 2, c. 1 (1661), certainly went beyond 25 Edw. 3, stat. 5, c. 2, but it did so in the same way that the Elizabethan acts or the interregnum act for Cromwell's safety had done. There were no Restoration statutes defining seditious libel, and at first, like many crimes previously prosecuted in the Star Chamber, seditious libel tended to be poorly understood by the justices of the King's Bench. Hale does not treat it separately, merely remarking in passing that a charge of speaking seditiously does not amount to a charge of high treason (*HPC*, 1, 11, 77). Instead of having a careful theory of the difference between utterances that constituted treason and utterances that constituted seditious libel, the crown seems to have chosen the more drastic indictment in cases where defendants were suspected of having also been involved in conspiracy or overt acts of treason or in cases where the general demeanor of the defendant was especially irritating.

This latitude is evident in a series of Restoration cases involving prosecution for words alone. In 1661 John James was convicted of high treason, apparently under 13 Car. 2, c. 1, for preaching, "That the king was a bloody tyrant, a blood-sucker and a blood-thirsty man, and his nobles the same," and, on the same occasion, for making various millennial remarks that might have been considered threatening.[55] James, however, was also suspected of having been involved in Venner's Rebellion, although no such accusation was made against him at the trial and although no evidence was presented of any act besides the preaching. The best evidence of the arbitrary distinction between treason and seditious libel is perhaps the contemporaneous prosecution in 1663 of John Twyn for printing *A Treatise of the Execution of Justice* and the prosecution of Thomas Brewster, Simon Dover, and Nathan Brooks for their involvement with the publishing of *The Speeches and Prayers of some of the late King's Judges.* Twyn was indicted for high treason; Brewster, a bookseller, Dover, a printer, and Brooks, a bookbinder, for seditious libel.[56] Not only was no distinction made between the political offensiveness of these two books, but Lord Chief Justice Hyde actually warned the misdemeanor defendants that they might have been prosecuted for treason: "And I will tell you all three, it is the king's great mercy you have not been indicted capitally; for every one of these books is filled with treason, and you for publishing of them, by strictness of law, have forefeited your lives and all to the king: It is his clemency towards you."[57] In 1678 William Stayley, said to be a Roman Catholic, was convicted of high treason under 13 Car. 2, c. 1. Two witnesses testified to having heard him say angrily, in a tavern, and in French, "The King of England is the greatest Heretick and the greatest rogue in the World. Here is the Heart, and there's the Hand, that would kill him I myself." Stayley denied the words and so did not raise the issue of whether such a speech could properly be said to be malicious and advised. He was accused of no acts beyond these words. The Lord Chief Justice remarked, "The Statute hath been read, which was made since the king came in, for the preservation of his person, and during his life: The parliament thought it reasonable, even to make desperate words to be Treason, although there was no other thing but words, that is, such words, as had the thing been done would be Treason, the speaking it is Treason."[58] John Brydall in *Decus et Tutamen* (1679) mentions Stayley's conviction without complaint.[59]

Gradually the power to prosecute for mere words against the king began to be doubted. In the reign of Charles I *Pines' Case* had already declared that words only disrespectful were not treasonable.[60] Brydall and Hale still maintained that to hold the king has no title to the throne is treason, but Hawkins, who discusses words more extensively, says, "perhaps this may be questioned, because it cannot certainly appear from such words whether the speaker had a design against the king's person or no."[61]

Hale and Brydall are sure that written or printed words may be an overt act of treason and have cases to support that contention. Hawkins, however, wonders whether prosecution for unpublished writing is not over severe. By Blackstone's time treason convictions for spoken words or unpublished writings occurred only in the dark past of "some arbitrary reigns"; "of late," he adds, treason prosecutions for published writings "have also been questioned" (4, 6, 80–81). Furthermore, some defendants in seditious libel cases began to argue that they had a right as citizens to say what they had said. When Samuel Johnson was tried for writing *Julian*, Lord Chief Justice George Jeffrey "upbraided Mr. *Johnson* for meddling with what did not belong to him; and scoffingly told him, he wou'd give him Text, which was, *Let every Man study to be quiet, and mind his own Business:* to which Mr. *Johnson* reply'd, That he did mind his own Business as an *Englishman*, when he wrote that Book."[62]

Other acts earlier considered treasonable also gradually became lesser crimes during this period. Most notably, riot. Various crimes against public order had from time to time become constructive treasons—highway robbery and arson, for instance. Early in the Restoration, in *Messenger's Case* (1668), several members of a mob of apprentices who had pulled down brothels were indicted for high treason. Pulling down brothels was construed as levying war by a line of reasoning most clearly expressed by Justice Kelyng: "the pulling down of houses upon pretence they were bawdy-houses, was high-treason, because they took upon them regal power to reform that which belonged to the King by his law and justices to correct and reform."[63] Hale alone of the justices said the apprentices were guilty of felony only. Several years later, however, as Stephen points out, the judges were divided five to five as to whether a riot by weavers to destroy engine looms was treason and the offenders were consequently prosecuted only for riot. (To destroy a brothel, or a loom, or to pull down an enclosure was never thought treasonous, but to tear down brothels, looms, or to pull down enclosures generally—especially as a matter of principle instead of because of some personal quarrel with the owner of the particular property—was thought of as threatening public order generally.)

The convictions of Algernon Sydney and Lord Russel for high treason in 1683 were critical episodes in changing contemporary ideas about treason. Sydney and Russel both denied guilt and were the subjects of a considerable pamphlet literature, some of it complaining about the injustice of the laws that contributed to their convictions. After the Glorious Revolution their attainders were repealed and they were hailed as Whig martyrs and patriots.

More generally, dissatisfaction with the treason laws and with the treatment of treason defendants was one of the grievances parliament sought to remedy after 1688. A new bill for the conduct of treason trials drafted in 1689 gave the treason defendant a significant number of procedural advantages he had not had before, including a copy of the indictment, a copy of the jury panel, and access to legal counsel. Two witnesses were required to the same overt act or to two overt acts of the same treason, and no evidence of any act not expressly laid in the indictment was to be admissible. Of particular interest is a provision that defense witnesses be sworn and subject to subpoena, though the significance of this is complex and will appear at length in a later chapter on oaths. This bill attempted to regularize the irregular concessions that had increasingly been made to defendants throughout the century and addressed itself to the "unfairness" of the treason law complained of by such defendants as Stephen College, Russel, and Sydney. The *Parliamentary History* praises it as a means "by which many hardships upon the liberty of the subject were removed or mitigated."[64] Ironically, as the ones most likely to be treason defendants after the Glorious Revolution, the Tories were the most ardent supporters of this bill. The Whigs were ashamed to argue openly against the principles of the bill, but once in power grew more reconciled to the older treason laws, tempted by the chance to use them as a bulwark against their enemies. Whigs, therefore, obstructed the passage of the treason bill until it was made law in 1696. The final form of the bill excepted parliamentary impeachments from the new procedures and so allowed the majority party one arena for the relatively untrammeled prosecution of its enemies. Nevertheless, as Samuel Rezneck says, "the statute of 1696 implied that a man might actually expect to be tried for his offense now, instead of being merely

indulging in the sexual assaults so characteristic of tyrants, finally provokes his subjects to revenge. Annius Minutianus moralizes:

> Proud tyrants who no bounds of law endure
> Are common foes; and never are secure;
> Their lofty thrones they seldom long enjoy:
> Fierce lions all men labour to destroy.
>
> [4:412]

If lovers of freedom perish, they do so in the "happy suicides" of Southerne's *Fate of Capua* (1700) or Addison's more famous *Cato* (1713). The chief virtue of warrior kings like Timoleon (1697) or Rowe's Tamerlane (1701) is apt to be that they disclaim the divinity of monarchy and insist firmly on their own humanity.

John Bancroft's *King Edward III, With the Fall of Mortimer* (1690) is dedicated to Henry Sidney, a Privy Counselor of William's who had played an active part in the revolution. Bancroft compliments him on being "a true bred Son of the Country, and a Person who has always valued the freedom of his Native Brethren, above the Temptations of a prejudic'd and designing Court."[67] The play itself parallels the abuses of Queen Isabella and Mortimer with the abuses of James II and the overthrow of Mortimer with the Glorious Revolution. Mortimer, for example, had used the Chancellor and the courts to stretch royal prerogative:

> He Summons the most Learned of the Robe,
> Begging their Kind Interpretation of it,
> Telling how necessary, nay how Loyal 'tis
> When the Prerogative o'th' Crown is pinch'd
> Within the Clutches of the Griping Law
> To ease the Royal Power, and give it freedom.
>
> [P. 3]

Justice is also corrupted when Mortimer removes uncooperative judges and uses perjured witnesses against his enemies. A comic subplot further insists on judicial abuses, such abuses also having been loudly complained of during James's reign. Parliament can no longer represent the nation because charters have been surrendered or confiscated. The queen refuses to call a truly representative parliament that might inquire into her conduct with Mortimer.

One of Bancroft's heroes is Lord Montacute, a young man who refuses to suffer Mortimer's rule. When Montacute talks of "usurpation," he uses the word to speak of the usurpation of the people's rights, not the usurpation of the throne by someone who has no hereditary right to it:

> All joyn the Nobles, Gentry and the Commons,
> The Chain is Rivitted, the wresty People
> Whose Rights and Priviledges are usurp'd
> No longer free, but all in Vassalage
> Are ripe for Mischief, ready for Rebellion;
> They wait from us the Signal when to Dole
> The act of Justice.
>
> [P. 36]

The traditional symbolic equation of kings and lions is abandoned when Montacute describes the reaction of another subject invited to join the rebellion:

> He like some Lyon almost stiff with ease,
> Lolling at length within his Antick Cave,
> Takes the Alarum of the Huntsmans sound,
> At which he stretches out his well-grown Limbs,
> Brustles his horrid Main and furls his Tail,
> Whetting his Crooked Talons on the Rock,
> Staulks to the Field, and swells to meet the Foe.
>
> [Pp. 35–36]

The other hero of the play is the young king himself. Edward III was a favorite king of the Whigs for several reasons, one of them being that his reign had produced the great Treason Act limiting constructive treasons. Lord de la Mere interrupted his defense of Lord Russel with a panegyric on Edward III, "a Victorious Captain, and a potent Prince":

But that which made his Name the Greater, and his fame more lasting, was those good and wholesome Laws which were Enacted in his Time; by which he restored and beautified the Government, that had been defaced and almost destroyed, by the Illegal proceding during his Father's Irregular Reign. And of all the Oppressions under which the

Nation Groan'd, there was none that lay heavier on the People, than the Extravagant License which the Judges took in the Interpretation of Treason.[68]

Even more important, Edward III was an English king "whose Accession to the Throne was occasion'd by the Removal" of a predecessor and whose claim to the throne could be said to be based not on conquest or hereditary right, but on the confirmation of parliament. According to the author of *A Letter from Oxford, concerning Mr. Samuel Jonson's late book*:

> No *Hypothesis* was invented to color his Accession to the Crown, than what was really true in Fact, which was no other than his being set up by the Statutes of the Realm, which had deposed his Father for his Misgovernment, upon formal articles of Impeachment. . . . Much less would the king have endured such as should charge him to his face with Usurpation, and that he was a king *de facto* only, but not *de jure*.[69]

Edward III was proclaimed king when he was only fourteen years old and so was at first king in name only. Bancroft chooses to show the events of 1330, when Edward was seventeen. In that year Edward responded to the arguments of Montacute and others that Mortimer was trying to capture power for himself and that the queen and her lover had reduced Edward to an ignominious position. Edward consented to a plot to have Isabella and Mortimer seized, allowed Mortimer to be executed for treason, announced his intention to rule personally, and summoned a new parliament. Bancroft includes some of the more colorful historical details, like the capture of the queen and her lover in Mortimer's locked chamber in Nottingham Castle by conspirators who enter through an underground passageway. Other facts he suppresses, mostly those that would complicate Edward's character or be extraneous to his emphasis on good government and the right political relationship between king and people. We hear nothing, for instance, of Edward's marriage to Phillippa of Hainault or of the birth of their son, both events that also apparently prompted Edward to want to rule independently. Bancroft chooses Edward as a hero because he cooperates in overthrowing the tyrannical Mortimer, because he summons a parliament immediately, and because he was a brave warrior king who fought valiantly against the French. All these

traits, of course, he shared with William III. When Queen Isabella
berates the peers, Edward rebukes her:

> Tho' Subjects, they have no dependance on us,
> And Majesty's adorn'd and serv'd by them,
> Much more then is at all times fit to own;
> 'Tis true they are not safe, but under Kings,
> Nor kings can't flourish but by such assistance.
>
> [P. 43]

Bancroft's play possesses neither great poetry nor political
profundity, but it is good propaganda in the service of good
political values. Bancroft recovers part of the English past for his
audience and, through a coherent story, sympathetic heroes, and
carefully drawn parallels between the later Middle Ages and the
later seventeenth century, succeeds in using the public theater to
consolidate support for judicial integrity, civic virtues, and the
"Rights and Privileges" of Englishmen.

Bancroft had earlier gone to Plutarch as the source of his
Tragedy of Sertorius and after the revolution Plutarch was used
several times by playwrights who found in *The Lives of the Noble
Greeks and Romans* heroes suitable to democratic romance. In
Behemoth Hobbes had complained that the study of classical
political philosophy in the universities had been one cause of the
Civil War: "For it is a hard matter for men, who do all think
highly of their own wits, when they have also acquired the learning
of the University, to be persuaded that they want any ability
requisite for the government of a commonwealth, especially
having read the glorious histories and the sententious politics of the
Greeks and Romans, amongst whom kings were hated and branded
with the name of tyrant."[70] Those same glorious histories of the
Greeks and Romans attracted playwrights in the 1690s and
throughout the eighteenth century. Even Dryden, who lost his
laureateship under William and who clung to the old formula of
true king restored in plays as late as *Don Sebastian* (1689) and *Love
Triumphant* (1694), wrote a *Life of Plutarch* (1683) for a five-
volume translation of the complete Plutarch commissioned by
Jacob Tonson.[71] Dryden also based *Cleomenes, the Spartan Heroe*
(1692) on Plutarch. The hero, albeit an exiled true king, embodies

republican virtues and suffers at the hands of Ptolomy, a true king
who is nevertheless decadent and irresponsible.

An anonymous play, *Timoleon: or the Revolution* (1697) uses
a story from Plutarch that has very obvious parallels with the
career of William III. Typically for the 1690s, the anonymous
author in his preface attacks the decadence of manners and of the
stage in the "late Reigns": "Our Poets, instead of attacking Vice
where it is, have sought to find it where it 'tis not, and hence it
comes to pass, that Frugality and Good-husbandry in the Citizen
(the strong Ligatures of the Commonwealth) and Vertue in the
Wife or Daughters, are the Chief Subjects of Ridicule."[2] His play,
on the contrary, will inculcate civic virtue and will show: "The
Dethroners of Tyrants, and the Restorers of Liberty, are the great
Benefactors of Mankind; whose Memories will ever appear Bright
and Glorious, notwithstanding all the Aspersions that Malice and
Ingratitude can cast on them." Timoleon, though not a Sicilian,
landed with a small force in Sicily and drove out the tyrant, as
William drove out James; Timoleon defeated the Carthaginians, as
William defeated the Irish in the battle of the Boyne; unsuccessful
attempts were made to assassinate Timoleon, as they were to
assassinate William, and so on. Opposition to Timoleon is based on
the same fears and jealousies that aroused suspicion of William:
Pharax, a counterrevolutionary, tells his henchmen: "Shew 'em the
Danger and Inconvenience of being governed by a Foreigner, when
Offices, Places, and Preferments must be bestowed on Strangers,
and they themselves excluded from having any Share" (p. 6). Less
selfishly motivated adherents of the old tyrant, like the Jacobites,
believe "that kings can't err":

> These Priest-ridden Fools,
> Incorigible under Stripes,
> Still court their own Destruction.
> [P. 38]

Timoleon goes further than *Edward III* or *Tamarlane* in insisting
on the value of self-government. Timoleon not only eschews absolute rule, he is reluctant to rule even in partnership with the
oligarchy and finally resigns his power altogether. Offered the
crown early in the play, Timoleon first asks why the Sicilians

cannot rule themselves and, when the Sicilians insist on his governing them, pledges:

> If I must Rule, then this you may expect,
> My End's your Rights and Freedoms to protect.
>   [P. 2]

Timoleon's heroism, unlike the heroism of Boyle's Henry V or Dryden's Almanzor, depends on his respect for law and the people's right, on his abhorrence of needless fighting, and on his modesty. Returning from victories over the Carthaginians, he proclaims:

> Sheath all your Swords, throw by your useless Arms,
> For War is now no more.
> Iron, and Steel, forget your killing Trade,
> And serve those ends for which ye first were made;
> Let all your force be now imploy'd in Earth,
> There use your Power, from whence ye took your Birth.
>   [P. 20]

If the Sicilians try to attribute supernatural prowess to him, Timoleon resists and reminds them of his humanity:

> Nor must this Vict'ry be ascrib'd to me,
> Heaven is the Patron of your Liberty.
>   [P. 20]

Like the old-fashioned usurpers, Timoleon quickly falls in love with the deposed monarch's daughter, Leonora. When she has scruples about loving him, however, the thought of violence toward her never crosses his mind. Instead, he offers to kill himself and she, responding to his virtues, offers him hope. Leonora receives a forged letter apparently from her father ordering her to follow the instructions of Timoleon's enemy. Like her sisters in earlier heroic romance, she is reluctant to betray her lover or her father and exclaims:

> Yet 'tis my Father's Will; who as a Prince
> And Parent, commands a double Duty.
>   [P. 61]

Leonora, however, has already made clear her opposition to her father's tyranny, earlier berating the leader of the counterrevolution for flattering the king "in all his Crimes" and for telling her "he was / No king, whils't bound or circumscrib'd by Law" (p. 13). Faced with the dilemma of divided loyalty to the old king and to Timoleon, she neither awaits a surprising revelation as the heroines of romance tended to do nor resigns herself to death, as the heroines of tragedy in the eighties so frequently did. Instead, Leonora betrays the plot to Timoleon, accepts Timoleon's love, and agrees to retire to private life with him. A particularly striking feature of this play is that we never do learn what finally happened to Dionysius, Leonora's father, the old tyrant who was overthrown. Upon abdicating in order to enjoy private life, Timoleon offers his vision of democratic political harmony and a warning to the newly liberated Sicilians, obviously a warning the author intended for the politicians struggling for places under William:

> Henceforth both Nobles and Plebians too,
> Shall each a just share of Government partake;
> The Rich no longer shall the Poor oppress,
> Whilst Justice flows with an uninterrupted Stream,
> But let not Pride or Avarice destroy
> The Freedom you have sought, and now enjoy.
>
> [P. 79]

A third democratic romance, Nicholas Rowe's *Tamerlane* (1701), further develops the civic virtue, humanity, and modesty of the new hero. Like the anonymous author of *Timoleon*, Rowe also makes explicit the parallels between his hero and William III.[73] Marlowe's Tamburlaine, as Eugene Waith has said in *The Herculean Hero*, is an important ancestor of the Restoration huffing heroes like Almanzor.[74] Marlowe's play itself also had a Restoration version in Charles Saunders's *Tamerlane* (1681). It is, therefore, of particular interest that Rowe does not follow Marlowe but relies instead on Richard Knolles's *General Historie of the Turkes*, an account that emphasized Tamerlane's lack of cruelty and his tolerance.[75]

"Man" is a crucial word in Rowe's play. Content with his humanity, Tamerlane does not share the desire of such earlier

heroes as Maximin or Almanzor to fight with gods. After defeating
Bajazet, he rebukes Axalla for praising him too extravagantly:

> It is too much, you dress me
> Like an Usurper in the borrow'd Attributes
> Of Injur'd Heaven: Can we call Conquest ours?
> Shall Man, this Pigmy with a Gyant's Pride,
> Vaunt of himself, and say, thus have I done this?
> Oh ! vain Pretense of Greatness! Like the Moon,
> We borrow all the brightness which we boast,
> Dark in ourselves and useless.
>
> [P. 80]

Later when Bajazet, seeing Tamerlane with Arpasia, rages
jealously at him, Tamerlane warns that insults to his honor may
provoke him:

> I am a Man,
> And have the frailties common to Man's Nature:
> The fiery Seeds of Wrath are in my Temper,
> And may be blown up to so fierce a Blaze
> As Wisdom cannot rule.
>
> [P. 123]

Throughout, Tamerlane, a man aware of his place on this
isthmus of a middle state, is contrasted to Bajazet, who pretends to
divinity but sinks to bestiality. Bajazet has broken his oath not to
invade Greece, provoking Tamerlane to exclaim:

> Let Majesty no more be held Divine,
> Since Kings, who are call'd Gods, profane themselves.
>
> [P. 66]

Bajazet, though, insists upon his prerogative to be above oaths or
leagues and taunts Tamerlane with having no understanding of his
own kingship:

> art thou a King
> Possest of Sacred Pow'r, Heav'n's darling Attribute,
> And dost thou prate of Leagues, and Oaths, and Prophets?
> . . . I am pleas'd we differ,
> Nor think alike.
>
> [Pp. 82–83]

Tamerlane retorts:

> No—for I think like a Man,
> Thou like a Monster.
> [P. 83]

Tamerlane's rejection of any pretense to divinity, his refusal to be above the rules of common humanity, is further underlined by the dervishes' antagonism toward him. Like Dryden's Montezuma, he is a natural man and a tolerant deist who emerges victorious in argument with sectarian priests. Unlike Montezuma, he survives and flourishes.

Two love plots inculcate the primacy of civic virtue over private emotion and even over familial duty. Axalla, an Italian prince who is Tamerlane's general, loves Selima, Bajazet's daughter. Seeing an opportunity, Bajazet tells Axalla the price for Selima will be Tamerlane's head. More public spirited than Boyle's heroes, Axalla simply refuses. Moneses, a Grecian prince, has fought for Bajazet, but only because Bajazet has captured the woman he loves, Arpasia. Bajazet has "married" Arpasia, raped her, and recognized her as his queen. Learning this, Moneses, an unusual prince, still wishes to marry her. He appeals to Tamerlane, who is fond of him and pities his misfortune, but nevertheless decides that to take Arpasia away from Bajazet would be an act of injustice. Both Bajazet's daughter and his wife defy him and ignore his authority—and the play endorses their resistance. Selima frees Axalla (taking care to get a guarantee for Bajazet's life) and Arpasia defies Bajazet's command to flee with him, and so contributes to his downfall.

Revolution and counterrevolution were central to the political experience of the late seventeenth century. The Restoration of Charles II was a counterrevolution, the Exclusion crisis a threat of revolution, and the invitation of William III an actual revolution threatened by counterrevolutionary Jacobite plots. It is, therefore, not surprising that the plots of Restoration serious drama so often turn on revolution or counterrevolution. Although the playwrights were not original political theorists, the evolution of Restoration serious drama shows their gradual assimilation of changing political ideology, especially of a changed understanding of the right relationship between sovereigns and subjects, and their ability to create new fictions to correspond to the new ideology. In the first stage, the heroic romance, dramatists like Boyle and Dryden use plots of usurpers defeated by true kings and develop elaborate arguments over legitimist issues such as the authority of hereditary claims versus the authority of force, the role of providence in declaring the true king, the limits of obedience to a usurper, and so on. The true king remains hedged about with some divinity: he seems set apart from more ordinary humanity even when his right to the throne is still unknown. His providential discovery brings grace and resolution to the confusions and misrule his subjects have endured in his absence. One function of the heroic romance seems to have been to assuage the guilt of the postwar generation over its abandonment of the legitimate monarch. In the second stage, political tragedy, the older systems of political authority are seen to be crumbling. Clashes between political, religious, and familial principles of authority result in questioning the legitimacy of each claim for obedience. Kings are too corrupt or too impotent to be divine, or, in a number of plays set in oligarchies or democracies, are absent altogether. Try as they will to preserve honor, the sympathetic characters are nevertheless destroyed by the failure of existing political authority to provide an adequate ground for ethical behavior. The third stage, the democratic romance, engages in another retreat from political reality, this time, though, rewriting the earlier plot of the legitimate king restored into a new plot of public-spirited resistance to arbitrary government. The democratic romances served principally to consolidate public support behind a secular and utilitarian contract theory of government—a theory undoubtedly even less historical in its account of the origins of government than the patriarchal and Adamic romance of Filmer, but a theory nonetheless better suited to free men.

3
SOVEREIGNTY IN THE FAMILY

I

For people who thought in terms of the hierarchical ordering of the great chain of being, the relations of sovereigns and subjects were analogous to the relations of parents and children and of husbands and wives. Such analogies still seemed natural during the late seventeenth century. A broadside of 1685, "The Husband's Instructions to his Family," captioned the pictures of a family by noting, "A Family well Govern'd is like a Kingdom well Rul'd" and "The Father's Love and Care of his Children, is like that of the KING's over his People."[1] Writers on marriage argued that were it not that men saw the "agreeableness of power" and "the advantages of order and subjection" in "particular Families," they might never have been able to grasp the advantages of sovereignty in the state.[2] More elaborately, Justice Hyde discussed the case of a runaway wife by comparing her to a subject who had forsaken his allegiance to the sovereign:

> When the wife departs from her husband against his will, she forsakes and deserts his Government; erects and sets up a new jurisdiction; and assumes to govern herself, *besides* at least, if not *against*, the law of God and the law of the land. Therefore it is but just, that the law for this offence should put her in the same plight in the petit commonwealth of the household, that it puts the subjects for the like offense in the great commonwealth of the realm.[3]

Restoration law itself still supported traditional analogies between kings and subjects, parents and children, husbands and wives. The Treason Act of Edward III discussed in the preceding chapter also defined the crime of petit treason, which included both counterfeiting and a form of aggravated murder, specifically the murder of a husband by his wife, a master by his servant, or an ecclesiastic superior by his inferior. Women who were convicted of petit treason were supposed to be burned alive. As Matthew Hale explained, "If the husband kills the wife it is murder, not petit treason, because there is subjection due from the wife to the husband, but not *è converso*" (*HPC*, 1, 39, 381). Hale clearly knew of petit treason prosecutions in his lifetime. The pamphlet literature also records cases of women sentenced to burning for petit treason during the Restoration. Elizabeth Ridgeway was burned in 1684 after she poisoned her husband by putting arsenic in his broth. The burning of Mary Hobry in 1688 was commemorated by Elkanah Settle in "An Epilogue to the French Midwives' Tragedy." Provoked apparently by her husband's cruelties and beatings, Mrs. Hobry strangled him, chopped up his body, and buried the pieces in a privy and other unsavory places. Officials seem increasingly to have sabotaged the punishment for petit treason by executing the women first and burning them only after they were already dead. By the end of the eighteenth century, Sir Benjamin Hammel denounced burning women as the "savage remains of Norman policy" and his "Act for discontinuing the Judgment which has been required by Law to be given against Women Convicted of certain Crimes" was passed without any substantive dissent.[4] Petit treason itself was abolished by 9 Geo. 4, c. 31 (1828). Restoration law was by no means consistent in regarding women as the subjects of their fathers or husbands— sometimes it regarded them as men's property, sometimes as possessing very specific property rights of their own with which husbands could not interfere—but a wife's disagreement with her husband could still often be perceived as like a subject's revolt against his king.

For reasons that can only be the subject of speculation, English law did not include a child's murder of his father in petit treason and has never recognized parricide as a crime distinct from homicide. In this and a number of other respects, the legal position of wives and children has never been exactly analogous. Though it may at first appear odd, seventeenth-century law usually credited the child with more independence of will than it accorded to the wife. For example, the law refused to punish wives for certain felonies committed in the presence of their husbands, presuming that they acted under coercion, but children committing felonies in the presence of their fathers could make no such plea. Wives could not testify against their husbands, but children could testify against their parents. (It might be argued that men making the laws found it easier to imagine the possible independent personhood of children than the personhood of wives since they themselves had been children; they had never been and could never be wives.) Nevertheless, wives and children remained similarly subjected to many forms of patriarchal authority. Husbands and fathers remained entitled to the proceeds of the labors of their domestic inferiors, entitled to collect damages if a wife or a child were abducted, and entitled to correct their misbehavior.

Because the traditional analogies between sovereign / subject relations and domestic relations persisted in the late seventeenth century, the dilemmas of sovereign / subject relations considered in the preceding chaper inevitably affected contemporary thought about authority and obligation in the family. The same questions that had been raised about the absolute authority of the king were now raised about the absolute authority of fathers and husbands. Portia in Otway's *Atheist* (1683) proclaims liberty "an English Woman's natural Right": "Do not our Fathers, Brothers and Kinsmen often, upon pretence of it, bid fair for Rebellion against their Soveraign: And why ought not we, by their Example, to rebel as plausibly against them?" (2:379). After rebellion became respectable at the Glorious Revolution, such questions were asked with increasing seriousness. In an early feminist tract now frequently quoted Mary Astell inquires:

> If Absolute Sovereignty be not necessary in a State, how comes it to be so in a Family? or if in a Family, why not in a State; since no reason can be alledg'd for the one that will not hold more strongly for the other? If the Authority of the Husband so far as it extends, is sacred and inalienable, why not of the Prince? The Domestic Sovereign is without Dispute Elected, and the Stipulations and Contract are mutual, is it not then partial in Men to the last degree, to contend for, and practice that Arbitrary Dominion in their Families, which they abhor and declaim against in the State?[5]

As the authority of the sovereign weakened during the later seventeenth century, so patriarchal authority weakened. Though such generalizations can apply only roughly, concern for the rights of domestic inferiors grew along with concern for the rights of subjects. The deepest causes of this process seem to lie in the ideas of the Reformation and in the practical growth of state power in the sixteenth and seventeenth centuries. Lawrence Stone, who in *The Crisis of the Aristocracy, 1558–1641* has traced a transfer of power from individual aristocrats to the state, observes:

> The most remarkable change inside the family was the shift away from paternal authority, a shift made possible by the extension of the power of the central government. As the state and law courts came to provide greater protection to wives and children, so the need for subordination to husband and father declined. The fact that these movements are inversely linked was not appreciated by contemporaries. . . . Owing partly to the growth of puritan opposition to the double standard and of puritan emphasis on contented Christian partnership in marriage, partly to the development of ideas about economic and political liberty, it was slowly recognized that limits should be set not merely to the powers of king or Church, but also to those of parents and husbands.[6]

Although Stone uses 1641 as a terminal date in the title of his book, he draws data from the later part of the seventeenth century and sometimes even refers to eighteenth-century sources. It is evident that the processes he describes were not fully accomplished before the Civil War and Stone himself has treated them further in his recent *The Family, Sex, and Marriage in England, 1500–1800*. In looking at the period 1660–1700 here, it is necessary to recognize that the weakening of patriarchal authority occurs not only as a result of events peculiar to the Restoration, but also as a consequence of the Reformation and the Civil War.

Nevertheless, Robert South voiced a common Restoration idea when he blamed the immorality and insubordination of domestic inferiors on the confusions of the Civil War. Those attaining middle age when South wrote in 1685 had grown up when things were hopelessly "topsy-turvy": "So that as soon as they were able to observe anything, the first thing which they actually did observe, were inferiors trampling on their superiors; servants called by vote of parliament out of their masters' service to fight against their prince, and so to complete one rebellion with another; and women running in whole shoals to conventicles, to seek Christ forsooth, but to find somebody else." Given such experiences, South thought, it was no wonder that in the later seventeenth-century parents had to complain "that their children pay them not that duty and reverence which they have heard and read that children used to show their parents heretofore." Speaking as a conservative Tory high churchman who found satisfactory older notions of both kingship and marriage, South was also forced to lament, "it is but too frequent a complaint, that neither are men so good husbands, nor women so good wives, as they were before that accursed rebellion had made that fatal leading breach in the conjugal tie between the best of kings and the happiest of people."[7]

The Civil War did indeed assault both monarchy and marriage. As the natural reverence of men for the monarchy, their almost instinctive loyalty, had been wounded, so also their sentiments toward marriage had been unsettled by the Civil Marriage Act of 1653 and the interregnum transfer of jurisdiction over marriage from the ecclesiastical courts to the state described in the first chapter. The interregnum legislation, of course, was in effect only until 1660. In fact, the first parliament of Charles II in order to avoid social chaos had to pass another act retroactively declaring all marriages contracted under the Civil Marriage Act legal. Nevertheless, both the Civil Marriage Act and the interregnum abolition of the ecclesiastical courts are of considerable importance to the history of marriage during the Restoration. First, the experience of civil marriage unsettled assumptions about the sacramental character of marriage. Second, during the interregnum the temporal courts and even the J.P.'s got into the habit of dealing with matrimonial cases formerly handled by the ecclesiastical courts. Since many justices served both before and after 1660, they were likely to remember these cases and to think of them as precedents. Jurisdiction once acquired is usually not easily relinquished. David Ogg points to the Duke of Norfolk's parliamentary divorce in 1700 as "an event which marked the beginning of the long process whereby the state took over control of divorce from the church," but in fact, as we shall see, the state

had already begun to attempt to regulate both divorce and
marriage itself through the secular courts and by acts of
parliament considerably before 1700.[8] Third, though the Civil
Marriage Act itself was repudiated, the protestant desire to
recognize marriage as a civil contract rather than a sacramental
union continued to affect ideas about marriage and eventually won
out. After the Glorious Revolution had effectively declared the
relationship between sovereigns and subjects contractual instead of
divine, Bishop Gilbert Burnet, one of the revolution's most enthusiastic supporters, had no trouble remembering the *Reformatio
Legum* and found it easy to declare that marriage was not a
sacrament and that its supposed indissolubility rested on misap-
prehending it as a sacrament instead of a contract: "For the end of
Marriage being the ascertaining of the Issue, and the Contract itself
being a mutual transferring the Right to one anothers Person, in
order to that End; the breaking this Contract and destroying the
End of Marriage does very naturally infer the Dissolution of the
Bond."[9] As I said in the first chapter, though the protestant
reformers had no desire to make marriage a secular institution in
the modern sense, their attempts to wrest control of matrimony
away from the church and into the hands of the civil magistrate
contributed substantially to its secularization.

Although the secularization of marriage continued throughout
the Restoration, the process was a tortuous one, and the larger
questions of authority and obligation in the family remained
problematic for several reasons. The analogies between political
and domestic authority retained much of their force, but since the
analysis of sovereign / subject relations was undergoing the
changes discussed in the preceding chapter, the first part of the
analogy was unstable. Also, as political theory became more
Whiggish, men did not necessarily wish to pursue the implications
of the analogies and impute to their wives and children rights like
those they themselves claimed as subjects. Many wished to preserve
natural law in the family long after they had made the transition to
natural right in the state. Indeed, one of the most telling lines of
argument employed by Tory controversialists against their Whig
opponents entailed the realization that even the Whigs did not wish
to accept all the domestic consequences of coupling their political

arguments with the traditional great chain of being analogies. George Hickes, for example, thought to refute those who held contract theories of sovereignty by showing that such theories make governance of women and children impossible and generally lead to domestic absurdities:

> They cannot tell us upon this hypothesis, whether the supreme Power belongs to all the people promiscuously, that have the use of reason, without any regard to Sex or condition, or onely to qualified persons, to Men onely, and men of such a condition and sort. If men only have a share and interest in the supreme Power, by whose order and authority, or by what Salique law of Nature were Women excluded from it, who are as usefull members of the Commonwealth, and as necessary for humane societies as the men are? Who gave the men authority to deprive them of their birthright, and set them aside as unfit to meddle with Government; when Histories teach us they have wielded Scepters, as well as Men, and Experience shews, that there is no natural difference between their understandings and ours, nor any defects in their knowledge of things, but what Education makes.[10]

Given these difficulties, some tried to escape by offering new accounts of authority in the family, while others began to deny that analogies between the state and the family had validity. Still others, of course, resisted the newer ideologies, clinging to more traditional views of authority both in the state and in the family. In this chapter I would like to explore the new secular accounts of domestic authority that emerged and to suggest that as the rights of subjects against the monarch increased so the rights of inferiors within the family also increased. The culture generally began to look at these domestic inferiors as persons with independent rights, not only natural law obligations. The drama in particular reflected the new attitudes explicitly through devices like the discussion of domestic relations in political language and implicitly by the increased representation of children and women, particularly married women. As we have seen the focus in political drama shift away from sovereigns and toward subjects, there is an analogous shift toward domestic inferiors, especially wives. Moreover, as kingship became "no more divine" so marriage also lost some of its sacred character. The secular courts nibbled away at the jurisdiction of the ecclesiastical courts over domestic relations. In

the drama as in life adultery became less a subject of tragic
eschatological import and more a topic of farce.

II

After the death of Cromwell but immediately before the
Restoration of Charles II, a very interesting comedy, *Lady Alimony*
(1659), was printed and claimed on its title page to be "Duly
Authorized, daily Acted, and frequently Followed." Although
supposedly set in Seville, the play obviously represents English life
at the end of the interregnum as seen by an opponent of the
parliamentary side. Trillo, an "illicentiate" playwright, plans a
satire on the consequences of the Civil Marriage Act:

> Divorces are now as common, as scolding at Billingsgate. O Alimony,
> Alimony a Darling incomparable dearer, then a seere-icy Bed possest a
> the spirit of a dull unactive Husband! He were a rare Justice in these
> times of Separation, who had the Ceremonial art to joyn Hearts
> together as well as Hands: but that Chymical Cement is above the
> Alchymy of his Office: or verge of his ministerial Charge.[11]

Six "alimony ladys" who are now attended by six gentlemen,
platonic confidants, ask these gentlemen to act as "Grave censors"
to hear their complaints against their husbands. The husbands
have been unsatisfactory in various ways, some of them grounds
for divorces *a vinculo* or *a mensa et thoro* in the old ecclesiastical courts (impotence, adultery), some of them not (stupidity, de-
formity, cowardice). The gentlemen sympathize with all complaints
and award the ladies a "moity" (or "moiety," probably half) of
their husbands' revenues as alimony. Madam Fricase, one of the six
ladies, comments:

> You did well
> In your proportioning of our *Alimony*,
> Moulded to th' moity of their estates
> Whom we have justly left: but we had less
> Alloted us in more Authentick Courts.
>   [E2v]

The rejected husbands, one of whom remarks that he does not mind
losing his wife but does object to the loss of his income, then
concoct a successful scheme to trick the ladies into dismissing the

platonic gentlemen. In a low comic underplot a lame country woman also demands a separation from her husband, telling him: "I have already fed a glib-tong'd Parret with a Coif on his head, that will trounce you . . . I will have *Ale-money*" [I4v]. An upper plot, a transparent allegory, concerns the restoration of the good Duke Eugenio who, having aided the Sicilians by punishing the pirates harassing them, returns to purge troublemakers and restore the old morality. At the end of the play, when the Duke hears the country woman complain that her "ale-money" has not yet been awarded, he rebukes the alimony ladies—"See what Examples, Ladies, you have given / To simple Women!"—and offers them a choice of returning to their husbands, "with a Conjugal Indeer'ment too," or entering convents. The ladies choose the husbands. The Duke also sentences the platonic lovers to rehabilitation through honest labor in the quarries and admonishes the gentlemen who awarded alimony:

> Sure such Decrees would not have relish'd well
> Your jealous Palats, had you so been us'd.
> "Wives to desert your Beds; impeach your Fames,
> "In Publick Courts discover your defects,
> "Nay, to bely your Weakness: and recover,
> "For all these scandals, Alimonious wayes
> "To feed their boundless riot!
>
>   [K3v]

The Sicilian consuls—unlike the British courts, as we shall see—agree to annul the alimony awards.

Although no other play deals so explicitly with the domestic consequences of the Civil War as *Lady Alimony*, a few other comedies, including Sir Robert Howard's *The Committee* (1662) and Sedley's *The Mulberry Garden* (1668) are also set in the interregnum. Unlike the author of *Lady Alimony*, however, Howard and Sedley both make the domestic rebels royalists and their guardians unsympathetic rebels against the king and so end by approving the domestic rebellions. With few exceptions—the exceptions including Lacy's *Sauny the Scot*, an adaptation of *The Taming of the Shrew*—the early Restoration plays prefer to focus on what was felt to be the easier case of children rebelling against their parents or guardians rather than the harder case of wives rebelling against their husbands. If we look at the plays of the sixties and early seventies generally, the tone of those that treat domestic difficulties seems approximately at least to match the tone of the early heroic romances discussed in the preceding chapter. Cheerfulness prevails from the idealistic Cavalier romance of Sir William Killigrew and Dryden's *Secret Love* through the Spanish intrigue of Thomas St. Serfe's *Tarugo's Wiles* to the more raucous city comedy elements of *Love in a Tub* and the farce of *Sir Martin Mar-all* and *Sauny the Scot*. John Harrington Smith was quite right to point to the sixties and early seventies as the real moment of "gay comedy" and to insist that the gay couples in these comedies are to be viewed sympathetically.[12]

The gay couples Smith discussed are also of interest to us here because they can be contrasted with the sympathetic but relatively undifferentiated young lovers of most Elizabethan comedy. They are drawn to each other not simply as attractive young people but for reasons that depend more on what we now call "personality": fondness for daring opinions, sense of humor, wit, intelligence. This contrast is especially evident in the Restoration plays that set off such a gay couple against a more old-fashioned pair of young lovers, Harriet and Dorimant versus Emilia and Young Bellair in *The Man of Mode*, for instance. The ideal of marriage in the Restoration came to depend less on traditional status where any well-behaved opposite-sex person of the correct age and class will do and more on a match of individuated personalities where not only character but even something so apparently frivolous as "taste" could be at issue. The author of *Lady Alimony* thinks women's complaints about the cowardice or stupidity of their husbands are frivolous, but by the end of the century such personal qualities are apt to be seen as making marriage intolerable. In these early plays, however, there is no final sense of pain over the problems of resistance, and political language appears rather casually. Nevertheless, words like *liberty*, *slavery*, *freedom*, and *tyranny* are frequently in the mouths of women and children.

Sir William Killigrew's *Siege of Urban* (1666) is a coherent example of the early romances. It begins with the heroine Celestina thinking of suicide as the only escape from forcible marriage: "Why then, should selfe slaughter be a sinne? When I am dead, my Father may relent, and teach other Parents more humanity, and so

free many Innocents from like slavery!"[13] Fearing no evil "beyond
the imbraces of that rich rotten Carcas, my unkind Father would
match me to," Celestina determines to adopt a masculine disguise
and to avoid the guilt of suicide by dying in honorable battle.
Sword in hand, she exclaims: "Why should not Womens hearts
agree with such a strength, as our Arms have to manage this
Sword? 'tis only custome, and a tender Education makes us lesse
bold, and active, then the bravest men;—the *Amazons* we read,
have done great things" (p. 6). She immediately rescues from
bandits a man who eventually turns out to be Lorenzo, Duke of
Florence; they marry in the fifth act and live happily ever after.

On a more humble plane, St. Serfe sets up his Spanish intrigue
Tarugo's Wiles (1667) as a problem comedy designed to test Don
Patricio's "Fantastick opinion . . . that a Woman's Will is easily
restrained."[14] Don Patricio intends to make his "experiment" on
his sister, Lavinia, but both Horatio, his sister's lover, and
Sophronia, whom Don Patricio says he loves, determine to employ
the clever Tarugo to free her from "her Brother's Tyrannous restraint." Sophronia is also concerned that Patricio's attitudes
toward his sister augur equally unfortunate behavior toward the
woman he will marry. The arguments are clearly drawn in the
second act when Don Patricio and Horatio talk with Sophronia, a
woman with "a vast knowledge in Masculine learning," who asks,
"is there any thing more certain then shut up a Woman against her
will, but like a fire of Coals cover'd with earth, which (though it
burns not clear) yet vents its heat in smoak, and in the end with
violent flames breaks thru the cloddy goal that smother'd its
natural course?" (p. 7). Instead of using analogies from natural
history to reinforce the hierarchical principles of woman's subjection to man, Sophronia uses them to make an opposite point.[15]
Don Patricio retreats to old truisms: "Madam, I know you have
store of Philosophy to maintain Paradoxes, therefore, I'le avoid to
reason with you upon the Argument, for I am sure that watchful
authority overthrows all hazards of that kind" (p. 7). Horatio
supports Sophronia by observing that in nature "strict Restraint
raises both passion and hatred against the Guardian; but most in
Women whose brains are continually busy'd, to acquire their
freedom" (p. 7). In the end Don Patricio is forced to acknowledge
his error and to agree with Sophronia that a woman's will cannot

The extent to which the Restoration began to see a match of personal qualities as opposed to status as crucial to a satisfactory marriage is evident not only in the development of the gay couple, but also in Dryden's *Sir Martin Mar-all* (1667), a play closer to farce than to comedy of manners. Dryden adapted Sir Martin from Phillipe Quinault's *L'Amant indiscret, ou le estourdy* and from Molière's *L'Etourdi*, following both to develop the comedy of a foolish master whose stupidity repeatedly baffles the clever schemes of his servant to win the heroine for him. Sir Martin was written for James Nokes and we have Cibber's account of how he played the role:

> In the Character of Sir *Martin Marr-all*, who is always committing Blunders to the Prejudice of his own Interest . . . what a copious, and distressful Harrangue have I seen him make, with his Looks (while the House has been in one continued Roar, for several Minutes) before he could prevail with his Courage to speak a Word to him! Then might you have, at once, read in his face *Vexation*—That his own Measures, which he had piqued himself upon, had fail'd. *Envy*—of his Servant's superior Wit. *Distress*—to Retrieve, the Occasion he had lost. *Shame*—to confess his Folly; and yet a sullen Desire, to be reconcil'd, and better advis'd, for the future![17]

Dryden departed from his sources in one way that is relevant here: he refused to allow Sir Martin to win the heroine at the end, instead awarding her to the clever servant, who is also made to say at the last moment that he used to be a gentleman himself. Dryden's changed ending has been much criticized, but Sir Walter Scott saw the point of it when he observed, "the decorum of the French stage would not have permitted the union of a lady with an intriguing domestic, nor would an English audience have been less shocked by seeing her bestowed on a fool."[18]

Of particular interest in the early Restoration are plays that accept the conventional analogies between the family and the state, indeed, that depend upon them for the degree of formal coherence they achieve, plays like Sedley's *Mulberry Garden* (1668) or Dryden's *Conquest of Granada* (1669–70). Apparently it sometimes seemed impossible to deal adequately with the issue of authority without having an upper plot involving sovereign / subject conflict and a lower plot involving domestic conflict. The use of double plots is especially striking since the writers who used them in theory professed admiration for the neoclassical dramatic unities. The upper plots of these plays are usually like the heroic romances discussed in the preceding chapter. Resolution commonly comes when the true king is discovered in the fifth act. In the lower plot, the blocking father or husband is usually simply converted to more generous views, though sometimes he may die or be exposed as having "usurped" his authority.

The Mulberry Garden expresses the euphoria of the early Restoration in its delighted acceptance of romance for the resolution of both the upper and lower plots, though the magical return of the true king in the upper plot happens to be the historical return of Charles II. The action is set in London of 1659; the heroes of the upper plot, Philander and Eugenio, are cavaliers being sought by the parliamentary forces. Philander loves Diana, Eugenio, Althea—both daughters of the politic Sir Samuel Forecast—but Forecast has forbidden the marriages because he wants to avoid being politically compromised by such sons-in-law. A rake hero, Wildish, attempts to pry Olivia and Victoria away from two men of the town who pretend to love them. Vivian de Sola Pinto, the only critic who has bothered to say much about this attractive play, is so put off by what he calls the "silly" heroics of the upper plot and by the supposed offense against the unities of the double plot itself, that he fails to see any connection between the two plots.[19] However, both plots are concerned with governance and honor, the upper plot with the governance of the state and men's honor, the lower with the governance of families and with woman's honor. Both plots contrast true liberty with the illusion of liberty and both also explore the possibilities and limitations of traditional analogies between love and war.

The first sentence of the play contains the word *govern*, but the governance there referred to is the governance of families. Sir Samuel Forecast and Sir John Everyoung debate how daughters should be governed. To Forecast's insistence on tight reins, Everyoung replies, "I think those women who have been least us'd to Liberty, most apt to abuse it, when they come to't."[20] When Forecast tries to marry Althea to a young man in the good graces of

the interregnum government, her dislike for proud usurpers in the
state finds an echo in her resistance to her father's tyranny:

> Under what Tyranny are Women born!
> Here we are bid to love, and there to scorn;
> As if unfit to be allow'd a part
> In choosing him, that must have all our heart;
> Or that our liking, like a head-strong beast,
> Were made for nothing, but to be opprest;
> And below them, in this regard we are,
> We may not flye the cruelty we fear.
> The Horse may shake the Rider from his back,
> The Dog his hated Master may forsake;
> Yet nothing of their native worth impair,
> Nor any conscious sting about them bear.
> But if a Virgin an Escape contrive,
> She must for ever in dishounour live,
> Condemn'd within her self, despis'd of all,
> Into worse mischiefs then she fled from, fall.
>
> [Pp. 131–32]

Sir John's daughters wander alone in the Mulberry Garden, but use
their freedom to discover the difference between the meaningless
flattery of Modish and Estridge and the genuine love of Wildish
and Horatio.

Nature, it seems, in the world of this sort of romance at least, is
so arranged that unjust governors lose their power both in the
public and the private worlds. The king returns and Sir Samuel is
also defeated. As his name indicates, Sir Samuel Forecast prides
himself on calculation and taking thought for the morrow. He
criticizes his daughters for their attachment to the hunted
cavaliers: "these young Wenches ... have less Forecast than
Pigeons, so they be billing, they look no farther, n'er think of
building their nests, nor what shall become of their little ones ... I
should be sorry to see any child of mine solliciting her Husbands
Composition at a Committee" (p. 127). For Sedley, whose own
mother had been arrested during her dealing with the Committee
for the Advance of Money, Sir Samuel's prudence is both
treacherous and absurd. The knight, who has nothing but contempt for "those unprofitable and foolish principles the

honourable Beggars of Former times Govern'd their lives by," uses his own relation to a judge to buy "a thousand Pounds worth of other men's Lands of him for a hundred" (p. 138). But all Sir Samuel's calculations are confounded. Though he protests his innocence and devotion to the republic, he is dragged off to the Tower for harboring Eugenio. In act 5 Monck has announced for the king and Sir John Everyoung brings an order for the release of all sufferers in the cavalier cause. Sir Samuel is thus rewarded for the crime he adamantly refused to commit. Under such circumstances, his opposition to a match between Althea and Eugenio dissolves.

Dryden similarly relies on romance formulas for solutions to the problems posed by public and private tyranny, though Dryden characteristically allows for pointed debate before rejecting skeptical challenges. Throughout his career Dryden used authority problems to link double plots in plays including *Secret Love* (1667), *The Conquest of Granada* (1669–70), *Marriage à la Mode* (1672), *The Spanish Friar* (1680), *Don Sebastian* (1689), and *Love Triumphant* (1694).[21] Some of these plays have a sharp separation between verse upper plots and prose comic plots, others, like *The Conquest of Granada*, do not. In the preceding chapter I discussed how in *The Conquest of Granada* obedience to public authority creates problems for subjects whose sovereign does not deserve to rule, but the play also shows the problems of children whose parents are arbitrary and of a wife whose husband is irrational.

There are three father / child pairs: Selin and Benzayda, Abenemar and Ozmyn, the Duke of Arcos and Almanzor. The first two are presented basically in terms of cavalier drama, but take on a slightly new cast because of the comparisons one is constantly encouraged to make to problems of political authority. Benzayda is in love with Ozmyn, who has killed her brother in one of the factional fights between the Abencerragos and the Zegrys. Ozmyn is captured and turned over to Selin, who commands his daughter to kill her lover in the language of the stage tyrant:

> You are to smile at his last groaning breath,
> And laugh to see his eyeballs roll in death.
>
> [4:89]

Before the deed can be done, Selin is forced to return to the fighting leaving his daughter to execute his command. But Benzayda defends the way of passive resistance:

> When parents their commands unjustly lay,
> Children are privileged to disobey;
> Yet from that breach of duty I am clear,
> Since I submit the penalty to bear.
> To die, or kill you, is the alternative;
> Rather than take your life I will not live.
>
> [4:91]

Benzayda appeals to the guards delegated to see Ozmyn killed, and her own willingness to die shown, Dryden allows the two lovers to escape.

In the next act Ozmyn's father, Abenemar, presents him with an ultimatum that provokes a similar crisis. He demands Ozmyn cease loving Benzayda or cease to be his son. His arguments are based on the analogies of the great chain of being:

> What piety canst thou expect from her,
> Who could forgive a brother's murderer?
> Or, what obedience hop'st thou to be paid,
> From one who first her father disobey'd?
>
> [4:102]

Ozmyn replies to his father's command even more strongly than Benzayda had ventured; he calls his father's will "a murdering will / That whirls along with an impetuous sway" and complains:

> Nature, that bids us parents to obey,
> Bids parents their commands by reason weigh.
>
> [4:102]

As his father leaves Ozmyn says bitterly:

> He does my honour want of duty call;
> To that, and love, he has no right at all.
>
> [4:102]

Nevertheless, Dryden will not require the sympathetic Ozmyn to make any active resistance to his father. In part 2, act 4, after Ozmyn, Benzayda, and Selin in turn each offers to sacrifice his life and his deepest desire, Abenemar is won over and ceases his opposition.

Within the conventions of the heroic romance, as I pointed out in the preceding chapter, it can sometimes happen that a subject's active resistance to a usurping sovereign turns out to be justified by the discovery that he himself is the true sovereign. However, since it can hardly be discovered that a wife is her own husband or that a child is his own father, we do not see much active resistance in the domestic plots of these fundamentally conservative romances. About the only circumstances under which resistance becomes possible are when a true king is in conflict with a man he wrongly thinks to be his father or when a child joins the forces of a true king while his father is fighting for the usurper. Dryden uses both of these cases in *The Spanish Friar*. In the upper plot the true king Torrismond wrongly thinks Raymond is his father; in the lower plot Lorenzo joins Torrismond's forces, though even there Lorenzo is not a particularly sympathetic character and never actually has to draw his sword against his own father.

The relationship between Boabdelin and his wife Almahide in *The Conquest of Granada* is also difficult and is also presented in terms of questioning the limits of authority and obligation. Almahide has married the king only because her father wished it and her husband is constantly suspicious of her love for him. Boabdelin's laments over the married state introduce a domestic note more like that usually associated with Restoration comedy:

> Marriage, thou curse of love, and snare of life,
> That first debased a mistress to a wife!
> Love, like a scene, at distance should appear,
> But marriage views the gross-daubed landscape near.
> Love's nauseous cure! thou cloyest whom thou should'st please;
> And, when thou cur'st, then thou art the disease.
> When hearts are loose, thy chain our bodies ties;
> Love couples friends, but marriage enemies.
>
> [4:155]

Almahide is strictly virtuous, but her loyalty is severely tried by the king's jealousy and by his irrational exercise of authority over her. Boabdelin commands her to invite Almanzor back to Granada, then as soon as she assents, regrets his command and claims that her assent reveals not obedience to him but love for Almanzor. She replies:

> This sudden change I do not understand,
> Have you so soon forgot your own command?
>
> [4:135]

Boabdelin reaches an apogee of unreasonableness in a couplet combining the pettiness of a neurotic tyrant with the sullenness of a spoiled child:

> Grant that I did the unjust injunction lay,
> You should have loved me more than to obey.
>
> [4:135]

Problems multiply until Almahide at last declares she will no longer share Boabdelin's bed and will retire to live with "vestals." It is not clear that there were any Moorish convents or that any convent, Moorish or Christian, would accept a queen against the king's will, but that does not matter, since once Almahide has established her willingness to renounce all to preserve her self-respect, Boabdelin is killed, Granada falls to Spain, and the kind Queen Isabella orders her to become engaged to Almanzor.

In *The Conquest of Granada* Dryden strips the commands of the fathers and the husband of all moral authority except that of status. The commands have force because of the status of the man who gives them; in all other respects they are unsympathetic, unjust, and—with the aid of the heightened rhetoric of heroic drama—blood-thirsty or irrational. Dryden still wants to insist that status does confer authority and demands at least nonresistance, yet he is also enough of his time to perceive those authorities as virtually empty forms. He averts tragedy only by containing the domestic conflicts within larger political conflicts and, like Sedley in *The Mulberry Garden*, finally dismissing the domestic authorities as rebels against the true king.

It would, of course, be foolish to argue that the spectacle of wives and children rebelling against their husbands and fathers was a novel invention of the Restoration. In comedy of all periods, young lovers regularly defy their tutors, parents, and guardians and expect the audience's sympathy. At least in comedy, sympathy is even frequently granted to lusty young wives restive under the rule of old and stingy husbands. Nevertheless, different meanings are attached to such rebellions at different times and the forms of the rebellions differ. To compare and contrast the treatment of domestic rebellion in prewar plays and postwar plays suggests both similarities rooted in the ideological shifts of the Reformation and differences based on the further development and heightening of these trends and on later influences from events and newer philosophies. As could be expected from what we have already said about the ideological interest in marriage from the beginning of the Reformation, earlier Tudor and Stuart plays also addressed themselves to issues raised by children and wives rebelling against patriarchal authority. Comedies like Thomas Dekker's *Shoemaker's Holiday* (1599), Michael Drayton's *Merry Devil of Edmonton* (1599–1604) or Thomas Middleton and Dekker's *Roaring Girl* (1611) all show worthy children in love resisting the commands of fathers who oppose their matches for unworthy motives. These plays are lighthearted and the fathers are all brought to relinquish their opposition; nevertheless, they are quite in accord with serious protestant belief in marriage for love as opposed to marriage for dynastic or acquisitive motives. Restoration couples also insist on the moral correctness of love matches, but they do so with more open attacks on their guardians and with more political self-consciousness. Rose in *The Shoemaker's Holiday* rejects her father's candidate for her hand and determines to marry the man she loves in spite of the class difference between them. At the beginning of the play she soliloquizes:

> O my most vnkind father! O my starres!
> Why lowrde you so at my natiuity,
> To make me loue robd of my loue?[22]

Gertrude in Shadwell's *Bury-Fair*, on the other hand, says to the suitor her father has sent: "my Father is no Outwork of mine: you may take him, but you are ne'r the nearer me. I am a free Heiress of *England*, where Arbitrary Power is at an end, and I am resolv'd to choose for my self" (4:339).

Although some late sixteenth- and early seventeenth-century

playwrights were willing to approve children's resisting their parents' commands to marry, they were considerably less willing to endorse a wife's resistance to her husband. Unfaithful or disobedient wives almost never triumph; adulteresses die and wives who try to rule their husbands are brought to repentance. Donna Margarite in Fletcher's *Rule a Wife and Have a Wife* (1624) sets out to marry a husband she can control, but though she finds one apparently the quintessence of docility and though he is her maid's brother, he ends by establishing his authority over her. Somber plays like the anonymous *Lamentable and True Tragedy of Arden of Feversham* (1585–92), based on an actual case of petit treason in which a wife murdered her husband, George Wilkins's *Miseries of Enforced Marriage* (1605–17), or Thomas Heywood's *Woman Killed with Kindness* (1603) all present disastrous marriages. Commenting on a group of these prewar unhappy marriage plays, Chilton Lathem Powell concluded, "The fact that where the wife is the offender the plays result in tragedy, but where the husband performs equal and worse crimes they result in forgiveness and reconcilliation, is no mere accident but in strict keeping with the domestic ideals of the day."[23] Restoration playwrights, as we shall see, were more likely to look at unhappy marriages from the woman's point of view, and, though they were still not willing to present a sympathetic adulteress as a central character, they did frequently use adultery outside of tragedy both in problem comedy and in farce. They also went further toward secularizing the issues. When Aphra Behn adapted *The Miseries of Enforced Marriage* as *The Town Fop* (1676), for instance, she avoided traditional religious arguments by simply eliminating the doctor of divinity from Oxford who enunciates such arguments in Wilkins.

If we follow a series of plays descending from *The Taming of the Shrew* we can glimpse a progressive loss of the ideological supports of the husband's sovereignty and a groping toward the protestant ideal of marriage as mutually helpful spiritual companionship. Shakespeare's Katharina is finally brought to moralize:

> Thy husband is thy lord, thy life, thy keeper,
> Thy head, thy sovereign . . . .
> Such duty as the subject owes the prince,
> Even such a woman oweth to her husband;
> And when she's froward, peevish, sullen, sour,

And not obedient to his honest will,
What is she but a foul contending rebel,
And graceless traitor to her loving lord?—
I am ashamed that women are so simple
To offer war where they should kneel for peace,
Or seek for rule, supremacy, and sway,
When they are bound to serve, love, and obey.[24]

Fletcher wrote a sequel to *The Taming of the Shrew* called *The Woman's Prize; or, the Tamer Tamed* (performed 1633, published 1649) that shows some awareness of a more thoroughly protestant point of view. There Petruchio marries a second time, but Maria, his second wife, determines from the beginning to repress her naturally sweet disposition in order to perform the heroic deed of taming Petruchio:

by the faith I have
In mine own noble will, that childish woman
That lives a prisoner to her husband's pleasure
Has lost her making, and becomes a beast,
Created for his use, not fellowship!

[5:271]

Organizing the other women to help, on her wedding night she barricades herself and her forces in part of Petruchio's house, lays in provisions for a long siege, and determines to hold out until Petruchio, whom she has admitted to loving in the first act, comes to a right understanding of marriage. In the middle of the play Petruchio decides to make at least a show of compliance, agrees to Maria's written demands for "liberty and clothes," but as she still refuses to sleep with him for at least a week and continues to tease him with extravagant wishes, they fall out again. When he appeals to her "obedience" she retorts:

That bare word
Shall cost you many a pound more. Build upon't!
Tell me of due obedience? What's a husband?
What are we married for? to carry sumpters?
Are we not one piece with you, and as worthy
Our own intentions as you yours? . . .

> Take two small drops of water, equal weigh'd,
> Tell me which is the heaviest, and which ought
> First to descend in duty?
>
> [5:337]

Petruchio in the fifth act determines to go abroad, declaring the bond of matrimony broken between them and leaving Maria half his house and all her jointure. She blandly compliments him on his desire to gain wisdom. Nevertheless, he attempts one final ploy. In hopes Maria will repent her behavior toward him he pretends to be dead. Confronted with his bier, however, she merely regrets that he wasted his life in such unreasonable and ungentle behavior. He gives up the pretense, laments his unhappiness, and Maria, declaring herself victorious, at last relents: "I have tamed you / And am now vow'd your servant" (5:397). The epilogue, whether written by Fletcher or not, correctly points the moral:

> To teach both sexes due equality,
> And, as they stand bound, to love mutually.

During the Restoration Shakespeare's *Taming of the Shrew* was transformed into the comedian John Lacy's *Sauny the Scot; or, The Taming of the Shrew* (1667). *The Woman's Prize*, more often called *The Tamer Tamed* in the Restoration, was popular during the early Restoration and performed without adaptation and apparently sometimes in tandem with *Sauny*.[25] Hazelton Spencer is severe on Lacy's "vulgar adaptation of the delightful Elizabethan farce," but it is significant that though Lacy in general preserves Shakespeare's plot and the substance of much of the dialogue, the more dignified aspects of support for a conservative view of domestic relations evaporate and the crucial fifth act is reconstructed. Although Margaret (Katharina) has submitted to Petruchio at the end of the fourth act as she does in Shakespeare, in Lacy once she gets safely back to town and to her father's house, she begins another revolt, declaring, like Maria in *The Woman's Prize*, "I'll make Petruchio glad to wipe my shoes or walk my horse ere I have done with him."[26] So challenged, Petruchio resorts to a brutal tactic suited to farce but not without its symbolic significance: he pretends Margaret's ill-temper is caused by an

infected tooth and sends for a barber to remove it. Sauny—
Petruchio's servant—jokes that the barber ought to make a mistake
and rip something else out of Margaret's body instead—her "tang"
(tongue), he suggests, reminding us of jokes about tongues as
stingers, but also suggesting a castrating assault on the woman who
aspires to usurp a man's authority. Margaret wins a reprieve from
this attack by hitting the barber. She has, however, vowed to give
Petruchio a version of what he wants in a wife by swearing herself
to two months of silence. Frustrated, he seeks revenge, by
proceeding to have her buried alive. When at last she cries out to
save herself from death, Petruchio has won. The final wager scene
from Shakespeare is included at the very end of the act, but instead
of Katharina's long verse speech quoted above, Margaret says
more shortly: "Fie! ladies, for shame! How dare you infringe that
duty which you justly owe your husband's? They are our Lords, and
we must pay 'em service" (p. 389). Though I must concede Lacy's
mind was less philosophical than Shakespeare's, his version on the
whole seems to reflect greater tension and even animosity in the sex
war and also some loss of belief in the traditional ideological
underpinnings of a husband's claim to authority.

It is not that the resistance of domestic inferiors is dramatized
after the Restoration and not earlier, but rather that the
justifications for patriarchal authority are weaker and the
resistance is more often politically self-conscious. Restoration plays
like *Tarugo's Wiles* or *The Gentleman Dancing Master* tend to
emphasize not simply that true love cannot be thwarted, but also
or even alternatively that inferiors cannot be subjugated. At the
beginning of the period most writers fight shy of the more drastic
consequences of their renderings of inferiors' complaints. St. Serfe
ignores the public implications of Lavinia's position and softens
even the domestic implications by having her resist her brother
instead of her father. A fundamentally conservative writer like
Dryden puts skeptical arguments in the mouths of his less sympathetic characters like Boabdelin and takes final refuge in
romance solutions. Assertions about the necessity of "liberty" and
"enfranchisement" for women are at first made more confidently
in pure comedy than they could be in the lower plot of a play with
an upper plot concerned with politics and the public world.

Restoration comedies frequently use political language to talk about marriage and the relations between men and women. In the last lines of *The Triumphant Widow* (1674) the Duke of Newcastle makes his Lady Haughty say she will not marry, but:

> sit alone,
> And triumph in the liberty I owne;
> I ne're will wear a matrimonial Chain,
> But safe and quiet in this Throne remain,
> And absolute Monarch o're my self will raign.[27]

Antonio in Joseph Arrowsmith's *Reformation* (1673) urges his co-conspirators to swear: "that you will, without respect of persons, endeavour the extirpation of Tyranny, that is, the government of Husbands and Fathers, by Sisters, Aunts, Nurses, and all other Officers depending upon that Usurpation."[28] As the political lines between Whig and Tory became more sharply drawn, the analogies between rebellious domestic inferiors and Whigs are also drawn. Crowne makes the factious Podesta in *City Politiques* (1683) ask if he is to blame that his wife is a strumpet. Florio, pretending to be a sympathizer to the faction in order to seduce Podesta's wife, replies: "Yes, she is a true Whig and has revolted from you because you did not pay her nightly pension well. . . . Our principles are: he is not to be regarded who has a right to govern, but he who can best serve the ends of government. I can better serve the ends of your lady than you can, so I lay claim to your lady."[29] Shadwell's women tend to be particularly self-conscious about the political analogies suggested by their attitudes even in the plays before 1688, as we shall see in a later discussion of *The Woman-Captain*, but the analogies are very striking after the Glorious Revolution. In *The Scowrers* (1690), for instance, when Clara complains that she has been sold to an "Alderman's most impertinent Nephew," Eugenia urges her to revolt: "thou art like those unreasonable, craven Fellows that would do nothing toward the Deliverance of *England*, and yet would have all the benefit of the change, nay that would keep those that did, out of government." In another scene, Eugenia says, "We are born free, and we'll preserve that freedom; we have learn'd more Wit than to call Self-defence Rebellion" (5:110).

III

Although some weakening of traditional notions of domestic authority is evident even in the early plays of the Restoration, more serious rethinking was going on elsewhere in the culture, particularly among the philosophers and the lawyers. Hobbes and Locke both tried to offer new accounts of paternal authority that would be consonant with their secular philosophies of political sovereignty. The common lawyers wrestled with problems left in the wake of the interregnum abolition of the ecclesiastical courts and invented various rationales for their continued encroachments on the traditional jurisdiction of the ecclesiastical courts after the ecclesiastical courts had been restored.

Especially after about 1670, many writers expressed fear that marriage itself was under attack. Obviously there has been adultery as long as there has been marriage and sins against domestic piety may be expected whenever there is any domestic piety, but writers in the late seventeenth century complained that contemporary sinners not only sinned but refused to accept any shame or guilt for their sins. Virtuous gentlemen like the author of *An Account of Marriage or the Interests of Marriage considered and Defended, against the unjust attacques of the Age*, observing that they had fallen "into such an age, where it is reckoned not only innocent enough, but a peculiar piece of gallantry and good breeding, to divert ourselves with holy wedlock," thought it necessary to write not only conduct books with advice on how to behave once married but also pamphlets justifying the very existence of the institution of marriage.[30] Another anonymous writer of the seventies tried to dissuade a young gentleman of his acquaintance from going to live in London by warning him against the opinions he was likely to find current there: "if you cannot mock at Vertue and prudence with a mene of scorn and contempt, you will not be able to keep company with these Heroes." A chief object of the wits' attack, he says, "is Marriage, which they treat most ingloriously, affirming it to be the clogg of generous minds; . . . they believe Mankind has suffered in nothing more, than in the restraints and captivities of Wedlock, and that no freedom ought to be more dear to his nature, than wild and rambling Lusts."

Moreover, he claims, the plays of the wits have contributed significantly to the current "contempt of Wedlock."[31] So frequently was contempt of marriage expressed that Wycherley used it as a humor for Lady Flippant in *Love in a Wood* (1671), and D'Urfey used it in Sir Philip Freewit of *The Marriage Hater Match'd* (1692).

In the nineties writers were still speaking of attacks on marriage as commonplace. The clergyman Joseph Fisher began his *Honour of Marriage: or, the Institution, Necessity, Advantages, Comforts, and Usefulness of a Married Life* by complaining the modern writers "have endeavoured from the Armoury of their Learning, some indulged Practices of Former Ages [probably polygamy among the patriarchs], and unwarry Expressions of Ancient and Modern Authors to overthrow the Laws of God and Man," later adding that these same writers attacked the holy institutions of God "as things either above, or below, or contrary to their Reason." In his *Discourse on Fornication*, Turner, a lecturer at Christ Church, London, explained: "the looseness of Mens Manners had corrupted their Judgements, and defaced their Sense of Good and Evil: So that instead of Humiliation before God, Men justifie themselves, and are so far from abandoning their Vices that they plead Innocence, and upon the Perpetration of the vilest Crimes, cry out with Solomon's Harlot, that *they have done nothing amiss.*" Even the facetious Tom Brown has some fictional ladies note in an equally fictitious petition of 1693: "You need not be reminded with what Scorn and Contempt the Holy State of Matrimony has of late years been treated: Every nasty Scribbler of the Town has pelted it in his wretched Lampoons; it has been persecuted in Sonnet, ridicul'd at Court, exposed on the Theatre, and that so often, that the Subject is now exhausted and barren."[32]

It is undoubtedly true that the more conservative gentlemen of the Restoration were apt to overreact and to consider some writing with a serious moral intention nothing but antimoral filth. The author of *Remarques on the Humours of the Town* himself thinks those who attacked *Marriage à la Mode* as libertine misinterpreted a satire on contemporary libertinism. Satirists are very often accused of approving the evils they represent. Though I think P. F. Vernon overstates his argument in "Marriage of Convenience and

the Moral Code of Restoration Comedy," I would agree that much
of the apparent hostility to marriage in the comedy is an essentially
moral protest not against marriage itself but against mercenary
marriages of convenience.[33]

Nevertheless, where there's smoke there's fire. The behavior and
writing of wits like the Earl of Rochester and Sedley did genuinely
shock their more conservative contemporaries and were meant to
do so. The Restoration divines who thought "Love a woman? You're
an ass!" did violence to fundamental feelings about the sanctity of
marriage were not seeing ghosts. The representation of libertine
sentiments and adultery in comic contexts, whether "approved" by
the playwrights or not, violated important decorums. An
anonymous poem like *Sylvia's Revenge* made an attack on
patriarchal authority reminiscent of the subversive attacks on the
aristocracy in the liveliest of the interregnum ballads:

> Tell me you grave Disputers of the Schools,
> You learned *Cocks-combs*, and you well-read *Fools*:
> You that have told us *Man* must be our *Head*;
> And made Dame Nature *Pimp* to what you've say'd.
> Tell me when *Husband* drench't in *Clarret* reels,
> And flips by th' Motion of his treach'rous Heels,
> That *Head* he has we all confess and own,
> But what's the Head, when once the Sense is gone? . . .
> Are these ye Gods!, the Sov'raign's we must own?
> Must we before these golden Calves bow down?
> Forgive us Heaven if we renounce the Elves,
> We'll make a Common-Wealth amonge our selves.[34]

Attacks on marriage as against reason or against nature were
particularly disturbing and I shall examine the grounds of these
attacks in chapter 5. Some of the complaining was undoubtedly
provoked by genuinely libertine behavior and attitudes, but much
of it also was conservative reaction against the impulses of the
protestant Reformation and their practical consequences, especially state interference with church and patriarchal authority.

Satisfaction with marriage was also undermined by practical
problems that some thought could be solved within the framework
of existing institutions and others thought required more drastic

remedies. For instance, clergy and laymen alike were worried about the frequency of clandestine marriages. Admitting the ecclesiastical registrars issued marriage licenses for profit, Humphrey Prideaux, archdeacon of Suffolk, nevertheless claimed that parliamentary interference would be unnecessary if the existing canon law were followed more scrupulously.[35] Others in parliament offered bills to prevent clandestine marriages in 1666, 1677, 1685, and 1691, though these bills were resisted by commons until the passage of Lord Hardwicke's Marriage Act in 1753.[36] There was also continuing worry about the ability of the ecclesiastical courts to secure compliance with the decrees and dissatisfaction with the procedure of having writs *de excommunicato capiendo* issued out of Chancery. Sir Leoline Jenkins, Judge of the Prerogative Court of Canterbury and perhaps the most distinguished civil and canon lawyer of his day, reflected this dissatisfaction when he prepared a bill to create a writ *de contumace capiendo*, in effect reserving excommunication for more serious offenses and creating a new, lesser punishment—one more likely to be enforced—for lesser offenses.[37] Such a bill was not enacted until 1813, but parliament did pass other legislation directly affecting marriage and the family. The state continued its encroachment on ecclesiastical control of marriage with several statutes taxing marriage licenses in William's reign. Parliament also reduced the prerogative of fathers by various acts and declarations. The House of Lords reversed a Chancery decision in *Hall and Keene* v. *Potter*, attacking all marriage brokage bonds, and in "An act for the further preventing the growth of popery" parliament allowed protestant children whose Roman Catholic parents denied them "fitting maintenance" to appeal to Chancery.[38]

The prominence of mercenary motives in marriage was almost universally lamented and it is probably true that the cost of marriage portions rose steeply in the late seventeenth century.[39] A "Person of Quality" in 1691 compared his degenerate times to less mercenary days: "There are some now living in these kingdoms, that remember when Money was the least part considered in Marriage, when that *Summ* would have been thought a Fortune

For a *Lord*, that is now despised by a Merchant; yet then there were few dyed without *Posterity*." Progressing beyond mere complaint, in *Marriage Promoted* he offers a scheme for encouraging people to marry by levying a heavy annual tax on men over twenty-one who have not yet married; widows and widowers who have had no children are also to be taxed while they remain unmarried, as are single women over eighteen who have control over their own fortunes. The money raised through these taxes is to be spent on marriage portions for virtuous single women under forty.[40]

Going beyond such attempts to tinker with matrimony, more profound philosophers were prepared to offer fundamentally new accounts of the family itself, though it is important to realize that they were motivated more by dissatisfaction with divine right theories of sovereign / subject relations than by any particular interest in the family for its own sake. Neither Hobbes nor Locke wished to support the political views of Filmer. Logically, one might suppose, they could simply have rejected the great chain of being analogies and argued that whatever elements of natural subjection there might be in domestic relations, domestic relations are irrelevant to the rights of sovereigns over subjects. Yet neither Hobbes nor Locke adopts this line simply. Each attempts to provide a new account of the relations between parents and children analogous to his new account of the relations between sovereigns and subjects; Locke also treats husbands and wives. That they should make such attempts is eloquent testimony to the power and pervasiveness of the great chain of being analogies even in the struggles to escape from them.

Hobbes believes he can show that the sovereign acquires dominion through the consent of his subjects, consent they give in order to preserve themselves from violent death. Similarly, he feels he should show that the "right of dominion" of parents over children does not derive from generation, "but from the child's consent, either express, or by other sufficient arguments declared" (2, 20, 130). Children give this consent for the same reason subjects do: to preserve their lives. If paternal authority did derive from generation, in effect, from nature, Hobbes argues, then it would be possessed equally by fathers and mothers. Yet that, he claims, is impossible: "for no man can obey two masters." (Hobbes is one of the funniest writers of the late seventeenth century, and quoting Scripture to destroy traditional religious beliefs is one of his favorite games.) The only reason fathers appear to have dominion over children, Hobbes says, is not that they are naturally "the more excellent sex," but simply because "for the most part commonwealths have been erected by the fathers, not the mothers of families" and their civil law has given dominion to fathers. In a state of nature, on the other hand, "either the parents between themselves dispose of the dominion over the child by contract; or do not dispose thereof at all." Then he introduces an ingenious example, hardly characteristic of human practice, but one that supports his case. The Amazons, he notes, continued their communities beyond the first generation by arranging to have intercourse with men in neighboring countries; they made contracts stipulating that the female offspring should go to the Amazons, the male to their neighbors. In a state of nature, Hobbes argues further, dominion ultimately belongs to mothers since there is no marriage and the identity of fathers cannot be known unless mothers declare it. If an infant remains in the power of its mother and she preserves it, she has dominion; if she exposes it and another finds and preserves it, that other has dominion: "For it ought to obey him by whom it is preserved; because preservation of life being the end, for which one man becomes subject to another, every man is supposed to promise obedience, to him, in whose power it is to save, or destroy him." Except to state that there are no matrimonial laws in the state of nature and to claim that in nature "there is not always that difference of strength, or prudence between the man and the woman, as that the right can be determined without war," Hobbes does not discuss authority in the relation between husband and wife. If the relationship is an artificial creation of the commonwealth, it is less vital to his argument.

Though Hobbes's remarks on the family were not addressed specifically to Filmer, Filmer realized their relevance and sought to counter them. The application of contract theory to parent / child relationships he finds incomprehensible: "How a child can express consent, or by other sufficient arguments declare it before it comes to the age of discretion I understand not, yet all men grant it is due before consent is given."[41] Hobbes's contention that the

mother originally has the government of her children he rejects
with the counterargument that "God at the creation gave
sovereignty to the man over the woman." Doubts about paternity
he dismisses with the statements that if a mother has no husband,
"the child is not reckoned to have any Father at all" and that "no
child naturally and infallibly knows who are his true parents, yet
he must obey those that in common reputation are so."

Filmer's position was still strong enough in the 1680s for Locke
to consider it necessary to refute him in *Two Treatises of Government*. Chapters 5 and 6 of the *First Treatise*, "Of *Adam's* Title to
Sovereignty, by the Subjection of *Eve*" and "Of *Adam's* Title to
Sovereignty by Fatherhood," and chapter 6 of the *Second Treatise*,
"Of Paternal Power" are devoted to demolishing paternal claims
to the obedience of children founded in natural law and to dif-
ferentiating between domestic relationships and sovereign / subject
relationships. Nevertheless, like Hobbes, Locke tries to offer an
account of domestic authority analogous to his own account of
political authority. Locke wants to show that subjects are born
free, not bound by nature to obey a particular sovereign. Similarly,
he tries to show that natural law theories about the subjection of
children and wives are incorrect. Like Hobbes again, he tries to
complicate the father / child part of the analogy by introducing the
mother: "For whatever obligation Nature and the right of
Generation lays on Children, it must certainly bind them equal to
both the concurrent Causes of it" (2, 52), that is, equally to fathers
and mothers:

> Had but this one thing been well consider'd without looking any deeper
> into the matter, it might perhaps have kept Men from running into
> those gross mistakes, they have made, about this Power of Parents:
> which however it might, without any great harshness, bear the name of
> Absolute Dominion, and Regal Authority, when under the Title of
> *Paternal Power* it seem'd appropriated to the Father, would yet have
> sounded but oddly, and in the very name shown the Absurdity, if this
> supposed Absolute Power over Children had been called *Parental*, and
> thereby have discover'd, that it belong'd to the Mother too.
>
> [2, 53]

Parental power properly understood, Locke argues, derives from
the duty both fathers and mothers have to take care of children

until they are able to reason for themselves. As Hobbes maintains that whoever preserves a child, not necessarily his natural parents, possesses authority over him, so Locke—less brutally—argues, "Nay, this *power* too little belongs to the *Father* by any peculiar right of Nature, but only as he is Guardian of his Children, than when he quits his Care of them, he loses his power over them, which goes along with their Nourishment and Education, to which it is inseparably annexed, and it belongs as much to the *Foster-Father* of an exposed Child, as to the Natural Father of another" (2, 65).

Even wives are not subject to the absolute authority of their husbands by positive divine law or by the law of nature. In the *First Treatise*, the one addressed directly to Filmer, Locke maintains that God's words to Eve in Genesis 3:16 ("And thy desire shall be to thy Husband, and he shall rule over thee") do not—as Filmer claimed and as seems obvious—imply any grant of authority to Adam over Eve:

> And if we will take them as they were directed in particular to her, or in her, as their representative to all other Women, they will at most concern the Female Sex only [whose freedom Locke is not so concerned to maintain], and import no more but that Subjection they should ordinarily be in to their Husbands: But there is here no more Law to oblige a Woman to such a Subjection, if the Circumstances either of her Condition or Contract with her Husband should exempt her from it, then there is, that she should bring forth her Children in Sorrow and Pain, if there could be found a Remedy for it. [1, 47]

In the *Second Treatise* Locke discusses marriage as a "voluntary compact," the end of which is procreation. He notes that the power of the husband is "so far from that of an absolute Monarch" that the wife retains "the full and free possession of what by Contract is her peculiar Right" and that she also has a "liberty" to separate from her husband "where natural Right, or their Contract allows it" (2, 82). (The legal validity of marriage contracts providing for separation was moot.) He even permits himself to wonder why when procreation and the education of children, which he considers the ends of the contract, are completed, husband and wife might not separate (2, 81).

While Locke offers accounts of domestic relationships analogous to the account of political relationships he wants to maintain, he does so in the process of arguing that the analogies traditionally seen between political authority and domestic authority are false.[42] Furthermore, Locke tries to limit his own analogies. The power of life and death over subjects, which he grants to the political sovereign, is not possessed by husbands or fathers. Filmer collects examples of fathers who have exercised the power of life and death over their children, examples Locke dismisses as monstrous, complaining that if such historical cases are to be used to imply natural law rights, then any crime ever committed, including sodomy, could be considered justified by natural law (1, 59). It is not fathers, Locke says, who give life to their children, but God. Fathers beget children to satisfy their own sexual appetites, not to confer obligation. This is a fairly common skeptical argument in the later seventeenth century and is also used by Lorenzo in *The Spanish Friar:*

> Bear arms against my father? he begat me;—
> That's true; but for whose sake did he beget me?
> For his own, sure enough: for me he knew not.
>   [6: 503]

Lorenzo uses the argument in the course of persuading himself of the legitimacy of armed resistance to his sovereign, and that, after all, is fundamentally the reason Locke—who had no serious difficulty with his own father, who never married, and who, as far as we know, never had any children of his own—interests himself in domestic relations.

It was not, however, only in plays and verse or the writings of such advanced thinkers as Hobbes and Locke that traditional natural law accounts of domestic authority were questioned. Even the law, among the most conservative of social institutions, gradually began to alter its views of patriarchal prerogatives. Blackstone says in discussing the degree of force a husband might justifiably use against his wife: "For, as he is to answer for her misbehaviour, the law thought it reasonable to intrust him with this power of restraining her, by domestic chastisement, in the same moderation that a man is allowed to correct his apprentices or children. . . . But, with us, in the politer reign of Charles the second, this power of correction began to be doubted" (1, 15, 444–45). Blackstone refers his reader to Lord Leigh's case (1674), and from the law reports we learn that Lord Leigh's wife, "upon affidavit of hard usage, and that she went in fear of her life, was granted security of the peace against her husband." This may seem a weak remedy, but had the justices been more conservative they would have refused any remedy at all, sending her into the ecclesiastical courts to sue for a divorce *a mensa et thoro* on the grounds of cruelty, and, if her fears were justified, by the time she secured that she might have been beaten to death. Chief Justice Matthew Hale opined that "the salva moderata castigione in the register not meant of beating, but only of admonition and confinement to the house, in case of her extravagance."[43]

One of the most significant domestic relations cases of the Restoration was that of *Manby* v. *Scott*. The facts in the case were that a wife had left her husband, then after a considerable interval, had offered to return to him. He refused. No specific immorality or extravagance was alleged against her. The husband had forbidden a certain merchant, the plaintiff, to sell his wares to the wife, but the merchant did supply the wife with necessities and then sued the husband for debt.

The issues in this case were complex and were debated at great length by the justices of both King's Bench and Exchequer. That it was generally considered an important case is evident from the fullness of the accounts and from the fact that many different law reports include it. The lawyers who argued for the defendant, that is, for the husband's refusal to pay his wife's debts, were apt to quote Scripture to prove the justice of women's subjection to men and also to lavish florid rhetoric on the anarchic horrors to be expected if runaway wives were allowed to charge necessities. Mr. Justice Hyde thought a decision for the merchant would put it in "the power of the wife (who by the law of God, and of the land, is put under the power of the husband, and is bound to live in subjection unto him) to rule over her husband, and undo him. . . . Is such power," he inquired, "suitable to the judgment of Almighty God inflicted upon women for being first in the transgression? . . .

Will wives depend on the kindness and favours of their husbands, or be observant towards them as they ought to be, if such a power be put into their hands?"[44] Orlando Bridgeman, Chief Justice of the Common Pleas, agreed:

> If this be not an encouragement to disobedience, I know not what is. O but, says my brother Twisden, she must not starve though she be an ill wife. I answer, when she voluntarily departs from him, if she will rather starve than not have her humour,—whose is the fault? The Scriptures say "He that will not work, let him not eat." So may I say, if she will not return with the prodigal, she must eat husks with the prodigal.[45]

Those for the plaintiff, on the other hand, argued that it was intolerable that the wife should starve. Justice Tyrrell, who had served on the parliamentary side as a colonel of horse and also as an interregnum M.P., took a particularly protestant line that showed more concern for the wife as an individual than for the social hierarchy. Invoking the law of nature and "the evangelical law, which saith, no man hateth his own flesh," he argued that though by common law the wife cannot compel her husband, "yet no reason hinders but that he may be charged by a third person collaterally . . . else it may fall out, that though he cannot murder her, yet he may starve her." Tyrrell had no sympathy for the husband's refusal to receive his wife again. He noted the parallel between this and the Old Testament story of Vasti, the queen who refused to obey her husband's command and was punished by the loss of her estate and her position in order that "all the wives shall give to their husband's honour." But to this story, which he dismissed as "but politick advice of heathens in their cups," he opposed the New Testament morality of 1 Corinthians 7:10, 11: "Let not the wife depart from the husband: and let not the husband put away his wife." Pointing out that the issue in *Manby* v. *Scott* was only the wife's bills for admitted necessities, "not for variety, or for jewels or money," he deprecated fears that a decision for the plaintiff would encourage wives generally to elope. Finally, although agreeing that the wife was subordinate to the husband, Tyrrell declared, "but yet her will is not so subject to his, that if his be unreasonable, yet it must be an uncontrollable law."[46]

Jurisdiction was a critical issue in *Manby* v. *Scott*. One of the strongest arguments for the defendant was that the wife should have sought her remedy in the ecclesiastical court, which, as Bridgemen and others maintained, was "the proper Court for matters of matrimony." If the wife could show cruelty on her husband's part she could get a divorce *a mensa et thoro* in the ecclesiastical court and would be entitled to alimony. Otherwise, she could sue him there for a restitution of conjugal rights. Not only was the ecclesiastical court traditionally the place for resolving matrimonial disputes—a sufficient legal reason in itself— but since ecclesiastical law emerged from civil law rather than from common law, a married woman had standing there to sue her husband herself. Furthermore, the conservatives hoped that the judges of the ecclesiastical courts, hearing cases without juries and in relative privacy, would be able to reduce the bitterness and scandal of matrimonial disputes. (In *Manby* v. *Scott* and similar cases snide remarks were sometimes made about the impropriety of allowing juries of tradesmen to decide the private disputes of their betters and, worse still, to decide whether other tradesmen had common-law remedies.)

To these strong arguments those for the plaintiff pointed out that during the interregnum the ecclesiastical courts had lost their powers and that the temporal courts had consequently handled such cases.[47] Twisden went so far as to maintain—quite unhistorically—that "alimony probably never was within ec- clesiastick jurisdiction," though he apparently changed his mind later. Moreover, the remedies belonging to the ecclesiastical courts were complained of as too feeble. Unlike the temporal courts, the ecclesiastical courts had no power to touch money or land, but could only issue writs *de excommunicato capiendo*, writs providing for the imprisonment of recalcitrant offenders. Thus Tyrrell argued, "they only excommunicate, not sequester the estate, as at common law, and to presume one will not lye in prison rather than pay debts, is contrary to experience, and the judgment of a learned Parliament that giveth execution against lands of the debtor dying in prison, in which case the wife hath lost all." Twisden agreed with this and also complained that the remedies of the ecclesiastical courts were insufficient in that alimony was only allowed after divorce.[48]

At a deeper level, the fundamental protestant dislike for the ecclesiastical courts themselves motivated the supporters of the plaintiff to try to take jurisdiction away from them.[49] The animus that led to the abolition of the courts in the first place did not evaporate at the Restoration. About the time of *Manby* v. *Scott*, for instance, Henry Cary published his *Law of England; or, A True Guide for all Persons concerned in Ecclesiastical Courts*. This is not a sympathetic statement of canon law but an elaborate guide showing how to frustrate ecclesiastical proceedings by claiming every last procedural right and by trying for prohibitions on the basis of various Reformation statutes. Excommunication, Cary says, used to be feared:

> But afterwards, when men began to give but small regard to the Flashes of this Spiritual Lightning, the Clergy (who have always had a great hand in molding our Laws) decided to make use of the thunder of the Secular Arm, and thereby render these their fulminations more formidable to the vulgar. Hereupon they introduced our cruel sanguinary Laws for casting the bodies of those men into Prisons, Earthly Purgatories, whose Souls they had by Excommunication given to the Devil.

Edward Hickeringill, who was chaplain to Lilburne's regiment of horse during the war and ordained in 1661 by Robert Sanderson, skirmished with the ecclesiastical courts throughout his career. He was suspended for three years for celebrating marriages irregularly, but claims in *News from Drs. Commons* that it is the duty of presbyters to marry people, not a crime, and that people from his part of the country often married without bans or licenses.[50] Even a sympathetic expounder of canon law like Henry Conset in *The Practice of the Spiritual or Ecclesiastical Courts* (1685) refers repeatedly to defendant's contempt for the courts and discusses techniques used to evade its sanctions.

The King's Bench judges, who first heard *Manby* v. *Scott*, "being divided in opinion" the case was adjourned to the Exchequer where long arguments finally resulted in a decision for the defendant. William S. Holdsworth points to the minority opinion in *Manby* v. *Scott* as the beginning of a process making an exception to the rule that married women could not make valid contracts. He cites *James* v. *Warren* (1707) where Justice Holt declared "that if a man wrongfully deserts his wife, and leaves her destitute, she is his "agent of necessity" and can pledge his credit for necessaries. Holdsworth comments that though the minority opinion in *Manby* v. *Scott* "was probably new law, and inspired by a desire to encroach on the province of the Chancery and the ecclesiastical courts, it . . . has become a settled principle of the modern common law."[51]

However, two important consequences of *Manby* v. *Scott* are evident before *James* v. *Warren*. First, the temporal courts were increasingly willing to continue the interregnum practice of handling matrimonial disputes formerly within the jurisdiction of the ecclesiastical courts. Gellert Spencer Alleman is incorrect when he says that "the common law courts refused to intervene in matrimonial cases."[52] Although there are cases in which they specifically refused to interfere and contemporary statements— especially from civil lawyers—that such cases were none of their business, they did in fact interfere on various occasions. Sometimes, as in *Manby* v. *Scott*, they became involved because questions of debt or the ownership of property arose, but at other times they intervened over pure questions of the validity of marriages. For example, in spite of explicit pleas from Dr. Richard Sterne, the Archbishop of York, Chief Justice Vaughan granted a prohibition in *Thomas Harrison & Ux.* v. *Dr. Burwell*, a case in which Harrison had been cited in the ecclesiastical court for incest in marrying his deceased great uncle's wife. Perhaps taking a leaf out of Cary's book, Harrison contended that 32 Hen. 8, c. 38 made his marriage valid and forbade any proceeding against him in the ecclesiastical courts. Vaughan considered that the statute applied and that it had been passed in the first place because "marriages were often dissolved and brought into great incertainty" when the "Court of the Bishop of Rome" had created unnecessary prohibited degrees merely to grant dispensations from them "for their lucre."[53] In *Boyle* v. *Boyle* (1687) a woman sued for jactitation of marriage in the ecclesiastical court asked for a prohibition on the ground that the man libeling her there had already been convicted of bigamy in Old Bailey.[54] Apparently in spite of protests from a civil lawyer present in court, this prohibition was also granted. Lord Leigh's case and other cases to be discussed below are also examples. John Godolphin even mentions a case where a wife who tried to sue her husband for a divorce based on cruelty was told to go to the temporal courts and get security of the peace against him.

A constant stream of cases like *Manby* v. *Scott* continued to be heard in the secular courts. As the judges drew upon obiter dicta in *Manby* v. *Scott* rather than simply upon the final decision for the defendant, a number of these cases before *James* v. *Warren* were decided for the plaintiff. In *Dyer* v. *East* (1669), where the wife apparently lived continuously with her husband, the court found for the merchant, noting that no specific prohibition had been issued to him: "and per Curiam the case of *Manby* and *Scott* was adjudg'd that the husband was not chargeable against his prohibition, nor upon an elopement, but else the court said it was agreed there the husband was chargeable for necessary wearing apparel, and so it was said per Curiam now."[55] In *Longworthy* v. *Hockmore* (1698) we find Holt ruling "that if the husband turns away his wife, and afterwards she takes up necessaries upon credit of a tradesman; the husband shall be liable."[56] An alternative would have been to tell the merchant that the wife could not make a valid contract and to send the wife to the ecclesiastical court to sue for a restitution of conjugal rights. In general, the cases after *Manby* v. *Scott* decide that the husband is liable for his wife's debts for necessaries so long as she is willing to live with him, though she "be ever so lewd," or if he leaves her or forces her away from him; he is not liable if she elopes with an adulterer unless he takes her back or if she goes away by herself unless she offers to come back.[57] The court's view of eloping wives appears to have been influenced by a statute rather than by canon law, 13 Edw. 1, c. 33, which deprives eloping wives of dower. The significance of these cases for my argument is not so much in the details of their resolution, as in the simpler fact that the temporal courts occupied themselves in hearing them, apparently ignoring the strong arguments raised in *Manby* v. *Scott*. Decisions for the merchant plaintiff in some of these cases also imply that the temporal courts were acknowledging a wife's right to support by her husband and acting to enforce such a right.

The second consequence of the line of cases descending from *Manby* v. *Scott* to become evident before *James* v. *Warren* is even more significant. The court discovered a class of married women it was willing to treat as though they had the autonomy of single women. Some of those wives who lived apart from their husbands had separate maintenance allowances. When merchants wished to recover the debts of these women from their husbands they began to be denied not on the ground that married women could not make contracts, but on the ground that these women had regained some of the legal personhood of a feme sole and so could be sued in their own right. In *Ferrars* v. *Ferrars* (1682) the court declared, "If the Wife, whilst she lives separate from her Husband, and has a separate Maintenance, buys Goods of Tradesmen who know of the Separation and Maintenance, they cannot sue the Executors of the Husband for these Goods."[58] In *Todd* v. *Stoakes* (c. 1695) an apothecary failed to collect from a husband whose wife had a separate maintenance allowance. Chief Justice Holt opined, "it is unreasonable that she should have it still in her power to charge him; and it is not to be presumed, but tradesmen that deal with her, trust her on her own credit, and not on the credit of her husband, and a personal notice is not necessary; it is sufficient that it be public and commonly known."[59] Commenting on the development of the law concerning a husband's obligation to maintain his wife after *Manby* v. *Scott*, Justice Strange noted in 1744 that where there was a voluntary separation agreement

> and there has been an allowance of a sufficient maintenance to the wife, recent determinations have not merely held the husband discharged from the obligation of contracts entered into by her, but have regarded her as being sui juris with regard to matters of property, in the same manner as she is by the civil law. They have considered her therefore as being so far emancipated by the agreement from the incapacities incident to coverture, as to be capable of contracting not only for necessaries, but for every other thing which can be made the subject matter of agreement, and consequently as being liable to be sued in the Courts of Common Law as if she were a feme sole.[60]

It seems that during the Restoration separate maintenance agreements became a popular way of resolving marital discord without recourse to the ecclesiastical courts. In the *School for Scandal*, of course, Sir Peter Teazle and Lady Teazle consider a separate maintenance agreement as a way out of their difficulties, but they are anticipated by Restoration couples like Mr. and Mrs.

Woodly in Shadwell's *Epsom-Wells* (1672) and Mr. and Mrs. Friendall in *The Wives Excuse* (1691). As Alleman points out, the Woodly's final parting is a parody of the better known proviso scenes in which gayer couples agree to marry:

> *Wood. Imprimis*, I Francis *Woodly*, for several causes me thereunto especially moving, do declare I will for ever separate from the company of *Sarah* my now Wife. And I will never hereafter use her like a Wife.
>
> *Mrs. Wood.* That is scurvily. Also all Obligations of conjugal affection, shall from henceforth cease, be null, void, and of none effect.
>
> *Wood.* Then, that I am to keep what Mistress I please, and how I please, after the laudable custom of other Husbands.
>
> *Mrs. Wood.* And I am to have no spies upon my company or action, but may enjoy all Privileges of other separate Ladies, without any lett, hindrance, or molestation whatsoever.
>
> *Wood.* . . . I restore you all your Portion, and add 2000£ to it for the use I have had on you . . . Faith, take a Kiss at parting for old acquaintance. [2: 180]

Alleman, however, incorrectly treats the law concerning separation as fixed in this period, consisting simply of ecclesiastical separation and voluntary separation with which the common-law courts had nothing to do. He notices that characters in the plays seem confused about points of law; this is not only because dramatists are "not satisfactory expounders of the canon law," but also because the law itself was changing. If the common-law courts had refused to have anything to do with voluntary separate maintenance agreements, they would not have been enforceable and there would not have been much point in entering into them.

The temporal courts began to circumvent the ecclesiastical alimony system by agreeing to enforce voluntary separate maintenance agreements and even by making their own decrees for separate maintenance as they had done during the interregnum. Such a development is striking because precedent gave the ecclesiastical courts jurisdiction over matrimonial disputes and, even more, because it flies in the face of the common-law principle that husbands and wives cannot make valid contracts with each other—especially not contracts in abrogation of the marriage contract itself—a principle reasserted in the later eighteenth century. In

Whorewood v. *Whorewood*, which was still being referred to as a "famous case" in the 1790s, a husband who had during the interregnum been ordered by Chancery to pay alimony appeared in 1662 to challenge the decree on the ground that only the ecclesiastical courts could award alimony. Contradicting the expectations of the author of *Lady Alimony*, the court replied that such decrees had been confirmed by the Act for the Confirmation of Judicial Procedings. In 1675 Mr. Whorewood again appeared in Chancery, this time asking that the same alimony award be revoked, now on the ground that he was willing to be reconciled with his wife. The Court refused to discharge the arrears of alimony, and Bridgeman told the wife that if she refused to return to her husband she would have to seek her remedy in the ecclesiastical court; if she did return to him, however, and he failed to treat her "as a Gentleman and a good Husband ought to do," Bridgeman promised to "hear the Wife's Complaint with favour, and lay on the Decree again, as Cause shall be."[61] In *Seeling & Eliz. Crawley* v. *Crawley* (1700) the Crawleys had agreed to separate and the husband had given the wife's father a note to pay him £160 on demand in consideration for the father's agreeing to be responsible for the wife's maintenance and debts. The father appeared in Chancery to ask them to compel payment. In this case although the husband tried to avoid payment by offering to take his wife back again, the court still found for the plaintiffs. By the time of *Oxenden* v. *Oxenden* (1705), *Whorewood* was being cited as a precedent, and though Chancery was still clear that it could not decree divorces itself, when the objection was raised that Chancery had no jurisdiction in alimony, "Mr. Pooley said (to which the *Keeper* agreed), that this was a proper, if not a properer Place than the Spiritual Court."[62]

The worst fears of the conservative justices in *Manby* v. *Scott* were justified in *Angier* v. *Angier* (1718) where the secular procedures for resolving matrimonial disputes obviously interfered with the operation of the ecclesiastical courts. The sordid scandal earlier justices had feared was also evident when the wife attempted to prove publicly that the husband beat her with a horsewhip and denied her necessities, and the husband offered evidence that she drank brandy to excess, was morose and malicious, and purposely wore her dirtiest clothes. The wife had begun a suit against her husband in ecclesiastical court, but while the suit was pending, the husband entered into a private separate maintenance agreement. As they appeared before the equity judges, the husband was refusing to pay the wife's allowance on the ground that he wanted her to come home again. The husband's lawyers denied that Chancery had any jurisdiction in such a case; the wife's lawyers, citing earlier precedents, argued "that though this court could not decree alimony, yet it might decree execution of articles according to the parties' own agreement" and that the separate maintenance articles had been "intended to supply the sentence in the Spiritual Court, and to prevent the charge and trouble of a solemn litigation there."[63] The Lord Chancellor agreed with the wife that "the intent of these articles was to save the expense of a suit in Spiritual Court" and found for the wife. This means that Chancery had developed its own procedures to rival the ecclesiastical divorce *a mensa et thoro* and suggests—surprising as it may seem to devotees of *Bleak House*—that equity procedures were simpler and cheaper. A mid-eighteenth century Chancery report states it as a settled principle of law that if a husband turns away his wife or behaves cruelly toward her, "Chancery will upon her own, or *Prochein Amy's* Application, decree her a separate Maintenance suitable to her Degree and Quality, the Fortune she brought, and her Husband's Circumstances."[64] Among the precedents there cited is *Ashton v. Ashton*, an interregnum case in which Chancery awarded a wife three hundred pounds a year so long as she and her husband lived apart.

Both the issue of whether Chancery could decree separate maintenance and the issue of whether Chancery could enforce voluntary separate maintenance agreements were hotly debated in the late eighteenth century. These separate maintenance agreements were extremely vulnerable not only as contracts between husbands and wives but also as contracts in abrogation of the marriage contract itself, and thus invalid just as a husband's contract to sell his wife to another man would be invalid. This is why it is so interesting that the courts should have had anything to do with them, so suggestive of the dislocations of the interregnum and of a new willingness to perceive married women as persons. The practices of the court in cases like *Seeling & Eliz. Crawley v.*

Crawley, Oxenden v. *Oxenden*, and *Angier* v. *Angier* were challenged or explained away in the later eighteenth century, but it seems reasonable to suppose that at the end of the seventeenth century and at the beginning of the eighteenth wives entering into voluntary separation agreements had reasonable certainty that they would be enforceable or judges could not have accepted separate maintenance agreements as exempting husbands from liability for their wives' debts and wives would not have entered into the agreements that produced the cases we have observed. There are also many subsidiary issues not immediately relevant to our discussion here, for example, whether separate maintenance agreements must be between the husband and trustees for the wife instead of the wife directly, whether the separation agreed to is understood to be temporary, whether provisions for separate maintenance may be made before marriage in the original settlement articles, and so on. Later developments are reflected in *Head* v. *Head* (1747), *Guth* v. *Guth* (1792)—which affirms the line taken in *Crawley*—and *Legard* v. *Johnson* (1797), which repudiates *Guth*. The other line of cases descending from *Todd* v. *Stoakes* was overturned in *Marshall* v. *Mary Rutton* (1800). It seems significant that in *Rutton* the merchant has simply gone ahead to sue the wife with a separate maintenance allowance directly, ignoring the husband. The court overturned the earlier opinions, declaring, "The ground on which the plaintiff in this case rests his claim, is an agreement between the defendant and her husband to live separate and apart from each other. That is, a contract supposed to be made between two parties, who . . . being in law but one person, are on that account unable to contract with each other: and if the foundation fail, the consequence is, that the whole superstructure must also fail."[65]

Traditionally the law had seen petit treason, actual murder, as the domestic analogue of high treason, which, of course, frequently did not involve murder. In a period of such a polite revolution as that of 1688, we are perhaps entitled to find a more appropriate domestic analogue to treason in separation and divorce. As parliament had declared the throne vacant in 1688 and allowed itself to choose another sovereign, so it was during the Restoration that parliament declared itself able to dissolve the bonds of marriage and permit a man to choose another wife. As the Glorious

Revolution entailed a secularization of kingship, so separate maintenance decreed or enforced in Chancery and parliamentary divorce entailed a secularization of marriage. Indeed, because there were mutual promises at the wedding and especially because in the upper classes there were actual documentary marriage contracts, it was even easier to think of the relationship between husbands and wives as contractual than it was to imagine sovereigns and subjects as having agreed to a contract. The analogy is certainly not exact since revolution was for the benefit of subjects and parliamentary divorce initially for the benefit of husbands rather than wives, but it does exist. Separate maintenance was often for the benefit of wives and enabled them to live free of unbearable husbands.

As we have noted, sentiment for regarding marriage itself as a civil contract subject to regulation by the state rather than by church courts had existed from the early years of the Reformation. Such Reformation thinking often also involved the belief that divorce and remarriage were allowable on various grounds. Some protestant thinkers advocated death as a suitable penalty for adultery and so did not have to worry about the issue of remarriage for the innocent party. In 1549 and 1552, however, bills to permit second marriages while the first partner lived were proposed in parliament, though not passed. The bigamy act of 1603 specifically exempted from punishment those who had remarried after divorces in the ecclesiastical courts and this statute continued in force through the late seventeenth century. That some confusion existed over whether second marriages could be valid is also indicated by the fact that in 1671 the Archbishop of Canterbury was still issuing a broadside "admonition" to those about to marry, warning "that they contract not anew with any other upon divorce and separation made by the Judge for a time, the Laws yet standing to the contrary." Henry Swinburne, a civil lawyer who died in 1623, says in his *Treatise of Spousals* (1686) that spousals *de praesenti* are "in truth and substance very Matrimony, and therefore perpetually indissoluble, *except for Adultery*" (my italics).[66] John Godolphin discusses the issue of second marriages extensively in *Repertorium Canonicum* (1678). Though remarriage was supposedly not permitted by canon law, instances of particular bishops allowing it are recorded. Matthew Parker, the Archbishop of Canterbury, in the early seventeenth century allowed John Stawell to remarry after a divorce. Thomas Wilson, the saintly bishop of Sodor and Man, in 1698 granted one Christopher Hampton permission to remarry after his wife had been sentenced to seven years penal servitude for lamb stealing.

In the debates over the Lord Roos divorce bill in the early 1670s proponents generally insisted on marriage as a contract rather than a sacrament, argued that the contract could be dissolved, and stigmatized divorce *a mensa et thoro* as a popish invention of the Council of Trent. Bishop John Cosin said that either adultery or malicious desertion were grounds for divorce and argued that marriage was

> a conjugal promise, solemnly made between a man and his wife, that each of them will live together . . . separation from bed and board, which is part of their promise to live together, doth plainly break that part of the bond, whereby they are tied to live together both as to bed and board. The distinction between bed and board and the bond is new, never mentioned in the Scripture . . . devised only by the canonists and the schoolmen . . . to serve the Pope's turn the better.[67]

Not wishing to deny a husband the right to forgive an adulterous wife if he decided to do so, supporters of the bill used contract analogies to deal with the problem. Lord Essex, for example, said, "the marriage bond was broken (like as peace betweene Princes) not when the fact was committed, but when the Injured party makes claim to the Judge, who cannot deny Justice being asked it. Soe that the act of Adulterie does but putt the husband in the advantage to take the forfeiture, if, and when, he pleases."[68]

Though no woman actually got a parliamentary divorce until Mrs. Addison's in 1801, radical protestant sentiment had supported a woman's right to divorce her husband and equal rights to divorce were defended by some during the Roos debates. The main grounds of the opposition to equal divorce rights for women had been cogently stated by Henry Hammond in 1644, "family inconveniences [concerning inheritance] do not follow the falseness of the husband as they do that of the wife" and "the wife hath by promise of obedience made herself a subject, and owned him a lord, and so hath none of that authority over him (an act of which putting away seems to be,) which he by being lord hath over her."[69] In the Roos debates, however, the Duke of Buckingham is reported to have argued—perhaps ingenuously, considering his private life—"that if this law did extend to the adulterye of the man as of the woman yet it may be there is no inconvenience therby but rather a better means to oblidge men as well as weomen [sic] to live more virtuously."[70]

The most elaborate published prodivorce argument seems to have been Sir Charles Wolseley's *The Case of Divorce and Re-Marriage Thereupon Discussed.* Wolseley is perhaps most remembered for his early advocacy of religious toleration and for his *The Reasonableness of Scripture Belief* (1672). He is on a continuum reaching from the Cambridge Platonists through Locke to the third Earl of Shaftesbury; "reason" and "the law of nature" are vital terms for him. Like the first Earl of Shaftesbury, Locke's patron, and others who supported Lord Roos's divorce, Wolseley had been a supporter of Cromwell during the war. Though his father had been a royalist, Charles married a daughter of Lord Saye and Sele, belonged to Cromwell's Council of State, and urged Cromwell to accept the kingship. The support of people like Shaftesbury and Wolseley for the divorce bill may have been partly inspired by the idea that it would serve as a precedent to allow Charles II to marry a more fruitful wife and so disinherit the Roman Catholic James, but it was also very much in keeping with protestant ideas about marriage. Wolseley cites the *Reformatio Legum,* insists that divorce *a mensa et thoro* is a Romish invention, and also that it is against "reason":

> For whatsoever can be sufficient to Justifie a Divorce from all the ends of Marriage, must needs be sufficient to justifie a Divorce from the obligation of Marriage, the one being but in order to the other; It seems no way reasonable to bring any man into that condition, that the obligation of marriage should remain, and the helps and advantages of it be taken away.[71]

Marriage to him is clearly a contract. When challenged to defend his idea that marriage should not continue if its advantages are taken away against the case of unfortunate spouses taken captive or fallen prey to disease—cases in which it is assumed he would not want divorce—he replies:

> When by providential disabilities in either party, the duties of marriage cannot be performed, yet the marriage-bond continues unbroken, though the ends cannot be attained. . . . Ability to perform is implied in all contracts, providential disability no way cancels the matrimonial obligation, because 'tis entered into with a supposition of them. [137–38]

On the issue of whether wives should be allowed to divorce their husbands he declines to take a position, but notes that Calvin "saith that although the Husband be superior in other respects, yet in the marriage bed the man and the woman are equal" and Paul "seems to put the matter between Man and Woman in even terms in all conjugal respects" (pp. 152–53).

It is not difficult to find affirmations of traditional religious views of domestic authority in the Restoration. In 1699, for example, John Sprint in *The Brides-Woman's Counsellor* was still quoting Genesis 3:16 to justify woman's subjection to man and asserting that barring commands to do the impossible or the sinful "God and Nature hath given the Husband Authority to Command, and the Wife is bound to obey, however unnecessary or unfit she may think it to be."[72] Indeed, these views were perhaps expressed more rigidly because they were felt to be under attack. Sprint was soon explicitly rebuked by Lady Mary Chudleigh in *The Ladies Defence: or, The Bride-Woman's Counsellor Answer'd* (1701). The point, however, is that alternative views were being articulated and, at least as importantly, institutionalized. Hobbes and Locke gave accounts of domestic authority that untethered it from its scriptural and traditional natural law moorings. Like the sovereign who ceases to provide his subjects with the benefits for which they yielded up their natural liberty, the domestic ruler who is impotent (a Hobbesian case) or tyrannical (the case of more interest to Locke) now finds that his subjects owe him no more allegiance. The law, long accustomed to punishing the petit treason of domestic inferiors, now takes an increased interest in curbing the exercise of authority by fathers and, especially, husbands. Ignoring the common-law tradition that made a feme covert incapable of making a contract either with her husband or a stranger, the temporal courts involved themselves in a long series of cases that violated these principles, developed a doctrine of a wife's right to maintenance, and constructed in separate maintenance a rival to the ecclesiastical alimony system. Animated by many of the same arguments that had led to the passage of the Civil Marriage Act, parliament went further than the courts and declared itself ready to accept divorce.

IV

As might be expected from these debates in contemporary controversial writing, politics, philosophy, and law, in the plays of the middle and late Restoration marriage is increasingly represented as a problematic institution. Marriage now becomes not so much the happy ending of romances like *The Siege of Urban* or cheerful comedies like *Tarugo's Wiles* and *The Mulberry Garden* but the beginning of tragedy or mordant and imperfectly resolved comedy. In their brilliant comedies of the seventies Etherege and Wycherley still use marriage structurally as a closure device, but the feasting, dancing, and marrying that traditionally announce the resolution of comedy undergo strange permutations and short-circuitings. Harriet tells Dorimant he may come to court her in the country if he likes, but we do not witness her final acceptance of him. Horner marries no one at all and stands alone at the center of the dance of cuckolds. The word *divorce* is heard in Shadwell's *Humorists* (1670), John Dover's *Mall; or, The Modish Lovers* (1674), Thomas Rawlins's *Tom Essence; or, The Modish Wife* (1676), and D'Urfey's *Fond Husband* (1677).[73] Lady Haughty in *The Triumphant Widow* (1674) persists throughout all five acts in preferring her natural freedom to the authority of another husband.

Of particular interest in the seventies and early eighties are comedies that begin with major characters already married or with their marriage in the early acts, plays including Dryden's *Marriage à la Mode* (1672), Aphra Behn's *Town Fop* (1676), Shadwell's *Woman–Captain* (1676), and Otway's *Atheist* (1683). Even the conservative Dryden takes notice of how problematic marriage has become when he opens *Marriage à la Mode* with a

song by a young woman who wonders whether her marriage vows
were "mere words," nothing but conventions antagonistic to
nature:

> *Why should a foolish marriage vow,*
> *Which long ago was made,*
> *Oblige us to each other now,*
> *When passion is decay'd?*
>
> [4:261]

Furthermore, even in those plays where the only characters
already married are secondary characters, in the comedies of the
seventies and eighties these characters are more likely to represent
problems than to be the simple butts of humor they tend to be in the
earlier comedies. Wycherley, for instance, in *The Country Wife*
shows that Pinchwife does not deserve his dominion over Margery,
but at the end of their brief adventures in London, Horner points
out that Margery is nevertheless permanently married to the old
whoremaster and must return to the country with him. Lady
Fidget and the virtuous gang are presented as hypocrites, but as
reasonably conscious hypocrites who are aware of the difference
between the universe of reputation and the universe of fact. When
Lady Fidget rebels against the neglect of Sir Jasper, whose involvement with money and business keeps her on very short
rations, Wycherley allows her to make her point:

> *Why should our damn'd Tyrants oblige us to live.*
> *On the pittance of Pleasure which they only give.*
>
> [P. 349]

Nor is Lady Fidget fooled by Horner, to whom she says, " 'tis to no
purpose to require your oath, for you are as often foresworn as you
swear to new women." In the world of *The Country Wife* this
much insight and this much honesty is enough to get her sexual
satisfaction from Horner and to secure her reputation with all
except the other coconspirators—Wycherley even gives her a pretty
piece of china. In the seventies so undistinguished a writer as
Joseph Arrowsmith treats with some seriousness secondary married
characters like Lysander and his unfaithful wife Juliana in *The
Reformation* (1673). Lysander discusses what "alimony" he will
pay to Juliana in the fifth act and she finally says to him, "Since
you are so cruel as to part, I must allow you truly noble" (p. 78).

The marriage of a cast mistress to a fool is a stock closing device of Restoration comedy, but in *Tom Essence* one of the main actions of the play opens with such a cast mistress now married to a milliner. Although the old milliner is predictably jealous, she becomes less predictable than one might expect when she says at the beginning, "I'le keep the Vows I made to my old Dotard, in hopes that Heav'n, to reward my Loyalty to him, will take compassion on my Youth, and by his death, make me capable of making a younger Brother's fortune" and does in fact remain faithful to him.[74] When another wife in this play is discovered to be guilty of adultery and her husband threatens to divorce her, she retorts: "The Portion must be paid, and Divorce where you will, the Prerogative-Court will give me Alimony, and the Chancery Separation money, enough to maintain a Gallant" (p. 62).

Although there was some general agreement that marriage had become problematic in the seventies and early eighties, not surprisingly, there was not much agreement about the nature of that problem. Some playwrights affirm traditional positions in practice, though even in the relatively conservative plays the sort of ringing affirmation of the ideological underpinning of domestic authority quoted earlier from *The Taming of the Shrew* is noticeably absent. As the opening song of *Marriage à la Mode* indicates, Dryden as usual entertains skeptical challenges to old values. Rhodophil and Doralice are already married at the beginning of the play. Bored with each other and suffering from jaded imaginations, they flirt with the possibilities of adultery. At the end, they reunite and Rhodophil and Palamede, Doralice's lover, agree not to invade each other's property. They also write themselves slightly revised contracts openly acknowledging their final solution may very well not be final:

> *Palamede.* . . . From henceforth let all acts of hostility cease betwixt us; and that, in the usual form of treaties, as well by sea as land, and in all fresh waters.
>
> *Doralice.* I will add but one *proviso*, that whoever breaks the league, either by war abroad, or neglect at home, both the women shall revenge themselves by the help of the other party.
>
> *Rhodophil.* That's but reasonable. [4:356]

Arrowsmith's *The Reformation*, appearing shortly after *Marriage à la Mode*, takes a brief swipe at Dryden's heroic drama and at the alleged bawdiness of his comedy, including the "double sense and brisk meaning Songs," yet Arrowsmith's plot progresses to more or less the same conclusion as Dryden's. A simple young man recently returned to Venice from England is persuaded by cleverer men with libertine motives to help establish a society to make Venetian women as free as English women. The two gay heroines show some enthusiasm for this scheme but do not really intend to allow themselves to be debauched. When they finally marry Ismena says, "I ever lov'd the talk of liberty, more than the thing it self" (p. 78). Both *Marriage à la Mode* and *The Reformation* are essentially satires on contemporary skepticism, even though Dryden as usual allowed the satiric objects so much room to speak their pieces that he opened himself to suspicion that he was sympathetic toward them. As satires they give evidence of the attitudes that provoked them, but they are also significant because the positive ideal so clearly articulated in *The Taming of the Shrew* no longer seems visible.

In Otway's *Soldiers Fortune* (1680) and its sequel, *The Atheist* (1683), almost everything seems out of joint: the hierarchies of state, class, and family are all awry. Beaugard and Courtine are brave soldiers returned from fighting abroad now without employment or money in London. Beaugard says, "Loyalty and starving are all one. The old Cavaliers got such a trick of it in the King's Exile, that their posterity could never thrive since." Like Otway himself, Courtine complains of having been disbanded and paid in debentures instead of ready money (1:22–24). London seems to be in the control of absurd characters like Sir Jolly Jumble, the whoremaster, and Sir Davy Dunce, a J.P. and "commonwealthsman," stupid, cowardly, and treacherous. A former seller of ale now with an officer's commission, a former sequestrator, and a former member of the rump parliament, all now rich and respectable, are paraded across the stage to provoke disgusted comments from the loyal soldiers. When in *The Atheist* Beaugard comes into money, Otway makes a running joke of the way his father, impecunious and addicted to gaming and drink, is dependent upon him and finally promises to be "obedient" (2:398). The atmosphere of these plays is similar to that of *The Plain Dealer*, though more politicized and somehow nastier. Like Manly, Courtine returns from service abroad to rail at a degenerate society: " 'Tis as unreasonable to expect a man of Sense should be prefer'd, as 'tis to think a Hector can be stout, a Priest religious, a fair Woman chast, or a pardon'd Rebel loyal" (2:122). Unlike Manly, however, Courtine is deep in London cynicism and lacks any naïve integrity of his own to make him sympathetic. In a scene with the woman he marries, for instance, he offers to swear "Upon the word of a gentleman, nay as I hope to get Money in my Pocket" (2:172).

Marriage, a central focus of both plays, partakes of the degeneracy of the society. Beaugard and Courtine were later appropriately selected as interlocutors by the anonymous author of "The Cornuted Beau: or a Satyr upon Marriage."[75] Even before the action of the play, we learn, Beaugard's father quickly spent most of his mother's portion, broke her heart, lived with a housekeeper mistress, and then threw young Beaugard out of the house when he called the mistress whore (2:304). The two main actions of *The Soldiers Fortune* are Beaugard's cuckolding of Sir Davy Dunce and Courtine's pursuit of Sylvia, an heiress with £5,000; both actions are given equal prominence. Having observed Lady Dunce's marriage to Sir Davy, Sylvia has resolved never to marry. Her first words in the play are sarcastically addressed to Lady Dunce:

> Indeed such another charming Animal as your Consort, Sir *David*, might do much with me; 'tis an unspeakable blessing to lie all night by a Horse-load of diseases; a beastly, unsavory, old, groaning, grunting, wheazing Wretch, that smells of the Grave he's going to already; from such a curse and Hair-Cloath next my skin good Heaven deliver me! [2:107]

Lady Dunce and Beaugard do succeed in cuckolding Sir Davy and the effect of this action is quite different from the effect of the aborted cuckolding attempts in early comedy or even from the effect of consummated cuckoldings in subplots. Beaugard's intercourse with Lady Dunce is the culmination of a main line of action in the play and occurs in the fifth act. It is not something he leaves behind as Bellmour in *The Old Bachelor* leaves Mrs. Laetitia Fondlewife for his more romantic courtship of Belinda; it is not even really subordinated to any more romantic element since Beaugard and Courtine are given equal prominence and since Courtine and Sylvia act more like estate agents than lovers.

Beaugard begins *The Atheist* persisting in his denunciations of marriage and has fortunately inherited two thousand pounds a year from his uncle so that he does not need to resort to marriage for subsistence. He makes a rendezvous with Portia, whose guardians "for base Bribes, betray'd, sold, and married" her, but who is now a widow confined by a tyrannical uncle with control of most of her fortune. This develops as a relatively normal gay couple plot; Beaugard and Portia, though originally attracted by their mutual antipathy to marriage, do use the word *love*. She tests his loyalty to her and proves him true. They intend to marry at the end and the only real deviation is created by Portia's being an aggressive widow.

Courtine, on the other hand, by the beginning of *The Atheist* has been married long enough to be depressed by marriage:

> For I am forced to call a Woman I do not like, by the name of Wife; and lie with her, for the most part, with no Appetite at all; must keep the Children that, for ought I know, any Body else may beget of her Body, and for Food and Rayment, by her good will she would have them both Fresh three times a day: Then for Kiss and part, I may kiss and kiss my heart out, but the Devil a bit shall I ever get rid of her. [2:305]

When he comes to London to return to whoring, Sylvia follows him with reproaches and advice to other women:

> Be warn'd by me, ye Virgins that are blest
> With your first native Freedom; let no Oaths
> Of perjur'd Mankind wooe ye to your Ruin.
> But when a creeping, fawning, weeping Crocodile
> Moans at your feet, remember then my Fall.
> [2:363]

Sylvia herself, however, shows a willingness to be interested in a "very handsom Youth" (2:369) and is otherwise not the idealized wife found in the later plays of Southerne and Cibber. In the fifth act Courtine discovers her in compromising circumstances with

Beaugard (though she is not guilty with Beaugard) and declares gleefully:

> I am only glad of this fair opportunity to be rid of you, my Dearest; henceforth, my Dearest, I shall drink my drink, my Dearest, I shall whore my Dearest; and so long as I can pimp so handsomly for you, my Dearest, I hope if ever we return into the Countrey, you'll wink at a small Fault now and then with the Dairy-Wench, or Chamber-Maid, my Dearest.

Her final words are, "I always was a Burden to your sight, and you shall be this time eas'd on't" (2:395). Beaugard does win Portia's consent to marriage at the end, but the spectacle of Courtine and Sylvia makes one wonder whether he has also won the right to live happily ever after.

The representation of libertine sentiments and adultery in comic contexts, whether "approved" by the playwrights or not, violated important decorums. Robert Hume has recently argued that no Restoration comedy "genuinely" attacks "marriage as an institution" or envisages "any serious alternative to marriage."[76] The importance of rakes and of libertinism in Restoration comedy, he thinks, has been greatly exaggerated. Pointing, for instance, to the frequency with which characters who articulate libertine values are shown to renounce them and / or themselves agree to marriages at the end of the plays, Hume thinks the comedies "support marriage as an institution, however horribly wrong it can go." Hume also wants to dissociate the keeping of mistresses from libertinism on the grounds that "mistresses were regarded as an inevitable part of the fashionable world," so that the mere keeping of a mistress does not in his eyes qualify a man or a character in a comedy as a rake. In so far as Hume differentiates between the more benign comedy of the sixties and the nineties on the one hand, and the harsher comedy of the seventies and early eighties on the other, I think he makes a valid point—indeed, one clearly made by John Harrington Smith in *The Gay Couple*. Distinguishing between one sort of rake and another is also a useful enterprise. It is true too, I think, that fashionable men kept mistresses and felt entitled to do so. According to Stone, in the sixteenth century gentlemen felt free "to beget bastards without any sense of shame and any attempt at concealment," making open provision for their education and frequent mention of them in wills.[77] Nevertheless, I think Hume is insensitive to the importance of representation and decorum. It is one thing to know fashionable men keep mistresses or even to have a mistress oneself and quite another to be prepared to have such a practice exhibited on the public stage. There is a difference between tacit acceptance of fornication and adultery as common practices and public approval of fornication and adultery as morally neutral acts. Hume is quite right that heroes in Restoration comedy usually take their right to have mistresses for granted, but instead of being evidence that the Restoration rake is a myth, this seems to me precisely the sort of thing seventeenth-century critics of Restoration comedy were upset about. As Stone has pointed out, protestant reformers were increasingly successful in giving men bad consciences about fornication and adultery and, though the reformers may not have affected the behavior of Restoration playwrights like Etherege and Wycherley, they certainly affected their critics. Furthermore, as the writers of the pamphlets quoted earlier in this chapter suggest, the keeping of mistresses or other forms of fornication and adultery were bad enough in themselves, but what was worse was the failure to acknowledge guilt. I certainly would not want to argue that Restoration playwrights "genuinely" envisaged "any serious alternative to marriage"— who has?—but I do want to maintain that real skepticism is expressed and that the center of interest in the plays characteristic of the seventies and early eighties is closer to skepticism and malaise about marriage than it is to affirming "support for marriage as an institution."

John Harrington Smith chose to describe the comedy of 1675–87 as "cynical" and that seems to me an appropriate term for plays so dominated by cuckolding, sexual intrigue without love, and antipathy to marriage. The better plays of the period are apt like *The Soldiers Fortune* and *The Atheist* to capture our attention by the strength of their contempt and the vivid language of their loathing. Wycherley's *Country Wife* and *Plain Dealer* are also like this, I think, though there has been much debate over their meaning and some critics have attempted to describe what they consider the attractive positive ideals in characters like Alithea and Harcourt.

The more tedious cuckolding plays like D'Urfey's *Fond Husband* and Ravenscroft's *London Cuckolds* (1681) seem to lack any particular anger and trade on what almost all writers in the late seventies discerned as a taste for farce and meaningless debauchery. Dryden responded to this taste with *Mr. Limberham; or, The Kind Keeper*, adding one more impotent lecher to a startling number of such characters in the 1677–78 season.[78] In this season Mrs. Behn produced *Sir Patient Fancy*, a comedy Allardyce Nicoll thought more than any other "has inclined the minds of critics to attribute a systematic looseness to the works of Mrs. Behn."[79] Shadwell in *A True Widow* (1678) has Lady Busy try to persuade Isabella to be kept by Bellamour: "Now I say since Custom has so run down Wedlock, what remains? . . . as long as you are true to one Man, Madam, you are in the manner his Lady, . . . 'tis a kind of Marriage, and great Persons most commonly co-habit longer with Mistresses, than they used to do with Wives" (3:304–5).

Three points seem worth making about this cynical comedy. First, in so far as it expressed denegration of marriage or ar-ticulated skeptical attacks on marriage—whether endorsed by the author or not—it reflected the debates on marriage described earlier. Second, contemporaries and older critics who applied epithets like "beastly impudence," "grossly indelicate," or "noisome," to these plays saw one of their key features: they violate important decorums by representing attitudes and behaviors that had not been represented before not simply because they were new—the more elaborate skeptical arguments were fairly new, but there was nothing new about successful cuckolding or even about adulterous wives showing contempt for their husbands—but because it had seemed improper to represent them. Third, the cynical comedy is markedly more realistic than the romantic gay couple or cheerful intrigue comedy that preceded it. Ideal visions of love and marriage are not confidently affirmed. It is perhaps significant that several authors insist that their lechers are also religious hypocrites, as D'Urfey does in *Trick for Trick; or, The Debauch'd Hypocrite* (1678) and Dryden does in *Mr. Limberham*. Obviously the accusations of debauchery are stock antidissenter satire, but there also seems to be a more general diffused anger and disillusionment at the failure of both religious and domestic ideals.

The greater realism of these domestic plays corresponds to the greater realism we noticed in the preceding chapter in the second phase of Restoration political drama, the political tragedies. In comedy as in tragedy, the original euphoria of the Restoration itself gradually evaporated. In the sixties it was possible to hope that the old ideas and the old myths that embodied them might be restored along with Charles II, indeed, the interregnum had allowed the older ideals to seem all the more shimmering from having been untarnished by daily contact. A king in exile can easily seem more attractive than a king who quibbles about money for the fleet, to say nothing of a king who makes secret treaties with the French or who spends his spare time as a notorious whoremaster. Similarly, the author of *Lady Alimony* can blame the wives' dissatisfaction with their husbands on the Civil Marriage Act, but once the church and the church courts were restored it was harder to think of them as solutions. The protagonists of the better cynical comedies are in some ways like the protagonists of political tragedy: they are quite sure that the older myths are no longer workable, but they have not yet discovered any newer ones.

V

Amidst such Juvenalian railing at the abuses of the marriage bed as Otway's, the more Horatian satire of Dryden's *Marriage à la Mode*, and the early farce of D'Urfey, however, we begin to find some writers more comfortable with the possibility of greater freedom for wives and children. Shadwell was always a natural choice for the Whig laureateship and in 1679, even before he received his official honors, he wrote *The Woman-Captain*, a play about liberty cast in domestic terms. In *The Woman-Captain* Sir Humphrey Scattergood has just come into his estate and vows to compensate himself for the "slavery" he endured while his father was alive. Soon he decides he wants to include the wife of the old and stingy Gripe among his delights. Mrs. Gripe longs for her own "liberty." "Will this Tyrannie never be at an end," she asks, "must

I be always thus abridg'd of Liberty? a cram'd Fowl has a better time on't, for that's fed well. . . . I will have the liberty of a She-Subject of *England*" (4:27–28). Mrs. Gripe outwits her husband, escaping from him in a captain's uniform that belongs to her brother, then bullying the cowardly Gripe into enlisting in the army. In a ludicrous scene, Gripe makes a feeble attempt to bribe the sergeant to release him, raising his bid from ten shillings to twenty, a shilling at a time, and finally provoking the exasperated sergeant to exclaim, "The Rogue bids for his Liberty, as if it were a stock at 12d Gleek." Gripe gets a taste of his own medicine as his wife in her captain's disguise orders him about and terrorizes him with threats of how she will exercise her authority over him. Finally Gripe is persuaded that in order to extricate himself from the army, and from the fear of sudden death in Flanders, he will have to agree to return to his wife her dowry of £3,000 or to pay her a separate maintenance of £400 a year. Sir Humphrey, showing some intelligence for the first time in the play, announces that he has married Phillis, his own mistress, upon whom he had foolishly settled his house. He thus regains the "liberty" he had complained of losing when she came into possession and declared that her authority was absolute in *her* house. (Once he marries her, of course, all her property becomes his.) At the end, the son is free of his father, the wife of her husband. Mrs. Gripe draws a primary moral of the play very clearly in the final lines when she warns the husbands in the audience:

> If you'd preserve your Honours, or your Lives;
> Ne'r dare be Tyrants o're your Lawful Wives.
>
> [4:85]

The title of Shadwell's play suggests a very important shift occurring generally in the culture: the hero turns into a heroine. In the 1660s the theaters had opened with martial protagonists like Clorimun in *The Generall* or Cortez and Montezuma in *The Indian Emperor*. Scenes were frequently set out of doors and often involved parties of soldiers running from one place to another. Many early comedies like Lacy's *Old Troop* or Howard's *The Committee* also have a decidedly masculine atmosphere; the girls are there principally to be won by the men. By 1676, though, Dryden was offering the more subdued Aureng-Zebe, a character of some *sensibilité*, and remarking in his dedication, "True greatness, if it be any where on earth, is in a private virtue." By 1676 too Otway had been inspired by Racine to strive for "tristesse Majestesse" and was saying in his own dedication, "this I may modestly boast of, which the author of the French Berenice has done before me in his Preface to that Play, that it never failed to draw Tears from the eyes of the Auditors, I mean those whose Souls were capable of so Noble a pleasure." In the seventies also a series of joking titles in comedy suggests some exploratory play with role reversal: *The Woman Made a Justice* (1670), Edward Howard's two Amazon plays, *The Woman's Conquest* (1670) and *Six Days Adventure; or, the New Utopia* (1671), *The Triumphant Widow* (1674), *The Woman Turned Bully* (1675), and, of course, *The Woman-Captain.*

Increased attention to the private and the feminine by 1680 produced that astonishing masterpiece of English opera, Purcell's *Dido and Aeneas*, originally written for the young ladies of Mr. Josias Priest's Boarding School. All awareness of Aeneas's public mission has evaporated from the Tate-Purcell version; Aeneas is a cardboard figure plotted against by local witches, not the gods. All the life and drama belong to Dido, who rejects Aeneas's offer to change his mind with heroic scorn and who sings the wonderful final aria, "When I am laid in earth." In 1682 Henry VIII finds himself merely an unattractive man and a subordinate character in Banks's *Vertue Betray'd; or, Anna Bullen.* By the nineties we see a marked fashion for female protagonists: the very popular *Prophetess* (1690), *Distressed Innocence; or, the Princess of Persia* (1690), *The Fairy Queen* (1692), *Bonduca* (1695), *Agnes de Castro* (1695), *The Roman Brides Revenge* (1696), *The Unnatural Mother* (1697), *Queen Katherine* (1698), *The Princess of Parma* (1699), *Iphigenia* (1699), and so on. We also see a taste for the claustrophobic interiors of *The Mourning Bride* (1697) and a very important series of domestic titles, some of them lugubrious: *The Wives Excuse* (1691), *A Very Good Wife* (1693), *The Married Beau* (1694), *The Fatal Marriage* (1694), *The Provok'd Wife* (1697), *Phaeton; or, the Fatal Divorce* (1698), and *The Reformed Wife* (1700).

In the final decade or so of the seventeenth century the culture generally seems preoccupied with the feminine. Queen Mary, who acted as sole sovereign during William's campaigns of the early nineties was generally popular, the subject of far more panegyric than satire.[80] Serious drama begins to turn to she-tragedy. The cynical comedy of triumphant rakes, as John Harrington Smith has noted, begins to give way to sentimental or exemplary comedy in which virtuous heroines redeem their weaker, wayward husbands. Similar changes occur outside the theater. Bertha M. Stearns has traced the development of John Dunton's *Athenian Mercury* into the *Ladies' Mercury*, appearing in 1693 as the first English periodical especially for women. Studying the pamphlet literature, A. H. Upham thought she found more than fifty titles between 1670 and 1700 that showed "the existence in the last years of the seventeenth century of a widely-extended movement to restore women to an equality of privilege in learning and literature rather than in affairs."[81] If we look at panegyric verse, the most successful panegyrics of the sixties are public poems like Waller's "On St. James's Park" and Dryden's "Astraea Redux" and "Annus Mirabilis." Dryden's best panegyrics of the eighties and nineties, on the other hand, are addressed to women and to masters of the affective and expressive arts: "To Mrs Anne Killigrew," "A Song for St. Cecelia's Day," "Eleonora," and "An Ode, on the Death of Mr. Henry Purcell." Controversialists increasingly insist that the apparent inferiority of women is the creation of custom rather than nature, and women writers like Mary Astell and women characters in plays articulate arguments for their own freedom. In the preceding chapter we saw the political drama shift focus from sovereigns to subjects. Here we see what appears to be an analogous shift from the masculine to the feminine. Women are no longer present simply as rewards for the masculine heroes or even as equals in lovers' games; the interest of these late plays is ostensibly in the women's sufferings and in their moral dilemmas as seen from their point of view.

Changes in emphasis are perhaps most evident in reworkings of older material. Though Aphra Behn's *Town Fop* (1676) is not as centered on female character as later exemplary comedies, if we compare *The Town Fop* with its source, George Wilkins's *Miseries of Enforced Marriage* (1605–7) we can see how she shifts the emphasis toward the woman. Her Bellmour, not himself the fop, is subject to his guardian Lord Plotwell, who by the terms of Bellmour's father's will has the power to deprive him of his estate unless he marries the woman proposed by Plotwell. Reflecting the debates over marriage we noticed in the seventies, Plotwell acknowledges that Bellmour is "none of the fashionable Fops, that are always in Mutiny against marriage," but maintains that his father, "seeing so many Examples in this leud Age, of the ruin of whole Families by imprudent Marriages," fixed upon this method to prevent the ruin of his family (3:32–33). Plotwell is made entirely unsympathetic by his tyrannical threats to Bellmour. Bellmour is already contracted to Clarinda, whom he loves, but he allows himself to be intimidated into marrying Diana, Plotwell's niece.

In Wilkins's play, where the basic circumstances are the same, when Clare, the protagonist's betrothed, learns of his marriage she writes a note saying, "Forgive me, I am dead," and kills herself. William Scarborough, the protagonist of *The Miseries*, berates himself in the harshest terms; abandoning all hopes of living a good life, he tries to seek forgetfulness in drunkenness and debauchery. In the fifth act Clare is forgotten. Dr. Baxtor of Oxford, the clergyman who has married William to Katherine, appears to finish William's reformation and to help reconcile him to living with Katherine and their two children. Mrs. Behn is unwilling to allow Clare, whom she calls Clarinda, to receive the short shrift she gets in Wilkins. Her Clarinda also writes Bellmour a suicide note, but instead of killing herself comes to town disguised as a boy. Bellmour and Diana have no small children to cry appeals to their father. Diana is given independent motives of her own and a former lover she has spurned for Bellmour returns to woo her. Mrs. Behn's saving Clarinda alive not only means that Clarinda is available to reunite with Bellmour in the fifth act, but also that, unlike William, Bellmour is never in the position of having the woman he was contracted to dead. Dr. Baxtor does not appear at all in the Restoration version. Mrs. Behn's resolution depends on Bellmour's never having consummated his marriage with Diana and on their hopes for attaining what both Diana and Lord Plotwell call a "divorce," meaning a *divorce a vinculo* on the grounds of precontract and/or consanguinity, the rough equivalent of our annulment. Given the realities of 1676, this is the only device that could yield her version of a happy ending, Wilkins's ending being obviously unacceptable to her.

Settle's *Fatal Love; or, the Forced Inconstancy* (1680) is interesting because it shows cavalier romance modulating into domestic tragedy and because it touches on the issue of the essential goodness or evilness of women. *Fatal Love* is set in the rather abstract purlieus of a neoclassical Cyprus; all the protagonists have romance names. Although Artaban is described as a "Prince," there are no issues of state. His wife, Oliza, believing him drowned at sea and threatened by her parents with marriage to "a Rich Nauseous Miser," has now privately married Philander. We have thus the same situation Southerne later used in *Fatal Marriage*, except that Settle, prompted by the impulse to baroque doubling that died away by the nineties, also makes Philander previously contracted to Penthea, a woman supposed to have been drowned. Of course, neither Artaban nor Penthea are actually dead and their return to Cyprus precipitates the tragedy. When Artaban returns to find Oliza remarried he breaks into a tirade against women, articulating the old idea that Eve and women in general were responsible for the fall of Adam and for man's fall, a view frequently offered to justify patriarchal authority:

> Woman damn'd the World,
> Her Treason drown'd it, and her Lust will burn it!
> When Nature shall all blaze, and the Poles crack,
> Hell gape, all its Sulphurous Mines burst out,
> 'Tis only Woman that must light the Fire-brands.[82]

However, though there is considerable talk of broken vows in *Fatal Love* and some acceptance of the guilt of perjury, particularly by Philander, it is clear that in the context of the play, the sinfulness of woman has nothing to do with the problem. Artaban himself is not very sympathetic—he left Oliza on their wedding day for a jealous whim and later starts to rape another woman—and finally relents, bequeathing Oliza to Philander, though partly because of the machinations of a fifth villain, all four principals die in an orgy of stabbing, shooting, poisoned swords, and suicide. Artaban's speech contrasts sharply with Jaffeir's more famous speech in *Venice Preserved*, one that points forward to the she-tragedy of the nineties and sets the tone of so much eighteenth-century sentimental drama and fiction:

> Oh Woman! lovely Woman! Nature made thee
> To temper Man: We had been Brutes without you;
> Angels are Painted fair, to look like you;
> There's in you all that we believe of Heav'n,
> Amazing Brightness, Purity and Truth,
> Eternal Joy, and everlasting Love.
>
> [2:214]

The best known of the so-called she-tragedies of the late seventeenth century are Banks's *Vertue Betray'd* (1682), *The Island Queens* (1684), and *The Innocent Usurper* (1684), discussed in the preceding chapter since they involve sovereign / subject conflict; Otway's *The Orphan*; Southerne's *The Fatal Marriage* (1694), to be discussed in chapter 5; and Rowe's plays beginning with *The Ambitious Stepmother* (1700). Charles Gildon's *Phaeton* (1698) and Dennis's *Iphigenia* (1699) and other late tragedies rely on stories from epic or myth; *Fatal Love* and, to a lesser extent, *The Orphan* contain significant romance elements. Banks moves a little toward more realism by basing his plays on British history, but it is really Southerne in *The Fatal Marriage* who invents bourgeois domestic tragedy. These she-tragedies and domestic tragedies are quite different from earlier domestic tragedies like *Arden of Feversham* or *A Woman Killed with Kindness* and even from the plays of Webster and Ford: they focus more on the woman's dilemma and suffering, and they depend more heavily on misfortune than on sin; indeed, Christian explanations of the heroine's fate are not only not accepted, for the most part they are not even considered.

The evocation of pity for the heroines of she-tragedy and domestic tragedy entails a view of woman as intrinsically good. It is significant that as in *Fatal Love; or, the Forced Inconstancy*, *The Orphan*, and *Fatal Marriage; or, the Innocent Adultery* the plots often turn upon misprision by men who wrongly believe the heroine is adulterous, treacherous, or otherwise guilty. In part this seems to be a dramatic projection of the culture's decision that women are not so evil as the patriarchal view of Eve insisted they were. The heated misogynist / antimisogynist debate of the earlier seventeenth century that Robert Ornstein has related to the treatment of women in the tragedies of Webster and Ford by the end of the century tipped in favor of the antimisogynists.[83] William Walsh, for instance, in 1691 published *A Dialogue Concerning Women, Being a Defense of the Sex*, set up as a debate between Philogynes and Misogynes. Philogynes is allowed to get the last word and much the better of the argument. His views are advanced, though expressed with some levity. When Misogynes complains that heiresses show their depravity by running away with the worst sort of men, Philogynes retorts, "If they do, Sir, it should rather deserve your Pity than your Anger; or if you must be angry, be angry with the Guardians whose severity frightens 'em away, and yet hinders 'em the sight of any Men of merit to run away with."[84] Philogynes professes himself convinced by Anna Maria Schurman's arguments in favor of learning for women and, like Nahum Tate in *A Present for the Ladies* (1693) and Defoe in his better known *Essay on Projects* (1697), blames custom rather than nature for many of the observed deficiences of women:

> We may tell you too, that granting the equal Capacities of both Sexes, 'tis a greater Wonder to find one Learned Woman, than a hundred Learned Men, considering the difference of their Education. . . . Will you by all your Laws and Customs endeavour to keep 'em ignorant, and then blame 'em for being so? And forbid all Men of Sense keeping 'em company, as you do, and yet be angry with them for keeping Company with Fools? Consider what Time and Charge is spent to make Men fit for somewhat; Eight or Nine Years at School, Six or Seven Years at University; Four or Five Years in Travel; and after all this, are they not almost all Fops, Clowns, Dunces, or Pedants? I know not what you think of the Women; but if they are Fools, they are Fools I am sure with less pains and less expense then we are. [Pp. 100-1]

One of the most striking examples of how far the 1690s were willing to go in this insistence on the intrinsic goodness of women is Gildon's *Phaeton: or, The Fatal Divorce* (1698). Gildon's tragedy is based on Euripides' *Medea*, not an obvious source of pathetic she-tragedy. In a preface Gildon tries to discuss the Greek cultural context in which the story of Medea could have made sense to Euripides, but announces that the Greek Medea would be too shocking for modern audiences, that she is worse than Nero and acts "contrary to all the Dictates of *Humanity* and *Motherhood*." Gildon changes the names of the characters and softens them considerably, specifically explaining why he changes Jason's behavior in a particular scene: "on his meeting after his forsaking her *Jason* wou'd seem too harsh, rough, and Ungentleman-like, to a Lady on our Stage." Medea is called Althea, "Wife to Phaeton" (Jason), and allowed to ask the gods:

> Do not my Husbands impious Deeds provoke you?
> He breaks thro all your sacred Tyes of Oaths,
> To the curs'd Joys of a new Bridal Bed.[85]

Unlike Medea, she refrains from cursing him. Althea's maids are allied with her in the "Quarrel" of "Womankind" and lament her fate:

> O! hard condition of poor Womankind!
> Made Slaves to mans imperious changeful Will!
> [P. 14]

The ghost of Althea's father appears, not to blame her for past murder or for eloping with Phaeton in the first place, but to blame her for suffering her present wrongs and—in accord with the patriotic spirit of the democratic romances discussed in the preceding chapter—to demand she revenge the slight to her country. Unlike Medea, Althea does not bargain with Aegeus, promising to give him children if he will swear to receive her after she makes her escape from Corinth. Althea does succeed in having Jason's bride poisoned (a softer Phaeton faints at her agonies), but instead of murdering her children as she does in Euripides, pleads sincerely for them to be allowed to stay in Greece. The children are killed by a mob that tears them limb from limb. Althea stabs herself, thus vindicating Gildon's notion of the behavior natural to mothers and making Euripides' terrifying play fit for the British audience of the 1690s.

Like the tragedies, the comedies and plays of the last decade or so of the seventeenth century generally insist on the goodness of the heroine. As Kathleen Lynch observed in discussing D'Urfey's *Virtuous Wife; or, Good Luck at Last* (1679) as the beginning of sentimental comedy, "D'Urfey's awareness that Olivia's virtue was something of an innovation in comedy may be inferred from an apologetic Prologue spoken by the heroine, in which she announces her unwillingness to play the part."[86] The most famous of the sentimental comedies, Cibber's *Love's Last Shift* (1695), shows the reform of a wayward husband by a virtuous wife. Sentimental comedy is the obvious analogue to the democratic romances discussed in the previous chapter, except that it offends by failing to use the usual distancing devices of romance and seems to be making claims of realism for its idealized Amandas. Ernest Bernbaum pointed to this when he observed, "Such virtuous characters as the eighteenth-century drama of sensibility was to place in the environment of ordinary life, were, previous to its rise, placed in romantic comedy, pastoral drama, and heroic tragedy,—types which did not profess to hold a true mirror up to nature."[87]

The other significant difference between sentimental comedy and older romance is that women are not present principally as obstacles or rewards in the hero's quest, not as false Duessas or Faery Queens. Instead, they are themselves actors and protagonists in their own quests, as Christiana is in *Pilgrim's Progress, Part II*. In the nineties we even begin to get comedies about women who reform, Thomas Dilke's *City Lady; or, Folly Reclaimed* (1696) and William Burnaby's *Reformed Wife* (1700), for instance. In Crowne's *English Friar* (1690) one of the plots concerns the reformation of Laura, Lord Stately's eldest daughter, "a great Gallant and Coquet." In *The Married Beau* (1694) Crowne adapted material from Cervantes's *Curious Impertinent* to show a husband who tries to test his wife's virtue by asking his best friend to try to seduce her. Although the wife eventually succumbs, Crowne rejects Cervantes's disastrous ending, allows her to repent, makes the husband repent too, and reconciles them.

A sentimental comedy like *Love's Last Shift* affirms the protestant demand that a husband be as chaste as his wife.[88] Most of the comedies of the nineties insist on more equal standards of behavior from husband and wife and idealize marriages where both partners are equally chaste and, perhaps more importantly, possessed of equally refined sensibilities. In the problem comedies like Southerne's *Wives Excuse* and Sir John Vanbrugh's *Provok'd Wife*, which modern critics like better than the sentimental comedies, similar ideals are invoked, but the playwrights emphasize the difficulty of achieving them under contemporary circumstances. One of the best of the problem comedies, *The Wives Excuse: Or, Cuckolds make themselves* (1691), picks up what had been a secondary comic subject in plays like *The Country Wife* and treats it as a primary problem. The *excuse* in the title has a double sense: wives have an excuse for making cuckolds of their husbands when their husbands are foolish and cowardly and good wives with foolish husbands are always having to make excuses for them. Mr. Friendall, the unworthy husband in this play, we eventually learn, has only married his wife for her estate and the better to carry on his own intrigues, "For having been so often abroad, and visiting with my Wife, I pass upon the formal Part of the Town for a very good Husband; and upon the Privilege of that Character, I grow intimate with all her Acquaintance . . . and deliver my Billets my self" (1:334). Mrs. Friendall is aware that marriage can be viewed as a contract voidable if its reasonably anticipated benefits fail to materialize: "in a marry'd State, as in the Publick we tie our selves up, indeed; but to be protected in our Persons, Fortunes and Honours, by those very Laws that restrain us in other things; for few will obey, but for the Benefit they receive from the Government" (1:292). Nevertheless, Mrs. Friendall says she has too much respect for herself to become an adulteress. Several recent critics have admired Southerne's attention to the psychology of the heroine, and although Anthony Kaufman exaggerates a little the novelty of this interest in 1691, he is right to argue that Mrs. Friendall's refusal of Lovemore depends upon her respect for herself and is not simply "the stubborn adherence to some conventional notion of virtue"; "she does not insist on her own virtue, or demand abasement from her erring husband—or virtue from her contemptible suitor."[89] Again, there can be only the partial solution of a separate maintenance, and Southerne's conclusion emphasizes that this is not entirely satisfactory:

Mrs. F. The unjust World, let what will be the Cause of our Complaint (as there is Cause sufficient still at home) condemns us to a Slavery for Life: And if by Separation we get free, then all our Husband's Faults are laid on us. . . . I must be still your Wife, and still unhappy. [1:345–46]

Vanbrugh's *The Provok'd Wife* (1697) presents another problematic marriage and shows more self-consciousness about the implications to be drawn from sovereign / subject relations for husband / wife relations. Lady Brute applies the social contract theory to her marriage: "I think I promised to be true to my husband. Well; and he promised to be kind to me. But he han't kept his word. Why then I'm absolved from mine. Aye, that seems clear to me. The argument's good between the king and the people, why not between the husband and the wife?"[90] Throughout, the play toys with the issue of how far such an argument might go to justify the rebellion of wives, though Vanbrugh is unwilling to press it so far as to allow his heroine to commit adultery with her gallant, Constant. The contract theory comes up again when Constant talks of her husband's bad behavior and Lady Brute replies, "But can his fault release my duty?" Constant also tries criticism of the double standard for men and women and the more traditional lover's argument that marriage is "slavery" where generous love is impossible. Lady Brute, of course, knows perfectly well that he offers the arguments from self-interest, and Vanbrugh will not risk losing his audience's sympathy for his heroine by allowing her to become an adulteress. As a playwright, Vanbrugh is content to dramatize these puzzles without pressing all the arguments that engage him to a conclusion. Closer to cynical comedy than Southerne, Vanbrugh even avoids the partial solution of separate maintenance, in the fifth act simply leaving us with an unrepentant Constant, a wife who is wavering though not yet fallen, and a cowardly Sir John too afraid to fight Constant.

Mary Pix's *Innocent Mistress* (1697) is not so much to the taste of modern critics as *The Provok'd Wife*, but in some ways is even more revealing of how weak the traditional obligations imposed by the religious vows of marriage could seem when the individuals they joined could not respect each other. Mrs. Pix departs from the more famous formula of *Love's Last Shift* to pair a virtuous husband, Sir Charles Beauclair, with an impossible wife. They were married, we are given to understand, when Charles was in his "Nonage": "Ruling Friends and [their] Curst Avarice joyned this unthinking youth to the worst of Women."[91] Lady Beauclair, interestingly, is not an adulteress; she is objectionable basically because she is ill-bred and grates on Sir Charles's more refined sensibilities. She does try to enrich her brother, Cheatly, by scheming to force a young heiress who does not like him to marry him, but the real issue is not her virtue but her taste. In a critical scene Sir Charles reproaches her:

> *Sir Cha.* Madam, you have not been abus'd; you know that I was in my Nonage married, saw not with my own Eyes, nor chose for my unhappy self; e'r I liv'd with ye, I possess'd an Estate nobler, a larger far than yours, which you have still commanded; nay, I have often urg'd ye to Diversions, in hopes it would have alter'd that unquiet mind, but all in vain.
>
> *La. Beau.* Divartions! what Divartions? Yes, you had me to the Playhouse, and the first thing I saw was an ugly black Devil kill his Wife, for nothing; then your *Metridate* King o' the *Potecaries*, your *Timon* the *Atheist*, the Man in the Moon, and all the rest—Nonsense Stuff, I hate 'em.
>
> *Sir Cha.* I need say no more,—Now, Madam, you have shown yourself. [P. 24]

Mrs. Pix expects the audience to understand that Sir Charles cannot live with a woman who says "Divartions!" and has no love of Shakespeare and Lee. This is a view of marriage quite beyond the comprehension of the ecclesiastical courts.

Furthermore, Sir Charles has fallen in love with Marianne, a young girl who reads romances and who has fled from her father's house in order to avoid a forced marriage with a man described as "Rich, but wanting all *Scuderies* Accomplishments." Marianne, the innocent mistress of the title, engages her heart to Sir Charles before she knows he is married and is careful to conduct her platonic relationship with him entirely in company. When she does learn of his marriage and of her father's distress over her running away, she soon resolves to return to the country. One of the other characters comments, "How strong are the Efforts of Honour where a good Education grounds the Mind in Virtue!" (p. 27). How to resolve such an impasse? Solutions in which the erring spouse reforms seemed possible when the erring spouse was an adulterous husband, but here a wife who is objectionable because she is stupid and vulgar cannot very well become more intelligent. Sir Charles has no grounds for divorce and even if he enters into a voluntary separate maintenance agreement he still will not be able to marry Marianne. In the fifth act he declares: "I'll act the uneasie part no longer, that Woman, the bar to all my Happiness, by Heaven, she's not my Wife: 'tis true, the Ceremony of the Church has pass'd between us, but she knows I went no further" (p. 47). Since this is of no practical use, Mrs. Pix adds a final discovery in the last lines of the play. The merchant Flywife bursts onto the stage chasing his kept mistress and is suddenly recognized as a former husband of Lady Beauclair's "thought dead in the *Indies*" (p. 49).

Despite its title, *The Innocent Mistress* differs from most of the comedies and tragedies we have been discussing in that they focus not on men but on women. Why should the culture of the last decades of the seventeenth century have been so interested in the feminine? Upham, in the study of the pamphlet literature mentioned earlier, thinks she finds a feminist movement "in practically all respects paralleling, and in part derived from the French activity of that period." Rae Blanchard, exploring Steele's ideas about women, describes the advanced reformers of the turn of the century as Cartesian enthusiasts for the new philosophy.[92] The most advanced French reformer noted by both Upham and Blanchard is François Poulain de La Barre whose book appeared in English as *The Woman as Good as the Man* (1677), though better known writers like François Fénélon, Charles Perrault, and Madame de Maintenon also dealt with the education of women and defended them. Both Upham and Blanchard, I think, overestimate the importance of a French influence. So distinguished a French scholar as Georges Ascoli thought French feminism did not really begin until the eighteenth century and found most of the seventeenth-century works on women going over old ground, repeating what had already been said. Many of the French works Ascoli discusses are, like a number of those Upham includes in her total of fifty English works, peripheral to any feminist movement, consisting of historical catalogues of good and bad women, Abelard-like *sic et non* displays of cleverness, or courtesy book advice.

(Blanchard takes account of this.) The seventeenth-century précieuses, Ascoli thinks, "loin d'avoir servi au progrès des idées véritablement 'feministes' le retarda plutôt, et qu'en particulier el ne fut guère favorable, á tout prendre, au dévelopement de l'instruction des femmes."[93] Furthermore, the sort of controversy over women Upham and Blanchard discuss has an analogue in England in the earlier seventeenth century. The controversy has been well described by Louis B. Wright in *Middle-class Culture in Elizabethan England.*[94] Indeed, some of Upham's titles are reprints of earlier English works. For example, *The Great Advocate and Oratour for Women* (1682) is William Heale's *An Apology for Women, or An Opposition to Dr. G. his Assertion Who held in the Act at Oxford Ann. 1608 that it was lawful for husbands to beate their wives* (1608). It would be foolish to deny that such a striking book as Poulain de la Barre's could have had any influence on English writers or that the French had any influence on the development of English rationalism, but French influence hardly seems the best explanation for British attention to women in the eighties and nineties.

If we looked only at the theater, the development of talented actresses would suggest itself as one fairly obvious reason for the shift toward heroines. Looking only at sentimental comedy, John Harrington Smith has argued that the responsibility of a change to female-oriented sentimental comedy should be divided between "Shadwell, who, in order to correct the dubious morality of the plays of his contemporaries, invented the exemplary method, and the ladies, who were revolted by the Wycherley phase of comedy and fought it by boycott until—as is always likely to happen in any age—they got their way."[95] To support this theory he cites prefaces, prologues, and epilogues that state or imply ladies did not like bawdiness and that less cynical comedy was written to please them. This theory has a certain plausibility, especially when it suggests that the ladies disliked cynical heroes who only married "with an air of lordly condesension" or who were simply cuckoldmakers who never married, though I do not really see that angry married women might not have enjoyed watching husbands like Old Moneylove in *Tom Essence* humiliated—after all, the wives get off scott free in these plays; it is the cuckolds who have to pay. But if cuckolding had been the problem, writers could simply have stuck to the gay couple comedy which Smith thinks the ladies did like.

The real problem with Smith's argument, however, is that it rests on sexist assumptions for which there is no evidence and that it begs the deeper questions. Politeness aside, in most ages the ladies have not got their way. More importantly, Smith fails to see that the crucial question is why ladies should not like bawdy as much as gentlemen liked it, indeed, why ladies should not be the most enthusiastic consumers of bawdy. When the English writers of the earlier seventeenth century catalogued the characteristics of women lewdness was frequently high on their lists. Classically, erotic female temptresses drag men away from the nobler pursuits to which their own natures draw them. Even in Wycherley's famous *Plain Dealer* scene where Eliza and Olivia discuss *The Country Wife*—which Smith uses as evidence that "respectable female society had put the play under a ban"—it is the immoral and hypocritical Olivia who condemns the play and the virtuous Eliza who maintains the truly modest "are least exceptious." The really interesting thing that is going on in the emergence of sentimental drama is not that drama is suddenly written to please the ladies, but that ladies were invented whom this drama was supposed to please.

If we step back from particular manifestations like sentimental comedy or feminist pamphlets to ask the broader question of why the culture was taking a new interest in women as independent persons no worse by nature than men it is obvious that explanations like the influence of French Cartesianism or professional actresses or the wishes of the ladies in the theater audiences will not do. The judges who thought it was better that disobedient wives should be maintained by their husbands than that they should starve and who were willing to provide temporal court remedies were not animated by Cartesianism or by a desire to please lady theatergoers. The members of parliament who voted to extend benefit of clergy to women criminal defendants in 1692 were not trying to ingratiate themselves with lady voters.[96]

The deepest reason for the increased interest in women seems to be protestantism, not only the protestantism of the sectaries but the spirit of the Reformation within the Church of England. William Heale, who wrote the *Apologie for Women* attacking the lawfulness of wife-beating, was an Anglican clergyman immediately provoked by the defense of wife-beating of a civil lawyer who held a variety of posts in the ecclesiastical courts. Heale condemns an obedience gained by force as servile, criticizes the civil law as too obdurate against wives, and speculates that its harshness arose from the lawgivers' having been unmarried. A protestant emphasis on a woman's having her own soul to save certainly lay behind *Pilgrim's Progress, Part II* (1684) where Bunyan, having shown Christian's salvation in Part I, then returns to chronicle the passage of Christiana and the Christian children to the heavenly city. Even François Poulain de La Barre, the author of *The Woman as Good as the Man*, though he did apparently study Descartes and began life as a Roman Catholic priest, in 1688 left the priesthood, went to live in Geneva, married, and raised his son to be a protestant minister.[97] Though sober Anglicans recoiled from the practices of the extreme sectaries who allowed women to preach, they nevertheless felt the impact of the protestant emphasis on the priesthood of all believers. It was, after all, a conservative and sober Anglican like Richard Allestree who produced *The Ladies Calling* (1673); that the advice contained therein is hardly revolutionary is not the point—what is significant is that he bothered to address himself exclusively to women. Mary Astell herself was an exceptionally pious Anglican.

Besides protestantism, I think, we have to look to politics for an explanation of the increased stress on the feminine in the last decades of the seventeenth century—though a distinction between protestantism and politics in this period is as much an expository convenience as a reality, and the protestantism at issue desired to wrest control over citizens' morals away from the church into the hands of a Christian state. Politics affects the culture here in two ways, one conscious, one unconscious. First, the analogies discussed at the beginning of this chapter all direct that when the culture starts to find the dilemmas of subjects more interesting than the dilemmas of sovereigns it will also begin to focus more closely on the problems of wives and children than on the problems of husbands and fathers. As the analogies would lead us to expect, we do in fact find a rough equivalent to the democratic romances discussed in the preceding chapter in "domestic romances" like Mrs. Behn's *Town Fop*, Mrs. Pix's *Innocent Mistress*, and the more ordinary sentimental comedies like Cibber's *Love's Last Shift*. Just as *Edward III*, *Timoleon*, and *Cato* focus on subjects instead of sovereigns, so Southerne's *Wives Excuse* and Vanbrugh's *Provok'd Wife* ask our sympathy for the wife instead of the husband. Also, as the religious conception of kingship is replaced by an idea of the sovereign's obligation to the interests of the people so the older hierarchic religious conception of marriage begins to give way to a newer idea of marriage as a contract intended to promote the interests of both partners. However, perhaps because there was no medicine for the wife's dilemma so strong as the Glorious Revolution had been for the subject's, domestic romances coexist with domestic tragedies and problem comedies through the end of the century.

At a deeper political level, I would suggest, the late seventeenth century's interest in women was aroused by the usefulness of seeing women as models for men. As the culture became more a bourgeois culture of men who rejected the personal use of violence, where better to look for examples of how people manage without violence than among women? Stone in *The Crisis of the Aristocracy* has shown how physical force gradually passed from the hands of individual aristocrats to the state, observing, for instance, how lords were forced to abandon their private armies and how the elimination of gangs of liveried retainers put noblemen and gentlemen on terms of equality. In 1670 an assault on Sir John Coventry provoked the passage of the first law against maiming. Later seventeenth-century satire against nonaristocratic characters constantly harps on their propensity for solving disputes through litigation instead of by the sword. Ordinary gentlemen, instead of admiring older aristocratic ideals, began to turn on them. As Irene Coltman suggestively observed, in the mid-seventeenth century political philosophy had begun to assume the attitude of classical comedy toward classical ideals. Naturally antiheroic attitudes appeared in comedy and ballads, but contempt of traditional heroism spread to sober prose. Anthony Ascham in *Of the Confusions and Revolutions of Governments* advised his readers not to endanger themselves by resistance and to change sides whenever it was safe to do so. Marchamont Needham in *The Case of the Common-wealth of England, Stated* argued the necessity of submitting to whatever government had seized power; those who resist revolutions in government are fortifying "Castles in the Aire against Fatall necessity, to maintain a Phanti'sie of pretended Loyalty", and in time may consider they have hazarded their lives and fortunes "for the satisfying an Opiniated Humour."[98] The citizen's only obligation is to obey his own individual need for safety and self-preservation. Such attitudes were, of course, excoriated by the cavaliers during the war and by many royalists afterwards, but expressed more moderately, they gradually gained respectability. Locke, for instance, wrote in *Of Education:*

> All the entertainment of talk and history is of nothing almost but fighting and killing; and the honour and renown that is bestowed on conquerors, (who for the most part are but the great butchers of mankind) farther mislead growing youths, who by this means come to think slaughter the laudable business of mankind, and the most heroic of virtues. [9:113]

At first, as we have seen in the preceding chapter, the heroic drama indulged in a fantasy of pure honor while simultaneously acknowledging such honor to be impossible. The ideal tried to preserve itself by retreating to a narrower and narrower sphere. Even while the tragedy of about 1680 admits the possibilities of strains on loyalty so great that no one can emerge as a man of honor, it reserves the right to present female characters who are able to preserve their own integrity in a limited private sphere. The female characters like Monimia in *The Orphan* or Isabella in *The Fatal Marriage* are incapable of organizing any effective resistance to those forces that threaten them with loss of integrity, but their experience of maintaining some kind of recognizable honor in spite of their passivity and helplessness becomes more and more central and more and more crucial to the culture in general as aristocratic protagonists are replaced with protagonists who have less and less access to individual power.

The most advanced marriage plays of the late seventeenth century present annulment or separate maintenance as the only solutions to unhappy marriage. The profound changes in the understanding of marriage over the course of the century are clearly indicated by the contrast between Dr. Baxtor's appearance in the fifth act of *The Miseries of Enforced Marriage* and the separate maintenance agreements in plays like *Epsom-Wells* and *The Wives Excuse*. Marriage is only tolerable as the union of like-minded persons; the condemnation of Lady Beauclair in *The Innocent Mistress* is not much more frivolous than Milton's justification of putting away an unsympathetic wife in *The Doctrine and Discipline of Divorce*. Only the later seventeenth century went beyond Milton by sympathizing with the wife's desire to part from her husband on similar grounds of personal dislike. The issue is not really adultery or even cruelty, the grounds for an ecclesiastical divorce *a mensa et thoro*, but loving or liking and such purely personal qualities as stupidity, coarseness, lack of taste, and cowardice. At the beginning of the period in *Lady Alimony* women who gain divorces from husbands who are unsatisfactory because of their personal qualities are vigorously satirized; the author obviously hopes the restoration of the king will bring an end to such puritan nonsense and a return to patriarchal notions. That anonymous author, however, was a poor prophet. By the end of the century audiences were prepared to sympathize with a Mrs. Friendall or a Lady Brute. Outside the theater the secular courts stood ready to enforce separate maintenance agreements in spite of the fact that they violated the old principle that husband and wife being in law one person are unable to contract with each other, a principle eventually reasserted in the more reactionary later eighteenth century.

The puritans appeared to have lost their battle for civil marriage and for the idea of marriage as a civil contract at the Restoration. In so far as the ecclesiastical court system was restored, it essentially continued its old practices in dealing with matrimonial cases, arguing against continued encroachments on its jurisdiction but acquiescing in assertions of state power when they were accomplished. As even expositors of canon law noted, many defendants showed contempt of ecclesiastical jurisdiction and successfully frustrated or evaded it.[99] Although the puritans failed to prevent the restoration of the ecclesiastical courts, they had more success in affecting the state directly. The temporal courts continued to nibble away at the ecclesiastical jurisdiction and continued to do some of the business the abolition of the ecclesiastical courts had forced them to do during the interregnum. Parliament, harranged by such scions of independency as Shaftesbury and Burnet and even by a bishop like Cosin, permitted divorce with remarriage and began to assert the state's control over marriage with various statutes. Although patriarchal and economic pressures continued to influence the selection of marriage partners, at about the same time subjects asserted their right to elect a sovereign in the Glorious Revolution women acquired an analogous right to elect husbands, a right often not secured to them in practice and in fact undermined by later eighteenth-century legislation, but a right finally acknowledged in theory not only by puritan fanatics and feminists but also by such different sons of the Church of England as the creators of Clarissa and Sophia. The cultural heroes of the eighteenth century were not to be brave men or warriors but peaceable, private ladies and gentlemen like Ralph Allen and Martha Blount.

4
OATHS AND VOWS

I

Oaths and vows are signs that legitimate obligation is recognized. If I take an oath of allegiance and supremacy, I say that I owe the sovereign my obedience and that he has a right to rule over me. Indeed, vows can create obligation where it did not exist before. If I promise to marry a certain man, I accept the obligation of being faithful to him and—in the late seventeenth century—give him the right to force me to marry him or to sue me for breach of promise. For a women, to utter the marriage vows is to give the authority of a husband to a man who previously had no particular power over her. Before the Marriage Act of 1753, the simple exchange of vows in the present tense itself constituted a valid marriage.

During the later seventeenth century oaths and vows were frequently the subject of public debate and parliamentary action. Quakers continued to be attacked for their refusal to swear, for example, by John Gauden, the Bishop of Exeter, in A Discourse Concerning Publick Oaths, and the Lawfulness of Swearing in Judicial Proceedings (1662). Parliament passed a law making it an offense to maintain that the taking of oaths was unlawful or contrary to the word of God or to attempt to persuade others to such an opinion by speaking or writing; a third offense was punishable by banishment or transportation.[1] Gentlemen assembled for the assizes apparently were frequently greeted with admonitory sermons like that of Thomas Comber, Prebendary of York, on *The Nature and Usefulness of Solemn Judicial Swearing with the Impiety and Mischief of Vain and False-Swearing* (1682). The clergy regularly lamented the sins of false swearing and vain swearing, which were sometimes said to be the characteristic sins of the age. The precise language of such oaths as the oaths of allegiance and supremacy and the oaths in the Corporation Act and the Test Acts were debated extensively, as was the government's fundamental right to impose such oaths at all or to require them as tests for public office holders. Swearing is also a pervasive theme in Restoration literature. Works as diverse as Sir Robert Howard's popular play, *The Committee*, Samuel Butler's even more popular *Hudibras*, Crowne's *City Politiques*, Otway's *Venice Preserved*, and Aphra Behn's story, *The History of the Nun; or, The Fair Vow Breaker* are all concerned in one way or another with oaths. These works and others like them may usefully be understood in the context of the specific historical anxieties of the Restoration.

The theme of swearing is more interesting and less narrow than may at first appear. The Restoration understanding of oaths offers a particularly focused and elegant example of how a nominalist universe of force and passion triumphs over an idealist universe of words. An early play like *The Committee* shows Howard still able to indulge himself in heroes who triumphantly uphold the reality of perfect loyalty, scorning the material world in which they are being robbed of their property as a reward for their faithfulness. Butler presents a more complex view in which Hudibras breaks through the bonds of one sacred oath after another; Ralpho meanwhile provides a counterpoint of authentic historic examples of perjurers who have prospered. Butler's specific satire on the Covenanters' slippery way with words spills over into a more general skepticism about the power of universals: "Oaths are but words, and words but wind, / Too feeble impliments to bind." Earlier works seem to fight shy of the lessons Butler drew from the experience of the war and the continued political struggles of the Restoration. But by the end of the period several writers feel their world is so chaotic and irrational that it corresponds to no ordered universe that can be expressed in language. In *Venice Preserved* and in Southerne's *The Fatal Marriage; or, the Innocent Adultery* the keeping of vows becomes so problematic that perjurers are the objects of the audience's sympathy.

Why did people who knew many examples of broken oaths still insist on regarding all sorts of loyalty and testing oaths as essential safeguards to the security of government? Edward Dering's account of the Commons debate over the rather trivial issue of whether the assessors for Charles's subsidy shoud be sworn provides a useful illustration. Those objecting pointed to "the multiplicity of oaths throughout the land" and "the great and evident dangers of perjury." They also claimed "that customary oaths were very little regarded, witness the oath of church wardens and constables" and therefore suggested a penalty of twenty pounds as more effectual. The advocates seemed to agree that perjury was rife, but maintained with muted optimism "that the age was not so deplorable but that we could not find 4 or 5 men in a hundred to make assessors who would reverence an oath." Opportunities for graft greatly exceeded twenty pounds. The advocates of the oaths won.[2]

Part of the explanation for the Restoration enthusiasm for loyalty and testing oaths, I think, may be discovered in the history of the criminal law concerning perjury in the period. As we shall see, the idea that sworn testimony must be believed because it was sworn was only very slowly abandoned. Words, especially the words used under oath, retained a good deal of their primitive magic power in the late seventeenth century. Enthusiasm for loyalty oaths is a corollary of faith in sworn testimony. Given that what I swear has to be believed because I swear it, if I can be made to swear that I will be loyal, then I will be loyal.

As I pointed out in the first chapter, during the interregnum government repeatedly tried to secure itself by using oaths as instruments of purges and to create obligation by forcing citizens to take particular oaths. The casuistry used to reconcile consciences to these oaths was frequently attacked, not only in mid-seventeenth-century pamphlet literature, but also after the Restoration in sermons, tracts, and satires of various kinds. In

1682, for instance, Dryden and Lee were still raking over the old coals. Melanax, who is literally a devil, temporarily disguised in a "Fanatick Habit," tells the Paris mob in *The Duke of Guise*:

> Therefore, go on boldly, and lay on resolutely for your Solemn league and Covenant; and if here be any squeamish conscience who fears to fight against the king,—though I, that have known you, citizens, these thousand years, suspect not any, let such understand, that his majesty's politic capacity is to be distinguished from his natural; and though you murder him in one, you may preserve him in the other. [7:89]

Bitter as many royalists were over interregnum attempts to tyrannize over their consciences, however, post-Restoration governments did not abandon the use of oaths to coerce allegiance and identify dissenters. The Corporation Act (1661) immediately imposed a quadruple test on the officers of corporate towns. Not only did these officials have to take the new oaths of allegiance and supremacy, they also had to abjure the Solemn League and Covenant and take a special nonresistance oath. The words of the nonresistance oath were designed to remove the threat of future revolutions:

> I, A. B., *do declare and believe, That it is not lawful, upon any pretense whatsoever, to take arms against the King: and that I do abhor the traitorous position of taking arms by his authority against his person or against those that are commissioned by him. So help me God.*

Many office holders in the sixties would earlier have sworn to the Solemn League and Covenant, but now all had to abjure it:

> I, A. B., *do declare, That I hold that there lies no obligation upon me or any other person, from the oath commonly called, The solemn league and covenant; and that the same was in it self an unlawful oath, and imposed upon the subjects of this realm against the known laws and liberties of the kingdom.*[3]

Just as the interregnum governments had done, the Cavalier Parliament proceeded to impose its oaths on an ever-widening circle of people and to add new oaths. The Act of Uniformity (1662) imposed the nonresistance oath of the Corporation Act on university fellows and tutors, schoolmasters, et al., on penalty of removal for nonconformity.[4] Teachers were thus bound to abhor the chief justifications that had been used by parliament during the war and to defend nonresistance. The Act of Uniformity also imposed on clergy a declaration of consent to "every thing contained and prescribed in and by" the Book of Common Prayer.[5] Another statute of 1663 proceeded to impose all five oaths on vestry men.[6]

Many who were still capable of tormenting themselves over particular words knew very well that oaths were regarded as political weapons by those who imposed them. Extreme statements could be included as a way of triumphing over one's enemies, forcing them to abase themselves by eating their own words, humiliating them with vague pledges to they knew not what. Burnet's *History of My Own Time* gives vivid examples of characteristic Restoration quarreling over oaths. In the Scotch parliament of 1662 the Presbyterians were nervous over the large ecclesiastical powers the new oaths of supremacy and allegiance seemed to give the king. They requested a Scotch Act of explanation, Robert Leighton arguing that "the words of this oath were certainly capable of a bad sense" and that "to act otherwise looked like laying snares for people and making men offenders for a word." Burnet remembers:

> Sharp took this ill from him, and replied upon him with great bitterness; and said, it was below the dignity of government to make acts to satisfy the weak scruples of peevish men: it ill became them, who had imposed their covenant on all people without any explanation, and had forced all to take it, now to expect such extraordinary favours. Leighton insisted that it ought to be done for that very reason, that all people might see a difference between the mild proceedings of the government now, and their severity: and that it ill became the very same persons who had complained of that rigour, not to practice it themselves,—for thus it may be said, the world goes mad by turns.[7]

After the passage of the Act of Uniformity, Burnet also recalls, many thought a blanket assent to "every thing" in the prayer book too hard. The revised prayer book itself was so slow in appearing that by the time of the deadline for taking the oath, few copies were available: "Many that were affected to the Church, but made conscience of subscribing to a book they had not seen, left their benefices on that very account. Some made a journey to London on purpose to see it." Yet, given the obvious political motivation of parliament's imposition of conformity and its relative disinterest in dogma and niceties of ritual, other clergy decided to interpret the oath "as importing no more but a consent of obedience."[8]

When passions cooled a little, thought might sometimes be given to softening the language of a particular oath. The royalist Dering reports an English parliamentary debate over repealing the clause demanding abjuration of the Solemn League and Covenant in the Act of Uniformity. Proponents, including Sir Robert Howard, wanted to strike the words "nor upon any other person." They observed that such a phrase was to be found in no other known oath and that it must necessarily be useless, "no man being either bound or loosed by any other man's opinion but his own." Nevertheless, the motion was defeated in a close vote, 132–141.[9]

Never certain of its security, Restoration government invented further testing oaths and declarations to expose and segregate its enemies. Texts that had been used both before the Civil War and during it to identify Roman Catholics were revived. The words of the new Test Act (1672) were carefully chosen to contradict major articles of Roman Catholic belief: "I, A. B. *do declare, That I do believe there is not any transubstantiation in the sacrament of the Lord's supper, or in the elements of bread and wine, at or after the consecration thereof by any person whatsoever.*"[10] Burnet describes the Test Act debates of 1675, commenting that the lords often sat until midnight in what he remembered as their "greatest and longest debate" in his time. Danby, Heneage Finch, and some of the bishops claimed that tests were necessary to separate good subjects from bad and to prevent the horrors of civil war. On the other side, "a great deal was said, to show that the peace of the world was best secured by good laws, and good government; and that oaths or tests were no security: the scrupulous might be fettered by them, yet the bulk of the world would boldly take any test, and as boldly break through it; of which late times had given large proofs."[11] This 1675 session of parliament was broken up by *Shirley* v. *Fagg*, but in 1677 parliament was still so far from repealing tests that it demanded a further declaration rejecting adoration of Mary and the sacrifice of the mass as "*superstitious and idolatrous*" in "An Act for the more effectual preserving the King's person and government, by disabling papists from sitting in

either house of Parliament." As an increased safeguard against
Jesuitical practices, takers of this oath had to declare that they took
it according to the *"plain and ordinary sense of the words read, as
they are commonly understood by* English *protestants, without any
evasion, equivocation or mental reservation."*[12]

The burdens placed on dissenters, Roman Catholics, and even
scrupulous members of the Church of England by these various
oaths were substantial, but the most dramatic Restoration crisis of
conscience over oath-taking came with William's invasion. Did
James's flight justify Englishmen who had pledged him their
allegiance in taking an oath of allegiance to William? The new oath
of allegiance was painstakingly streamlined to avoid unpleasant
references to the past. Unlike the Restoration oaths, it did not ask
subjects explicitly to abjure any earlier oaths; it did not even make
any assertion of William's right to rule. It said simply: "I A. B. *do
sincerely promise and swear, That I will be faithful, and bear true
allegiance to their majesties King* William *and Queen* Mary, *So
help me God."* An oath of supremacy revived the pledges of earlier
Tudor oaths when it had the taker declare he abhorred and abjured
the doctrine that princes excommunicated by the Pope "may be
deposed or murdered."[13]

When in March it was proposed to administer the new oath to
Commons the members acquiesced readily enough. But in the
House of Lords only eight bishops and no more than ninety temporal peers complied. The Duke of Newcastle, the Earl of
Clarendon, Lord Godolphin and many other noblemen "retired
into the Country upon various Pretences, but really because they
were unwilling to own the present Government."[14] Eventually at
least 400 nonjuring clergymen lost their livings. The loyalty of
these nonjurors was certainly futile and they have been treated
rather roughly. Macaulay snapped, "the nonjuror sacrificed, not
order to liberty, not liberty to order, but both liberty and order to a
superstition as stupid and degrading as the Egyptian worship of
cats and onions."

Nevertheless, the position of divines like Archbishop William
Sancroft had been based on the defense of hereditary monarchy
and on the nonresistance oath. Regarding the obligation of an oath
as sacred and binding might be superstitious, but Sancroft had

spent years defending that superstition and refused to abandon it
suddenly because circumstances changed. Also, the questions of
exactly when a conqueror had actually conquered and exactly
when all resistance became futile were enormously difficult. Nor
was it necessary to be a religious man to find the country's utter
abandonment of James disconcerting. From his position as
diplomatic resident in Ratisbon, Etherege watched William's plans
for an invasion with alarm. The behavior of the opposition at home
seemed to him strongly reminiscent of parliament's behavior on the
eve of the Civil War; the claims of the Seven Bishops and their
followers seemed as absurd as those of the puritans had been.
Though he worried about the loyalty of James's subjects, even after
William was on the throne and Etherege had decided to join James
in Paris, he was not certain that the Glorious Revolution would be
permanent:

> While his person is not in their power, it will mark the place where all
> his faithfull subjects may rally, whose number cannot but be con-
> siderable tho' the perfidious and ungratefull have seduc'd many with
> them. . . . Impostures cannot be long conceal'd. Mankind is unconstant,
> especially the humour of a whole Nation. The face of affaires cannot be
> long the same in Christendom, so that a powerfull assistance may be
> had in case it be requisite.[15]

Many of William's supporters, lay and clergy alike, sought to
persuade the nonjurors by arguing that William deserved their
allegiance by right of conquest. Clergymen now began to observe
that the early Christians had yielded their obedience to emperors
who had gained power by unscrupulous means including poisoning
and assassination as well as conquest. The obedience parliaments
had shown to various English usurpers, especially Henry VII, was
pointed to as offering precedent. Though such arguments would
have been branded as treasonous by the spokesmen for the Stuarts,
now, "in nearly every Williamite pamphlet, it was broadcast that
allegiance could be given to the king in being, however infirm his
title might afterwards appear, for the law itself protected subjects
from future retribution."[16] In fact, most of the arguments used to
defend Cromwell were now revived for William's benefit.

In his *Discourse concerning the Unreasonableness of a new
Separation on Account of the Oaths* (1689) Edward Stillingfleet

distinguished between usurpers, kings *de facto*, and kings *de jure*. He insisted that oaths might be taken to kings *de facto*. The oath taken to James, he argued, was not merely an oath to a person, but entailed prior obligation to the nation and the church. Advancing to a position that might be described as casuistical—but that also reflects the shifting doctrines of sovereignty discussed in chapter 2—he claimed that the taker of the oath to James was not obliged to the specific words but to the real function of the oath, which was to ensure the general good: "For, there is a Common Good of Human Society, which mankind have an obligation to, antecedent to that obligation to particular persons. For, as magistrates were designed for a general Good, so the obligation to them must be understood." Stillingfleet's invocation of the general good to justify abandonment of a useless monarch is not too far from one of Milton's favorite lines of argument.

Any claim that sovereignty could be derived from force had been anathema to the royalists during the interregnum and in the years immediately following the Restoration. It is Dryden's villain Boabdelin who says in *The Conquest of Granada*, " 'Tis true from force the noblest title springs." Hobbes especially had been excoriated for maintaining that subjects owed obedience to successful usurpers and conquerors. As recently as 1683 the Convocation at Oxford had attacked certain "damnable doctrines" and burned the books that expressed them. Among the propositions condemned was one ascribed not only to Hobbes but also to Owen in his sermon before the regicides: "Possession and strength give a right to govern, and success in a cause or endeavour proclaim it to be lawful and just; to persue it is to comply with the will of God, because it is to follow the conduct of his providence."[17] Hobbes had not been as interested in providence as he was in the individual's right to self-preservation, but the puritans had regularly argued that Cromwell's successes in battle showed God's providence favored his cause. Even Marvell, in the "Horatian Ode," had concluded, " 'Tis madness to resist or blame / The force of angry heaven's flame." Now heaven appeared to have elected William. Writers like Sherlock in *The Case of Allegiance* and William Lloyd in *God's Ways of Disposing of Kingdoms* found that such election itself gave William a right to the subject's obedience. "It is all but

Providence still," Sherlock argued, "and I desire to know why the Providence of an entail [i.e., hereditary succession] is more Sacred and Obligatory than any other Act of Providence, which gives a Settled Possession of the throne?" Considerable attention naturally had to be paid to explaining why, if William had gained title to the throne by conquest, Cromwell had remained an illegitimate usurper. A contemporary illustration shows a picture of Cromwell with William's head and satirists played with the equation O. P. (Oliver Protector) = P. O. (Prince of Orange).[18]

As opponents of William were happy to point out, the new king's advocates were themselves resorting to Hobbist arguments. Since Sherlock had at first joined the nonjurors and only took the oaths after the battle of the Boyne and James's flight to Ireland, he was a favorite target. Satirists accused Sherlock of being converted by opportunism and fear and particularly resented his justificatory *Case of Allegiance:*

> For there he has plainly made it appear,
> That strength gives a right; therefore we may swear
> To him in possession, though not the right heir,
>   Which nobody can deny.

> Besides, he has proved the mighty convenience
> Of subjects transferring their faith and allegiance
> To those that can crush 'em all into obedience;
>   Which &.

> So let O. P. or P. O. be King,
> Or anyone else, it is the same thing,
> For only Heaven does that blessing bring.
>   Which &c.[19]

The necessarily anonymous *Examination* (of Dr. Sherlock's *Case*) discovered after much detailed comparing of the texts that "Mr. Hobbes and the Doctor teach . . . the same doctrine about the legal right and possession of sovereignty, and the transferring of allegiance to usurpers." Another anonymous pamphlet, *Dr. Sherlock's Case of Allegiance Considered,* observed, "Mr. Hobbes makes power and nothing else give right to dominion. And pray does not the Doctor do the same? I am much mistaken if this be not the design of his whole book."[20]

Once William's government was settled parliament allowed itself to be appalled by the further expression of such theories, theories that on the one hand provided philosophical justification for obeying conquerors and on the other hand left the door open for alarmingly absolutist claims from the conquerors so justified. In January 1693 parliament condemned Charles Blount's *King William and Queen Mary Conquerors* and Bishop Burnet's *Pastoral Letter* to be burned, resolving "that the assertion of king William's and queen Mary's being king and queen by conquest was highly injurious to their majesties, and inconsistent with the principles, on which this Government is founded, and tending to the subversion of the rights of the people."[21]

The question might fairly be asked why the usurpation of power by Cromwell or William III should have had any effects different from the effects of Henry VII's defeat of Richard II on Bosworth field. We are arguing that the changes of dynasties in the late seventeenth century contributed to men's perceiving the universe to be a materialist universe of force and sensation instead of an idealist universe of words, but why should Cromwell's or William's illegitimate succession have had effects any different from those of all the other illegitimate successions in English history? As Stillingfleet pointed out to the nonjurors, Englishmen had frequently shifted allegiance

> or else the whole Nation was perjur'd in most of the Reigns from the Conquest to H[enry] 8, for the two Williams, six at least of the seven Henries, King Stephen, and King John were all Kings *de facto* . . . for they came not in as next Heirs in a lineal Descent. But still Oaths of Allegiance were taken to them; and no such Scruples appear to have been made all that time; nor any charge of Perjury, on those who did what our Law and Constitution required.[22]

But there must have been some differences between the "illegitimate successions" of the seventeenth century and earlier ones or there would have been more charges of perjury and more prominent nonjurors at the accession of those earlier kings. The effects of Cromwell's refusal to declare himself a king have often been remarked; other usurpers clothed their naked power with the mantle of kingship as rapidly as possible, whereas Cromwell refused the sanction the title could help bestow. Any attempt by Cromwell to claim hereditary relationship to earlier dynasties would have been particularly ludicrous. Even Henry VII was at least the great-great-great-grandson of Edward III. Of still greater importance, I think, was the extent to which ordinary people had been brought to have opinions on political and religious questions. There were no pamphlet wars in 1485. Especially during the interregnum, printing and protestantism had combined to help the citizen see himself as an individual creature apart from the state. The soldiers of Cromwell's army debated religion and political ideology; dissenters of all sorts protested any attempts to constrain their beliefs. It did not occur to fifteenth-century parliaments to pass laws imposing loyalty oaths on all male citizens over eighteen. As we have seen though, both interregnum and Restoration governments sought to force declarations of principle from larger and larger classes of citizens.

On the other hand, the gentry and common people loyal to church and king endured eighteen years during which the government in power was not their government. The more faithful they were, the more likely they were to develop "subversive" attitudes and to feel justified in defying the law. Thus, we find one Sir Willoughby Aston, a gentleman of Chester, accused in 1683 of frequenting conventicles and harboring Nonconformist ministers. Aston replied that his neighbors would laugh at such a charge, for the only conventicles he ever attended were those of the Church of England during the war. "When I came to London," he confessed, "I did frequent a sort of conventicle at Exeter House, and another private house in Fleet Street, where Dr. Gunning at the first place and one Wild at the other did use the common prayer. These I did frequent to the hazard of my liberty, if not of my life and estate, and other than those conventicles, for such they were in those times, I never was at any."[23]

Furthermore, ordinarily English usurpers did not suffer counterrevolutions; whatever counterrevolutionaries there were simply faded away. At the Restoration, though, when these seventeenth-century counterrevolutionaries got back into power they indulged themselves in exposing the false premises of their enemies, hardened traditional positions concerning the possibilities of revolt against unjust rulers, and coerced abjurations and sworn consent to nonresistance from large numbers of citizens. Extreme forms of oaths, including abjurations and oaths asking for declarations about other persons, are also not found in earlier periods. As early as the 1640s it was realized that such attempts to bind men's consciences by forcing them to swear to a succession of oaths or to risk their worldly interests was likely to increase cynicism. Pamphleteers complained, "it is an imperious tirannizing over men's consciences, forcing upon them Oath after Oath, Covenant after Covenant, till they have hardened themselves into a senselessness of what is just and right."[24] Later, even as Bishop Gauden argued against the Quaker's refusal to swear, he paused to admire their willingness to take swearing seriously and to pity them because "they were scared from *all Swearing* by the frequent forfeited *Oaths* and repeated *Perjuries* of those Times" in which men were "daily imposing, as any new Partie or Interest prevailed, the *Superfœtations* of new and *illegal Oaths, monstrous Vows, factious Covenants, desperate Engagements,* and *damnable Abjurations.*"[25] Eventually, for many, the oaths themselves lost their power.

II

In the decade immediately following the Restoration, royalist satirists looked back on the evil days of the interregnum to see villainous puritans invariably justifying the most transparent perjuries with jesuitical casuistry and noble cavaliers heroically refusing to take the Solemn League and Covenant. As should be evident from chapter 1, considerable mythmaking ability was needed to create this pleasing contrast.

After 1660, though, it was easier to forget that most of the king's supporters had compromised themselves by taking the Negative Oath and Covenant and otherwise acknowledging the sovereignty of the usurping forces. Sir Robert Howard's very popular comedy *The Committee* (1662) provides a good example of early Restoration romance in which idealized royalists take oaths seriously, reject material considerations for the pursuit of their ideals, and are finally rewarded with both money and women. Two gentlemen, Col. Careless and Col. Blunt, want to retrieve their estates from the Committee of Sequestration, but their principles forbid them to take the Covenant. Told he will have no land unless he swears, Blunt cries, "Then farewel acres, may the dirt choak them."[26] The audience's favorite character in the play was Teague, a simple-minded loyal Irishman whom Careless takes on as a servant. Understanding that his master's happiness is blocked by his unwillingness to "take the covenant," Teague good-naturedly decides to do it for him. When he hears a bookseller crying his wares, "*Mercurius Britannicus, or the Weekly Post; Or, The Solemn League and Covenant*," Teague simply knocks him down, snatches the paper from his hand, and thus has "taken the covenant" for his scrupulous master (p. 84). Obviously the joke was dear to the Restoration audience who would have liked nothing better than to beat up the parliament men who made such hurly-burlies about liberty of conscience and then tried to tyrannize over the consciences of other men. That Teague is so simple as not to understand the difference between the literal and symbolic meaning of "taking the covenant" only adds to the delightfulness of the joke; it mocks the seriousness of the issues and allows the powerful parliamentary side to be quickly defeated by a man who is both powerless and stupid.

The chief enemies of the two cavaliers are Mr. Day, a member of the Sequestration Committee, and Mrs. Day, his loquacious wife. The plot of *The Committee* achieves a certain coherence when it is seen as the Days' attempt at a triple usurpation. First, they are trying to usurp power in the state that Howard thinks legitimately belongs only to the nobility and gentry; they even try to occupy the property of their betters. Second, the Days have "captured" Ruth, the daughter of a dead cavalier and illegitimately exercise the authority of parents over her. She explains:

> 'Tis too long
> To tell you how this rascal being a Trustee,
> Catch'd me and my estate, being the sole Heir unto my
> Father into his gripes; and now for some Years
> Has confirm'd his unjust power by the unlawful
> Power of the Times.
>
> [P. 83]

Third, they want to marry their idiotic son Abel to the beautiful Arbella, a rich heiress of a cavalier who died in the king's service and left his estate under sequestration. This marriage would put Abel in a position of authority over Arbella and Arbella's property, a position Howard again thinks rightly should belong only to someone of her own class. (Marriage was, in fact, used by both sides to get control of property during the interregnum; after General Fairfax had been granted a large share of Buckingham's estate, Buckingham returned to England in 1657 and married Mary Fairfax.)

Although the Days have already usurped paternal authority over Ruth and seem well on the way to securing Abel's authority over Arbella, Ruth and Arbella retain a true cavalier spirit and fall in love with Col. Careless and Col. Blunt when the gentlemen refuse the oaths and defy the authority of the committee. Careless echoes the pamphleteer quoted above when he refuses the Covenant and complains, "This is strange, and differs from your own principle, / To impose on other mens consciences" (pp. 92–93). More prescient about the eventual fate of the interregnum government than most of Howard's audience had been, Careless and Blunt remain loyal to the king:

> C. Car. No, we will not take it [the Covenant]; much good may it do them
>   That have Swallows large enough;
>   'Twill work one day in their stomachs.
> C. Bl. The day may come, when those that suffer for their
>   Consciences and honour may be rewarded.
> Mr. Day. I, I, you make an idol of that honour.
> C. Bl. Our Worships then are different: you make that
>   Your idol which brings you interest:
>   We can obey that which bids us lose it.

[P. 93]

In life, of course, things were more complicated. Though Howard was so dedicated a royalist as to have been knighted on the field as a teenager and later imprisoned, in 1656–57 he was willing to negotiate with Cromwell's government for the renewal of a family grant of the post-fines. It was, also, impossible totally to undo the property arrangements of the interregnum, as Howard well knew since he was a Commissioner for Concealed Lands trying to see what could be done.[27] Nor, in the long run, did Charles possess either the means or the will to reward those who suffered for their consciences as they thought they deserved to be rewarded. Nevertheless, Howard himself had already received substantial tokens of the king's favor and no doubt in 1662 the majority of the audience still felt sympathy enough for the restored monarch to cheer the words of Careless and Blunt.

The resolution of Howard's play naturally shows the Days foiled, Arbella and Ruth in possession of all the property, and about to marry Careless and Blunt. Ruth, whose true name turns out to be Anne Thorowgood, steals the writings belonging to her own estate and those belonging to Arbella's. She also finds papers incriminating Mr. Day in various rogueries and uses them to blackmail him into allowing the cavaliers to have their own estates back on easy terms and without taking the covenant. Arbella and Blunt, Anne and Careless, all adopt a relatively tolerant attitude toward the defeated Days, possess all the contested property, and end by dancing and singing cavalier songs in celebration of their approaching weddings.

One puzzling note, however, is sounded at a temporary impasse between Ruth and Careless. Ruth loves Careless, but is unwilling to be debauched by him. Careless loves Ruth, but makes it a point of honor not to marry a traitor's daughter. Careless proposes that he will marry her on condition that the Days are not really her parents:

> *Ruth.* Will you believe me if I swear?
> *C. Car.* Ay that I will, though I know all the while 'tis not true.
> *Ruth.* I swear then by all that's good,
>   I am not their daughter.
> *C. Car.* Poor kinde perjur'd pretty one, I am beholding
>   To thee; wou'd'st damn thy self for me?
>
> [P. 126]

What could have prompted Howard to invent such a colloquy? Perhaps in part he wanted to strengthen the link between his public plot and the private adventures of the lovers by introducing the theme of swearing into both. Beyond that, though, Careless's statement that he will believe Ruth's oath even though he knows it to be untrue is likely to strike the modern reader as such a flat logical contradiction that it can only be nonsense. However, as will appear more fully later in this chapter, the seventeenth century still attached a kind of magic power to the words of an oath that gave them a force above that of a mere claim to be proven true or false with empirical evidence. Even in courts of law the idea persisted that evidence given under oath must be believed because it was so given. Careless does not seem to understand an oath to be "mere words." It is itself a "real thing," a fact not to be subjected to comparison with physical facts for proof of its validity.

Howard's play remained in the repertory throughout the Restoration, but the real *locus classicus* of Augustan antipuritan, antidissenter satire is *Hudibras*, Samuel Butler's even more popular burlesque. This poem has evoked contradictory readings. Early readers usually assumed that *Hudibras* was a spirited and malicious attack on the puritans; later readers express doubts. Dr. Johnson's view is typical of early interpretations. Distributing praise and blame with his accustomed judiciousness, he admired Butler's "inexhaustible wit," but worried that much of the "humour which transported the last century with merriment is lost to us, who do not know the sour solemnity, the sullen superstition, the gloomy moroseness, and the stubborn scruples of the ancient Puritans."[28]

Modern criticism, however, resists accepting any Augustan satirist as a brilliant and spiteful reactionary. Many critics now choose to avert their eyes from the Dryden who was appalled at the idea of religious toleration or the Swift who advocated whipping beggars from one parish to another, preferring to lift their gazes to a more abstract level where the major Augustans are discovered to be affirming order against chaos. Satires that common readers long supposed to be virulent and funny attacks on some specific person or policy are now discovered to be judicious works rising far above contemporary feuds or politics into the philosophical empyrean.

William Hazlitt, himself a Whig, early decided that *Hudibras* was too entertaining to remain the sole property of Church of England Tories. Butler, he argued, was above ridiculing a particular party, directing himself instead to the foolish "principles, which may belong, as time and occasion serve, to one set of solemn pretenders or another."[29] Hazlitt is quoted approvingly both by Ian

Jack in *Augustan Satire* and by Michael A. Seidel in a recent article, "Patterns of Anarchy and Oppression in Samuel Butler's *Hudibras*."[30] Both also quote from Butler's prose *Characters and Passages from Note-Books*, where Butler is indeed sometimes given to a vision of universal folly rather like La Rochefoucald's. Seidel, for instance, offers the following equitable epigraph from the *Notebooks:* "Men of Different Parties, and Factions are never so good as they make themselves nor so bad as they are rendered by their opposites, therefore they easily deceive those that consider but one thing at once." Such quotations, though, do not determine the meaning of *Hudibras*.

Jack sees hypocrisy generally as the satiric target of *Hudibras* and argues that the poem does not question the values of "Augustan conservatism." Rhetoric itself is not under attack, only "the pedantic affection of rhetoric"; classical epics are not parodied, only the more modern heroic romances and romantic epics like those of Ariosto and Davenant. Seidel does find Butler genuinely hostile toward the "heroic," but otherwise agrees "the extreme royalist partisanship and topical backbiting associated for so long with Butler reflect badly and wrongfully on the nature of his satiric art." According to Seidel, the poem revolves around the extravagances of anarchy at one extreme and oppressive tyranny at the other. Hudibras is at once "a brawling revolutionary" and "a church and state tyrant." The madness of society consists in its tendency either to ignore social sanctions altogether or to invent hopelessly restrictive institutions.

But does this make sense? The "restrictive institutions" and "tyranny" Butler attacks are attacked because they are the creations of the Presbyterians and Independents, not because Butler is opposed to "restrictive institutions" and government control generally. To use words like "oppression" and "tyranny" is to beg the question; anyone is opposed to anything he is willing to call "oppressive" or "tyrannical." The Solemn League and Covenant and the Engagement were oppressive in the same way that the Corporation Act, the Act of Uniformity, and the Test Acts were oppressive. Butler satirized such measures in the interregnum governments and not in Restoration governments because he thought the Presbyterians and Independents were crazy, lower-class fanatics who had absolutely no right to impose their wills on respectable people, not because he was an enlightened person "who felt antipathy towards all forms of social oppression."

In fact, *Hudibras* is crammed full of exactly that "topical backbiting" that Seidel disdains—and very trenchant and funny topical backbiting it is.[31] Like Sir Robert Howard in *The Committee*, Butler lambastes the parliamentary side and chooses to ignore the weaknesses of the cavaliers. His detailed recollections of the casuistry parliament men had employed to deal with oaths is also a major subject of his satire. As Butler tells it, "the cause at first begun / With perjury" went on from one perjury to another.[32] The royalists "who to their Faith . . . [so] firmly cleav'd," barely appear in the poem, but when they do they are treated encomiastically, their noble faithfulness being sharply contrasted with puritan treachery:

> For though out-number'd, overthrown,
> And by the Fate of War, Run down:
> Their Duty never was defeated,
> Nor from their Oaths and Faith Retreated:
> *For Loyalty is still the same,*
> *Whether it win or lose the Game:*
> *True as a Dyal to the Sun,*
> *Although it be not shin'd upon.*
>   [3, 2, 169–76]

Most of part 1 of *Hudibras* was probably written during the interregnum; part 1 was published in 1663, part 2 in 1664, and a corrected version of parts 1 and 2 in 1674. John Wilders argues convincingly that most of part 3, published in 1678, was written after the Restoration, some of it as late as 1675. This third part does venture into more general satire aimed at marriage and the law, but it does not abandon the animus against dissenters or attempt an attack on the court faction.

The adventures and debates of Hudibras and his Squire Ralpho as they journey about the countryside are recapitulations in little of the grander adventures of the parliamentary party in the Civil War, and so allow for repeated references to their alleged perjuries. Hudibras's famous attack on bear-baiting in the first canto, for example, is a miniature social reform movement in imitation of the larger reforms in church and state demanded by parliament.[33] For Hudibras the attack on bear-baiting is a necessary continuation of the reforms begun so nobly in 1642. To desist from this attack would be to give up the original cause and to allow unbelievers to consider it simply a temporary outburst of brawling against religion:

> The *Cause*, for which we fought and swore
> So boldly, shall we now give o'er?
> Then because Quarrels still are seen
> With Oaths and Swearing to begin,
> The *Solemn League and Covenant*,
> Will seem a mere *God-dam-me* Rant;
> And we that took it, and have fought,
> As lewd as Drunkards that fall out.
>   [1, 2, 505–12]

Though the reformers swear for their cause more boldly than they fight for it, their solemn vows mean no more than drunken imprecations. Hudibras himself is aware of the accusations the enemies of the cause could make. He knows that the Solemn League and Covenant entailed promising to reform the church according to the best reformed churches, but that there was no agreement on the identity of the best reformed churches:

> They'l say our bus'ness to *reform*
> The Church and State is but a worm;
> For to subscribe, unsight unseen,
> T'an unknown Churches Discipline
> What is it else, but before-hand
> T'ingage, and after understand?
> For when we swore to carry on
> The present *Reformation*,
> According to the Purest mode
> Of Churches, best Reform'd abroad,
> What did we else but make a vow
> To do we know not what, nor how?
>   [1, 2, 635–46]

He knows about the canon oath of 1640:

> And is indeed the self-same case
> With theirs that swore *Et cæteras*.
>   [1, 2, 649–50]

And he knows and confesses how many devious devices were used
to ease men's consciences into breaking oaths they had formerly
sworn, about some dissenting ministers who absolved their
followers of the oaths of allegiance and supremacy, and about
others who argued that the holy spirit would not let them keep
their word.

The action of part 2 is more dramatically concerned with
swearing and forswearing than is the bear-baiting episode.
Hudibras and Ralpho are confined in the stocks when the Widow
says she will strike a bargain with them. She offers to release them
and to marry Hudibras on the sole condition that he bring her "an
Oath, a fair account" of his undergoing a whipping. This whipping
is an intriguing device. It may at first appear puzzling and, indeed,
Dr. Johnson singled it out as the one incident in the poem that
violated "such probability as burlesque requires." It was, he
thought, "so remote from the practice and opinions of the
Hudibrastic time that judgment and imagination are alike of-
fended." Nevertheless, as Wilders notes, the Widow is aware that
itinerant beggars who had wandered out of their native parishes
were whipped, given testimonials of their punishment, and
escorted back to the parishes in which they were born:

> And in their way attended on
> By *Magistrates* of ev'ry Town;
> And all respect, and charges pay'd
> They'r to their ancient *Seats* convey'd.
> [2, 1, 822–25]

As Ruth Nevo perceptively observed, the whipping is also "a hint at
puritan mortifications of the flesh as opposed to Cavalier gallantry
and wickedness . . . and a reminiscence of the mental and
emotional abberations of fanatical flagellants of all creeds."[34]
Finally, since perjury was a misdemeanor during the Restoration,
whipping was also sometimes used as a punishment for perjury.

In stipulating such a punishment the Widow herself is partly
inspired by her familiarity with romance epics, including *Ibrahim*
and *Don Quixote*. During her conversation with Hudibras in the
stocks, the Widow has suggested that the knight could only appear

to be in such a plight if he were under an enchantment. In *Don Quixote* Sancho Panza resorts to a theory of enchantment to save himself from being punished for lying. He does not have to produce the beauteous Dulcinea for his master since he is able to persuade him that an evil spirit makes her seem to be the rather ugly peasant girl they meet on the road. Later, the decadent Duke and Duchess produce a fake Merlin who, administering a certain rough justice, proclaims that Dulcinea can only be freed from the enchantment if Sancho endures 3,300 lashes.

Butler's attitude toward Hudibras is markedly less genial than Cervantes's attitude toward Sancho and Hudibras's perjuries are more repellent than Sancho's lies. Hudibras is supposed to be a justice of the peace, but his activities produce neither justice nor peace. We laugh at Sancho's desire to be made governor of an island and are likely to consider the warning that he would then turn his back on his humble friends appropriate, yet when Sancho does at last actually govern Barataria Cervantes astonishes us with his true humility and Solomonic administration of justice. The Duke, the Duchess, and the inhabitants of Barataria who have been let in on the joke are all foiled when the schemes they devise to expose Sancho's folly lead instead to the revelation of his wisdom. As Johnson noted, however, for the purposes of this episode, Butler forces the squire's part upon his knight. Quixote himself is reasonably brave and has already proved his sincerity in being willing to suffer his self-inflicted "madness" penance in part 1. Butler wants to make Hudibras both cowardly and false. Even Sancho in his unwillingness to give himself the 3,300 lashes retains some sympathy: we know that the penalty has only been proposed by the steward masquerading as Merlin and that, until Quixote promises to trade ducats for lashes, Sancho himself will get nothing for having suffered. Sancho finally solves his problem by going into the woods out of Quixote's sight and inflicting the strokes on trees, all the while screaming in pain to increase the authenticity. This is a cowardly trick, but it pleases Quixote and does as much good as the real thing.

Butler's animus against Hudibras also prompts him to reverse the sex roles in this episode: the gentleman is bewitched, not the

lady, and the lady must decide to rescue him. The Widow confesses
to some reservations about the propriety of this reversal:

> But for a *Lady* no ways *Errant*
> To free a *Knight*, we have no warrant
> In any Authentical *Romance*,
> Or *Classique Author* yet of *France.*
> [2, 1, 784–88]

Hudibras has got himself into the stocks in the first place by suffering defeat at the hand of the warlike Dame Trulla. Like
Spenser's Radigund after she has conquered Artegall, Butler's
dame also insults Hudibras by forcing him to wear her mantle.
Showing considerably more respect for chivalric codes than the
men in the poem, Dame Trulla not only gives Hudibras quarter but
proceeds to defend the knight when her allies threaten him:

> She brandisht o're her head his sword,
> And vow'd they should not break her word.
> [1, 3, 939–40]

At the beginning of the second canto of the second part the freed
Hudibras is about ready to submit to the lashing. Suddenly a
scruple occurs to him and he wonders whether whipping is not so
sinful that he might be justified in forswearing himself. Ralpho
obligingly argues that lashing must indeed be sinful since, as every
one knows, it was practiced not only by the heathen but also by the
more dreadful papists. The squire offers to demonstrate that the
saints are entitled to forswear themselves. Pointing out that the
devil has the power to perjure himself, he inquires whether by
denying themselves this privilege the saints would not sinfully
acknowledge that the devil is more powerful than they. His
opening assertion deliberately announces a radically skeptical
position:

> *Oaths* are but *words*, and *words* but *wind,*
> Too feeble impliments to *bind;*
> And hold with *deeds* proportion, so
> As *shadows* to a *substance* do.
> [2, 2, 107–10]

Nevertheless, Ralpho's appeal to the facts of recent history appears to support his claim. The saints did take and break the oaths of allegiance and supremacy; they did "take and break the Protestation"; they did "take th' *Engagement*, and disclaim it"; and they did swear to preserve the House of Lords and later vote to abolish it. First one oath was enthusiastically taken, then another that flatly contradicted it. Their perjuries were defended with imaginative casuistry:

> Did they not swear at first, to *fight*
> For the KING's *safety*, and his *Right?*
> And after march'd to find him out,
> And charg'd him home with *Horse* and *Foot?*
> And yet still had the confidence,
> To swear, it was in His *defence?*
>
> [2, 2, 159–65]

Even Milton had complained about parliament's failure to pay the debts it had secured with the "public faith," lamenting in his sonnet to Fairfax:

> For what can war but endless war still breed,
> Till truth and right from violence be freed,
> And public faith cleared from the shameful brand
> Of public fraud?

Agreeing that the public faith of the saints has meant nothing, Ralpho concludes that it is therefore absurd for individuals to be bound by private oaths:

> And if that go for nothing, why
> Should *Private faith* have such a tye?
>   *Oaths* were not purpos'd more then *Law*,
> To keep the *Good* and *Just* in awe,
> But to confine the *Bad* and *Sinful*,
> Like Moral Cattle in a *Pinfold*.
>
> [2, 2, 195–200]

Again, oaths are but words, so:

> it is no *perjury*,
> But a mere *Ceremony*, and a breach
> Of nothing, but a form of speech,
> And goes for no more when 'tis took,
> Then mere *saluting* of the *Book*.
>
> [2, 2, 206–10]

The immediate thrust of Butler's satire is at the puritan's slippery way with words; their promises are not to be trusted. He brilliantly mimics the argumentative style of the puritans, sometimes pushing premises just a shade beyond anything that actually occurred to them, and playing logic games as Swift did later in A *Tale of a Tub*. As Hazlitt noticed, "it would be possible to deduce the different forms of syllogism in Aristotle, from the different violations of them or mock-imitations of them in Butler." The most damning admissions are made as minor premises on the way to convenient conclusions. Hudibras is especially fond of arguments that turn on puns; identical words seem to him to show identical cases. We speak of the "court of conscience" so:

> Why should not *Conscience* have *Vacation*
> As well as other Courts 'oth' Nation?
>   [2, 2, 317–18]

We can talk of "broken" laws or of "broken" oaths, so what is true of laws must be true of oaths:

> A broken Oath is, *quatenus Oath*,
> As sound t'all purposes of *Troath*,
> As broken *Laws* are ne're the worse,
> Nay till th' are broken, have no force.
>   [2, 2, 277–80]

In cases like these Butler invites us to laugh at literalism and at the insanity that comes from mistaking words for things.

Yet the irony goes deeper than the attack on puritan casuistry during the war, suggesting that not only the puritan's words but words themselves are shadows. Men did take solemn oaths that turned out to have absolutely no effect on their behavior and they did violate their oaths without apparent consequence. In spite of the handy rationalizations Hudibras and Ralpho use to cloak their perjuries, in practice they never mistake words for things. They understand very clearly that "*Oaths* are but *words*, and *words* but *wind*" and guide their behavior by this understanding. The satire finally becomes confused because Butler himself no longer feels that words are any more powerful than wind. In the poem ideals are everywhere exposed as flimsy covers for self-interest. Ideals exist as words, but here words are unreal compared to black puddings, leeks, and broomsticks. Butler asks us to despise Hudibras and Ralpho for ignoring words for things, yet his poem offers a world in which only things seem real. Aristophanes also debunks grand-sounding heroism in favor of the more substantial attractions of food, warmth, and sex. But Aristophanes asks us to laugh at Lamachus and with Dicaeopolis.

When Ralpho finally concludes his ingenious argument, Hudibras, satisfied, surprises the squire by asking him to take the beating in his master's place. Ralpho refuses, the two argue, and then draw upon each other. Before they can engage, they are interrupted by the loud noises of a shouting procession of boys with pots and drums. This turns out to be the skimmington, a noisy procession ridiculing a henpecked husband and his wife. Hudibras quickly redirects his energies into an assault on such a heathenish custom, noting that as the husband and wife ride on a "raw-bon'd steed" so the whore of Babylon rides on a horned beast, and chivalrously adding that since women were the first puritan apostles, "It is an Anti-Christian opera / To scandalize that sex for scolding." Like most of the discourses in the poem, Hudibras's speech in defense of women is cut short by violence. The crowd attacks with smelly rotten eggs, driving off both the knight and his squire. Hudibras ends the canto by hoping the Widow will hear of his chivalry and by deciding to swear falsely that he has suffered his lashing.

One scruple remains to him. Hudibras is loath to pursue his courtship and perjure himself if the outcome is too uncertain:

> For though an *Oath* obliges not,
> When any *thing* is to be got,
> (As thou hast prov'd) yet 'tis *profane*,
> And *sinful*, when men *swear* in *Vain*.
> [2, 3, 101–4]

He therefore decides to seek the advice of Sidrophel, a Rosicrucian astrologer. Prophets, though, as Cassandra said, can tell the past and the present as well as the future. Much to Hudibras's discomfiture, Sidrophel decides to speak of the humiliations the knight has already suffered at Brentford. Hudibras calls him a liar and beats him up. Weak but wily, Sidrophel scares his enemy off by pretending to be dead.

Part 2 continues the satire on Hudibras's general faithlessness and introduces new attacks on the perfidies of lawyers and the perjuries of witnesses. Significantly, the Widow and Hudibras really do agree that trust is only to be placed in material facts (especially money); it is simply that Hudibras's circumstances make him more reluctant to admit it. After the encounter with Sidrophel, he rushes off to swear to the widow that he has suffered the whipping she demanded:

> And if you make a question on't:
> I'll pawn my Soul, that I have don't.
> [3, 1, 201–2]

She immediately doubts that his soul is very good security for his debt, since "few make any account, / Int' what incumbrances they run't" [3, 1, 211–12]. Hudibras retorts:

> For Oaths are th'only *Tests*, and *Seals*,
> Of *Right*, and *Wrong*, and *True*, and *False*,
> And there's no other way to try
> The Doubts of Law, and Justice by.
> [3, 1, 231–34]

In so saying, it will be seen, the knight is not very far from the contemporary justices of the King's Bench. This idea that oaths are essential to the determination of right and wrong and even to the very order of society was a common one in the late seventeenth century. John Tombes, for instance, writes in *Sephersheba: or the Oath-Book*, "Controversies cannot be well determined without Oaths, not only because the forme of Lawes and Judicial proceedings do require it, but because also, as men are, there is little security and confidence in many mens Testimony without a Solemn Oath, and if there be no Judicial proceedings there will be no peace nor Government."[35] Butler, however, gives the statement an air of paradox and makes it appear that if indeed oaths are the only way to try the doubts of law and justice, then law and justice must be very unsatisfactory. The world presented in his poem certainly seems to support the Widow's skepticism.

The third part of *Hudibras* was not published until 1678 and, I think, in the first and third cantos leaves behind the specific quarrels of the interregnum to engage in more contemporary Restoration satire on marriage and the law as social institutions. Oaths—whether Hudibras's oaths, the oaths of witnesses, or the oaths of lovers—are again seen as mere words to be exposed as fraudulent by apparently stronger material realities. Marriage, of course, is a relationship created by the taking of vows and dependent upon faithfulness to them. One facet of the attitudes toward marriage expressed in the cynical comedy discussed in chapter 3 was the observation that marriage vows and the oaths of lovers generally were honored more in the breach than in the observance. Skeptical heroes like Dorimant repeatedly proclaim that faithfulness to oaths and vows is unnatural. As he says to Mrs. Loveit when she reproaches him for his perjuries, "Constancy at my years? 'Tis not a virtue in season; you might as well expect the fruit the autumn ripens i' the spring."

After swearing to the Widow, Hudibras proceeds to tell her a wild story in which he alleges that Sidrophel appeared as an evil spirit warning him in a magically loud voice that he must be whipped. The magician, he claims, first turned into a bear and then into a goose which disappeared into a pond. The Widow lets Hudibras spin his absurd story for several hundred lines, then interrupts to say Sidrophel has already given her a true account. Hudibras raises his "affidavit hand" and again swears to his truth, but the Widow now demands ocular proof of his welts. When he refuses, the two engage in a long argument on the nature of marriage. Again, like all long arguments in the poem, this one is ended by violence. The Widow's servants disguised as spirits enter noisily to terrify Hudibras and punish him for his *"horrid Perjuries."* Hudibras confesses and submits to be catechized by the spirits:

> *What makes all Doctrines Plain and Clear?*
> About two hundred Pounds a Year.
> *And that which was prov'd true before,*
> *Prove false again?* Two hundred more.
> *What Makes the Breaking of all Oaths.*
> *A Holy Duty?*—Food, and Cloathes.

[3, 1, 1277–82]

Foiled by the Widow's skepticism and scared by Sidrophel's accusations of robbery, Hudibras decides to sue her for breach of promise of marriage and to bring some sort of action against him. Since Hudibras is only interested in the Widow's money anyway, collecting monetary damages will be as satisfying as marrying her. The law turns out to be a weapon with which the bourgeois knight is considerably more at home than he was with his horse, his sword, and his rusty guns. He goes to seek legal advice and is quite able to discuss not only breach of promise of marriage, but also the possibilities of an action of trover and conversion against Sidrophel, claims of false imprisonment, and the filing of cross bills. At first Hudibras seems a trifle worried at the failure of the facts to support his allegations, but the lawyer quickly reassures him:

> But you may swear at any rate,
> Things not in Nature, *for the State*:
> For in all *Courts of Justice here*
> A Witness is not said *to swear*,
> But *make Oath*, that is, in plain terms,
> *To forge whatever he affirms.*
> [3, 3, 701–6]

The lawyer also explains that there are many skilled false witnesses and artistic forgers to be had cheap. The professional perjurers, called knights of the post, may be found near the Temple and near Lincoln's Inn:

> Where *Vowchers, Forgers, Common-bayl,*
> And *Affidavit-men,* ne'er fayl
> T'expose to Sale, all *sorts of Oaths,*
> According to *their Ears, and Cloaths.*
> Their only *Necessary Tools,*
> Besides the *Gospel,* and *their Souls.*
> [3, 3, 765–70]

The two agree to begin by accusing Sidrophel of magic and Hudibras plies the Widow with love letters to entrap her into an answer that can be used against her or improved by forgery. Though the poem does end with "an Heroical Epistle of Hudibras to his Lady" and "The Ladies Answer to the Knight," the Widow is too crafty for Hudibras and seems to escape him forever. The earlier parts of Butler's poem focus their satiric attack on the hypocrisy and perjury of the sectaries during the interregnum; the later parts show perjury infecting so fundamental a social institution as the law.

III

Lawyers, the law, and the rhetoric of special pleading are, of course, eminently traditional satiric targets. In *The Clouds* Strepsiades listens to the agon between Right Logic and Wrong Logic and decides to send his son Pheidippides to Socrates' think-shop to learn to argue his creditors out of their money. Confidence in his son's rhetoric allows Strepsiades to defy oaths and witnesses, but Pheidippides turns on his father, beating him up and offering irrefutable arguments to justify it. Perjury also was obviously not limited to the seventeenth century. Yet perjury as we now understand it is a special sort of crime, an artificial crime that cannot exist independently of institutionalized justice. Like treason, adultery, or sodomy, it is neither a crime against persons nor a crime against property, but a crime against order. As treason is a subversion of the political order, perjury is a subversion of the legal order. Society protects its critical institutions by declaring criminal behavior that interferes with their operation: bribery of officials, threatening officials, or perjury. Like a number of other crimes against order we are concerned with, certain perjuries were once punished in the ecclesiastical courts and were thought of more as crimes against God's order than as crimes against the order of the state. The ecclesiastical courts in the fifteenth century, for instance, still clung to jurisdiction over actions upon contracts that had been confirmed by oaths or vows. Both the treatment of perjury in the ecclesiastical courts and the use of various oaths in these courts are complicated subjects, certainly poorly understood by the late seventeenth-century commentators I have read and, I think, by modern scholars. Though I agree with Christopher Hill that imposing conflicting loyalty oaths on large numbers of people contributed to increased skepticism toward oaths and also that a loss of confidence in oaths is symptomatic of increased secularization, I think he is mistaken in emphasizing so much the oaths of the ecclesiastical courts as almost cynical devices of social control over the lower classes. A better understanding would come from looking also at what was happening to the understanding of oaths in secular court procedure, as I shall try to do.[36]

Different systems of justice create different sorts of perjury. Twentieth-century American criminal procedure encourages defendant perjury; medieval ecclesiastical courts encouraged it even more.[37] But defendant perjury did not exist in seventeenth-century British felony trials because defendants and their witnesses were not permitted to be sworn. So long as perjuries in criminal trials were primarily produced by lower-class criminals testifying against their associates à la Peachum's gang, society was not likely to be very upset. People even seem able to accustom themselves to routine perjury in civil cases, in modern divorce cases, for instance. The numerous and highly publicized political trials of the Restoration, on the other hand, saw the government using perjured testimony to take the lives of gentlemen. Government anxious to convict people of crimes that frequently had not even been perpetrated had no other recourse. The out-of-court perjuries of puritans and dissenters were early established as satiric targets, but as political trials increased, society became very conscious of witness perjury. Many of the critical cases in forming modern ideas about witness perjury come from the Restoration, and Restoration ideas about witness perjury reveal with peculiar vividness the degree to which the late seventeenth century effected a transition between traditional and modern perceptions, not only perceptions of oaths and evidence, but, ultimately, perceptions of reality.

In primitive societies oaths are felt to have magic power.[38] To swear an oath is to utter a conditional curse: "May my foot rot if I step on your land." There is no question but that the swearer will suffer the stipulated punishment if he violates his promise. Suffering a particular fate may even reveal that one is a perjurer. Among the ancient Greeks, who thought that perjury was punished by being struck by lightning, all those who were killed by lightning were refused proper burial. That a man died by lightning proved he was a perjurer, whether or not he was known to have sworn a particular oath. In theistic cultures the gods may be invoked to enforce oaths, but the words of the oath themselves seem to retain a magic power.

Both classical and Germanic legal traditions have oaths that are quite different from our modern testamentary oaths. Roman civil law had a decisory oath that could be proposed by one party to the other; if taken, such an oath resolved the issue. There was also a suppletory oath that the judge could offer to one party after there had been evidence in his favor; again, if the oath were accepted, it was understood to supply the rest of the defense. In the Germanic tradition, the defendant was invited to take a carefully prescribed oath concerning the disputed facts.[39] He could either purge himself by accepting the oath or suffer the consequences, which, along with the words of the oath, had been stipulated beforehand by the court. The witnesses were not there to testify to facts, but as the defendant's oath helpers. They were often members of his clan and swore that his oath was pure. Perjury in the modern sense did not exist; only one side (the defendant's) was allowed to swear and no counteroaths were permitted. The system understood all oaths to be true. Sometimes a specific number of oath helpers was stipulated and a defendant's oath might "fail" if he could not produce a sufficient number. Sometimes foreigners were allowed to strengthen their oaths by taking them repeatedly—six times in six churches, for instance—in place of the usual number of compurgators. Canon law also had a decisory oath in the form of a *purgatio canonica*. This replaced the ordeals of water and fire in 1215. One reason why benefit of clergy was so sought after by criminal defendants was that the ecclesiastical courts continued to allow defendants to purge themselves with oaths.

The modern oath administered to defendants and witnesses, an oath *de veritate dicenda*, is obviously very different from these decisory oaths. It is nonsense to dispute a decisory oath, but sensible to ask whether a witness who has promised to tell the truth has actually done so. Much confusion arose in the sixteenth and seventeenth centuries because of a failure to understand this distinction. The old impulse was to assert that the law refuses to contemplate the possibility of a false oath, the new to argue that oaths are merely words to support testimony that might or might not correspond to facts. The old view accepted the authority of an oath; the new challenged it and looked for corroboration from facts.

Not surprisingly, the privilege of purging oneself with a decisory oath was relinquished reluctantly. When Lilburne was about to be tried before the Star Chamber he was asked to swear that he would make "a true answer to all things" that were asked him. He called this an unlawful "oath of inquiry" and refused to take it. Instead he offered to take a decisory oath that would "be the end of all controversy."[40] In an action of debt during the reign of William and Mary a defendant insisted on "waging his law." Counsel for the plaintiff argued that if he swore falsely the court was not bound to accept his oath, but though the court was willing to "admonish" the defendant, Chief Justice Holt opined, "if he will stand by his law, we cannot hinder it, seeing it is a method the law allows." The man then swore he did not owe the money and was supported by compurgators.[41]

The fundamental conflict between decisory oaths and oaths *de veritate dicenda* was manifest in the debate over the status of perjury at common law. As Sir James Stephen has pointed out, "the conclusion that all perjury in a judicial proceeding is a crime" was arrived at by very "slow degrees" (3:247). One reason for this was the law's reluctance to contemplate the possibility of false oaths. Sixteenth-century lawyers did not consider witness perjury a common-law crime; they knew only of jury attaint as a way of correcting verdicts. In sixteenth- and seventeenth-century felony trials, judge, jury, and prosecution witnesses were all under oath, but the defendant and his witnesses were not. A statute of Henry VII complains that "perjury is much and customarily used within the City of *London*," but the statute obviously means jury perjury and sets about establishing remedies such as property qualifications for jurors to make them less susceptible to bribery.[42] A later statute of Henry VII was regarded as having given the Star Chamber authority to punish witness perjury as a misdemeanor— all crimes punished in the Star Chamber were misdemeanors.[43] 5 Eliz. 1, c. 9 (1562) sets a fine of twenty pounds for perjury itself and forty pounds for subornation of perjury, allows the injured party to sue the suborner, and, for those perjurers who cannot afford twenty pounds, sets the notorious penalty of the pillory, "there to have both his ears nailed."[44] Two later Elizabethan cases are said to show reluctance to punish witness perjury. In *Onslowe's Case* the court insisted that before Henry VII there was no remedy for perjury except jury attaint and that the Star Chamber's authority to punish perjury had lapsed in the nineteenth year of Henry's reign.[45] In *Damport* v. *Sympson* the court refused to allow a plaintiff to recover damages from a perjurer whose testimony had cheated him out of three hundred pounds, arguing that "the law intends the oath of every man to be true" and that because of the statute of 5 Eliz. 1, c. 9, he might be subject to being punished twice.[46] The Star Chamber itself supposedly refused to punish perjury in witnesses whose testimony had led to felony convictions and, therefore, executions.[47] The reasons for this seem to have included a lingering sense that oaths were decisory as well as rationalizations that justice would be scandalized and prosecution witnesses discouraged. Witnesses, like oath helpers, were thought of as supporting one "side" or another; a "side" was not supposed to try to impeach its own witnesses. In Titus Oates's perjury trial his counsel argued in arrest of judgment "that a witness sworn in behalf of the king in a process of high-treason, cannot be punished for perjury by the king." The Attorney General replied that "had Mr. Oates been indicted upon the statute, it [the objection] had been something; but at the common law, certainly he may be prosecuted by the king, though he was a witness for the king before."[48]

The modern reader of Restoration trials is likely to be struck by the "unfairness" of allowing prosecution witnesses to be upon oath while defendants and their witnesses remain unsworn. With monotonous regularity the judges summing up point out to juries that prosecution testimony has more weight than testimony for the defense.[49] Oaths are more powerful than affirmations; three oaths more powerful than two. Almost no thought was given to obtaining physical evidence. Trials still have the atmosphere of oath ordeals in which only one side is allowed to swear—except that the privilege of swearing has now been turned over to the prosecution. In 1680 a very old and very deaf Roman Catholic gentleman, Sir Thomas Gascoigne, was tried for high treason. He was accused, among other things, of conspiring to establish the Roman Catholic religion in England and of agreeing to pay money to one Robert Bolron to kill the king. The defense demonstrated the likelihood of malice in the crown witnesses. Nevertheless, Justice Jones told the jury, "I leave it with you upon the credit of the witnesses for the king, who have sworn it upon their oaths, and the others that go upon their words, and not upon their oaths, whether they have taken away the force and strength of the king's evidence, which is as full, express, and positive as can be by two witnesses." (Two witnesses were required to prove treason.) Justice Dolben even agreed that Bolron's testimony was "a very improbable thing to be true," yet he still instructed the jury that papists were treacherous and that "where there are two men that positively tell you anything that lies within their own knowledge, and swear it is true, it is scarce any improbability that should weigh against such evidence."[50] As a substantial helpless old gentleman Sir Thomas received relatively polite treatment from the court and, the evidence verging on the ludicrous, was acquitted by his neighbors. In the treason trial of Thomas Rosewell, a dissenting preacher, it was obvious that either Rosewell was innocent or three women witnesses had conspired to commit perjury. Jeffreys told the jury they must remember that the defendant's statements could only have the force of affirmations, not oaths, otherwise no criminals would ever be convicted: "But . . . the denials of the prisoner at the bar, with all the imprecations that he has made, and all the affirmations that he has offered of what he has formerly done; and all these things of his appealing to the great God of Heaven about his innocency, that I must tell you, of themselves, they are not to weigh with you."[51]

In most of the Popish Plot trials it was obvious that either crown witnesses were perjured or defendants were innocent. Many Roman Catholics went to their deaths on perjured testimony which juries credited. Ironically, after Titus Oates had appeared so often as a crown witness in these trials, he turned up as a defense witness for Stephen College.[52] This entire trial was a swearing contest in which notorious lies were told. College was accused of writing "The Raree Show" and of riding armed to Oxford to foment rebellion and seize the person of the king. At one point the pattern of the swearing contest becomes especially clear. The justices warn College that he his not proving his case and College complains that he could only prove a particular point with the testimony of one of the witnesses he contends is perjured:

> *Justice Jones.* Would you have the jury to believe you upon your word?
> *College.* There is no more than his oath against me; and why my oath, being an Englishman and a protestant, should not be taken as well as his that is an Irishman, and hath been a papist, I know not.
> *L. C. J.* You go upon the ground that your word is to be taken . . . but I must tell you . . . no justice against malefactors were to be had if the word of him that is accused should pass for proof to acquit him.[53]

Dugdale and Bryan Haynes, who had appeared against the papists, now appeared against the protestant joiner. College tried to impeach them. One of his defense witnesses, a cabinetmaker named Henry Hickman, testified that when Haynes came to visit a papist widow who was his tenant, he overheard him say, "God damn me . . . I care not what I swear, nor who I swear against, for it is my trade to get money by swearing."[54] One John Lun testified that Haynes had abused parliament, calling them rogues who refused the king money, "but he would help him to money enough out of the fanatics estates" and "they would damn their souls to the devil before their Catholic cause should sink."[55] Oates himself testified that another crown witness, Turbervile, had first told him he could give no evidence against College, then changed his mind, explaining, "Why, said he, the protestant citizens have deserted us," and, " 'God damn him,' he would not starve." Dugdale was accused of claiming to have been poisoned when he had only got the clap. He swore this was untrue and boasted, "My lord, I say further, if any doctor will come forth, and say he cured me of a clap or any such thing, I will stand guilty of all that is imputed to me." After College was hanged, a doctor did just that, backing his testimony with bills and the testimony of the apothecary. Dugdale was never indicted for perjury.

The judges seemed a little puzzled as to how to deal with the contradictions between the crown witnesses and their old ally Oates, but ended by ignoring the improbability of much of the sworn testimony against College and by reaffirming the weight of sworn testimony and multiple oaths. With a terrible unconscious irony, Serjeant Jeffreys said to the jury, "I must take notice to you, that it is strange to me, that ever you, upon your consciences, should perjure three men, who positively upon their oaths deny any such discourses as Mr. Oates speakes of against them." How could the "bare affirmation" of Oates, he asked, "convict three men, upon whose testimony the lives of so many as have suffered have been taken away, and, as we protestants do believe, justly"?[56] After all, the Solicitor General argued, the testimony of Dugdale and Turbervile had already sent no less a peer than Stafford to his death.

Though, as has been said, the modern reader is apt to feel the Restoration practice of not swearing defendants was quite unfair, it was actually a demand of enlightenment law reformers that defendants not be sworn. From a modern, secular point of view, of course, there is little reason to insist that any testimony be sworn. For example, Beccaria in the eighteenth century objected to the continental practice of administering oaths *de veritate dicenda* to defendants: "there is a palpable contradiction . . . between the laws and the natural sentiments of mankind in the case of *oaths*, which are administered to a criminal to make him speak the truth, when the contrary is his greatest interest."[57] During the period of the French Revolution the Constituent Assembly abolished the required oath for defendants and in England Bentham objected to oaths in *Swear not at all* (1813) and *The Rationale of Judicial Evidence* (1827).

If oaths are decisory and if they have a power beyond mere affirmation, then it does not make sense to allow witnesses to retract testimony given under oath. There were, in fact, Restoration attempts to establish a rule that an attesting witness cannot be allowed to repudiate his attestation. Several cases arose under 19 Car. 2, c. 3, "An act for Prevention of Frauds and Per-juries," a complicated statute dealing with leases and contracts of various kinds and setting a requirement of three witnesses to make a valid will. In *Hudson's Case* two witnesses to a will swore that the testator had not been competent and that their original signatures on the will had been perjuries. Litigants then argued that the will itself was invalid under the three witness rule of the Statute of

Frauds. The court denied their claim, reasoning, "otherwise it would be in any man's power to destroy another's will."[58] The Statute of Frauds itself, on the other hand, shows parliament moving toward a more modern understanding of oaths and evidence because it tries generally to replace parol leases and contracts, that is, those confirmed by verbal promises, with written or documentary leases and contracts.

The two witness rule also shows how slowly the early ideas of trials as oath ordeals was abandoned. Star Chamber proceedings generally demanded two witnesses for proof and the medieval principle *testis unus testis nulus* retained considerable authority. After the Restoration though, according to Pollock and Maitland, "the rule that one witness is sufficient is stated as a positive point of law."[59] Other than exceptions made by particular statutes, the only exceptions to this new rule were treason and perjury. In perjury trials the justification of the rule was that there should be no conviction when there is oath against oath. Perjury trials are unusual in that the defendant has already sworn, although in the earlier trial rather than in the one in which he is a defendant. The two witness rule is not now considered satisfactory even in perjury trials.[60]

Although some Restoration judges were still telling defendants that they could not be sworn because a trial in which there was oath against oath would be absurd, there was, in fact, no English statute that prohibited defendants and defense witnesses from being examined under oath. Hale, with his relatively advanced views, can no longer even understand why such should be the practice: "Regularly the evidence for the prisoner in cases capital is given without oath," he says, adding, "tho the reason thereof is not manifest" (*HPC*, 2, 37, 283). Hale, no longer thinking of oaths as decisory, does not perceive a trial in which there is oath against oath as nonsensical. Instead, he begins to think about cases where oath evidence is contradicted by other evidence and about witness credibility. In discussing rape, for instance, Hale argues that infant rape victims should be allowed to testify, sworn or unsworn: "for the excellency of the trial by jury is that they are triers of the credit of the witnesses as well as the truth of the fact; it is one thing, whether a witness be admissible to be heard, another thing, whether they are to be believed when heard" (*HPC*, 1, 58, 635). He also contemplates the possibility of physical evidence contradicting sworn testimony, as in an account of a trial before him in Suffolk where a man was about to be convicted of raping a young girl until he finally offered to show the jury he was incapable of rape, "for all his bowels seemed fallen down into those parts, that they could scarce discern his privities, the rupture being full as big as the crown of a hat" (*HPC*, 1, 58, 636). Like Hale, William Hawkins can see no good reason why defendants and their witnesses should not be sworn. Unable to reconstruct any rationale, Hawkins simply attributes the practice to hoary custom, "judges being always tender of departing from the settled practice of their predecessors, and generally choosing rather to presume it originally founded on some statute or other good foundation, than to suffer the reasonableness of it to be nicely inquired into."[61] The Treason Bill of 1696, discussed in chapter 2, gave treason defendants the right to testify under oath and to have their witnesses so testify. The bill is thus not only evidence of more modern ideas about sovereignty, but also of more modern ideas about trials, oaths, and evidence. The right there accorded to treason defendants was soon extended to other felony defendants by 1 Anne, c. 9 (1702).

In Anglo-Saxon trials a man whose oath once failed lost the privilege of waging his law for ever after. So long as one thinks of oaths as having absolute power and thinks that testimony given under oath must be believed because it is so given, there also seems to be sense in thinking that a witness who has once committed perjury ought not to be allowed to testify again. If, on the other hand, testimony given under oath is simply affirmation that may inspire various degrees of credence according to the character of the witness, his apparent motives, its conformity to other testimony, and so on, then there is no reason why perjurers should not be allowed to testify. Indeed, to bar them as witnesses may make it impossible for innocent people to defend themselves in court. Modern law allows their testimony. Not surprisingly, though, Restoration jurists found the question of whether perjurers could testify problematic. When the Earl of Castlemaine was being tried for treason the prosecution attempted to swear Thomas Dangerfield as a witness against him. It was objected that although Dangerfield had received a pardon, a man convicted of felony could not testify. Justice Jones of the King's Bench thought a pardon restored a felon "to wage battel, and . . . makes him *'liber et legalis home.'* " A long discussion ensued during which Justice Raymond was sent down to the Court of Common Pleas to learn their opinion. Scroggs, then Lord Chief Justice, allowed Dangerfield to testify but also allowed the defense to introduce evidence of his felonies. Perjury appeared to him a different matter: "if a man stands convict in court for perjury, no pardon can ever make him a witness, and set him upright again."[62] In Titus Oates's perjury trial the attorney general wanted to swear William Smith to give evidence that he had perjured himself at an earlier trial. Jeffreys objected: "I tell you truly, Mr. Attorney, it looks rank and fulsome, if he did forswear himself, why should he ever be a witness again"?[63] The Solicitor General argued that perjurers had always been allowed to testify against those who had suborned them and complained that Smith's testimony would be best evidence against Oates. Jeffreys, who presumably also wanted to see Oates convicted, nevertheless rejected Smith as a witness and insisted, "he that has once forsworn himself, ought not to be a witness after that in any cause whatsoever." Several cases around the turn of the century made a distinction between perjury convictions at common law and perjury convictions upon the statute and generally show the justices' increased willingness to allow perjurers and forgers to testify. Lord Chief Justice Holt in *Rex* v. *Ford* (1700) opined that an irreversible part of the judgment set by the statute was that the perjurer be "infamous and lose the credit of his testimony," but that the king's pardon might restore the credit of a witness convicted at common law.[64] Hale, not surprisingly, disagreed with Holt's position, thinking that the king's pardon could restore any convicted perjurer's ability to testify.

For the sake of discussion, four cultural stages in the understanding of oaths may be distinguished. In the first and most primitive stage, the words of an oath are magic; oaths are decisory and cannot be false. In the second stage, oaths are understood as direct appeals to the gods who will themselves punish any perjury. There is no need for any social penalties for perjury. In the third stage, oaths are still understood as appeals to God and punishable by him, but the state admits the possibility of perjury and imposes its own criminal penalties. Supernatural powers are invoked to sanction oaths, but are not relied upon. In practice, the Restoration was more or less at this state, though elements of earlier thinking survived, particularly in the courts where precedent had special power. Restoration divines stress the essentially religious nature of oath-taking and the inevitability of punishment for perjury. Thomas Comber, for instance, defines an oath as "an Appeal to a Higher Power, to one Greater in Knowledge, who sees if we deceive, and cannot be deceived . . . to One Greater in Power, who can as easily punish as find out Perjury, and cast the Perjur'd wretch into Hell Fire."[65] Quoting Plutarch with approbation, he adds, "*Every Oath contains, either expressly or implicitly, a Curse on the Taker, if it be false*" (p. 32). As Comber himself sees when he notes that the Romans did not punish perjurers but left them to the "more terrible vengeance of the *gods*," this third stage is contradictory. If the penalty for perjury is eternal damnation, minor social penalties like twenty pounds or a whipping appear at best trivial and superfluous and at worst blasphemous. "One would imagine," said Comber, "nothing could tempt a Rational Man" to perjury, "if the too frequent and sad Experience of *Opposite*, yea of *Contradictory Oaths* (in this Impious Age of ours) did not convince us, that nothing is too monstrous or unreasonable for an *Ill Man* to do" (p. 39). It is significant that the early witness perjury statutes are the inventions of Tudor parliaments. Protestant parliaments took cognizance of perjury as they began to take cognizance of other crimes previously thought to be the exclusive concern of God and his church courts, bigamy and sodomy, for instance. Changes in the treatment of perjury during the Restoration reveal the slow process of secularization of the culture perhaps more profoundly than the secularization of ideas of sovereignty or marriage discussed in chapters 2 and 3. Such changes, moreover, have special significance for literature, since they reflect changing perceptions of the possible powers of words themselves. In a fourth and final stage in the understanding of oaths, testimony is not given under oath, divine sanctions are not invoked, and verbal evidence is regarded as inferior to written evidence and physical evidence. Oaths are "mere words," less convincing than "facts." This is the stage advocated by secular law reformers like Bentham. The Restoration began to move toward it, though, obviously, even twentieth-century British and American courts have not yet done away with oaths altogether.

In short, the legal history of the Restoration generally shows waning confidence in the decisory power of oaths. The frequently repeated argument that defendants could not be allowed to testify under oath because then no criminals would ever be convicted depends on a contradiction. On the one hand, given the necessary conservatism of the law, the justices cling to the idea that sworn testimony must be believed because it is sworn. On the other hand, as men of some experience in the world, they are aware that criminals are apt to perjure themselves to save their necks. The judges of medieval ecclesiastical courts also knew about human frailty and took pains to warn principals and witnesses of the dangers of perjury, yet for centuries they allowed defendants to exculpate themselves with oaths. The Restoration method of not swearing defendants really did eliminate defendant perjury, but left the justices to severe puzzlement when they were confronted with civil perjury or prosecution witness perjury. They struggled, as we have seen, with questions of what authority there was to punish perjury, of whether improbable or contradicted sworn testimony should be believed, whether witnesses might retract testimony given under oath, whether two witnesses should always be required, and whether convicted perjurers might testify again. These Restoration trials and cases show both the remaining strength of older ideas about oaths and the beginnings of a more modern understanding of sworn testimony as mere verbal evidence the value of which must depend on the character of the witness, agreement with physical evidence, and so on. The important Statute of Frauds also struck at the evidentiary value of oaths, attacking a wide variety of parol leases by forbidding legal action to parties who had only verbal contracts instead of written ones. A man with a parol lease, of course, can defend his claim only with oaths, his own and those of witnesses, if he has any. In this serious attempt to avoid civil swearing contests, parliament demanded documentary evidence as the price of admission to court. Furthermore, one reason for the agitation against the ecclesiastical control over marriage discussed in chapter 3 was that the church recognized verbal spousals as constituting valid marriage. Reformers called attention to the possibilities of perjury after such verbal contracts and demanded written documentation in the form of the marriage registers required by statute in the reign of William and Mary. Lord Hardwicke's Marriage Act finally repudiated the principle that valid marriages could be contracted by words alone.

By the Glorious Revolution, both Whigs and Tories could agree that they had seen an unprecedented series of judicial murders and lesser injustices in political trials. Abuses came from partisan juries ignoring their oaths and intemperate judges as well as from perjured prosecution witnesses. The Popish Plot trials were "balanced" by court prosecutions of the city Whigs for civil crimes and misdemeanors. Thomas Pilkington and Oates, for instance, were fined £1,000 each for *scandalum magnatum* against the Duke of York, a fine that amounted to a sentence of perpetual imprisonment. The Rye House Plot trials that sent Sydney and others to their deaths were followed by the Bloody Assizes where thousands were sentenced to death or transportation. Whig historians vilified the justices appointed by Charles and James, especially Jeffreys and Scroggs; revisionists now try to whitewash them.[66] More sobering are the conclusions drawn by legal historians who have argued that the law was generally applied in these treason trials with little departure from precedent and statute. Miscarriages of justice were created not so much by brutal, unprincipled justices as by the system itself. As A. F. Havinghurst remarks on the College trial, "The point is not that this case offers an outstanding example of judicial narrowness or subservience, but rather that it offers one of the best illustrations of the imperfect understanding of judicial evidence and of the disadvantages under which the accused in the seventeenth century defended themselves."[67] The only alteration I would suggest in this statement is to replace "imperfect understanding" with "older understanding."

Contemporaries expressed both outrage at individuals and unhappiness with the system, which was changed in some important ways during William's reign. The vilified justices themselves professed, I think sincerely, to be shocked at the results of their own justice. In his charge to the jury in Titus Oates's perjury trial, Jeffreys observed, "I confess, I cannot without horror and trembling, reflect upon the many mischiefs and inconveniences we have been run into, if the testimony given this day in the cause against Oates prove true . . . I cannot, I say, but bewail, that so many innocent persons (to the reproach of our nation be it spoken) have suffered death upon this account."[68] Justice Withins at the sentencing lamented that the law did not permit him to hang Oates for killing with "a malicious, premeditated, false oath": "For, if we consider those dreadful effects which have followed upon your perjury, we must conclude our law defective; they are such as no Christian's heart can think of, without bleeding for that innocent blood which was shed by your oath."[69] Twice during William's reign there were bills in the lords to make perjury a felony, though they were defeated. The law of treason, as has been pointed out, was substantially modified to demand narrower definitions of the crime and more rigorous proof. Such reforms not only made wrongful convictions of criminal defendants less likely but also reflected a more modern attitude toward oaths and evidence.

IV

Oaths and vows and perjury itself play important roles in the drama of the last few decades of the seventeenth century, particularly in the political tragedy described in chapter 2 and in the cynical comedy described in chapter 3. The greatest of the political tragedies, *Venice Preserved* and *Lucius Junius Brutus*, both offer sympathetic protagonists who find it impossible to be faithful to sacred oaths they have sworn. Their faithlessness contributes to the disastrous outcomes, but does not necessarily deprive them of the audience's sympathy. The protagonists of cynical comedy are equally guilty of perjury, though of private perjuries in love. For the cynical lovers, oaths and vows lose their power to oblige because they are seen as "mere words" and contrasted—not to documentary evidence or physical evidence as it appears in the law courts—but to physical facts nevertheless. As Doralice sings in *Marriage à la Mode*:

> Why should a foolish marriage vow,
>> Which long ago was made,
> Oblige us to each other now,
>> When passion is decayed? . . .
> But our marriage is dead, when the pleasure is fled:
>> 'Twas pleasure first made it an oath.

[4:261]

Private perjuries are also important in the sort of domestic tragedy exemplified by Southerne's *The Fatal Marriage*. Like the changing understanding of oaths and perjury in Restoration law, the treatment of oaths and perjury in these plays suggests a loss of confidence in the authority of words.

Considerations of oaths and perjury in the drama of the later seventeenth century, however, might best begin with Crowne's *City Politiques* (1682), where the contemporary political references are clearest. Crowne's comedy deals principally with false swearing and the use of law as a political weapon, though it also involves a successful cuckolding plot like many cynical comedies, and, in fact, makes an explicit connection between political perjury and private perjury when Florio remarks, "A lover is a swearer, a private one; he is not a public evidence, a swearer-general."[70] Major conflicts between the City and court are clearly reflected in the play: the contested London elections, the controversy over the City's charter, *ignoramus* juries, Titus Oates, the government's Irish witnesses, and the Protestant Association. *City Politiques* is conventionally regarded as a Tory attack on the defeated City Whigs. Crowne himself, who later wrote prefaces and plays sympathetic to the Glorious Revolution, is accused of being another Restoration Vicar of Bray. Even John Harold Wilson believes that the satire on corrupt lawyers is limited to Whig lawyers. He also praises the play for its "amusing characters in absurd situations" and for its "gay, light-hearted tone."[71] However, though Crowne is certainly attacking the Whigs, it seems to me that *City Politiques* shows a pervasive distaste for the machinations of politicans and lawyers of all persuasions and that it is considerably less cheerful and pleasant than Wilson suggests. Indeed, in giving an account of his own career in the dedication to *The English Friar* (1690), Crowne asserts, quite plausibly, it seems to me, "Nay, in what I wrote for the Court, I spar'd not their tampering with knavish lawyers, magistrates, and Irish evidence" (4:19).

Crowne concentrates on the abuses of oaths that marked contemporary political conflicts. Oates himself, who was not indicted for perjury until 1685, appears as the despicable Doctor Sanchy. The central satiric victim is Paulo Camillo, who at the beginning of the play is elected chief magistrate or Lord Podesta of Naples.

Podesta, as he is usually called, bears some relation to Slingsby Bethel, the Whig sheriff of London Dryden attacked as Shimei, though some of his deeds mirror those of other City Whigs. Like Bethel, Podesta is interested in the rabble-rousing potential of Popish Plots and fond of the casuistry that allows him to justify his lies and general bad faith. Indeed, one line of satire in the play simply applies Butler's attacks on the puritan abuse of logic to the dissenters. Hudibras, it will be remembered, in trying to avoid the beating he has sworn to take, insists that he objects to "vain swearing"—by which he means swearing that does not get him anything. Similarly, Podesta is brought to agree with his more intellectual friend, the Bricklayer (Stephen College, who had been hanged in 1681):

> *Podesta.* . . . What need we lie to no purpose?
>
> *Bricklayer.* By your favor, 'twill be to good purpose; a lie will give it the stamp of our party. Lies are the supporters of our arms and the great seal of our corporation.
>
> *Podesta.* If a lie will do the nation any service, I shall not scruple.
>
> *Bricklayer.* You would ha' no reason, for that lie that does as much good as truth is as good as true; ergo, 'tis true. *Quicquid est idem, est idem* is a rule in logic, but you know no logic.
>
> *Podesta.* But I know a rule in divinity that says you are not to do evil that good may come thereby.
>
> *Bricklayer.* Ay, that good may come, and not come. But the evil that does good is a good evil; but no evil is good; ergo 'tis no evil at all.
>   [Pp. 82–83]

As Wilson has pointed out, Slingsby Bethel himself in *The Present Case of England Stated* argued against "that rule which forbids doing evil that good may come of it." Podesta, who has turned to rabble-rousing in the first place because he has been denied a knighthood, in act 5 immediately offers to betray all his friends when he is invited to court. Bethel and his running mate Henry Cornish as dissenters were both supposed to be barred from office by the Corporation Act, but both decided to accept the sacrament of the Church of England and to accept the Corporation Act and Test Act oaths. Similarly, when Podesta is asked at court if he will take some oaths to qualify to be lord treasurer, he immediately replies, "Nothing, I'll refuse nothing, sir, for such honor as this" (p.

126). The hypocrisy of the dissenters' principles and piety is also underlined by the ease with which Florio and Artall, two debauched courtiers out to do a little cuckolding, are able to counterfeit reformation and be accepted into Podesta's household.

Crowne lavished special attention on the lawyer of the play, Bartoline. In "To the Reader" he compliments himself on having taught Anthony Leigh how to speak the part and on inventing a system to show in print how an old man without teeth could pronounce words: "As, for instance, *th* is pronounced by thrusting the tongue hard to the teeth; therefore that sound they cannot make, but something like it. For that reason you will often find in Bartoline's part instead of a *th* a *y*, and *yat* for *that, yish* for *this, yosh* for *those*; sometimes a *t* is left out, as *houshand* for *thousand, hirchy* for *thirsty*." Bartoline's part, Crowne tells us, was thought by everyone to be "the most divertising in the comedy." Bartoline, it seems to me, is certainly a wonderful grotesque, but a frightening one. Through him the law itself is rendered grotesque.

Like many of the old men Anthony Leigh played (Squire Old-sapp, Limberham, et al.), Bartoline is a desiccated lecher who has married a pretty young girl. His true ruling passion, however, is avarice. He has absolutely no principles or feelings; so he uses his legal talents strictly in the service of whoever will pay him the highest fee. In his second appearance on the stage, we learn that since his brother has offered him only a ten pound retainer in a murder case against him and the woman who wants to prosecute has offered twenty, Bartoline will work for the prosecution. His young wife Lucinda objects that such behavior is against the law of nature. He replies, "Ye law of natchure belongsh cho pchivilians, woman; we common lawyersh yon't shtudgy ye law of natchure, 'tish none of our shtudgy" (pp. 60–61). In the same act, Bartoline first allows himself to be retained by Podesta and his friends to draw up articles against the Viceroy; immediately afterward he takes money from a courtier to help indict the City leaders for "several crimes." In the next act a courtier returns wondering whether a clause in the City charter does not allow Podesta to fortify the City without the Viceroy's permission. Bartoline tells him: "Shir, if yere be shuch a claush, 'twill overthrow yeir charcher; 'twill argue the King was descheived, so his grant will be void. 'Tish against ye peyogative, ash I'll prove outch common law, and clea shatchute law" (p. 86). No sooner does the gentleman leave, than Podesta and the Bricklayer enter to receive precisely contradictory advice. They are worried because another lawyer has told them their fortifications were illegal. But Bartoline flatters them, then says, " 'Twash not ye lawyer, 'Twash hish fee, and fees will shay anything," explaining, "Yer'sh no shuch hing ash a clea shtachute. Han't we lawyersh the penning of 'em, and do you hink we won't make work for ourshelvsh? We hate a clea shtachute as a housebreaker yoesch a clea night" (p. 87). The Bricklayer repeats the very argument Bartoline had offered the courtier, but the lawyer now refutes it: "If such a power in your charcher should overthrow it, 'twould argue the King had yesheived you, mun, and who dares shay yat?" (p. 87). Crowne himself says he is attacking the general corruption of lawyers, and though we are certainly not obliged to believe everything Restoration playwrights say in their prefaces, I do not see that this sort of satire is directed strictly at Whig lawyers. Both court and City have recourse to the same law and the same lawyer to maintain their rights. The political world represented in *City Politiques* is infected not only by greedy lawyers who can make the words of charters and laws mean what they will, but also by witnesses for hire who will swear away the lives of men. Justice is ostensibly restored in the final minutes of the play by the appearance of a benevolent governor who tells the tradesmen to cease meddling with government, but it is the possibilities for treachery in political life and the contempt men have for oaths and the meaning of words themselves that Crowne dramatizes.

As we noted in chapter 3, Restoration dramatists were fond of double-plotted plays in spite of theoretical opposition to them. Though *City Politiques* does not have the obvious verse / prose double plot of plays like *Marriage à la Mode*, Crowne does develop both public and private actions. Podesta has a lusty wife, Rosura, and a son Craffy, who has been brought up to be a poet and who, in spite of the fact that he writes answers to Dryden's political poems, is profoundly bored by family politics. Craffy borrows both the fashionable cynicism of the libertines and the tactics of City politics and applies them to his love life. Since the oaths of public men mean so little, he sees no reason why private vows deserve any more confidence: "as for marriage promises, they are but church-mouth-glue, they won't hold a couple together three days" (p. 33). Because Craffy lusts after Rosura, his attractive stepmother, he is tempted not only to ignore her marriage vows but also the prohibitions against incest. "Incest," he declares, is only a word, and marriage vows are only mere words, equally meaningless. "Prithee," he tells Florio,

> don't trouble me with hard names, I don't think it is any more incest to lie with the same woman my father does than to drink in the same glass, or sit in the same pew at church. . . . Not that I think his wife more sacred than his pew, for the locking of a man to a woman in marriage, or in a pew at church, are only a couple of church tricks to get money, one for the priest and t'other for the sexton. [Pp. 21–22]

Since Florio also lusts after Rosura, he thinks to eliminate a rival by threatening Craffy with exposure. Craffy, though, knows how to defend himself and effectively silences Florio by reminding him that he can easily obtain swearers who can convict Florio himself of lying with Rosura. It is clear enough that we are not supposed to think Craffy deserves his stepmother. On the other hand, since he sees the hypocrisy of his father and the Whigs so clearly and is used to satirize them, we do not entirely despise him. He also seems a more fully developed version of the shoemaker in *The Man of Mode*, a lower-class character to be laughed at for affecting the vices and libertine rhetoric of the aristocracy, but one who also makes us think about the merits of libertinism itself. Again, though *City Politiques* is an attack on the Whigs, it does not present the courtiers in a very attractive light either, allowing Florio and Artall to be parodied by Craffy, just as they themselves parody the dissenters.

City Politiques treats the abuses of oaths characteristic of the late seventies and early eighties satirically, but two important political tragedies see broken vows as causes of tragedy: Nathaniel Lee's *Lucius Junius Brutus* (1680) and Thomas Otway's *Venice Preserved* (1682). These tragedies are often supposed to be opposite plays, the Whig view of the Popish Plot versus the Tory view. Nevertheless, it seems to me that even as political plays the two are more alike than they are different. Both ultimately despair of the possibility of preserving personal integrity in the public sphere and both offer sympathetic heroes who repeatedly perjure themselves.

The word *swear* occurs fifty times in *Lucius Junius Brutus*; related words are also frequent (for example, *swore* or *sworn* twenty times, *oath* or *oaths* six times, *vow* or *vows* six times, *forswear* three times). Ritualized swearing produces some of the most vivid scenes in the play. Lucrece stabs herself after being raped by Tarquin; on stage, Brutus pulls the bloody dagger from her corpse so that all the conspirators can kiss it as they swear to avenge her. He uses the same bloody dagger when he forces his son Titus to swear to renounce his new wife Teraminta. After Brutus has driven Tarquin from the city, a priest appears to swear very formally that Tarquin will remain quiet in exchange for his property. Perjuring himself, the priest brings Tarquin's promise sealed with his signet in "sacred tables" and curses himself if he should be forsworn:

> But if I act, or otherwise imagine,
> Think, or design, than what I here have sworn. . . .
> Let me alone be struck, fall, perish, die,
> As now this stone falls from my hand to earth.[72]

The most spectacular scene is the oath-taking ritual of Tarquin's supporters. These conspirators have captured two of their enemies to sacrifice: "The *scene draws, showing the sacrifice: one burning and another crucified; the* Priests *coming forward with goblets in their hands, filled with human* blood" (p. 64). As the victims moan, the conspirators swear and drink wine and blood from the goblets.

Similarly, John Robert Moore long ago pointed to the prominence of oath-taking in *Venice Preserved*, observing, "In addition to frequent references to vows, repeated protestations of loyalty, and a fair proportion of ordinary swearing for the sake of emphasis, no less than nine passages—129 lines in all—are devoted to the formal act of swearing, only one of which is derived from Otway's source."[73] Moore considered much of the swearing served "no apparent purpose in the story" and was interested in it simply as one aspect of the play's allusions to the Popish Plot. *Venice Preserved* also associates a dagger with the ritual of swearing,

though the dagger is stained with blood only at the end of the play.
Jaffeir gives the conspirators his own dagger when he yields
Belvidera as a hostage, vowing, "When I prove unworthy. . . .
Then strike it to her heart" (2:229). Renault threatens her with the
same dagger. Pierre returns the dagger to Jaffeir after he has
betrayed the conspirators, swearing to renounce him forever. In a
long scene Jaffeir then futilely attempts to redeem his pledge by
using the dagger to stab Belvidera. Finally, Jaffeir successfully uses
it to kill both Pierre and himself. Though one cannot be certain, he
also seems to yield it to a bystander urging him to bear it to
Belvidera as a sign of his blessing (2:285, line 475), the same
dagger, "well remember'd" with which he gave "a solemn vow of
dire importance" (2:263).

The sympathetic perjurers in *Lucius Junius Brutus* and *Venice
Preserved* are very similar. Both Titus and Jaffeir were played by
Betterton; Mrs. Elizabeth Barry played both Teraminta and
Belvidera. Titus is quite truthful when he swears concerning the
present or past, but perjures himself when he attempts promisory
oaths. He lurches to and fro like a wreck in the tempests he
imagines:

> like seamen in a storm,
> My reason and my faculties were wracked,
> The mast, the rudder, and the tackling gone;
> My body, like the hull of some lost vessel,
> Beaten and tumbled with my rolling fears.
>
> [P. 65]

First he marries Teraminta and swears never to desert her, then he
swears to Brutus to abandon her and deny her the consummation
of their marriage. That very night he returns to sleep with her.
Titus also swears to Teraminta he will never join Tarquin's friends,
then joins them, then "vows to lay their horrid treasons open" (p.
73). Similarly, Jaffeir vows to join the conspirators against the
Venetian state, then betrays them to the Senate. He pledges that
Belvidera shall be stabbed to death if he is unfaithful, but then fails
to kill her. Titus and Jaffeir both find their devotion to their wives
stronger than any desire to preserve their faith with the conspirators.

William McBurney quarreled with Moore's emphasis on oath-
taking in *Venice Preserved*, noticing instead the verbal eroticism of
the play and finding "a staggering number of passionate embraces
. . . they key symbolic action of the play."[74] We do not, however,
have to elect either the swearing or the sensuality in these plays as
the more significant. The two are related by both Lee and Otway.
Cynical public figures in both plays are as willing as Hudibras to
swear if anything can be got by it. Tarquin and the priest perjure
themselves in *Lucius Junius Brutus*. In *Venice Preserved*, Otway
follows his source in having the senators swear to preserve the lives
of the conspirators in exchange for Jaffeir's revelations. Adding to
Saint Réal, he also has Antonio swear to save Pierre for Aquilina.
In a bizarre parodic inversion of the dagger drawn on Belvidera,
Aquilina draws a dagger on Antonio and vows to plunge it into his
heart unless he swears to save Pierre. He agrees but obviously does
not have the slightest intention of keeping his promise. In the eyes
of worthier characters, on the other hand, oaths themselves are
discredited. Conscious of an opposition between vows and feelings,
they choose feeling.

Sensitive characters in both plays early show reluctance to swear
or to force their loves to swear because they believe their feelings
are more authentic than words. Oaths seem crude, inexpressive
forms quite inadequate to represent the sublime feelings they
experience more directly than any words. In both plays oath-taking
itself is degraded by the nasty, secret rituals associated with the
papists. When Teraminta asks Titus to swear constancy, he swears,
but adds:

> This night, this night shall tell thee how I love thee,
> When words are at a loss, and the mute soul
> Pours out herself in sighs and gasping joys,
> Life grasps the pangs of bliss, and murmuring pleasures.
> Thou shalt confess all language then is vile,
> And yet believe me most without my vowing.
>
> [P. 11]

When Titus tells Teraminta he has "rashly sworn" against his love,
she says she will believe his love, his manner, and his tears rather
than his words:

> Nay, should you swear,
> Swear to me now that you forswore your love,
> I would not credit it.
>
> [P. 41]

Belvidera tells Jaffeir in act 1:

> If Love be Treasure, wee'l be wondrous rich:
> I have so much, my heart will surely break with't;
> Vow's cannot express it.
>
> [2:214]

Jaffeir himself is initially reluctant to express his loyalty to Pierre with an oath:

> When thou would'st bind me, is there need of Oaths?
> (Green-sickness Girls lose Maiden-heads with such Counters)
> For thou art so near my heart, that thou may'st see
> Its bottom, sound its strength, and firmness to thee.
>
> [2:220]

Later, when Jaffeir is about to tell Belvidera of the conspiracy, she offers to swear not to betray him, but he refuses:

> No: do not swear: I would not violate
> Thy tender Nature with so rude a Bond.
> [2:238]

The natures of characters like Titus, Teraminta, Belvidera, and Jaffeir are indeed more adequately expressed in passionate embraces than in ritualistic oath-taking.

Lee and Otway were both beloved in the eighteenth century for very good reason. Titus and Jaffeir are private men of feeling without any serious public ambition. Like Uncle Toby or Harley they communicate most effectively through sighs, embraces, and tears, not reasoned public statements. Part of their goodness is a simplicity like Heartfree's which makes it quite impossible for them to realize beforehand the possibilities of faithlessness and cruelty in others. Brutus remarks on Titus's "sweetness." That they are deceived about their fellow conspirators proves the purity of their hearts, just as later Parson Adams and Squire Allworthy show their goodness by being imposed upon.

Titus, Jaffeir, and other protagonists of the political tragedy described in chapter 2 are not fit for the public world and must be destroyed by it. The public world is the world of history, of change, but these sensitive protagonists recoil from change and, before they are chastened, hope to escape it. Teraminta initially begs Titus:

> Swear that your love shall last like mine forever;
> No turn of state or empire, no misfortune,
> Shall e'er estrange you from me.
>
> [P. 10]

By the end of the second act, though, she has already been forced to adopt an old cavalier attitude, releasing Titus and insisting that his honor must be paramount:

> What, on the shock of empire, on the turn
> Of state, and universal change of things,
> To lie at home and languish for a woman!
> [P. 42]

These perjurers seem sympathetic because the worlds in which they find themselves seem too kaleidoscopic to be fixed in the words of any vow. Titus and Jaffeir swear in good faith, but sudden shakings of the kaleidoscope make what they have sworn to appear to change its nature. Their vows are made under great emotional pressure. Brutus has been assuming a disguise of madness for twenty years; now, abruptly, he decides to drop his disguise and use the rape of Lucrece to organize resistance. Startled and grateful for his father's apparently sudden recovery, Titus allows himself to be forced into swearing. Jaffeir has been evicted from his home by a senator and forced to contemplate the prospect of Belvidera's starving to death. Action takes place under the additional pressure of the Restoration version of unity of time. Intense feeling may be an adequate guide in the private world, but the political world is more complex. Furthermore, as I argued in the second chapter, older legitimist ideals have lost their credibility and there is not yet a newer democratic ideology that succeeds in inspiring political loyalty.

The major difference between *Venice Preserved* and *Lucius Junius Brutus* is obviously the presence of Brutus in Lee's play.

Brutus, of course, finally defends resistance to tyrants in the name of a "freeborn people," yet his demands for Titus's loyalty rely not on an appeal to Titus to fight for his own liberties but on a Filmer-like insistence on a son's sacred obligation to obey his father and a promise that the father can take upon himself any guilt entailed by the son's acts in obedience to his commands (p. 38). Unlike Titus and Jaffeir, Brutus does remain faithful to his vow and kills his sons. In his dedication to Dorset, Lee confides that "nothing ever presented itself to my fancy with that solid pleasure as Brutus did in sacrificing his sons. Before I read Machivel's notes upon the place, I concluded it the greatest action that was ever seen throughout all ages on the greatest occasion."[75] However, Lee also justly compliments himself on writing thought-provoking plays, and it is difficult to manage the simple enthusiasm for Brutus's acts interpretations of the play as Whig propaganda seem to demand, especially when *Lucius Junius Brutus* is compared with democratic romances like *Edward III*, *Timoleon*, or *Tamerlane*. Lee exerts himself to make Titus sympathetic, even bringing a mother and a child on stage to plead for his life. Unlike Octavia's children in *All for Love*, Junius, Titus's little brother, is even allowed to make a speech filled with pathos.

Lee collaborated with Dryden on *Oedipus* (1678) and on *The Duke of Guise* (1682) and, like Dryden, I think, is interested enough in ideas for their own sake to explore both sides, whichever one he finally allows to win. Early in the play Tiberius is allowed to make a monarchist argument contrasting the mercy prerogative affords with the harshness of impersonal law. He seems to have a strong point, that, since he and Titus are later condemned by law, achieves dramatic irony:

> A king is one
> To whom you may complain when you are wronged;
> The throne lies open in your way for justice. . . .
>   O, 'tis dangerous
> To have all actions judged by rigorous law.
> What, to depend on innocence alone,
> Among so many accidents and errors
> That wait on human life?
>   [P. 26]

Though Vinditius and the mob are allowed to catch a courtier who confesses to "seducing the citizen's wives to court," surely the Restoration gentlemen in the audience could not regard Vinditius's comment as the courtier is dragged off to be hanged without ambivalence: "this is law, right, and justice; this is the people's law; and I think that's better than the arbitrary power of kings. Why here was trial, condemnation, and execution without more ado" (p. 30). Generally the rabble who support Brutus do not come off much better than rabble usually do in Dryden.

Brutus's own conduct does not seem to be absolutely above reproach; his final sacrifice of his sons is at best an ambiguous gesture. Publicly he ascribes his return to his senses to a miracle of the gods, an untrue claim made for rhetorical and political effect. With a naïveté like Titus's own, Brutus also tells the rabble they must expel Tarquin's family "without damage to their persons." He promises Teraminta that he will not be cruel, though she naturally understands this to mean that he will not kill Titus. He also promises Titus to take care of Teraminta at the end of act 4, but Teraminta appears wounded at the beginning of act 5, having been whipped and dragged through the streets by the rabble. Though human sacrifice has already been shown to be the loathsome practice of the conspirators, Brutus imagines the sacrifice of his sons is necessary to the future greatness of the state:

> It has been found a famous truth in story,
> Left by the ancient sages to their sons,
> That in the change of empires or of kingdoms,
> Some sudden execution, fierce and great,
> Such as may draw the world to admiration,
> Is necessary to be put in act
> Against the enemies of the present state.
>
> [P. 87]

G. Wilson Knight, one good critic who has praised Lee, looks at the final scene of *Lucius Junius Brutus* and asks: "What then is our conclusion? Simply this: that commonwealths no less than kingdoms may be built on appalling horrors and that there are opportunities for tyranny in both."[76]

Lee and Otway destroy Titus, Teraminta, Jaffeir, and Belvidera, but significantly allow the heroines to die without having been unfaithful to their vows. Aphra Behn and Thomas Southerne go one step further by offering perjured heroines. In their work even private vows prove impossible to keep. The heroic drama abounds in grand villainesses who gleefully perjure themselves, but Behn and Southerne end the century by presenting unfaithful women as victims. Mrs. Behn indulges in some hostile moralizing, but Southerne seems simply to ask for our sympathy for his heroine.

During the Exclusion crisis Aphra Behn took a strongly Tory position, contributing such plays as *The Rover* (Part 1, 1677; Part 2, 1681), *The Roundheads* (1682), and *The City Heiress* (1682). After William's accession she was invited by Gilbert Burnet to write a panegyric to the new king, but refused, presumably out of principle. Several of the novels Mrs. Behn wrote in the interval between the Exclusion crisis and her death in 1689 focus on the issue of faithlessness to vows: *The Fair Jilt; or, the History of Prince Tarquin and Miranda* (1688), *The History of the Nun; or, the Fair Vow Breaker* (1689); and *The Nun; or, the Perjured Beauty* (1698), and *The Unhappy Mistake; or, the Impious Vow Punished* (1700).

Mrs. Behn's treatment of the perjured fair ones in these stories seems to vacillate between exculpation and moralistic con-demnation. The reader is told that love, apparently an irresistible force, makes them act as they do. Yet they are scorned as though they were responsible for their behavior. *The Fair Jilt*, for instance, offers an ambiguous panegyric to love, "the most noble and divine Passion of the Soul . . . to which we justly attribute all the real Satisfactions of Life" but also a passion that in some hearts may reign "like *a Fury from Hell*."[77] Miranda, enjoying the homage of her admirers but not wishing to marry, joins the Beguines, a mild order of nuns who take simple vows for a stipulated number of years instead of vows of perpetual chastity. After she becomes a nun, though, Miranda is afflicted with a serious passion for a handsome and noble friar: "Love, who had hitherto only play'd with her Heart . . . resolv'd, either out of Revenge to those Numbers she had abandon'd, and who had sigh'd so long in vain, or to try what Power he had upon so fickle a Heart, to send an Arrow dipp'd in the most tormenting Flames that rage in Hearts most sensible" (5:78). From this point her character seems to degenerate rapidly: she falsely accuses the friar who is the object of her passion of rape;

calling *The History of the Nun* "a quite remarkable study in the psychology of crime and guilt."[78] Frederick Link, however, rightly complains of some incoherence since, while both "the narrator and Isabella insist that the catastrophe arises as a result of the nun's broken vows," the narrator also claims that passion is irresistible. The moralizing directed at Isabella is thus spurious and imposed.[79]

Southerne borrowed the plot of *The History of the Nun* for his tragedy, *The Fatal Marriage, or the Innocent Adultery* (1694), but he makes numerous changes to redeem the character of Isabella. His earlier plays, including *The Wives Excuse*, discussed in chapter 3, had shown wives who preserved their virtue in spite of temptations. In *The Disappointment* (1684) a jealous husband spies on his wife and falsely accuses her, but she refuses to cuckold him. *The Fatal Marriage* treats Isabella very gently. Although she leaves the convent to elope with her first husband Biron, "they say they had the Churches Forgiveness" (2:110). Southerne uses his considerable skill to heighten the pathos of her position. As John Wendell Dodds pointed out, we first see her being driven away from her father-in-law's house: "Soon her creditors descend like vultures to seize her few remaining household goods, and she is saved from financial ruin only by the intervention of Villeroy, whom she marries more out of kindness and gratitude than love."[80] When the creditors threaten, Isabella's nurse asks what she will do; she replies, "Do ! nothing, no, for I am born to suffer" (1:119). Mrs. Behn has Isabella remain single for three years after the supposed death of her first husband. Southerne prolongs the interval to seven years. Significantly, the Bigamy Act of James I exempted from prosecution not only those who had been granted an ecclesiastical divorce *a mensa et thoro*, as noted in chapter 3, but also those whose first spouses had been absent for seven years, desertion being considered a valid ground of divorce by certain protestants. Most importantly, Southerne completely alters the ending. Mrs. Behn's ending recalls Grimms's fairy tales. The wife strangles her first husband, persuades the second to throw the sack containing the body over a bridge into a river—but tricks him by stitching the sack to his coat so that he throws himself into the river as well. Southerne's Isabella, momentarily insane and raving, draws a dagger on the sleeping Biron, but he wakes and she returns to her senses. Biron is killed instead by his treacherous brother Carlos, who for years has hidden the letters in which Biron begged to be released from foreign slavery. Isabella then relapses into madness and kills herself.

The Fatal Marriage was admired in its original version and in Garrick's version (which cut the comic subplot) and continued to be a popular play throughout the eighteenth century. One theatergoer in 1694 remarked that it "is generally admired for one of the greatest ornaments of the stage, and the most entertaining play has appeared upon it these 7 years."[81] Mrs. Barry, who had earlier created Teraminta and Belvidera, now appeared as Isabella to move this spectator to tears. Later Mrs. Sarah Siddons also regularly brought tears to spectators' eyes as the distressed Isabella. One commented that the enthusiasm she aroused was almost idolatrous: "Everything she did had the look and tone of truth, her laugh as she plunged the dagger into her heart so electrified her audience that they forgot to applaud, and the curtain went down with a profound silence that a couple of seconds later was rent with a fury of voices struggling to express admiration."[82]

The pathos of the maddened Isabella contrasts sharply with the gaiety of Arbella and Ruth in *The Committee*. Literature in the sixties and seventies shows considerable interest in oaths, but does not generally regard oaths themselves as hopelessly problematic. Characters in heroic drama may get into awkward situations because of their regard for the sanctity of vows, but there is usually some convenient *deus ex machina* to extricate them with honor. Thus Almahide in *The Conquest of Granada* has obligations to Boabdelin, but Boabdelin is conveniently killed and Queen Isabella, whom it would be wrong to defy, commands her to accept Almanzor. Even in comedy, characters like Howard's Careless and Blunt are admirable largely because of their scrupulosity. In satire like Butler's *Hudibras* and in satiric comedy one's enemies are lambasted for faithlessness; faithlessness itself is not embraced as the human condition. The plays and fictions of the eighties and nineties, however, reflect a more nominalistic universe in which words have become "mere words" and passion and sensation the most convincing realities. This is the new universe Swift attacks in the third voyage of *Gulliver's Travels* when he has one sect of the projectors, refusing to depend on words and even to utter them, converse by carrying around bundles of things. A similar movement may be observed in the law, especially in attempts to rely less on sworn testimony for evidence and generally in the treatment of perjury in this period. In 1696 parliament even decided to stop insisting that Quakers swear, permitting them instead to give evidence of loyalty or evidence in civil cases by declarations or affirmations rather than by oaths.[83] Perjured protagonists like Titus in *Lucius Junius Brutus*, Jaffeir in *Venice Preserved*, and Isabella in *The Fatal Marriage* ask for our sympathy because vows and words generally have been devalued. Oaths and vows—whether the loyalty oaths like those Englishmen swore to keep to James II, the oaths of political conspirators in life or on the stage, and even private marriage vows—all seemed not only brittle, but irrelevant.

5
THE AUTHORITY OF
NATURE'S LAWS

I

The authority embodied in persons is especially immediate. Every child knows what demands for obedience his father makes; every subject can at least see his king, if, like the cat, he cares to journey to London to look at him. Yet authority is usually supposed to belong not only to persons, but also to relative abstractions like the law, morality, or the law of nature. Indeed, obligations to particular persons are often derived from the authority of these abstractions. The law of nature, for example, is supposed to oblige children to obey and to care for their parents. The law of nature is also supposed to forbid incest, sodomy, and suicide. When in the late seventeenth century obligations to particular persons were questioned, it is not surprising that serious questions should also have been raised about the authority of natural law from which many of these obligations were derived.

Questions about the laws of nature vexed a great many people during the Restoration: what exactly were the laws, how could they be known, on what did their authority depend, could man discover them without supernatural aid? Divines insisted that nature and nature's laws demanded obedience to conventional morality. Libertines experimented with using nature and nature's laws to justify fornication and adultery. Filmer considered that the laws of nature required obedience to the sovereign; Locke believed the law might in some cases justify rebellion. The thought of the Restoration appears fragmented so long as the emphasis is on its content and on the diversity of opinion expressed on various subjects, but even on this difficult subject of natural law we will see some connectedness if we focus not so much on answers as on ways of framing the questions.

The idea of natural law itself contains a paradox that the Restoration was quick to appreciate: nature and law are first understood as opposed to one another. It is, therefore, useful to look briefly at the classical origins of natural law if we want to understand what it came to mean in the late seventeenth century. Some Restoration writers themselves were clear about the Greek roots of their controversies, especially Ralph Cudworth, who in *The True Intellectual System of the Universe* (1671) regarded Hobbes's philosophy as a revival of sophism, Epicureanism, and other Greek atheisms. The effect of the Peloponnisian War on the sophists was, also, perhaps, not unlike the effect of the Civil War on Restoration skeptics and libertines.

Prephilosophic societies have no idea of nature. Robert Boyle, who considered that many seventeenth century uses of the word *nature* were nonsensical, noted with pleasure that Moses had given his account of the creation without mentioning nature: "And I do not remember, that in the Old Testament, I have met with any one Hebrew word that properly signifies *Nature*."[1] In such prephilosophic societies, "the characteristic behavior of any thing or class of things was conceived of as its custom or its way."[2] It is the way of dogs to bark, the way of the sun to rise in the East, the way of men to die, and also the way of men to bury (or burn, or eat, or float out to sea) their dead. The idea of nature begins when a distinction is made between some things, which are natural, and other things, which are not. One immediate consequence of such a distinction is that the things that are not natural become stigmatized as only customs or mere conventions and seem to have less authority than they did before. Thus, *physis* ("nature") and *nomos* ("convention, custom, law") begin as opposites.

In the minds of the sophists, the laws were unnatural, only artificial conventions created by men. *Physis* was a weapon to use against the falseness and hypocrisy of *nomos*. Callicles in Plato's *Gorgias* argues that the laws are made by weak men who want to protect themselves from stronger men. In his opinion, on the

contrary, nature decrees that it is right for the strong to rule over
the weak:

> It is obvious in many cases that this is so, not only in the animal world,
> but in the states and races, collectively, of men—that right has been
> decided to consist in the sway and advantage of the stronger over the
> weaker. For by what manner of right did Xerxes march against Greece,
> or his father against Scythia? . . . Why, surely, these men follow na-
> ture—the nature of right—in acting thus.[3]

A man should let his desires be strong, not curb them as the
morality invented by the impotent suggests. The truth is, "luxury
and licentiousness and liberty, if they have the support of force, are
virtue and happiness, and the rest of these embellishments—the
unnatural covenants of mankind—are all mere stuff and nonsense"
(492C). Callicles actually uses the idea of "the law of nature,"
claiming that the conventionally unjust and immoral strong man
who gratifies his own desires acts according to the law of nature.
This use, of course, apparently the first appearance of the phrase, is
opposed to the usual sense of natural law in later philosophy. In
The Clouds, Aristophanes makes Pheidippides, who is under the
influence of sophists, deprecate nomos to justify beating his father.
Since the maker of the law against sons beating their fathers was
only an ordinary man, why should Pheidippides, another ordinary
man, not make his own law to permit father-beating.[4]

The word nomos, however, could be used not only to stand for
the written laws or the conventional norms current in a particular
place at a particular time, but also for the unwritten laws that had
authority in all places at all times. In the famous passage where
Antigone condemns Creon for his edict forbidding the burial of her
brother, she protests that neither Zeus nor Justice ordained these
human laws. Yet the gods have ordained eternal, unwritten laws
that Creon cannot annul and that she does fear to disobey (lines
450–57). With a bleaker view of what these unwritten laws were,
the Athenians tell the Melians, whom they have defeated and
whom they are about to destroy:

> For of the gods we think according to the common opinion; and of men,
> that for certain by necessity of nature (ὑπὸ φύσεως ἀναγκαίας) they
> will every where reign over such as they be too strong for. Neither did
> we make this law (νόμον), nor are we the first that use it made: but as we

found it, and shall leave it to posterity for ever, so also we use it:
knowing that you likewise, and others that should have the same power
which we have, would do the same.[5]

Many of Socrates' interlocutors attack morality as mere convention and, like Thrasymachus in *The Republic* or Gorgias, offer
instead what they consider more fundamental laws. Socrates, on
the contrary, tried to derive law from man's nature as a sociable
and reasonable being and to show that cynical principles were not
consonant with man's nature. The laws of the just city described in
The Republic are meant to be in perfect harmony with man's
nature. Cicero continued this tradition, arguing that law is
grounded in nature, not mere opinion: "For those creatures who
have received the gift of reason from Nature have also received
right reason, and therefore they have also received the gift of Law,
which is right reason applied to command and prohibition."[6]
Thus, the development of natural law theory is complex and paradoxical because what begins as an opposition between nature and
law ends in a fusion of the two in which law, "properly understood," is discovered to be based in nature, "properly understood."

Natural law theory is vulnerable not only because of this
paradox, but also because of the problem of selectivity that arises
when we are urged to follow nature's laws. At least listened to
casually, nature does not seem univocal, especially on the ethical
questions usually at issue. If we wish to imitate nature, shall we
imitate the lions who care for their young or the fish who devour
theirs? Or, to quote Nathanael Culverwel in *Of the Light of Nature* (1652), "Does the wolf oppress the lamb by a law? . . . That
amorous poet, Ovid, shows that these sensitive creatures, in respect
of lust, are absolute Antinomians."[7] If we put the question this
way, one answer is not more obvious than another. Thus, one
characteristic skeptical strategy was to pick out animal behavior
that defied traditional moral laws for man and to suggest that it
ought to be imitated. When Pheiddipides argues that he ought to be
able to beat his father, he points out that roosters beat their
parents. More generally, libertines could claim that the existence of
an appetite in nature implied that it ought to be gratified.
Rochester, for instance, told Gilbert Burnet that it seemed
unreasonable to suppose natural appetites "were put into a man

only to be restrained, or curbed to such a narrowness: This . . .
applied to the free use of wine and women."[8]

There were, of course, counterarguments. Pheiddipides' father
retorted:

> Look, if you want to imitate the roosters,
> Why don't you go eat shit and sleep on a perch at night?[9]

Burnet replied to Rochester, "if Appetites being Natural was an
argument for indulging them, then the revengeful might as well
alledge it for Murder and the Covetous for stealing." Responding
directly to the problem of selectivity and following the hints of
Plato and Aristotle, Aquinas had seen that the nature of a particular creature might be defined as its characteristic end. Given
such a teleological system, to follow nature became to do whatever
realized that creature's particular excellence. Since the characteristic excellence of a rooster was different from the characteristic
excellence of a man, a rooster's behavior could furnish little
guidance to man. Many Restoration philosophers and divines
simply followed Aquinas, also agreeing that man's characteristic
excellence was reason.

The questions of whether nature had authority for men, and, if
so, what the principles of natural law were had special interest
for the late seventeenth century. Problems associated with the
authority of natural law might seem confined to the narrowest
circles of technical philosophy. After all, most men at most times
simply defer to the customs that happen to be current and do not
reflect upon them. But revolution and civil war encourage thought
on moral issues. Custom offers limited help in determining which
side of a civil war you ought to join, especially when the war is not
even a clear struggle between North and South or East and West.
Custom said you paid your taxes to the king, but what if
parliamentary soldiers were at your door demanding your money
and plate? Custom said you married in church, but what if parliament had created civil marriage?

The scare of antinomianism was severe enough to drive almost
every systematic thinker of the late seventeenth century into trying
to find some way to describe obligation that would cut the ground
out from under people like the Diggers and the Quakers, and even

the Presbyterians. Traditionally, it had not seemed very necessary to argue out the claim that man was obliged to obey God, his creator. The notion that God in creating man, the natural world, and the happiness of heaven had conferred inestimable benefits on man, and was, therefore, entitled to obedience seemed to make sense. The Civil War, however, offered the spectacle of different individuals claiming radically different acts constituted obedience to God and God's law: fighting for the king against parliament; executing the king for treason; declaring the unholiness of property; insisting that God wished his saints to go naked; and so on. Obedience to God had seemed simple enough, but the sectaries made God turn out to be a very slippery concept. God could be invoked and was invoked to authorize virtually any behavior. Obedience to God's word as expressed in Scripture might seem a more satisfactory test, but the same sectaries often combined bibliolatry with their other enthusiasms and managed to convince themselves that their behavior found warrant in Scripture. The Quakers, for example, quoted Scripture to justify their refusal to take judicial oaths. Anyone who was inclined to forget the experience of the Civil War had his memory refreshed by the problems nonconformists continued to cause after the Restoration.

Furthermore, the younger cavaliers who had grown up with a contempt for the authority of the interregnum laws, and many of whom had had some contact with French libertinism, had their own brand of antinomianism.[10] The more pious writers on natural law frequently remark that their arguments are designed to overcome the objections of modern Epicureans, skeptics, libertines, or atheists. Samuel Parker, for instance, prefaced his *Demonstration of the Divine Authority of the Law of Nature* by observing, "we are grown so subtile as to suit our Notions to our Vices, and will not be so rash and unadvised as our dull Forefathers were, to be wicked and not be able to justify it on principle." The vulgar, both the ordinary vulgar and the "unlearned and barbarous" "Men of Title," he claimed, "declare they would not be so wicked as they are, if they thought that they lay under any obligation to be good." Similarly, James Tyrrell in his *Brief Disquisition of the Law of Nature* says he has written for an audience more general than a

Latin treatise might appeal to and that the arguments advanced are "chiefly" designed for people with skeptical and Epicurean principles.[11] Thus, given both the radical protestant forms of antinomianism and the secular Epicurean forms, the temptation to look for some incontrovertible source of obligation, one more immanent than God and easier to make everyone recognize, became nearly irresistible. Natural law seemed an obvious candidate.

During the Restoration the Greek debates over nature and law recurred, though, obviously, in an altered form. Like Callicles, the libertines scorned ordinary morality and were willing to argue that by right of nature strong men might indulge their appetites. Like Callicles, too, Hobbes considered that "by nature" the strong man would gratify himself at the expense of anyone who got in his way. So far, Hobbes's contemporaries were correct to see him as reviving sophistic attitudes. Hobbes, however, unlike Callicles, identified with the weak man who would be conquered and insisted on the undesirability of such a state of nature. Rejecting the traditional view of the state as originating naturally from the family, Hobbes sought to show that the state was an artificial creation of rational men seeking escape from the horrors of nature. The figure of the tyrant who commits "unnatural" crimes fascinated both Greek sophists and Restoration playwrights, raising for each the question of whether these crimes were really so "unnatural" as commonly supposed. In *The Gorgias* Polus tries to argue that Archelaus, usurper of Macedonia, though unjust, is an exceptionally happy man: formerly a slave, he seized the throne, murdered his uncle, his cousin, and his half-brother, and now has the power to indulge his desires. On the Restoration stage still more sensationally criminal hero / villains expressed contempt of slave virtues, achieved power by similarly unnatural murders of their relations and superiors, and then proceeded to gratify their appetites by adultery, rape, incest, and still more murders.

Though the skepticism of a Rochester or a Hobbes may appear modern in the Restoration context, in so far as they saw human nature as originally selfish and hostile to conventional morality, they were in agreement with the older view of man as fallen, a view that was to lose ground steadily during the later seventeenth century. The Cambridge Platonists, on the other hand, followed

Plato in trying to show that morality was grounded in nature, including human nature, and that man's nature "properly understood" was in harmony with conventional morality. A wide range of Restoration writers asked, "Is there a law of nature that binds every man?" In one way or another, people as different as Cudworth, More, Hobbes, Dryden, Locke, and Bishop Samuel Parker all agreed not only that the question was significant, but that there was such a law. Furthermore, though the question can be stated in an abstract and conventional philosophic form, as far as the Restoration was concerned the practical issue behind this question was whether the law of nature bound every man to conventional morality—conventional morality entailing obedience to civil magistrates and parents, faithfulness to oaths and covenants, respect for property, and avoidance of murder, adultery, incest, sodomy, fornication, and suicide.

Of course, questions about the authority of natural law did not appear suddenly in 1660. At the end of the sixteenth century Montaigne had subjected nature, custom, and natural law to provocative examination in various essays, including, "Of Custom," "Of Cannibals," and "Of the Custom of Clothing Oneself." Though "Of Custom" is overtly a tribute to the power of custom over nature and a caution against tampering with tradition, his "facts" gleaned from classical sources and from travelers are difficult to reconcile with the idea that natural law as described by Aristotle is universally observed:

> [There is a Place where] . . . they boil the Bodies of their Dead, and afterwards pound them to a pulp, which they mix with their Wine, and drink it. . . . Priests put out their own Eyes to be better aquainted with their *Daemons*. . . . Where a Man may get his own Mother with Child, and Fathers make use of their own Daughters, or their Sons, without Scandal or Offence. . . . In one Place Men feed upon human Flesh, in another, 'tis reputed a charitable office for a Man to kill his Father at a certain Age.[12]

Montaigne was translated into English by John Florio in 1603 and translated again by Charles Cotton in 1685. Cotton's translation went through several editions, each adorned with a dedication to Halifax and Halifax's response, confessing Montaigne's *Essays* to be "the book in the World I am best entertained with."

French libertines flourished in the earlier seventeenth century, and, of course, some skeptical and libertine questioning of the natural law tradition may also be found in English Jacobean literature. Mordant skeptical paradoxes torment characters in Ford, Marston, and Middleton. Even in Beaumont and Fletcher's *King and No King* (1611), the King Arabaces, one of the ancestors of the Restoration Herculean heroes, burns with what seems to be incestuous love for his sister (who turns out not to be his sister), and so is led to want to overthrow natural law and to lament its hold on man:

> Accursed man,
> Thou bought'st thy reason at too dear a rate,
> For thou hast all thy actions bounded in
> With curious rules when every beast is free:
> What is there that acknowledges a kindred
> But wretched man? Who ever saw the bull
> Fearfully leave the heifer that he lik'd
> Because they had one dam?
>
> [12:235]

Similar sentiments can be found in the poetry of the earlier seventeenth century, in Donne's "Confined Love" or his "Elegie XVII," for example.[13]

Moreover, we can find institutional changes in the late Renaissance that demonstrate earlier attempts to begin to dissociate natural law from theology. Almost from its beginning the protestant Reformation in England slowly made what had been crimes against God, logically punished in the ecclesiastical courts, crimes against the state, now punished in the temporal courts. For example, as early as 1533, within six years of Henry's beginning the dissolution of the monasteries, parliament passed "An act for the punishment of the Vice of Buggery committed with Mankind or Beast," making sodomy a felony without benefit of clergy. The preface to the act laments, "There is not yet sufficient and condign punishment appointed and limited by the due course of the laws of this realm."[14] Since the ecclesiastical courts punished with fines, penances, and excommunication for the unrepentant, parliament may have thought more severe penalties were needed. The Bigamy Act and the Civil Marriage Act discussed in chapter 3 also reflect the same impulse to claim the state's jurisdiction in areas that had previously belonged to the ecclesiastical courts and reflect the same desire to erect a Christian state. Sodomy between "consenting adults," to borrow the modern phrase, is neither an assault against persons nor an interference with property rights. Like treason, adultery, bigamy, and perjury it belongs to our class of crimes against order. If it is a crime, it is initially and logically a crime against God, who has forbidden it in his revealed word. Punishing sodomy as a sin in the ecclesiastical courts made sense. It is harder to understand how "unnatural offences" can be construed as crimes against the state to be punished in temporal courts, though, as we shall see, Restoration jurists addressed themselves to that problem and offered a theory.

Nevertheless, though questions about the authority of natural law did not appear all at once in 1660, and though the dissociation between natural law and theology was not effected suddenly, we can, I think, see both a changed character in the questioning and the development of a new natural law theory. The Jacobean characters who struggle with unnatural impulses do so in an atmosphere of tragedy or at least torment. Giovanni in *'Tis Pity She's a Whore* (pub. 1633) is accorded some sympathy, and his incestuous passion seems to have a certain integrity seen against the corruption of churchmen who declare it a monstrous sin. Still, Giovanni's criminality is apparent and he and Annabella have to be destroyed. The Restoration stage, on the contrary, prefers to remove religious figures like Friar Bonaventura altogether and to replace the tragedy surrounding criminal passion with comedy. Fornication and adultery, as we noticed in chapter 3, are often treated lightly; incest and sexual perversion are apt to become jokes. As Cibber pointed out and as has been increasingly recognized by modern scholars, even the Herculean heroes of Restoration "serious" drama are themselves not without an element of the ludicrous; they are phantasmagoric and exotic figures who from time to time provoke a laugh at the extravagance of their passions and sentiments, certainly not somber human beings like Giovanni.

In this chapter I shall try to show first how the relatively systematic thinkers of the later seventeenth century tried to build new systems on grounds cleared by skepticism of what had come to be regarded as fallacies of the natural law tradition, and how those new systems dissociated natural law from theology; second, how and why Restoration jurisprudence developed a theory to justify the punishment of crimes against God and nature in the secular courts instead of in the ecclesiastical courts, thereby confirming in the structure of contemporary institutions the philosophical dissociation between natural law and theology; and third, how the changes in the treatment of the rake and the Herculean hero on the Restoration stage also show the assimilation of a new idea of natural law.

The philosophical dissociation between natural law and theology was accomplished largely by attacking the crucial question of what created the obligation to obey this law. Some claimed that the obligation was created by God's will. Expressing a Calvinist point of view in *Of the Light of Nature*, Culverwel maintained that, though good acts are good in their own nature and though there is a natural law that can be discovered by reason, natural law obliges because it is commanded by God. Locke, who in his early *Essays on the Law of Nature* seems partially under Culverwel's influence, argues, in part, "no one can oblige or bind us to do anything, unless he has right or power over us," also deriving the authority of natural law from its being God's command.[15] Bishop Parker concurred, "without a Lawgiver there can be no Laws; so that if there be no Deity, or if the Deity that is, have no regard to or knowledge of humane Affairs, he can neither prescribe anything to our Actions, nor abet his Prescriptions with Rewards and Punishments." At this point in his *Demonstration of the Divine Authority of the Law of Nature and the Christian Religion* (1681) Parker was arguing with the atheistical Epicureans, whose philosophy, he thought, must inevitably "take away all natural Obligation to Religion, Justice and Honesty."[16]

Given the existence of God, the claim that his will created obligation seemed fairly sensible. The difficulty with this position, however, especially in the wake of the interregnum experience, was that in practice the will of God turned out to be liable to such inconsistent interpretations. Radical protestantism considers that God may command behavior that appears "wrong" by all the standards of the world, moral or natural law standards as well as legal ones. God's command to Abraham to kill Isaac was a favorite example, and like Kierkegaard more recently, the radical protestants of the seventeenth century were willing to dwell on the paradox of the divinely ordered murder, including, of course, the divinely sanctioned execution of the king. Contemporary Calvinists sometimes argued that it was God's will alone, his arbitrary will, that defined good and evil. The problem, therefore, as the Restoration saw it at first, was to use natural law to prove that conventionally immoral behavior, especially disobedience to the civil magistrate, could never under any circumstances be justified. Concern for the authority of Scripture sometimes modified this to "could never be justified in modern times, no matter what had happened in the age of miracles."

Hobbes, Locke, and the Cambridge Platonists all wished to use natural law to erect barriers against antinomianism. Hobbes, whose opinion of religious fanaticism is perhaps sufficiently well-known, begins the third part of *Leviathan* by pronouncing sardonically, "though God Almighty can speak to a man by dreams, visions, voice, and inspiration; yet he obliges no man to believe he hath so done to him that pretends it; who, being a man, may err, and, which is more, may lie" (3, 32, 244). High on Hobbes's list of false opinions that are apt to cause the dissolution of commonwealths are: *"That every private man is judge of good and evil actions,"* that *"Whatsoever a man does against his conscience, is sin,"* and *"that faith and sanctity, are not to be attained by study and reason, but by supernatural inspiration, or infusion"* (2, 29, 211–12). Locke, who took the trouble to go down from Cambridge to London to witness the examination of James Nayler, devoted a chapter of *An Essay Concerning Humane Understanding* to enthusiasm, remarking:

> Immediate revelation being a much easier way for men to establish their opinions, and regulate their conduct, than the tedious and not always successful labour of strict reasoning, it is no wonder that some have been very apt to pretend to revelation, and to persuade themselves that they are under the peculiar guidance of heaven in their actions and opinions, especially in those of them which they cannot account for by the ordinary methods of knowledge and principles of reason. [4, 19, 5]

With the exception of Culverwel, the Cambridge Platonists were "puritans" sympathetic to independency. Nevertheless, they also strongly disliked the antinomian element of radical protestantism. Whichcote affirmed, "Enthusiasm is the Confounder, both of Reason and Religion: therefore nothing is more necessary to the Interests of *Religion* than the prevention of Enthusiasm." He also warned, "If, under the pretence of *Spirit*, any one produces what is inferior to Sense, Reason, or the improved perfections of man in a natural way; he is certainly deserted of God." As scholars they were disturbed by claims that learning was superfluous for true believers. Cudworth considered it necessary to tell an interregnum parliament that the study of ancient languages in Scripture was worthwhile at the universities. Culverwel lamented, "If you do but make a syllogism, they will straightway cry it down for formal reasoning."[17] They opposed blind reliance on Aristotle and what they considered the excesses of scholasticism, but they also tried to use their learning to recover the truths of Scripture and early Christianity.[18] Even that most mystical of Cambridge Platonists, Henry More, bothered to write *A Brief Discourse of the Nature, Causes, Kind and Cure of Enthusiasm* (1656). From his own experience he describes various political enthusiasts he had met in England. One was a German who thought he was David sent to deliver the Jews, and who "seemed to be a very religious man, and a great hater of Tyranny and Oppression." Another spoke rationally and piously and "seemed to have his wits very well about him"—"nor could I discover the least intimation to the contrary, onely that he had this flaw, that he conceited he was by God appointed to be that fifth Monarch of which there is so much noise in this age." Though More does say there may be "presages in a man's own heart from a supernatural impulse not properly enthusiasm," his account of the causes of enthusiasm strongly resembles Swift's in *A Tale of a Tub*: the spirit of the enthusiast is nothing but flatulency rising into the head to quicken the imagination, "he being as it were drunk with new wine drawn from that Cellar of his own that lives in the lowest region of his Body."[19]

Hobbes chose to extricate his system from the fallacies of the enthusiasts by saying that, in civil society, right is defined by the will of the sovereign—an admirably unambiguous test so long as it is clear who the sovereign is. (He does recognize some obligations in the state of nature, obligations to keep certain covenants, for instance.[20]) Fond of bravura philosophizing, Hobbes was willing to discuss the most awkward cases avoided by others who rejected traditional theories of obligation. Suppose, he allows, your sovereign is not only himself a pagan but commands you to pay obeisance to pagan gods? Surely then it would be right to defy the will of the sovereign, at least by refusing to do the overt act and allowing yourself to become a martyr? Not at all, replies Hobbes, true to his principle that right is determined by the will of the sovereign, "whatsoever a subject . . . is compelled to do in obedience to his sovereign, and doth it not in order to his own mind, but in order to the laws of his country, that action is not his, but his sovereign's" (3, 42, 327). Naaman bowed down to the idol Rimmon to comply with his master's will and was excused by the prophet Elisha; Christians have the same liberty. If it be objected that then according to him all the martyrs have died needlessly, adds Hobbes, advancing his cause by an original definition, only those who were witnesses of the resurrection can be martyrs. (The behavior of the early Christians under the pagan emperors was, in fact, much debated during the Exclusion crisis, Whig writers like Samuel Johnson trying to show that the early Christians defied the commands of Julian, reproached him openly, threatened violence toward him and his pagan priests, and prayed for his destruction.)

Hobbes shared with many Restoration divines the desire for a nonslippery, categorical test of right, though it must be admitted that he was not especially interested in the elements of conventional morality beyond obedience to civil magistrates and faithfulness to covenants. He speaks politely of natural law, but sacrifices the individual positive law obligations traditionally seen within natural law in what he thinks is the interest of the state's stability. Apparently, according to Hobbes's system, the sovereign can make some conventionally immoral and "unnatural" acts obligatory. For example, to take a hypothetical case Hobbes does not consider, if the sovereign should take it into his head to order all male citizens to engage in sodomy, they would be obliged to do so. Indeed, in *Sodom*, the infamous play conventionally if un-convincingly attributed to Rochester, King Bolloxinion does pro-claim, "Buggery we choose and Buggery we allow," thus per-mitting acts conventionally prohibited by natural law—though it must be admitted that the citizens of Sodom seem willing enough to try buggery even in the absence of state coercion. However, when King Bolloxinion abandons Queen Cuntigratia for Fuckadilla, one of the maids of honor, Fuckadilla justifies her adultery as a political obligation: "my duty was to obey my King." Just as Hobbes's sovereign is entitled to require a citizen's presence at services of the Church of England, he seems equally entitled to declare that the state, even, if he likes, the state religion, requires the practice of sodomy. It is true that at some points Hobbes appears to shy away from such a conclusion. Speaking of divine positive law in *Leviathan* he says, "in all things not contrary to the moral law, that is to say, to the law of nature, all subjects are bound to obey that for divine law, which is declared to be so, by the commonwealth" (2, 27, 188). But Hobbes has already articulated his own version of the laws of nature—beginning with "every man, ought to endeavour peace"—and that list does not include prohibitions against sodomy or a large variety of other acts conventionally thought to be prohibited by natural law. At the end of the list he comments that the nineteen laws "dictating peace" are those concerning civil society and adds, "There be other things tending to the destruction of particular men; as drunkenness, and all other parts of intemperance; which may therefore also be reckoned amongst those things which the law of nature hath forbidden" (1, 15, 103). Sodomy, it could certainly be argued, does not fall into the class of acts "tending to the destruction of par-ticular men." In *De Corpore* sovereigns are said to be obliged by the law of nature to forbid certain acts, including "such copulations as are against the law of nature," because they are "prejudicial . . . to the improvement of mankind."[21] It is not clear why such copulations should be against the laws of nature as defined by Hobbes and, since in civil society a subject has yielded his right to the practical interpretation of both positive divine law and Scripture to the sovereign, he has no way of establishing that sodomy is against divine law or Scripture if the sovereign says that it is not. (I say "practical interpretation" because Hobbes does not care what subjects believe as long as they act in accordance with the commands of the sovereign.) Furthermore, if it be argued that a subject will damn himself to eternal death by such an act, and so— given that the sovereign's powers do not extend to commanding suicide—that therefore the command cannot oblige, not only does the subject have no way of knowing that such damnation will occur, but Hobbes also assures him that whatever sin he commits at the sovereign's command will be imputed only to the sovereign and that salvation depends only upon belief and intention, not on acts. Even if the sovereign be under an obligation not to command his subjects to engage in sodomy, the subjects appear to be obliged to engage in it anyway and not to murmur at the sovereign's injustice while they are about it. Tyrrell makes this point in his *Brief Disquisition*, objecting to what he takes to be Hobbes's principles, that "if the Civil Sovereign should make a Law, that every one might knock his Father on the Head, when he came to such an Age, and marry his Mother. . . . All these Wicked Actions will become lawful to be done, nay, every man were obliged to do them (p. 389). No doubt Hobbes considered it unlikely that sovereigns would impose such unconventional whims on subjects; the real issue was their right to impose the particular form of Christianity they fancied. The point is that Hobbes seems indifferent to conventional religious and natural law obligations if there is any prospect of their interfering with the peace of civil society and tries to remove the possibilities of resistance to the sovereign in the name of such obligations.

Dissatisfied with the teleological and utopian character of the natural law tradition, Hobbes thought he could deduce laws more likely to be obeyed. Instead of urging men to live up to their highest potential, to subdue the base promptings of passion, Hobbes "realistically" tried to derive his natural laws from the most powerful passions themselves, and so considered he had increased the probability that they would be obeyed: "the same laws, because they oblige only to a desire . . . are easy to be observed" (1, 15, 104). He abandoned the traditional idea that man is a naturally social animal and offered instead an account of man's artificial creation of civil society. He postulated a social contract, the terms of which oblige every citizen to obey the sovereign. Though men enter into the contract because they seek to escape the miseries of the state of nature, Hobbes considers the obedience they afterwards owe the sovereign is his by right, not simply a matter of expediency.

The Cambridge Platonists were not willing to leave the creation of right to the "arbitrary" will of God; they were even less willing to let it depend upon the arbitrary will of whoever happened to be sovereign. Instead, they argued, right depended upon the nature of things and could be discovered by reason alone, reason unaided by revelation and unaided by positive law promulgated by the civil magistrate. In a way, this was a traditional position. Medieval natural law theory had, after all, also maintained that the general principles of natural law could be discovered by all men who used reason, and also that what was right or good for each creature depended on its own nature and on what God had made its characteristic excellence. The tradition, I think, said simultaneously that good was what it was because God willed it to be so and because of the nature of things, things God had created in a certain way, not caring to make one or the other of these accounts primary; they were simply two aspects of the same fact. In another way, however, the Cambridge Platonists, by shifting their emphasis to the power of man's reason to know natural law, were really creating a new and quite original theory in which God's role seemed to disappear. The distinction between prelapsarian reason and postlapsarian reason also faded. Cudworth, for example, insisted aggressively, "Moral good and evil are what they are, not by will but by nature." Speaking before parliament in 1647, he used language that must have seemed startling: "Now, I say, the very proper Character, and Essential Tincture of God himself, is nothing else but *Goodnesse.* Nay, I may be bold to adde, That God is therefore God, because he is the highest and most perfect Good: and Good is not therefore Good, because God out of an arbitrary will of his, would have it so."[22] Though these statements about the nature of good may at first seem mere semantic games, they had practical ethical consequences. If good is what it is independent of will, you can examine the nature of things and deduce a consistent and certain ethic immune from any possibility of sudden surprises or exceptions produced by special revelations from God or the sovereign.

The Cambridge Platonists' views on natural law are significant as responses to the problems of antinomianism to which their English experiences made them peculiarly sensitive, quite independently of whether their views were original. Nevertheless, it might be objected that any discussion of natural law in the seventeenth century should give more attention to Hugo Grotius, conventionally regarded as the father of modern natural law. Grotius was certainly read in England throughout the seventeenth century, his works were published in England in Latin and in English translations, and his name and works were cited with approbation by a wide range of English writers (and with strenuous disapprobation by a few, including Filmer). Grotius is also conventionally thought to have effected precisely the dissociation between natural law and theology that is a principal theme of this chapter. In the *Prolegomena* to *De Jure Belli ac Pacis* (1625) Grotius seeks to refute skeptical arguments like those of Carneades that "there is no law" and remarks, "What we have been saying would have a degree of validity even if we should concede that which cannot be conceded without the utmost wickedness, that there is no God, or that the affairs of men are of no concern to him." This is the famous *etiasmi daremus* frequently quoted as evidence of Grotius's secularization of natural law. Also sometimes cited is his remark in the opening chapter of *De Jure Belli*, "Now the law of nature is so unalterable, that it cannot be changed even by God himself."[23]

However, recent scholarship has demonstrated that Grotius's *etiasmi daremus* was a neoscholastic commonplace and persuasively argued that Grotius cannot fairly be said to have established natural law on new foundations, though in other ways his contributions remain significant.[24] In *De Jure Belli* Grotius is principally concerned to establish explicit rules of international law and does not feel that a proof of the mere existence of natural law is a serious problem. He offers his argument for the existence of a law of nature briefly—from a later perspective, cursorily—relying on an argument from the consent of the more civilized nations (bk. 1, chap. 1, especially sec. 12). The English writers in whom I am interested, on the other hand, understand proof of the existence of a law of nature to be a problem, worry elaborately about how this law can be known and how it can create obligation, are conscious of skeptical challenges more elaborate than those of Greek sophists like Carneades or Callicles (particularly Hobbes's), are aware that arguments from consent are vulnerable, and, finally, devote more considerable sections of their books to these issues than Grotius does. Though the English writers often cite Grotius as an honored earlier laborer in the vineyards they wish to work, they also often comment explicitly on the weaknesses of his arguments for the existence of natural law and on other aspects of his work with which they must disagree. Culverwel in his *Of the Light of Nature* finds it necessary to discuss "What Nature Is" before he feels prepared to discuss the law of nature and observes at one point, "And so some, and Grotius among the rest, would understand that place of the Apostle, 'Does not even nature itself teach you' . . . of a general custome. But that word, 'nature itself,' does plainly refuse that interpretation; and the learned Salmasius does grant and evince that it cannot be meant of custom there." Culverwel, who was attracted to Grotius's description of the law of nature as a streaming out of light from the candle of the Lord, is prepared to give some weight to consent, but he is more conscious of difficulties with this than Grotius and says explicitly that the obligation to obey the law of nature cannot be derived from consent. The inadequacy of Grotius's arguments for the existence of the law of nature is also commented upon by Samuel Pufendorf in *De Jure Naturae et Gentium* where he devotes a lengthy chapter to establishing the existence of the law of nature. *De Jure Naturae* was first published in 1672, the same year as Richard Cumberland's *De Legibus Naturae*. Both of these works are lengthy and based on elaborate scholarship; they seem clear cases of parallel publication. Pufendorf does not cite Cumberland in the first edition of *De Jure Naturae*, but in later editions he cites Cumberland approvingly to develop further his own argument "On the Law of Nature in General" and also remarks that the law of nature as stated by Cumberland does not differ from his own fundamental law. James Tyrrell, adapting Cumberland's *De Legibus Naturae* for the Latinless reader, praises Grotius's work as "worthy of enduring as long as Vertue and Justice shall be in esteem among Mankind," but laments that his proofs of the existence of a law of nature will only convince those "naturally disposed to Vertue and right Reason," so that Cumberland and he have thought it "more useful, as well as certain, to seek for a firmer and clearer Demonstration thereof, from a strict search and inquisition into the Nature of things, and also of our own selves."[25]

There is perhaps no more powerful testimony to how desperately philosophers in the late seventeenth century wanted to create an objective source of obligation than the multitude of logical difficulties very intelligent people created for themselves with the new theories. Hobbes certainly wanted to create an absolute obligation, but there has been much doubt as to whether he succeeded in doing so. He himself recognizes a difference between his own laws of nature and what are usually called laws, observing at the end of a summary of his laws that they are actually "dictates of reason," improperly called laws: "for they are but conclusions, or theorems concerning what conduceth to the conservation and defence of themselves; whereas law, properly, is the word of him, that by right hath command over others."[26] Yet it is clear that Hobbes wishes these rules to be obligatory, not merely convenient guides for those who happen to desire certain ends. He adds that "if we consider the same theorems, as delivered in the word of God," then they are properly called laws. Later in *Leviathan* he notes that God's commands oblige because God's power is irresistible. (As we saw in discussing parents and children in chapter 3, Hobbes starts from his ideal sovereign / subject relationship and makes other great chain of being relationships analogous to that; here he abandons the idea that God's authority derives from his having created us—he cannot say that the sovereign has created us—and derives divine authority instead from absolute power.) If we try to pursue the connection between the claim that God's commands oblige because his power is irresistible and the claim that the fundamental law of nature is that every man ought "to endeavour peace," the second claim is not derived from the first in an ordinary way. Unlike most seventeenth-century writers on natural law, Hobbes does not begin by demonstrating the existence of God.

Indeed, he does not demonstrate God's existence at all and does not in the first book of *Leviathan* use scriptural proof. *Leviathan* begins with a book "Of Man," and the fundamental law of nature appears to be derived from the analysis of man's nature. Furthermore, when the account of God's commands is finally offered in the later books, it is developed in such a bizarre fashion that the practical impact of those commands is nullified. For example, atheists are said not to be obliged by God's law; each man in the state of nature interprets God's law for himself and all disagree; the natural law only becomes actual law when it is enacted as civil law and the sovereign's command obliges (2, 26, 174); Scripture in civil society has authority only because it is recognized by the sovereign; and so on.

Not without provocation, therefore, Hobbes's contemporaries ignored his grounding of obligation in God's will and focused instead on his more original account of the rights of man in a state of nature and the law of nature that supposedly obliged every man "to endeavour peace" and to preserve himself. Many felt that Hobbes had created only conditional obligations. Probably having Hobbes in mind, Locke in his *Essays on the Law of Nature* complained that law and binding obligation could not be derived from mere right: "For if the source and obligation of all this law is the care and preservation of oneself, virtue would seem to be not so much man's duty as his convenience. . . . The observance of this law would be not so much our duty and obligation, to which we are bound by nature, as a privilege and advantage, to which we are led by expediency" (p. 180). Even if we agree that citizens who allow the sovereign to release them from the miseries of the state of nature are obliged to obey him, suppose some strong men actually enjoy the war of each against each, that some men do not want peace, or even that some men do not wish to survive? How can these men be obliged? Hobbes says that all men desire self-preservation and peace, but does he actually prove that they do? He admits that rebels secede from civil society and revert to a state of nature; he also admits that sovereigns are in a state of nature with respect to each other. Why cannot a subject then rebel against his sovereign, risking death, and seek to regain his natural liberty by becoming a sovereign himself? Hobbes says he cannot because the odds of success are so poor that rebellion is a form of suicide, but again we are thrown back to his claim that all men wish to survive. In *The True Intellectual System of the Universe* (1678) Cudworth offers a form of this objection, arguing that Hobbes's laws are not laws at all, "but only conclusions or theorems, concerning what conduces to the conservation and defence of themselves, upon the principle of fear; that is, indeed, the laws of their own timorous and cowardly complexion, for they, who have courage and generosity in them, according with this hypothesis, would never submit to such sneaking terms of equality and subjection, but venture for dominion; and resolve either to win the saddle or lose the horse."[27]

Hobbes does say in *Leviathan* that "good" and "evil" are merely names for the objects of any man's desire or aversion and that there is no "common rule of good and evil, to be taken from the nature of the objects themselves" (1, 6, 32). He also stipulates that obligation is created when a right is either renounced or transferred; in fact, this seems to be his definition of obligation.[28] He defines justice as the performance of covenant, suggesting that before there are covenants there can be no justice. Statements like these and, more generally, Hobbes's nominalism led his contemporaries to conclude that Hobbes considered not only society but also *good, obligation, justice,* and probably also *law* artificial, not natural and eternal. Since obligation was to be created by the renunciation of rights, it appeared that Hobbes wished to derive obligation from right and the "necessity" for self-preservation. Thus, Cudworth cannot understand how the citizens of Hobbes's state, even those who want to preserve themselves, become categorically obliged to keep the covenants they make. If a man becomes obliged to the civil sovereign by renouncing his natural rights, and if natural justice does not exist, why cannot the man voluntarily undo what he has voluntarily done? Cudworth also accuses Hobbes of saying simultaneously that justice is by natural law and that justice is artificial and not by natural law. He complains, "our atheistic politicians plainly dance around in a circle":

> But though it be true, that if there be natural justice, covenants will oblige; yet, upon the contrary supposition, that there is nothing naturally unjust, this cannot be unjust either. . . . Wherefore, these justice makers are at last necessitated to fly to the laws of nature, and to

pretend this to be a law of nature, that men should stand to their pacts and covenants. Which is plainly to contradict their main fundamental principle, that by nature nothing is unjust or unlawful; and if there be laws of nature, then there must be something naturally unjust and unlawful.[29]

Though Hobbes makes a distinction between rights and duties, he sometimes speaks of self-preservation as a right and sometimes allows it to appear a duty. A right he defines as "liberty to do, or to forbear" and a law of nature as "a precept or general rule, found out by reason, by which a man is forbidden to do that, which is destructive of his life" (1, 14, 84). Self-preservation is said to be an inalienable right (1, 14, 86). But if the right to self-preservation is inalienable, and we have no liberty to forbear preserving our lives, does not the right then become a law? The *ought* of the first law of nature, "every man, ought to endeavour peace," cannot be the same *ought* as the one created by a renunciation or transference of rights; it can only be more than an *ought* conditional on a desire for self-preservation if self-preservation is a duty, not a right. If self-preservation is a right, then Hobbes seems to be saying:

1. There is a natural right to self-preservation.
2. Justice is necessary to self-preservation.
3. Therefore, there is a natural obligation to justice.

This would only make sense as:

1. There is a natural obligation to self-preservation.
2. Justice is necessary to self-preservation.
3. Therefore, there is a natural obligation to justice.

But Hobbes merely announces the obligation to self-preservation, he does not show how it originates, and, given his system, it is hard to see where it could originate.

Furthermore, as Clarendon pointed out, by making the right of self-preservation inalienable, Hobbes destroyed the moral basis of national self-defense.[30] If the sovereign is attacked, the citizen would seem to have the right to flee to any safe place, as Hobbes did during the civil wars. He insists that subjects are not bound to sacrifice their lives, or to hurt themselves, or to go to war unless they voluntarily undertake it (2, 21, 142). But earlier he said that if a man seeks voluntarily to alienate his right to self-preservation, "he is not to be understood as if he meant it" (2, 14, 87). Seeing the practical problem, Hobbes rather feebly adds that when the commonwealth itself is in jeopardy and requires everyone able to bear arms to defend it, then everyone is obliged, "otherwise the institution of the commonwealth . . . was in vain." But he does not explain why the subject should prefer immediate danger of death in battle to the chance of living peaceably under a new sovereign. Elsewhere he claims that the obligation of subjects ceases when the sovereign's power to protect them ceases.

Nor was it only Hobbes who was led into logical difficulties by his intense desire to create categorical obligation independent of the will of God. Just as it is difficult to see in Hobbes's philosophy how we can move from, "In order to preserve yourself you must keep contracts" to "You are obliged to keep contracts," so in the systems of the Cambridge Platonists it is difficult to see how we can move from, "What is good is good by nature, and may be discovered by reason," to "You are obliged to do what is good." Hume called attention to this difficulty, now called the *is-ought* problem, in a classic passage of his *Treatise of Human Nature:*

> In every system of morality which I have hitherto met with, I have always remarked, that the author proceeds for some time in the ordinary way of reasoning, and establishes the being of a God, or makes observations concerning human affairs; when of a sudden I am surprized to find, that instead of the usual copulations of propositions, *is*, and *is not*, I meet with no proposition that is not connected with an *ought* or an *ought not*. This change is imperceptible: but is, however, of the last consequence. For as this *ought* or *ought not*, expresses some new relation or affirmation, 'tis necessary that it should be observ'd and explain'd; and at the same time that a reason should be given, for what seems altogether inconceivable, how this new relation can be a deduction from others, which are entirely different from it.[31]

Twentieth-century philosophers continue to debate both whether it is possible to move from is-statements to ought-statements and whether Hume meant to condemn all such moves or only to complain that earlier philosophers had not made them with sufficient care. It is not necessary to recapitulate this debate here, except to note the persuasive contention of G. E. M. Anscombe that ought-statements themselves create difficulties in modern contexts because they are "survivals, or derivations from survivals, from an earlier conception of ethics which no longer generally survives." She agrees with a number of Restoration divines in claiming that the moral uses of *ought* (for example, "You ought not to commit sodomy") as opposed to the factual uses of *ought* (for example, "You ought not neglect to water the rhubarb or it will die" or "You ought not to break contracts or you will risk your life") depend upon the belief in a divine law and a divine lawgiver. For the concept of moral obligation to survive after the idea of a divine lawgiver has died is "as if the notion of 'criminal' were to remain when criminal law and criminal courts had been abolished and forgotten."[32] Whether one agrees with this contention or not, it is at least clear that the Cambridge Platonists altered the meaning of moral obligation when they forced it to depend upon the nature of things instead of directly on the fulfillment of divinely decreed law.

As much as the Cambridge Platonists berated Hobbes for making justice and right depend upon the will of the sovereign, they shared his desire to remove any justifications for disobedience to the civil magistrate, and this desire also led them into inconsistencies. Cudworth cannot deny that "evil persons may and do sometimes make a pretense of conscience and religion, in order to sedition and rebellion."[33] However, he argues conscience can only be a pretense in these cases, since natural law demands that no commands of the sovereign, lawful or unlawful, may be resisted. He thus lays himself open to the objection that in the case where a sovereign orders a subject to do something not naturally good and perhaps even naturally evil, the will of the sovereign has made the act good, a possibility he strenuously denies in his criticism of Hobbes. As J. A. Passmore says, "if all law-abiding acts are moral, then no other class of acts can be either moral or immoral, because any particular act might come to be commanded or forbidden by law."[34]

Locke, in many ways an heir of the Cambridge Platonists, developed his own natural law theories, theories that laid the foundation for the hedonistic benevolence so widely satisfactory in the eighteenth century. Though he is not usually thought of as a moral philosopher, and though he did not publish a single treatise devoted exclusively to moral philosophy, Locke's interest in such

problems began early, continued throughout his career, and undoubtedly was an important stimulus to his work in epistemology
and political philosophy. As early as 1664 he lectured on natural
law at Christ Church, Oxford; the essence of these lectures is
probably represented in the *Essays on the Law of Nature* which
remained in manuscript until 1954. In 1671 he was at the first Earl
of Shaftesbury's London house involved in discussions centering on
"the principles of morals and revealed religion and on natural law
as the basis of morality."[35] These discussions appear to have raised
so many problems that they helped provoke Locke into exploring
the epistemological questions treated in *An Essay Concerning Humane Understanding* (1689).

Like the Platonists, Locke claimed that reason unaided by
revelation was able to discover the being and goodness of God, the
nature of man, and also the moral obligations of man under
natural law. Yet Locke's willingness to admit that many individuals and even entire societies seem oblivious to the principles
of natural law coupled with his desire to maintain that the law of
nature can be known by reason led him into what seems to me a
paradoxical position. Sounding like Montaigne, both in the *Essays
on the Law of Nature* and in *An Essay* he recites instance after
instance in which the hallowed customs of one people or another
appear direct violations of natural law, sanctioning theft, oppression, lechery, polygamy, and so on: "What," for example, "is
one to believe about duty towards parents, if whole nations have
been met with where grown-up offspring kill their parents . . .
where each is the executioner of his parent and parricide is considered one of the duties of piety?"[36] Even the law of self-
preservation is not everywhere observed. More willing to look at
facts than the deists, he explicitly criticizes Lord Herbert of
Cherbury, arguing not only that Lord Herbert's principles are not
universal, but that not a single moral principle is everywhere
acknowledged (*Essay*, bk. 1, chap. 3, par. 14–19). That there is no
general consent to the law of nature, however, proves to Locke only
that the law is not innate, not that it does not exist. Men who are
ignorant of it have not sufficiently exercised their reason. Since
Locke believed that a law must be knowable before it can oblige, it

is essential to his position that reason be able to discover the precepts of the law of nature. Furthermore, reason also discovers the goodness of God, and it is incredible to him that a good God would torment men for disobedience if he had given them only a reason so dim as to be an *ignis fatuus* leading into error. The paradox emerges when we realize that though the precepts of natural law must be knowable by reason, in fact, not only are there whole societies that commend unnatural crimes, but apparently no one anywhere unassisted by revelation has ever succeeded in compiling an accurate list of the precepts of natural law. As Locke says in *The Reasonableness of Christianity:*

> But natural religion, in its full extent, was nowhere, that I know, taken care of, by the force of natural reason. It would seem, by the little that has hitherto been done in it, that it is too hard a test for unassisted reason to establish morality in all its parts, upon its true foundation, with a clear and convincing light.
>
> 'Tis plain in fact, that human reason unassisted, failed men in its great and proper business of morality. It never from unquestionable principles made out an entire body of the law of nature.[37]

To this natural law theory Locke added a hedonistic element.[38] God, he claimed, had created the universe and man in such a way that obedience to the law of nature produced pleasure and disobedience pain. In the *Essays on the Law of Nature* he says that though it is in every man's self-interest to obey the law of nature, that law cannot be derived from self-interest. Only the command of a superior entitled to obedience can oblige. Aligning himself with the Platonists and distinguishing his position from what he apparently regarded as Hobbes's position, he complains that natural right is powerless to create obligation: "Utility is not the basis of the law or the ground of obligation, but the consequence of obedience to it" (*Essays*, p. 215). Nevertheless, while man's self-interest and appetite do not create obligation to natural law, in Locke's system, they do motivate his obedience to it.[39] Like Hobbes, Locke has so far abandoned utopianism and created an ethic consonant with the satisfaction of the most intense passion experienced by man (though his analysis of the passions differs from

Hobbes's): "Nature, I confess, has put into man a desire for happiness, and an aversion to misery: these indeed are innate practical
principles, which (as practical principles ought) do continue
constantly to operate and influence all our actions without ceasing:
these may be observed in all persons and all ages, steady and
universal; but these are inclinations of the appetite to good, not
impressions of truth on the understanding," that is, not innate
ideas (*Essay*, bk. 1, chap. 3, par. 3). At one point he goes so far as to
declare, "Things then are good or evil, only in reference to pleasure
or pain" (*Essay*, bk. 2, chap. 20, par. 2; and cf. bk. 2, chap. 21, par.
42; bk. 2, chap. 28, par. 5), recalling Hobbes's declaration that
good and evil are only names for the objects of man's desire or
aversion. But this crude hedonism is variously qualified: pleasure
arises from purely mental sensations as well as from those that are
originally physical; we are to consider not only immediate pleasure
but also what procures or preserves another good, or the absence of
another evil; moral good and evil are to be distinguished from
natural good and evil and are fundamentally ideas of relation,
relation between acts and law, though it happens that acts that
conform to natural law also produce pleasure. A further twist is
given to this hedonism by Locke's assertion that all law must entail
rewards and punishments, "not the natural product and consequence of the action itself" (*Essay*, bk. 2, chap. 28, par. 6). The
calculus of pleasure and pain, therefore, becomes very complex,
and Locke nowhere works it out in any detail.

Locke maintains that not only the precepts of natural law but
also the fact that it obliges men may be discovered by reason
without revelation. He further tries to show that obedience only
requires man to gratify his appetite for pleasure. Nevertheless, he
appears quite as dubious at the power of reason and passion to
motivate men to obey the law as he does at the power of reason to
discern the law's precepts. Even when a pagan philosopher did
succeed in discovering some part of natural morality, he was
unlikely to be able to convince others that it obliged them: the
complexities of his reasoning lacked intelligibility or certainty, one
error in his system rendered the rest suspect and robbed the system
of authority, the philosopher himself had no personal authority,
and so on. It is a signal advantage of Christianity, Locke urges, that

it remedies this defect of philosophy by having "one manifestly sent from God, and coming with visible authority from him" announce the content of natural law and "as a king and law-maker" require obedience (*Reasonableness*, p. 139). Only when Christianity had revealed the rewards and punishments of the afterlife (a vision he insists was also available to reason, though reason never properly discovered it) did virtue become "visibly the most enriching purchase, and by much the best bargain. . . . Upon this foundation, and upon this only, morality stands firm, and may defy all competition" (*Reasonableness*, p. 150).

Nevertheless, one is tempted to accuse Locke of suborning religion to support natural morality, especially since—though natural morality seems too feeble to make its way in the world without the support of religion—any peculiar tenets of religion not consonant with reason and natural morality are rejected as superstition. Locke scrupulously refrains from discussing the Abraham and Isaac dilemma, but it seems clear that he refuses to allow the possibility of any clash between natural morality and the will of God. Revelation must be judged by reason and can never be contrary to it. He does quote Paul's praise of Abraham's faith and even cites Genesis 15:6, "He believed in the Lord," when talking about faith. Yet if Abraham had read Locke on the correct relation between reason and revelation and on the dangers of religious enthusiasm, he would have had to reject a revelation purporting to come from a merciful and sane God telling a ninety-nine-year-old man to circumcise himself and promising that his ninety-year-old wife would bear him a son—to say nothing of a revelation telling him to murder that son. Murder, especially the murder of children by their own parents, is elsewhere treated by Locke as clearly against the natural law. We know this by reason more certainly than we know anything by revelation; to commit the murder Abraham would have to act contrary to reason, not simply to accept a revelation above reason. If Abraham had never existed, Locke would have laughed at any enthusiast who declared that such a revelation had been made to him. As it is, the writer in Genesis says that Abraham and Sarah laugh at God's promise, though since the writer avoids psychologizing, we cannot be sure whether this is the laughter of rejoicing or the laughter of amused

Tyrrell repeats Cumberland's rule that the fundamental law of nature is to endeavor the good of the whole system of rational agents (God is considered as part of the system of rational agents) and describes the moral universe so that it seems strongly to resemble the physical universe as described by Newton:

> So that, if we consider the Nature of Mankind, in the whole course of their Lives, it ought to be considered as one entire System of Bodies, consisting of several particular parts; So that nothing almost can be done in Relation to any Man's Life, Family, or Fortune, which doth not some way or other, either benefit or prejudice, those things which are most dear to others also: as the motion of any one Body in the System of the World, Communicates itself to many others. [Pp. 50–51]

Though Tyrrell does in fact abstain from theological dispute and does not invoke scriptural proof texts, like the later eighteenth-century benevolists and like Newton himself, he finds God a necessary hypothesis (or "postulate," as he says). He is still closer to the earlier Cambridge Platonists' emphasis on right reason and to an older sense that right reason and passion are opposite terms than he is to the later benevolists, but he does claim that one reward for obeying the law of nature is "that inward Satisfaction the Soul enjoys . . . that inexpressible Pleasure, called *Peace of Conscience*." The "good-natured" person has not only the single pleasure of helping himself alone, but the multiple pleasures of helping others (p. 128).

The third Earl of Shaftesbury went still further than his mentor Locke in articulating a moral philosophy independent of the will of God and revealed religion. His first published work was a laudatory preface to *Select Sermons of Dr Whichcot* (1698), whom he honors as "The Preacher of Good-nature." Shaftesbury there argues that not only has God created man and the universe in such a way that virtue entails pleasure and vice pain, but that virtue entails pleasure and vice punishment *"in this State"*: "There is *inherent Punishment* belonging to all Vice; and no power can divide or separate them." He accuses both Hobbes and the divines who stress the corruption of man's nature of making war on virtue. In *An Inquiry Concerning Virtue and Merit* (1699) Shaftesbury introduces his doctrine of the moral sense. This sense is a faculty like hearing, pleased by virtue as the sense of hearing is pleased by harmony and pained by vice as the ears are pained by cacophony. Ethical development thus becomes the development of taste, and here we see one good reason why Hume, who also thought there was a moral sense, felt it imperative to show that taste was not arbitrary, that there was a "standard of taste." Shaftesbury also says explicitly that moral ideas like justice and goodness are known *before* the idea of God can be known: "Before . . . a Creature can have any plain or positive Notion one way or the other, concerning the Subject of a *God*, he may be suppos'd to have an Apprehension or Sense of *Right* and *Wrong*, and be possess'd of *Virtue* and *Vice* in different degrees."[41] As Ernest Tuveson pointed out in distinguishing between Shaftesbury and Restoration Latitudinarian divines like Isaac Barrow, in Shaftesbury the need for salvation or special grace disappears.[42]

In keeping with this idea that virtue and vice are known prior to and independently of the idea of God, Shaftesbury's mode of argument in the *Inquiry* is quite unlike that of most earlier seventeenth-century writers on ethics, who depend heavily on Scripture. Even Hobbes proceeds amidst a panoply of biblical quotations in the later books of *Leviathan*, though often his use of them seems a form of black humor. Locke cites Scripture rather sparingly, except when he is actually talking about Christianity, using it occasionally to buttress a point, sometimes forcing the verses into a Procrustean bed he has already created independently of religion, and not infrequently simply refusing to mention conflicts between his claims and traditional interpretations of the Bible. But Shaftesbury conducts his argument in the *Inquiry* without appeal to Scripture. Though he acknowledges that correct ideas about God are supports to virtue, they are not necessary to it; wrong or superstitious religious ideas turn out to be more destructive of virtue than atheism itself. His later writings included in *Characteristicks* (1711) show the impact of the new criticism of the Bible. There biblical verses have quite lost the talismanic quality they have even in Hobbes and Locke; they are no longer abstract sacred sayings that must be treated as givens. Instead, Shaftesbury sees scriptural accounts as imperfect and frequently confused or biased reflections of historical events, transmitted by a process that multiplied whatever initial confusions there were. He laments the cruelties and superstitions of the Jews and treats Judaism in the context of other contemporary early religions. When he speaks of Abraham, he does so in the context of discussing the unfortunate influence of the Egyptian religion on the Jews. Abraham, he notes, had been in Egypt where, according to historians like Herodotus, circumcision was a national rite (*Characteristicks*, 3:52). Primitive religions generally are said to tend toward "the dark part of Superstition," including human sacrifice, and Shaftesbury speculates that "something of this nature might possibly be deduced even from Holy Writ." In a footnote he refers the reader to the stories of Abraham and Isaac and of Jephthah's sacrifice of his only daughter, remarking, "These Places relating to Abraham and Jephthah are cited only with respect to the Notion which these primitive Warriours may be said to have entertain'd concerning this horrid Enormity, so common among the Inhabitants of *the Palestine* and other neighbouring Nations. It appears that the elder of these *Hebrew* Princes was under no extreme Surprize on this trying Revelation" (*Characteristicks*, 3:124). Shaftesbury, who argued extensively that humor had an important place in religious discussion, here anticipates the tones of Voltaire and Hume. Abraham, it would seem, had a defective moral sense.

We have seen some of the difficulties Hobbes, the Cambridge Platonists, and Locke encountered in trying to move in new directions. Shaftesbury, who had the enlightenment's contempt for rationalistic systems, was a much sloppier philosopher than either Hobbes or Locke and his ideas are open to even more numerous objections. He invokes general consent, ignoring Locke's evidence and arguments that there is no such thing. He divides the affections into: (1) the natural and good affections, which predominate, afford the highest delight, and contribute to the well-being of society, (2) the self-affections, also legitimate and natural, but which need to be subordinated to the social, and (3) the "unnatural affections" like delight in torture, moroseness, and "unnatural Lusts," which conduce neither to the happiness of society nor to the happiness of the individual. Even if it be admitted that these "unnatural affections" lead to misery, since their existence is acknowledged and no account of their having been created artificially offered, it is unclear why they should be stigmatized as "unnatural." If natural is defined as "productive of social or individual happiness," then to say that the natural affections produce happiness is merely tautological. Furthermore, Shaftesbury's moral sense is ultimately as subjective as direct revelation. It is as hard to contradict a homosexual who testifies that his moral sense draws him to the beauty and virtue of other men as it is to contradict the religious enthusiast who says God has told him directly that homosexuality is pleasing in His eyes—probably harder, since Scripture cannot be invoked to limit possibilities of what the moral sense may feel. Shaftesbury also has little understanding of the problem of obligation; he begins the second book of his *Inquiry* by promising that he will show "what *Obligation* there is to Vertue; or *what Reason* to embrace it," treating the two phrases as though they were equivalent. Nevertheless, in spite of its logical flaws, the eighteenth century found benevolism more agreeable and convincing than Roman Catholicism or Calvinism.

All these various late seventeenth-century ethical theories strove to disentangle the fundamental principles of morality from revealed religion and to make them immanent rather than transcendent. The stress the Cambridge Platonists put on reason was one step toward freeing the good from dependence upon the will of God or the will of the sovereign. My discussion has emphasized Cudworth because his *True Intellectual System of the Universe* and *Eternal and Immutable Morality* are among the most philosophically sophisticated writings of the Platonists, because his rejoinders to Hobbes are so pointed, and because he was an influence on Locke and Shaftesbury. But Cudworth's ethical concerns were characteristic of the Platonists, and I might almost equally well have discussed More's *Enchiridion Ethicum* (1667), translated by Edward Southwell as *An Account of Virtue* (1690) and apparently the most popular of More's works during the Restoration, or Cumberland's *De Legibus Naturae* (1672). More's treatise identified something roughly analogous to Shaftesbury's moral sense, a boniform faculty able to discern virtue and incline us toward it. Cumberland's *De Legibus Naturae* stresses benevolence and "the common good of the whole system of rational agents" as the end of morality; Passmore considers that it articulates "distinctly a utilitarian criterion of morality" and that it is "an important influence in English ethical speculation."[43] Like the enlightenment sages who followed them, the Cambridge Platonists were able to look to classical antiquity for ideas unencumbered by considerations of Christian doctrine, including early theories of natural law. Unlike some of the eighteenth-century enlightenment sages, however, they exemplified the kind of piety and learning capable of attracting many clergymen to their philosophical attitudes. As Simon Patrick said in his *Brief Account of the New Sect of Latitude-men* (1662), "I shall always think him most conscientious who leads the most unblameable life, though he be not greatly scrupulous about the externals of Religion; and for their lives I think the *Latitude-men* were never taxed by their greatest enemyes."[44] The Platonists were able to inspire Latitudinarian divines like Patrick, George Rust (*A Discourse of Truth*, 1677), and Archbishop Tillotson who gave their rational morality, their emphasis on ethics rather than the nicer points of doctrine, and their arguments for toleration a wider circulation than the writings of the Platonists themselves could have obtained. Though the Platonists were unwilling to press their ideas to their logical political conclusions, Locke did see how to use natural law and the independent existence of justice and good to defend rebellion against an unjust sovereign, and the Latitudinarian divines like Patrick and John Tillotson followed him in this.

Yet a purely rationalistic ethic was bound to be unsatisfactory in an age when ideas were felt to have less and less reality as compared to sense experience. Following the hints of the Platonists and Locke, Shaftesbury's doctrine of the moral sense took virtue out of the world of ideas, out of heaven, and located it firmly within the feeling breast of each individual man. No longer does a man have to consult Scripture; no longer does he have to attend to an uncertain chain of ratiocination. Now he may know what virtue is as surely and as immediately as he tastes honey and feels pleasure. Much as Shaftesbury quarreled with Hobbes's analysis of the passions, like Hobbes he felt the passions to be most real, most trustworthy, and most likely to influence behavior: "For let us carry element of wrong to other persons or to property. On what grounds can the state pretend to punish them? Or, to recall the issue raised in the account of perjury, why should offenses against God alone not be punished directly by God? Or at least only by the church? During the Restoration the secular courts developed new law allowing them to proceed against such offenses as open lewdness and blasphemy. Crimes against God and crimes against nature were declared to be subversive of public order. This new law did not represent increased influence of religion. On the contrary, it represented the encroachment of the secular courts on what had been the domain of the ecclesiastical courts and the determination of the secular state to define and to enforce morality for itself.

It is simplest to begin with a concrete event. Students of Restoration literature will recall that on a certain day in 1663 Sir Charles Sedley, Lord Buckhurst, Sir Thomas Ogle, and their friends had too much to drink at a tavern in Covent Garden. According to the law reports, after a while Sedley appeared "naked in a balkony" and threw down upon the heads of a crowd that had gathered "bottles (pist in) vi & armis."[46] While naked, he probably also made a speech that was considered blasphemous. It seemed obvious that such behavior ought to be punished, but it was by no means obvious who should proceed to punish it.

The interregnum statutes voided and the ecclesiastical courts enfeebled, Restoration society had no formal legal controls over various kinds of offensive "unnatural" behavior, except those few that remained from the reigns of protestant sovereigns before the war and whatever could be derived from reflection on the common law. From 1660 to about 1727, therefore, the courts were bothered with questions of whether they could proceed against such offenses. Sedley's case, besides being among the more notorious adventures of the Restoration rakes, is of importance in legal history. When Sedley appeared before the justices of the King's Bench, the justices realized that such an offense would have been punished in the Court of High Commission. The Court of High Commission having been abolished, they declared, "ils voil fair luy de scaver que cest Court est custos morum de touts les subjects le Roy, et est ore haut temps de punnier tiels profane actions fait encounter tout modesty queux sont cy frequent sicome nient solement Christianity."[47] Sedley was, therefore, fined by the temporal court.

Three other Restoration cases show the further development of this principle that the secular courts are *custos morum*, the guardians and enforcers of natural law and God's law, the punishers of heresy and blasphemy. In 1676 one Taylor was indicted for claiming that religion was a cheat, that Christ was a bastard and a whoremaster, and that he Taylor was Christ's younger brother (accounts of his exact words vary). At that time, the blasphemy statutes of the interregnum having been repealed, there was no particular statute that made these opinions indictable, so Chief Justice Hale, really making new law, opined that Taylor's words constituted a misdemeanor at common law: "These words though of ecclesiastical cognisance, yet that religion is a cheat, tends to dissolution of all government, and therefore punishable here, and so of contumelious reproaches of God, or the religion establisht." The court agreed and declared, "An indictment lay for saying the Protestant religion was a fiction for taking away religion, all obligation to government by oaths, & ceaseth, and Christian religion is a part of the law it self."[48]

Sedley's case combined with Taylor's case to create a significant precedent, but, as two other cases of interest to students of literature show, the position of King's Bench as the enforcer of moral law was established only gradually. In Anne's reign the crown attempted to proceed against Read, the publisher of an allegedly obscene book, *The Fifteen Plagues of a Maidenhead* (R. v. *Read*, 1708). Taking a conservative position, the court freed the defendant, declaring that the crime seemed punishable by the ecclesiastical courts and that there seemed to be no precedents for proceeding against it in King's Bench.[49] The precedent of *R. v. Read*, however, was overturned in *R. v. Curll*, the Curll now most familiar from his success in book 2 of *The Dunciad*, where, "obscene with filth," he wins the race of the booksellers through the sewers. The Attorney General moved against Curll for the publication of *Venus in the Cloister, or The Nun in Her Smock* and a *Treatise of Flogging*, but it was moved in arrest of judgment "that however the defendent may be punishable for this in the Spiritual Court as an offence contra bonos mores, yet it can't be a libel for which he is punishable in the Temporal Courts."[50] The court was clear that *R. v. Read* was a relevant precedent, and, therefore, had to decide whether it was willing to go so far as to overturn it. The Attorney General argued that there were three classes of offense against good order which, though without the element of force, were offenses at common law: (1) seditious words or writing, (2) libels against religion, and (3) public immoral acts destructive of morality in general. He cited Taylor's case in support of his second class of offense and Sedley's in support of the third, the third class being relevant to the proceedings against Curll. The justices easily agreed that it was "much to be lamented" if Curll's offense were not punishable, but they still raised the question of whether the temporal courts were entitled to proceed against him. Significantly, the common lawyers in 1727 seem very unclear about precisely what the spiritual courts did and do. The Attorney General argued that there could be no way of punishing the defendant outside the temporal courts, "for if the Spiritual Court had done it, instances might be given." The Chief Justice agreed that the spiritual courts did not punish writing. One justice noted, correctly, that "drunkenness and swearing were punishable in the Spiritual Court before the Acts which made them temporal offences," but another justice claimed that the spiritual court had taken no notice of drunkenness or swearing. The conservative position was forcefully summed up by Justice Fortescue: "I own this is a great offence, but I know of no law by which we can punish it. Common law is common usage, and where there is no law there can be no transgression." Nevertheless, relying heavily on the precedent of Sedley's case which considered the court as *custos morum*, King's Bench consciously overturned *R. v. Read*, extending the prerogative of the temporal courts from the right to proceed against open lewdness and blasphemy to the right to proceed against obscene publication. Curll was found guilty and set in the pillory. The principle may be seen firmly established when, in *R. v. Woolston* (1728), Woolston having written skeptical discourses on Christ's miracles, the justices of the King's Bench "would not suffer it to be debated, whether to write against Christianity in general was not an offence punishable in the Temporal Courts at common law."[51] Woolston himself claimed to be a Christian, so the secular court put itself in the position of pronouncing his interpretation of Christianity unsatisfactory when they imposed a jail sentence on him.

It may seem as though the development of common-law prosecutions against immoral and blasphemous writings in this period is counterevidence to the argument of chapter 4 about the later seventeenth century's devaluation of words as opposed to physical facts and actions. However, when it is considered that Woolston could earlier have been prosecuted in the spiritual courts for the more serious crime of heresy, before 1676 a potentially capital crime, a misdemeanor prosecution for blasphemous libel will be seen as a lesser sanction. The same movement noticed in chapter 2 from prosecuting writing as treason to prosecuting it as seditious libel is evident here. Furthermore, writing here also comes to be more frequently differentiated from speaking, writing being more like an "overt act" than speaking. Thus, by the beginning of the eighteenth century three things have happened in the law concerning immorality and blasphemy: (1) the death penalty for heresy has finally been eliminated and the severity of the penalties for purely religious crimes generally has been greatly reduced, (2) the secular state has encroached importantly on the prerogative of the ecclesiastical courts, and (3) the secular state has declared itself responsible for the definition and enforcement of God's law and natural law.

III

The same general movements we have been observing in the philosophical and legal thought of the period may also be traced in the literature. The imaginative writers of the period invent device after device to play with the puzzles of distinguishing between nature and custom, usually, though not always, in order to commend whatever is discovered to be natural. Many Restoration heroes are heroes precisely because they owe their allegiance to nature as distinguished from custom. In the sixties and seventies writers tend to try out sophistic attitudes, questioning conventional morality as merely custom, not supported by nature. In the eighties and nineties, however, nature is discovered to be the foundation of conventional morality. Heroes are finally led to virtue not by clergymen or religious influences, but by their own analysis of pleasure and pain.

Perhaps most obviously, Restoration writers loved to abstract characters from ordinary society and then speculate how they would behave in a state of nature. The behavior of such characters usually implied that customs of English society were more arbitrary and less grounded in nature than might otherwise have appeared. The fictions were sometimes inspired by the adventures of real voyagers and sometimes developed along more self-consciously theoretical lines. Henry Neville, a republican and close associate of James Harrington, in 1668 published his popular *The Isle of Pines, or, A Late Discovery of a forth Island near Terra Australis, Incognita*, a proto-Crusoe adventure chronicling the settlement of a remote island by one Englishman and four English women. The man sleeps with all the women in turn, and after a while ceases to feel guilt, "custom taking away the shame, there being none but us, we did it more openly, as our lust gave us liberty."[52] He later sleeps with a Negro servant. After sixteen years he has forty-seven children and the island is well on its way to being populated.

Edward Howard's *The Six Days Adventure, or the New Utopia* (1671) also imagines isolated survivors from shipwrecks, and Howard is very conscious of setting up his artificial community as a way of trying to differentiate between mere custom and nature itself. He says in the preface:

> For what can be objected against my introducing the several commonwealths of men, and women, grounded on suppos'd custome, by affirming it to be novel, and consequently unalowable, the objection is not at all solid, because it is not more impossible that such a manner of rule might be practis'd, than that there were *Amazons*, in one or more parts of the world . . . and perhaps it is more the authority of usage and manners, than the law of nature, which does generally incapacitate the Rule of women, there being not seldome to be found as great abilities in them (allowing for the disadvantage they have in not being suitably educated as to letters,) as are to be observ'd in men of greatest comprehensions.[53]

There is much emphasis on sexual appetite even in women who have never seen men before. When the question of a government arises, one of the women proposes, "Say, we elect a Monarchess amongst our selves." Another woman objects, "I Dissent by your favour Madam, because not so natural / In our Sex to endure a superior." A woman retorts:

> The very reason, that induces not a few of us
> To be out of love with Matrimony, which doth rather establish
> The Tyranny of men, than the Law of Nature.
>
> [P. 27]

Earlier English plays like Shakespeare's *Tempest* (1611) and Fletcher and Massinger's *Sea Voyage* (1622) yielded Restoration versions that developed further the original elements concerned with natural man—and, of course, natural woman.[54] Dryden tells us in the preface to the *Tempest* he wrote with Davenant that Davenant suggested Miranda, the woman who had never seen a man, might be complemented with an additional character, "a man who had never seen a woman." Dryden added, "I confess from the very first moment it so pleased me, that I never writ any thing with more delight" (3:106). The Davenant-Dryden *Tempest* also adds Dorinda, a younger sister to Miranda who has also never seen a man, and Sycorax, a sister for Caliban named after the mother of Shakespeare's monster. Certainly part of the motive behind adding these characters is the neoclassic aesthetic of symmetry, but another part is a desire to work out all the possible permutations and combinations of characters untouched by custom. Hippolito, the young man who has never seen woman, has been brought up by Prospero confined to a rock cave on the island. When he finally does see Miranda and Dorinda, he reveals a Hobbist longing for universal dominion:

> I mean to fight with all the men I meet,
> And, when they're dead, their women shall be mine.
>
> [3:190]

Caliban and Sycorax appear accustoned to consoling themselves for their servitude by incestuous love-making (3:195).

Works like these by Neville, Howard, Davenant, and Dryden show contemporary self-consciousness about nature and custom, but the significance of nature as a source of authority is perhaps most evident in the development of two very important types of Restoration character, the Herculean hero and the rake. Both

Herculean heroes and rakes are natural men who live freely in accord with strong passions and strong wills, not in accord with law, custom, or conventional morality. What makes them heroic is their fearless, single-minded pursuit of gratification for their appetites and their contempt for the hypocrisy of conventional morality. Both the Herculean heroes and the rakes are double-edged characters, at once heroes and villains, exciting because they are daring and defiant, but vulnerable to moral condemnation.

Eugene Waith's term, "Herculean hero," is more useful here than "heroic hero," because the characteristics at issue are not shared by all the protagonists of heroic drama. Discussions of heroic drama tend to amalgamate two quite different kinds of plays. One kind of heroic drama has protagonists who are, to borrow Dryden's phrase, "patterns of perfect virtue" and who might be called "scrupulous heroes." Among the plays listed in *The Key to the Rehearsal*, for instance, several fall into this class, including a number of cavalier plays, some written before the Restoration: Sir William Berkeley's *Lost Lady* (1639), Davenant's *Love and Honour* (1649), and Sir William Killigrew's *Love and Friendship* (1666), first published as *Ormasdes* in 1665. Nicoll in generalizing about the heroic drama remarks, "The hero is above smaller scruples such as might affect ordinary mortals," but the heroes of these plays, on the contrary, are exquisitely scrupulous, never governed by appetite, and often even Christian.[55] Alphonso in Davenant's famous *Siege of Rhodes* rejects Villerius's claim that there is no reason for him to endure the siege when he is only a guest whose new bride waits for him in Sicily:

> Honour is colder virtue set on fire;
> My honour lost, her love would soon decay.
> Here for my tomb or triumph I will stay.
> My sword against proud Solyman I draw,
> His cursed prophet, and his sensual law.[56]

Even the allegedly barbarous Solyman shows himself amazingly magnanimous when he releases Ianthe after his troops have captured her and grants her and Alphonso safe-conduct away from Rhodes. Ianthe is moved to remark, "He seemed in civil France, and monarch there," and Alphonso to exclaim, "O wondrous enemy!" *The Siege of Rhodes* is certainly a heroic play, but it does not have any Herculean heroes and this kind of heroic play is not relevant to our discussion of natural law.

Another kind of heroic play does have those irregularly great protagonists Waith calls Herculean. The impression is sometimes given that *The Conquest of Granada* is typical of a large class of such plays, all with heroes as magnanimous and as essentially good as the noble savage Almanzor, though also as contemptuous of the rules of decadent civilizations. In fact, Almanzor is an unusual character in Restoration drama and has few peers outside of Dryden's own work. Almanzor is above the smaller scruples, but follows impulses and passions that are fundamentally generous and noble. Most of the protagonists in the more Herculean heroic dramas, however, are libertines whose selfish passions drive them to poisoning, rape, infanticide, and incest. The protagonists of many of these heroic plays more strongly resemble Lyndaraxa than they do Almanzor: Dryden's own Maximin, Settle's Cambyses and the Empress of Morocco, Mrs. Behn's Abdelezar, Samuel Pordage's Herod, Lee's Nero, and so on. Many of these plays also have characters as correct as Ozmyn in *The Conquest of Granada*, but as the titles and casting suggest, their main focus of interest and excitement is the Herculean hero, criminal or not, rather than the more virtuous characters.

These Herculean protagonists usually justify their deviations from conventional morality by appeals to nature. Like the rakes, they are ruled by passion and appetite, not by law or conventional morality. Dryden's Maximin says to St. Catherine in *Tyrannic Love* (1669):

> I can no more make passion come or go,
> Than you can bid your Nilus ebb or flow,
> 'Tis lawless, and will love, and where it list;
> And that's no sin, which no man can resist.
>
> [3:433]

In Settle's very popular *The Empress of Morocco* (1673), the empress boldly declares, "My Will's my King, my Pleasures are my Gods."[57] She has her lover poison her husband, personally stabs her eunuch, tricks the young queen into stabbing the king (who is the empress's own son), murders the young queen, and finally commits suicide when her lust is frustrated. Crimilhaz, her confederate, proclaims:

> This work, which we so roughly do begin,
> Zeal and Religion may perhaps call Sin.
> No; the more Barbrous garb our Deeds assume,
> We nearer to our First perfection come.
> Since Nature first made Man wild, savage, strong.
>
> [P. 33]

The rhetoric of these heroic plays consistently likens the Herculean protagonists to grand natural objects and forces: blazing comets, stars, burning suns, thunder, tempests, oceans, winds, and the earth itself. One point of these comparisons is usually that such forces simply cannot be confined within the decorums of conventional morality.

The nature to which these hero / villains owe their allegiance is fundamentally a nature of independent individual appetite, not an hierarchical nature where "natural" obligations like those between parent and child can exist. The lascivious queen in Mrs. Behn's *Abdelezar: or the Moor's Revenge* (1676) literally attempts to exorcise a hierarchical nature in favor of a nature of individual appetite as she prepares for the murder of her son:

> Nature, be gone, I chase thee from my Soul,
> Who Love's almighty Empire does controul:
> And she that will to thy dull Laws submit,
> In spite of thee, betrays the Hypocrite.
>
> [2:31]

The nature possessed of "dull Laws" in the third line here is an hierarchical nature that abhors a mother's murdering her own child, the same nature Ozmyn in *The Conquest of Granada* finds "bids us parents to obey." But *thee* in the fourth line is also nature, the natural appetite only hypocrites repress in favor of morality. Tyrants in these plays commit sensational crimes that might be expected from people whose lust and anger are absolutely without restraint: numerous rapes and murders; Lee's Nero having Otho's tongue pulled out; his Mithridates having molten gold poured down the throats of his enemies; Settle's Cambyses showing

Mandana the supposed body of her lover while the executioner stands by with the lover's head in a bucket of blood.

Perhaps the acts most characteristic of these protagonists, however, are still more "unnatural" ones: mothers and fathers murdering their own children, children murdering their own parents, siblings murdering each other, incest, homosexuality, and suicide. Mrs. Behn's Queen Isabella has her lover poison her husband and then cheerfully agrees to the murder of her son. Settle's Cambyses orders his younger brother Smerdis killed and his Machiavellian accomplice Prexaspes observes:

> The Laws of Nature, and the tyes of blood,
> Are things *Cambyses* never understood.[58]

Lee's Nero has committed incest with his mother Agrippina and orders her poisoned. Glorying in his homosexuality, he seems in revolt against nature's having any categories or laws:

> Who but a GOD, like me, could Sexes change?
> Sporus be witness of my Mighty art,
> Sporus, now Lady, once Lord of my heart.
>
> [1:32]

Shadwell's Don John in *The Libertine*, a character somewhere between a Herculean hero and a rake, announces, "There's nothing good or ill, but as it seems to each man's natural appetite" (3:45). His libertine credentials and those of his friends are established when we learn that they have systematically trampled down all taboos in pursuit of his principle. The catalogue of their prior crimes includes not only theft, rape, and murder, but also fratricide, parricide, and incest.

The Restoration dramatists seem endlessly fascinated by imagining the lengths to which natural passions and ambitions might go if there were no such things as natural morality or natural obligation. It may seem paradoxical to say that the most characteristic acts of these heroes who claim to live according to nature are unnatural, but their "unnaturalness" depends upon assuming some moral order in nature that disallows incest, matricide, and so on—and, as we have seen, it was precisely this assumption that was being questioned. The point is not that playwrights like Lee or Settle "approved" of incest or of mothers who murdered their sons. They show their "disapproval" clearly enough by meting out horrible deaths to their characters, usually unrepentant, who commit such acts. The point is that Nero and the Empress of Morocco seemed to them exciting and interesting characters.

Similarly, the Restoration rake tries to remain faithful to appetite and individual will and re-creates the sophistic attack on conventional morality as mere custom.[59] High on the list of decencies for which the rakes have no regard—at least until the fifth act when they wish to secure a virtuous wife—are chastity, marriage, and fidelity to oaths. All of these are likely to be attacked as unnatural. Wildblood in Dryden's *An Evening's Love* (1668) reacts with horror to a rumor that he is engaged: "Marriage, quoth a! what, dost thou think I have been bred in the deserts of Africa, or among the savages of America? Nay, if I had, I must needs have known better things than so; the light of nature would not have let me go so far astray" [3:260]. The rakes invoke the authority of nature to justify flaunting conventional morality, characteristically using analogies. Sometimes the analogies serve to explain the vagaries of rake psychology, and by implication to justify them as natural. Wildblood and Bellamy see the pretty daughters of Don Alonzo in the first act and then open the second act by discussing what they are going to do about it:

> *Bell.* Nay, it may be I care as little for her as another man; but, while she flyes before me, I must follow: I can love a woman first with ease; but if she begins to fly before me, I grow *opiniatre* as the devil.
>
> *Wild.* 'What a secret have you found out? Why, 'tis the nature of all mankind: we love to get our mistresses, and purr over them, as cats do over mice, and then let them go a little way; and all the pleasure is, to pat them back again.
>
> [3:272]

Such analogies also insist on the rake's perception of the relations between the sexes as fundamentally appetitive, not Platonic ways of transcendence. So, even when Longvil in Shadwell's *Virtuoso* (1676) wishes to declare himself Miranda's lover and she accuses him of being simply another keeper, he retorts, "I was never one of those Madam. . . . I had rather kill my own Game than send to a

Poulterers. Besides, I never eat tame things, when wild of the same kind are in season" (3:132). Often the analogy serves directly to excuse the rake from the obligations of conventional morality, as when Dorimant tells Mrs. Loveit it is unreasonable for her to expect him to be faithful either to her or to the vows of eternal love he has so frequently uttered: "Constancy at my years? 'Tis not a virtue in season; you might as well expect the fruit the autumn ripens i' the spring."[60]

It is not accidental that the rake heroes are so often provided with fops as foils. The heroes themselves are in some danger of being considered affected; so the playwrights insist on their naturalness by contrasting them with monstrously affected humors characters, who, as Horner says of Sparkish, "force nature, and would be still what she forbids 'em." Ranger in *Love in a Wood* (1671) is allowed to laugh at Dapperwit, Gerrard in *The Gentleman Dancing Master* (1672) at Monsieur de Paris, and Valentine in *Love for Love* (1695) at Tattle. Many plays have early set scenes in which the rake amuses himself, and, often, his brother rakes, by drawing out the follies of the fop, sometimes encouraging him to expose himself further by agreeing to some scheme. Not infrequently, a side effect of the rake's plot will be the fop's final discomfiture, though the fop's self-conceit is usually powerful enough that he is not likely to be fully conscious of his humiliation. While the rakes are like Callicles men of strong natural passions, the fops are also contrasted with them and made more ridiculous by having only the feeblest of sexual appetites. At the end of *The Man of Mode*, Mrs. Loveit, obedient to Dorimant's wish, publicly scorns Sir Fopling, who simply concludes she is mad and reflects philosophically, "An intrigue now would be but a temptation to me to throw away that vigor on one, which I mean shall shortly make my court to the whole sex in a ballet" (p. 142).

Both the Herculean hero and the rake further re-create the sophistic attack on morality by trying to subvert morality's religious foundations. Not only baroque love of spectacle decrees that the heroic plays are usually set in pagan lands. When their pagan heroes express contempt for whatever the local religion is, they are likely to appear reasonably sympathetic, and their English creators cannot be accused of anti-Christian sentiments. Dryden takes the freedom this exoticism gives further than most playwrights when he allows the famous debate between his deistic Montezuma and the representatives of Spanish Catholicism in *The Indian Emperor* (1665). More typically, the issue of Christianity in any form is simply not raised, and what religion there is seems suitable only to the timid and credulous. Nero declares:

> Virtue's a name; Religion is a thing
> Fitter to scare poor Priests, than daunt a KING.
> [1:32]

The Empress of Morocco also shows herself grandly scornful of religious restraints on her desires. When she falsely accuses Mully Hamet of attempting to rape her, he warns: "Know, Madam, on such Crimes there waits a Hell." She replies with one of her more memorable rants:

> Hell! No, of that I scorn to be afraid:
> I'le send such throngs to the infernal shade,
> Betray, and kill, and damn to that degree,
> I'le crowd up Hell, till there's no Room for Me.
> [P. 24]

The more criminal protagonists, in fact, are apt to use the credulous beliefs of others to their own advantage, as Abdelezar does when he gets the queen of Spain to call in her confessor and declare the rightful heir to the throne a bastard:

> And zealously pretend you're urg'd by Conscience,
> A cheap Pretence to cozen Fools withal.
> [2:42]

Even in comedy, one element of the excitement generated by the heroes is the feeling that they are living dangerously in defiance of God. Part of the rake's bravado seems to come from the nagging suspicion that his sins may really be damning him. One of the earliest Restoration rakes, Dryden's Loveby in *The Wild Gallant* (1663), actually makes a mock alliance with the devil. The California editors point to parodies of the Book of Common Prayer and avow, "that Loveby is an unbeliever is in fact only too obvious."[61] Yet unless some belief in the reality of the prayer book tags remains, not only in the audience, but also in Loveby, half the fun goes out of the device. Part of the thrill the audience gets out of watching Loveby and part of his own excitement in playing with the powers of darkness comes from the idea that those powers might—just might—react. As critics of the license of the stage never tired of observing, contempt of religion seemed to be an essential attribute of the rake hero. Rakes swear and blaspheme, make assignations in churches, and regard religious devotees as fools, or, more often, venal hypocrites. Not infrequently they disguise themselves as parsons or friars, the better to minister to the gratification of their own appetites and the better to mock the hypocrites. Harcourt masquerades as a parson in *The Country Wife*, Lorenzo as a friar in *The Spanish Friar*, and Bellmour as a "fanatic" in *The Old Bachelor*. Critics like Jeremy Collier were right to consider these rakes hostile to religion and to protest that the fact the clergy represented were usually Roman Catholics or dissenters was no defense.

IV

Both the Maximins of heroic drama and the Dorimants of comedy fade away as the century draws to a close. Dryden himself renounces his Maximins as extravagances; Collier and other reformers demand the immoral rake be banished from the stage. It might seem as though custom and conventional morality had succeeded in reestablishing themselves as superior to nature, and as entitled to curb natural passions. Yet that is not what happens. Instead, the sophistic antithesis between nature and conventional morality is itself abandoned and morality is now seen to rest on nature. The final criticism of libertinism is not that the libertines were wrong to trust the authority of natural appetite, but that they had not known what natural appetites were. Man, it is decided toward the end of the seventeenth century, is not essentially a creature of lust and vengeance, but a tranquil social animal animated by benevolence. The nature by which he is to order his behavior is not a transcendent and hierarchical nature of abstract forms, but an immanent nature of the passions and sensations familiar to him within himself.

The Herculean heroes are stripped of their emphatic couplets and have to express themselves in more subdued blank verse. The three new tragic playwrights who dominated the stage during the eighties—Banks, Lee, and Otway—each began with a play in heroics and then moved toward a drama increasingly domestic and pathetic. The first plays of Lee and Otway, *Nero* (1674) and *Alcibiades* (1675), are their only plays in heroic couplets. King Massinissa in Lee's *Sophonisba* (1675), his Mithridates, King of Pontus (1678), and Otway's King Philip of Spain in *Don Carlos* (1676) are no longer simply tyrants who proceed gleefully to rape and murder, but monarchs who struggle fitfully against their lusts and suffer some anguish of conscience. Banks's relatively heroic *Rival Kings* (1677) and *Destruction of Troy* (1678) are followed by the pathetic *Vertue Betray'd* (1682), *The Unhappy Favourite* (1681), *The Innocent Usurper* (1683), and *The Island Queens; or, the Death of Mary, Queen of Scotland* (1684).

The Herculean heroes seem to be replaced by two characters, a generous and noble hero and selfish, passionate villain. Maximin is supplanted by the pairing of Aureng-Zebe and Morat, Torrismond and Bertran, Don Carlos and Don Juan, Jaffeir and Pierre. Or, to look at what happens another way, in the earlier plays an irregular hero is accompanied by a subordinate correct character (Almanzor and Ozmyn, the Empress of Morocco and Mully Hamet, Nero and Britanicus), while in the later ones a good hero is accompanied by a subordinate villain. But the good heroes who dominate the serious drama of the eighties and nineties are unlike the patterns of perfect virtue in the earlier heroic drama. No matter how intricate the honor puzzles set for Alphonso or Ozmyn, they confront them in an atmosphere of daylight and either triumphantly solve them themselves or are released with honor unblemished by some fortunate turn of events. Their descendents, though equally desirous of virtue, are tormented by darker puzzles and often lack the light to solve them.

The catalogue of crimes daringly and consciously committed by the protagonists of earlier heroic drama also figures prominently in the tragedies of the eighties and nineties: disobedience and revolt against sovereigns; usurpations; murders, including the murders of children by parents and parents by children; adultery; and incest. The same *behavior* is at issue, but the relationship of the later protagonists to that behavior is changed profoundly. In the plays of the eighties and nineties the sympathetic heroes and heroines commit the crimes unwillingly or—perhaps most powerfully—are falsely accused of having committed them. Leonora's "half-murder" of King Sancho in *The Spanish Friar* (1680) seems pivotal. The incident itself is unsatisfactory, but it seems to grope toward a feeling that became more clearly focused as the century drew to a close. Leonora has given the order for the king's death, and at the end of the play it appears that Torrismond, who has been revealed to be Sancho's son, therefore cannot marry her. We then are surprised to discover that Bertran has, after all, cautiously neglected to murder the old king, correctly suspecting that Leonora might blame him. With what many have considered something less than strict delicacy, Torrismond proceeds to marry the usurper who only intended to have his father killed. In the more satisfactory tragic plots, there is always some critical mistake connected with the crime, but the later mistakes leave us with characters less culpable than Leonora. Monimia in Otway's *Orphan* (1680) is unwittingly guilty of adultery and of the incest of having slept with her husband's brother, marriages between in-laws being within the degrees prohibited by canon law. Polydore did mean to trick Monimia into sleeping with him, but had no idea he would finally have to confess:

> By me last night the horrid deed
> Was done; when all things slept, but Rage, and Incest.
>
> [2:82]

Polydore runs on Castalio's sword, making Castalio in turn exclaim:

> I've murder'd too my Brother.
> Why wouldst thou study ways to damn me further
> And force the sin of Parricide upon me?
>
> [2:83]

The Earl of Essex in *The Unhappy Favourite* is unjustly executed for treason. Queen Elizabeth is even tricked into thinking him so contemptuous of her power as to refuse to ask her to spare his life. In *Vertue Betray'd* Anna Bullen is falsely accused not only of

adultery with Piercy, but also of incest with her brother Rochfort.
Since Lady Blunt and Cardinal Wolsey have tricked Rochford into
writing love letters to Lady Blunt addressing her as "sister" and
signing himself "brother," there is even documentary evidence of
this alleged incest, and Henry sentences Anna and her brother to
death. In *Don Sebastian* (1682), Sebastian and Almeyda do not
know of their relationship on the night of their marriage, but are
guilty of brother-sister incest. Isabella in Southerne's *Fatal
Marriage* is deceived into believing that her first husband is dead
and so becomes guilty of adultery when she marries again.

These plots are quite peculiar. Clearly the playwrights of the
eighties and nineties and audiences into the eighteenth century
found them deeply moving. Undoubtedly thinking of such pathetic
tragedies, Shaftesbury commented that the spectacle of virtue "in
the midst of surrounding Calamitys" afforded intense pleasure:

> For thus, when by mere Illusion, as in a *Tragedy*, the Passions of this
> kind [i.e., the social affections] are skillfully excited in us; we prefer the
> Entertainment to any other of equal duration. We find by our-selves,
> that the moving of our Passions in this mournful way, the engaging
> them in behalf of Merit and Worth, and the exerting whatever we have
> of social Affection, and human Sympathy, is of the highest Delight, and
> affords a greater Enjoyment in the way of *Thought* and *Sentiment*, than
> any thing besides can do in a way of *Sense* and *common Appetite*.
>
> [*Inquiry*, pp. 106–7]

Making heroes and heroines of these unwittingly guilty and unjustly accused characters is a way of denying the image of man as
an aggressive creature who selfishly seeks to gratify his appetites.
The most intense moments in these plays affirm the innocence of
the suffering heroes and heroines. *Innocence* is itself a key word
in pathetic tragedy. "Oh she's innocent," cries Polydore just as
Monimia announces she has poisoned herself (2:83). "*Castalio's
innocent, / And so's Monimia*," he repeats as he himself dies (2:85).
Wolsey in *Vertue Betray'd* watches Anna's first entrance and says:

> And in her heedless Innocence she sails,
> Shunning no Rocks, no Quick-sands, nor no Danger,
> But runs into her Ruine faster than We wish.[62]

Piercy gets Anna's letter explaining how she was deceived and forced into marrying the king and rejoices:

> She's Innocent! Oh! you Immortal Powers!
> She's Innocent!
>
> [P. 53]

When she is condemned to death, he laments:

> A greater Innocence this Day is fallen,
> Than even blest the Walks of Paradise.
>
> [P. 63]

Anna herself goes to her beheading moralizing: "For Innocence is still its own Reward" (p. 75). These pathetic tragedies affirm the essential innocence of their central characters, and, by extension, the essential goodness of human nature against all who would malign it. The emotions in which spectators luxuriate are not only pity for the victimized protagonists, but also the selfconscious approbation that arises from feeling generous sentiments within their own breasts and from recognizing their own goodness. The benign nature within man may be trusted and its laws observed with confidence that they are the foundation for social harmony.

In comedy, too, by the end of the century, heroes are innocent and good-natured. They continue to be enemies of falsehood and affectation and exemplars of truth and nature. Nature, however, is revealed to be the friend of conventional morality, not its antagonist. Rakes like Lorenzo in *The Spanish Friar* or Bellmour in *The Old Bachelor* assume clerical disguises the better to commit their adulteries and to expose the hypocrisies of the pretenders to religion. But when Mellefont in *The Double Dealer* appears in the final scene disguised in a parson's habit, it is to further his own marriage and to perform the function of a true parson, exposing and rebuking vice. His words to Maskwell could never be uttered by Lorenzo or Bellmour: "Do you hold down your head? Yes, I am your Chaplain; look in the Face of your injured Friend, thou wonder of all Falsehood"[63] Significantly, the one person in orders in the play, Saygrace, is a compliant tool of Maskwell. Mellefont is not a rake who needs religious salvation. There is no hint that he has had previous amours; in the play he scorns the advances of Lady Touchwood and wants to marry Cynthia from the very beginning. The humane, good-natured hero now proves quite capable of working out his own salvation.

The movement from the libertine rake to the good-natured hero can most conveniently be observed in Shadwell, who wrote comedies during the eighties and early nineties, after Etherege and Wycherley had withdrawn from the stage and before Congreve had begun his career. In an early play like *Epsom-Wells* (1672) Shadwell basically accepted the libertine ethos. His rake heroes, Raines and Bevil, are friends who agree to gratify their appetites, scorn a country life, and condemn marriage as "an Ecclesiastical Mousetrap." Their principles are established early on:

> *Bevil.* . . . we should no more be troubled at the Feavers we get in drinking, than the Honourable wounds we receive in Battle.
>
> *Raines.* 'Tis true, the first are the effects of our pleasure, and the last of our honour; which are two things absolutely necessary to the life of a Gentleman.
>
> *Bevil.* Yet your dull spleenatick sober Sots will tell you, we shorten our lives, and bring Gouts, Dropsies, Palsies, and the Devil and all upon us.
>
> *Raines.* Let 'em lie and preach on, while we live more in a week, than those insipid-temperate Fools do in a Year.
>
> [2:108]

Bevil is in the midst of an affair with his friend Woodly's wife. One of the chief characters in the play, indeed, the one who structurally replaces the fop, is Clodpate, a man who abhors London as Sodom, spends all his money in the country on principle (preferably among his own tenants), serves as a local magistrate, makes the surveyors mend the local roads, and otherwise attends to country affairs. These activities are ridiculed. Rains explicitly attacks him: "That men should be such infinite Coxcombs to live scurvily to get reputation among thick-scull'd Peasants, and be at as great a distance with men of wit and sense, as if they were another sort of Animals" (2:112). An extended dialogue in which Clodpate tries to woo Lucia for himself and a "pretty, innocent, huswifely life in the Country" evokes and mocks the quotidian realities of rustic life:

Luc. To see my Ducks and Geese fed, and cram my own Chickens.
Clod. Ay.
Luc. To have my Closet stink, like a Pothecaries shop, with Drugs and
    Medicines, to administer to my sick Neighbours, and spoil the next
    Quack's practice with the receipt-book that belongs to the Family.
    [2:121]

Though such a country life will later be idealized, here Clodpate is
rejected by Lucia, later robbed and tied up in a graveyard by two
bullies who impress him by disguising themselves as countrymen,
and finally married to Mrs. Jilt, who also tricks him by pretending
to be a lover of the country.

In Shadwell's comedies of the eighties, on the other hand, we can
see the libertine hero gradually replaced by the good-natured
gentleman who reaches his apogee in Mirabell and then continues
to sputter across the sky of eighteenth-century comedy. Already in
The Lancashire Witches (1681) Clodpate has been redeemed and
transformed into Sir Edward Hartfort, "a worthy Hospitable true
English Gentleman, of good understanding, and honest Principles"
(Dramatis Personae). Sir Edward's country life in Lancashire,
admittedly less penurious than Clodpate's, is lauded by the young
heroes in the play, Belfort and Doubty. At their first appearance in
The Lancashire Witches Belfort and Doubty have already forsworn
rakedom; they come to the country to woo and to marry two
gentlewomen they saw at Scarborough. Once the excitement over
the local witches develops, they join Sir Edward in expressing
skepticism. Although their doubts lay them open to accusations of
infidelity, in the context of this play it is clear that Smerk, the
Church of England clergyman who calls them "damn'd Hobbists
and Atheists," is himself the disreputable and shocking figure.

The play is slightly incoherent as to whether there are or are not
supernatural interferences in nature. Witches do appear on stage—
though sometimes they are supposed to be invisible—seem to
summon up thunder and lightning, cause objects to move without
apparent cause, ride through the air, and paralyze musicians so
they cannot play their instruments. This machinery was partly
responsible for the popularity of the play, as Shadwell anticipated
when he devised it. One of the witches' songs welcomes the Devil:

> O're Nature's Powers thou canst prevail,
> Raise Winds, bring Snow, or Rain, or Hail,
> Without their Causes, and canst make
> The sturdy Course of Nature shake.
>   [4:151]

Nevertheless, these witches are merely part of an entertaining operatic and comic spectacle, not seriously believed in. The admirable characters in the play agree with Belfort when he says, " 'Tis a little odd; but . . . I shall not fly from my Belief, that every thing is done by Natural Causes, because I cannot presently assign those Causes" (4:166). Shadwell's preface also supports the idea that, although he represents the witches on stage, he doubted their existence in reality:

> For my part, I am (as it is said of *Surly* in the *Alchymist*) somewhat costive of belief. The evidences I have represented are natural, *viz.*, slight, and frivolous, such as poor old Women were wont to be hang'd upon.
>   For the Actions, if I had not represented them as those of real Witches, but had show'd the ignorance, fear, melancholy, malice, confederacy, and imposture that contribute to the belief of Witchcraft, the people had wanted diversion, and there had been another clamour against it, it would have been call'd Atheistical, By a prevailing party who take it ill that the power of the Devil should be lessened, and attribute more miracles to a silly old Woman, than ever they did to the greatest of Prophets, and by this means the Play might have been Silenced. [4:101]

As it is, the attack on religion in *The Lancashire Witches* is bolder than is usual even in the comedies of the sixties and seventies; the censors forced heavy cuts in the part of Smerk, who was a clergyman of the established church, not a fanatic or a Roman Catholic priest. Yet, unlike the comedies of the sixties and seventies, *The Lancashire Witches* shows no interest in attacking conventional morality. On the contrary, Sir Edward, Belfort, and Doubty behave like paragons, speak out in praise of morality, and find no tension between virtue and the gratification of their natural appetites.

The Squire of Alsatia (1688) and *Bury-Fair* (1689), Shadwell's
two comedies produced immediately after the Glorious Revolution,
play the old ideas of the libertine rake off against the newer ideas of
the good-natured hero. In *The Squire of Alsatia* Shadwell borrows
from Terrence to develop a plot in which two brothers are
educated according to radically different principles. Sir William
Belford brings up his elder son, Belford, Sr., in the country,
denying him all pleasures and training him only to understand
agricultural business. His younger son, Belford, Jr., is adopted by
an uncle, Sir Edward Belford, who brings him up in London and
treats him with the greatest imaginable liberality. At the beginning
of the play, Belford, Sr., has fled from the country to run riot
among the cheats of Alsatia, while Belford, Jr., justifies his uncle's
confidence in his good nature by cultivating music and literature,
shunning cheats and bullies, and indulging in wenching and wine
only in moderation. His music master has set *Beatus ille* at his
request, and his friend Truman sings it on stage in the scene that
introduces the two benign rakes. Belford has been willing to
disguise himself as a Quaker to get access to a pretty Quaker he
fancies and shows some nervousness when he begins to approach
the heights of a sententious Mirabell, remarking to Truman after
an interval of moralizing, "Faith *Truman*, we may talk of mighty
matters; of our Honesty and Morality; but a young Fellow carries
that about him that will make him a Knave now and then in spite
of his Teeth" (4:226). Nevertheless, he sometimes strikes poses that
would not be uncomfortable for Young Bellair of *The Conscious
Lovers*, exhibiting the greatest possible deference toward his foolish
father, and protesting when accused of lying, "I scorn a Lye, 'tis
the basest thing a Gentleman can be guilty of" (4:229). Belford, Jr.,
has seduced the pretty daughter of an attorney before the play
opens, but, like Mirabell, feels obliged to make provisions for her:
"For how can a good natur'd man think of ever quitting so tender,
and so kind a Mistriss. . . . But I will better her condition" (4:252).
At the end of the play, he proclaims to Isabella, "*I* look on
marriage as the most solemn Vow a Man can make; and 'tis by
consequence, the basest Perjury to break it" (4:279).

When Shadwell's later heroes are converted from their libertine
ways, they are never converted by clergymen. No one suggests they

should abandon their natural appetites. Instead, they are converted because they recognize with Shaftesbury that the life of a sober gentleman yields more pleasure, more freedom from pain, and more gratification of natural appetites. The kindly Sir Edward tells Belford, Jr., "there's nothing but Anxiety in Vice: I am not streight Lac'd; but when I was Young, I ne'r knew anything gotten by Wenching, but Duels, Claps, and Bastards: and every drunken fit in a short madness, that cuts off a good part of life" (4:238). Later, after struggling with the rage of his cast mistress, Mrs. Termagant, Belford, Jr., himself reflects, "Well, say what they will, the life of a Whore-master is a foolish, restless, anxious life; and ther's an end on't" (4:269).

In *Bury-Fair* Shadwell presents Lord Bellamy, a country-loving hero still more virtuous than Belford, Sr., and allows him to argue with his town-loving friend, Wildish, who retains some affection for the rake's life. This pair of heroes may be contrasted with a pair in Shadwell's first comedy, *The Sullen Lovers* (1668). In *The Sullen Lovers* Lovell, fond of the town, and Stanford, who hates the town, are both gentlemen and friends, but Stanford, so tormented by the fools of London that he wishes to retire to some uninhabited place, is a humors character who can be manipulated by his gayer friend. In *Bury-Fair*, on the other hand, the relationship is reversed, with the sober Lord Bellamy understood to have achieved insights his gayer friend Wildish will only attain toward the end of the play. (Shadwell uses the eighteenth-century trick of introducing a lord into comedy to lend weight to his moral pronouncements and to make him an even more attractive catch for the virtuous heroine.) When the two friends debate, Bellamy praises country life and paints vivid pictures of the miseries of debauchery:

> *Bell.* But I have pleasure in reading the *Georgics*, and contemplating the Works of Nature.
> *Wild.* I contemplate the chief Works of Nature: fine Women; and the Juice of the Grape, well concocted by the Sun.
> *Bell.* Your fine Women, are a Company of proud, vain, Fops and Jilts, abominably Daub'd and Painted. . . . And, besides, many of them are so unsound, that making Love is become as dangerous as making War; and the Wounds and Scars are dishonorable to boot. Then, for your Wine, 'tis attended with such Surfeits, Qualms, Head-akes, late

Hours, Quarrels and Uproars, that every Scene of Drunkenness is a very *Bedlam*.

Wild. . . . Oh, the sweet of a Brimmer at Midnight! The Night was made for Beasts to sleep in, and for Man to Watch in.

Bell. And if I have no other misfortune but the Head-ake, and Puking in the morning, to hear of this Friend breaking a Collar Bone with a fall, that having his Scull crack'd by the Watch, another run through the Lungs by drunken Bullies; and all this to Treasure up Diseases, if you shall arrive to a miserable Age.

Wild. Who would not be sick ten Days for one good Night, with Men of Wit and Sense?

Bell. There's no true Pleasure but in Health. [4:337, and cf. 309–10, 336]

Bellamy is so scrupulous he will not read a rival's letter to the woman he loves when it falls into his hands, and even Wildish scruples to allow his animus against Lady Fantast to go so far as her marriage to a wigmaker. After Wildish and Bellamy realize they are rivals in love, they begin to fight a duel but almost immediately realize they could not possibly hurt each other, embrace, and, "like men of Reason," decide to let the lady choose freely. Gertrude chooses Wildish, whom she has loved before she knew Bellamy, but Bellamy discovers that Gertrude's equally beautiful sister has romantically disguised herself as his page for love of him, and so is happy to marry her instead.

The Scowrers (1690) focuses directly on the rehabilitation of Sir William Rant, a violent, lewd, and drunken rake. We learn immediately that he has added to his father's miseries by getting the parson's daughter pregnant when last he visited at his home in the country. His scowring includes not only the usual breaking of windows and attacking constables, but also beating up the women he finds in the taverns. Sir William's conversion is triply motivated. First, he discovers that Eugenia will not have him unless he forsakes "lewd company," limits his intake of wine to "three Glasses at a Meal," and turns into "the pattern of Vertue for the whole Town." Having heard her terms in the second act, he considers reformation but continues to scower. Second, he sees that his cousin Whachum, a lowly attorney's clerk, and Whachum's equally middle-class friends have all taken up what he had thought were aristocratic vices. Punishing Whachum and his friends by nose-tweaking, kicking, and cudgeling for their indiscretions can only provide partial solace for a thoroughgoing snob like Sir William, whose appetite for vice further weakens. Finally in the sort of climactic blank verse scene to become a fixture of sentimental comedy, Mr. Rant appears and rebukes his kneeling son—who by this time is prepared to agree with his critique of vice. Drunkenness and lewdness are discovered to be "wrong" not for religious reasons, but for hedonistic, pragmatic, and social ones. Drunks will lose their friends, lechers their noses. "God" is not involved, but "common sense," "Nature," and "morality" are. In one rather tangled section of his oration, Mr. Rant observes:

> Nature has prudently contrived each Man,
> In the worst miseries of humane Life
> Would be himself, and I would be I still,
> But sordid Drunkenness makes you differ more
> From your lov'd self, than from another Man.
>
> [5:138]

Shadwell's final and posthumous comedy, *The Volunteers* (1692) has gone beyond the problem of converting the rake and simply offers two good-natured, virtuous heroes and a heroine remarkable for her own "good Nature" (5:179), satisifed with country life, and exceptionally fond of her kind father.

The mutations Shadwell's comic heroes undergo are simply one sign of a more general transformation in Restoration culture. Nature and natural law retained their authority, but by the beginning of the eighteenth century nature and natural law were very differently understood than they had been before the Civil War. Older ideas of natural law were bound—perhaps inextricably bound—to a vision of a divinely created and managed hierarchical universe. The precepts of the law were determined by the end God had intended for man; its obligatory character depended on its being God's command. Natural man, after the fall, lacked the resources to fulfill the law without supernatural aid. Partly because political experience had made a law dependent on God's will seem so untrustworthy and partly because nature itself began to seem less divine, less hierarchical, and less teleological, the later seventeenth century looked for a more secular idea of natural law. Philosophers tried to show how natural law could exist independently of the will of God and generally attacked the utopian character of the older tradition. Parliament struck out at the powers of the ecclesiastical courts, while the secular courts declared themselves the interpreters and defenders of morality. So strong was the influence of the religious tradition and so multitudinous its assumptions, that it is not surprising the new theories contained many anomalies. Questions like whether *ought* can ever be derived from *is* and whether the state has a right to punish homosexuals, people guilty of indecency, or publishers of obscene literature have still not been entirely resolved. Even the older natural law tradition itself survives in twentieth-century encyclicals on birth control and in some arguments against such things as homosexuality and suicide. Nevertheless, the ideas of nature and natural law were significantly secularized by the beginning of the eighteenth century. The literature of the Restoration shows not only a variety of attempts to imagine nature without hierarchy and without obligation, but also finally some acceptance of the early modern image of man as so fundamentally good-natured and innocent that he is able to conform to law and to abide by conventional morality not only without divine help and without pain, but with pleasure. Such men no longer require the authority of a divinely appointed sovereign but may be trusted to form their own government and to decide under what circumstances the executive they have appointed should be relieved of that authority delegated to him.

NOTES

Notes to Introduction

1. Benjamin Whichcote, *Moral and Religious Aphorisms*, ed. Samuel Salter (London, 1753), Century 10, 942.

2. John Gauden, *A Discourse Concerning Publick Oaths . . . In order to answer the scruples of the Quakers* (London, 1662), p. 16.

3. Samuel Butler, *Hudibras*, ed. John Wilders (Oxford: Clarendon Press, 1967), 2, 2, 107–10. References are to part, canto, and line numbers.

4. A. H. Scouten, "Notes Toward a History of Restoration Comedy," *Philological Quarterly* 45 (1966): 62.

5. Robert D. Hume, "Diversity and Development in Restoration Comedy," *Eighteenth-Century Studies* 5 (1972): 365, 379.

6. Robert D. Hume, *The Development of English Drama in the Late Seventeenth Century* (Oxford: Clarendon Press, 1976), p. 30.

7. Hume, *Development of English Drama*, p. 190.

Notes to Chapter 1

1. Charles Blitzer, ed., *The Commonwealth of England: Documents of the English Civil Wars, the Commonwealth, and Protectorate* (New York: Putnam, 1963), p. 85.

2. David Hume, *The History of Great Britain: The Reigns of James I and Charles I*, ed. Duncan Forbes (Harmondsworth, Eng.: Penguin, 1970), p. 682.

3. Margaret, Duchess of Newcastle, *The Life of William Cavendish, Duke of Newcastle* (1667), ed. C. H. Firth (New York, 1886), pp. 149, 152.

4. Richard Baxter, *The Autobiography of Richard Baxter*, ed. N. H. Keeble (Totawa, N.J.: Rowman and Littlefield, 1974), p. 43; this is an accessible reading edition prepared from *Reliquiae Baxterianae* (1696).

5. Maurice Ashley, *Charles II: The Man and the Statesman* (London: Weidenfeld and Nicolson, 1971), p. 50; see also W. A. Horrox, *A Bibliography of the Literature Relating to the Escape* (Aberdeen: Aberdeen University Press, 1924).

6. Baxter, *Autobiography*, p. 126.

7. Quoted in C. V. Wedgewood, *Poetry and Politics under the Stuarts* (Cambridge: Cambridge University Press, 1960), p. 69.

8. Thomas Jordan, quoted in Wedgewood, *Poetry and Politics*, pp. 92–93.

9. George Fox, *The Journal of George Fox*, ed. Rufus M. Jones (New York: Capricorn Books, 1963), pp. 75, 76; most of the *Journal* was not actually written by Fox but was dictated to other Quakers and polished by them. (Subsequent citations in the text are to this edition.) Christopher Hill, *The World Turned Upside Down* (London: Temple Smith, 1972) is a recent exploration of the more radical "revolt within the revolution."

10. John Bunyan, *Grace Abounding to the Chief of Sinners*, ed. Roger Sharrock (Oxford: Clarendon Press, 1962), p. 10.

11. *A Relation of the Imprisonment of Mr. John Bunyan*, printed by Sharrock with *Grace Abounding*, p. 124.

12. 5 *S.T.* 801–42.

13. Thomas Ellwood, in *Lives of Lord Herbert of Cherbury and Thomas Ellwood*, ed. William D. Howells (Boston, 1877), pp. 223, 218.

14. *Lex, Rex* (1644), quoted in A. S. P. Woodhouse, *Puritans and Liberty: Being the Army Debates . . . with Supplementary Documents* (Chicago: University of Chicago Press, 1951), p. 199. Woodhouse's introduction is an excellent discussion of the general issue.

15. Baxter, *Autobiography*, p. 22.

16. John Rushworth, *Historical Collections*, part 3, vol. 1 (London, 1691), pp. 180, 181.

17. Ibid., p. 184.

18. 9 *Parl. Hist.* 321 (1641).

19. Ronald A. Marchant, *The Church under the Law: Justice, Administration, and Discipline in the Diocese of York, 1560–1640* (Cambridge: Cambridge University Press, 1969), p. 240.

20. Henry Swinburne, *A Treatise of Spousals or Matrimonial Contracts* (London, 1686), pp. 15, 223; this is the 1st ed., but Swinburne died in 1623.

21. Christopher Hill, *Society and Puritanism* (New York: Schocken Books, 1967), esp. chap. 8.

22. Quoted in English translation in George Elliot Howard, *A History of Matrimonial Institutions*, 3 vols. (1904; reprint ed., New York: Humanities Press, 1964), 1:389.

23. "An Ordinance for the punishing of Blasphemies and Heresies," 1 *Acts & Ords. Interregnum* 1133–36.

24. "An Act against several Atheistical, Blasphemous, and Execrable Opinions," 2 *Acts & Ords. Interregnum* 409–12.

25. "An Act for suppressing the detestable sins of Incest, Adultery and Fornication," 2 *Acts & Ords. Interregnum* 387–89. See Arthur Cleveland, "Indictments for Adultery and Incest before 1650," *Law Quarterly Review* 29 (1913): 57–60, for evidence of Middlesex County proceedings against ten defendants before 1650 and two in the reign of James II. Records are fragmentary and show only one sentence, a finding of guilty where the offender was carted. Cf. Lawrence Stone, *The Family, Sex, and Marriage in England, 1500–1800* (New York: Harper and Row, 1977), pp. 632–34.

26. John Milton, *Considerations Touching the Likeliest Means to Remove Hirelings Out of the Church* (1659), in *The Works of John Milton*, 18 vols. in 21 (New York: Columbia University Press, 1931–38), 6: 72–73.

27. "An Act touching Marriages," 2 *Acts & Ords. Interregnum* 715–18; cf. "An ordinance for the taking away the Book of Common Prayer," 1 *Acts & Ords. Interregnum* 599–601.

28. Arthur Robert Winnett, *Divorce and Remarriage in Anglicanism* (London: Macmillan and Co., 1958), p. 28f., and appendix to chap. 2.

29. 20 *Parl. Hist.* 217–18 (1653).

30. 13 Car. 2, c. 12.

31. Felex Makower, *The Constitutional History and Constitution of the Church of England* (New York, 1895), p. 446.

32. Hill, *Society and Puritanism*, p. 377.

33. David Underdown, *Royalist Conspiracy in England, 1649–1660*, Yale Historical Publications, 19 (New Haven, Conn.: Yale University Press, 1960).

34. Facts about Davenant are drawn from Arthur H. Nethercot, *Sir William D'Avenant* (Chicago: University of Chicago Press, 1938).

35. C. H. Firth, "Sir William Davenant and the Revival of Drama during the Protectorate," *English Historical Review* 18 (1903): 319–21.

36. The account of Waller draws upon *State Trials*; Samuel R. Gardiner, *History of the Great Civil War, 1642–1649* (London, 1898); C. Thorn

Drury, "Introduction," *The Poems of Edmund Waller* (London, 1893); and Warren L. Chernaik, *The Poetry of Limitation: A Study of Edmund Waller* (New Haven, Conn.: Yale University Press, 1968).

37. *Poems of Waller*, p. 140.

38. Quoted in Wedgewood, *Poetry and Politics*, p. 92.

39. Paul H. Hardacre, *The Royalists during the Puritan Revolution* (The Hague: Nijhoff, 1956), p. 1.

40. Quoted in Hardacre, *The Royalists during the Revolution*, p. 1.

41. Edward, Earl of Clarendon, *The History of the Rebellion and Civil Wars in England*, 3 vols. in 6 (Oxford, 1819), 2: 53–55.

42. John Wilders, "Introduction," in *Hudibras* (Oxford: Clarendon Press, 1967).

43. Charles Cotton, *Poems of Charles Cotton*, ed. John Buxton (Cambridge, Mass.: Harvard University Press, 1958), p. 113.

44. John Evelyn, *The Diary of John Evelyn*, ed. E. S. De Beer, 6 vols. (Oxford: Clarendon Press, 1955), 3: 58–59.

45. John Aubrey, *Aubrey's Brief Lives*, ed. Oliver Lawson Dick (London: Secker and Warburg, 1949), p. 125.

46. Wedgewood, *Poetry and Politics*, p. 103.

47. Abraham Cowley, *English Writings of Abraham Cowley*, ed. A. R. Waller, 2 vols. (Cambridge: Cambridge University Press, 1905–6), 1: 192; other facts about Cowley's life are drawn from Arthur H. Nethercot, *Abraham Cowley: The Muses's Hannibal* (Oxford: Oxford University Press, 1931).

48. Cowley, *English Writings*, 1: 455; printed only in the 1st folio of 1656, omitted in 1668.

49. Text in J. P. Kenyon, *The Stuart Constitution, 1603–1688: Documents and Commentary* (Cambridge: Cambridge University Press, 1966), p. 264.

50. Samuel R. Gardiner, *History of the Great Civil War*, vol. 1, chap. 11.

51. *The Plain-Meaning Protestant; Or, An Honest Defence of the Taking the Covenant* (Oxford, 1644), p. 11. Faulconer Madan, *Oxford Books: A Bibliography of Printed Works Relating to the University and City of Oxford*, 3 vols. (Oxford: Oxford University Press, 1895–1931), 2: no. 1643, identifies this pamphlet as a London counterfeit.

52. Evelyn, *Diary*, 2: 81–82.

53. Quoted in Hardacre, *The Royalists during the Revolution*, p. 22.

54. Kenyon, *Stuart Constitution*, p. 341; and see John M. Wallace, "The Engagement Controversy, 1649–1652," *Bulletin of the New York Public Library* 68 (1964): 384–405.

55. Quoted in Hardacre, *The Royalists during the Revolution*, p. 47.

56. G. E. Aylmer, ed., *The Interregnum: The Quest for Settlement, 1646–1660* (Hamden, Conn.: The Shoe String Press, 1972), p. 111.

57. Basil Willey, *The Seventeenth Century Background: Studies in the Thought of the Age in Relation to Poetry and Religion* (1934; Garden City, N. Y.: Doubleday, Anchor Books, 1953), p. 161.

58. James Bass Mullinger, *The University of Cambridge*, 3 vols. (Cambridge: Cambridge University Press, 1873–1911), 3: 287; facts in this section on Cambridge are drawn from Mullinger.

59. Simon Patrick, *A Brief Account of the New Sect of Latitude-Men*, The Augustan Reprint Society no. 100 (1662; Los Angeles, 1963), p. 5.

60. Henry More, "Preface" to *Tetractys Anti-Astrologica*, quoted and discussed in Mullinger, *University of Cambridge*, 3: 383.

61. Mullinger, *University of Cambridge*, 3: 302–3, 596; though there was a committee supposed to issue certificates that the Covenant had been accepted by each man who filled a new vacancy, Whichcote was apparently exempted from this requirement; he also generously gave half the income from his new post to the ejected Collins.

62. Mullinger, *University of Cambridge*, 3: 649.

63. G. E. Aylmer, *The State's Servants: The Civil Service of the English Republic, 1649–1660* (London: Routledge and Keegan Paul, 1973), pp. 29–33.

64. Facts about the judges in this section are drawn from Edward Foss, *The Judges of England* (London, 1857), vols. 6 and 7.

65. *Memorials of the English Affairs*, 4 vols. (Oxford, 1853), 1: 238, and quoted in Foss, *Judges of England*, 7: 243.

66. David Underdown, *Pride's Purge: Politics in the Puritan Revolution* (Oxford: Clarendon Press, 1971), pp. 204, 205.

67. Gilbert Burnet, *The Life and Death of Sir Matthew Hale* (London, 1682), pp. 36–37.

68. Gerald Hurst, "Sir Matthew Hale," *Law Quarterly Review* 70 (1954): 344.

69. Mary Cotterell, "Interregnum Law Reform: The Hale Commission of 1652," *English Historical Review* 83 (1968): 689–704.

70. Evelyn, *Diary*, 2: 475.

71. Martha Ornstein, *The Role of Scientific Societies in the Seventeenth Century*, 3rd ed. (Hamden, Conn.: The Shoe String Press, Archon Books, 1963).

72. George B. Parks, "Travel as Education," in *The Seventeenth Century: Studies in the History of English Thought and Literature from Bacon to Pope* (Stanford, Calif.: Stanford University Press, 1951), p. 279.

73. William Wynne, *The Life of Sir Leoline Jenkins*, 2 vols. (London, 1724), 1: v–vi.

74. John Dryden, *Essays of John Dryden*, ed. W. P. Ker, 2 vols. (Oxford: Clarendon Press, 1926), 1: 56; subsequent citations in the text are to this edition.

75. See, e.g., Arthur C. Kirsch, *Dryden's Heroic Drama* (Princeton, N.J.: Princeton University Press, 1965), and John Wilcox, *The Relation of Molière to Restoration Comedy* (New York: Columbia University Press, 1938).

76. Nethercot, *D'Avenant*, p. 312.

77. David C. Douglas, *English Scholars, 1660–1730* (London: J. Cape, 1939), pp. 64, 31–59.

78. Earl Miner, *The Cavalier Mode from Jonson to Cotton* (Princeton, N.J.: Princeton University Press, 1971), p. 187.

79. Nethercot, *Cowley*, p. 123.

80. Cotton, "The Retirement: Stanzes Irreguliers to Mr. Izaak Walton," in *Poems*, p. 50.

81. Cowley, "Preface" to *The Cutter of Coleman-Street*, in *English Writings*, 2: 262–63.

82. John Lacy, *The Dramatic Works of John Lacy, Comedian*, ed. James Maidment and W. H. Logan (1894; reprint ed., New York: B. Blom, 1967), pp. 194, 201.

83. Cf. Michael West, "Shifting Concepts of Heroism in Dryden's Panegyrics," *Papers on Language and Literature* 10 (1974): 378–93.

Notes to Chapter 2

1. Henry Neville, *Plato Redivivus* in *Two English Republican Tracts*, ed. Caroline Robbins (London: Cambridge University Press, 1969), p. 147.

2. See also Max Beloff, *Public Order and Popular Disturbances, 1660–1740* (London: Oxford University Press, H. Milford, 1938), for smaller scale uprisings. Michael McKeon, *Politics and Poetry in Restoration England: The Case of Dryden's "Annus Mirabilis"* (Cambridge, Mass.: Harvard University Press, 1975), chapters 2 and 4, offers a useful account of plots, allegations of plots, and political dissatisfaction generally during the sixties and his book reveals an admirable awareness of Dryden's rhetorical strategies, his exaggeration of Englishmen's happiness with Charles, and the general fictionality of his political poetry.

3. James Yonge, *The Journal of James Yonge, Plymouth Surgeon, 1647–1721*, ed. Frederick N. L. Poynter (Hamden, Conn.: Archon Books, 1963), p. 192.

4. John Loftis, *The Politics of Drama in Augustan England* (Oxford: Clarendon Press, 1963); Anne T. Barbeau, *The Intellectual Design of John Dryden's Heroic Plays* (New Haven, Conn.: Yale University Press, 1970); Geoffrey Marshall, *Restoration Serious Drama* (Norman, Okla.: University of Oklahoma Press, 1974).

5. Bonamy Dobrée, *Restoration Tragedy* (Oxford: Clarendon Press, 1929), p. 13; Louis Teeter, "Political Themes in Restoration Tragedy" (Ph.D. diss., Johns Hopkins University, 1936), p. 434; D. W. Jefferson, "The Significance of Dryden's Heroic Plays," *Proceedings of the Leeds Philosophical and Historical Society* 5 (1940), reprinted in *Restoration Dramatists*, ed. Earl Miner (Englewood Cliffs, N.J.: Prentice Hall, Twentieth-Century Views, 1966), p. 34; Eric Rothstein, *Restoration Tragedy* (Madison, Wis.: University of Wisconsin Press, 1966), p. 109; Anne Righter, "Heroic Tragedy," in *Restoration Theatre*, ed. John Russell Brown and Bernard Harris (New York: Capricorn Books, 1967), p. 135.

6. Dryden is most notably defended in Louis Bredvold, *The Intellectual Milieu of John Dryden* (Ann Arbor, Mich.: University of Michigan Press, 1934), and Philip Harth, *Contexts of Dryden's Thought* (Chicago: University of Chicago Press, 1968). Cf. John Wallace, *Destiny His Choice: The Loyalism of Andrew Marvell* (Chicago: University of Chicago Press, 1968).

7. Frances Barbour, "The Unconventional Heroic Plays of Nathaniel Lee," *Studies in English: University of Texas* (1940), 115; Thomas B. Stroup and Arthur L. Cooke, "Introduction" to *The Works of Nathaniel Lee*, 2 vols. (New Brunswick, N.J.: Scarecrow Press, 1954–55), 1: 17.

8. Frank C. Brown, *Elkanah Settle: His Life and Works* (Chicago: University of Chicago Press, 1910), p. 69; Elkanah Settle, *A Narrative: Written by E. Settle* (London, 1683), p. 25; Brown, *Elkanah Settle*, p. 26.

9. Adolphus Ward, *A History of English Dramatic Literature*, vol. 3 (London, 1899), p. 399; Loftis, *Politics of Drama*, pp. 23–24; Clifford Leach, "The Political 'Disloyalty' of Thomas Southerne," *Modern Language Review* 28 (1933): 421.

10. Willard Thorp, "Henry Nevil Payne, Dramatist and Jacobite Conspirator," in *Essays in Dramatic Literature: The Parrott Presentation Volume*, ed. Hardin Craig (Princeton, N.J.: Princeton University Press, 1935), pp. 347–81.

11. Milton C. Nahm, ed., *John Wilson's The Cheats* (Oxford: B. Blackwell, 1935), p. 187; this edition is prepared from a MS with deletions and marks for revision by Sir Henry Herbert, then Master of the Revels.

12. I would have to disagree with Geoffrey Marshall's claim that all the protagonists of Restoration serious plays are flawed (*Restoration Serious*

Drama, p. 138). I think his analysis suffers from conflating what I am treating as separate categories of romance and tragedy. At a later point he elaborates upon the meaning of flawed by adding "at least to the extent that they are unable to bring about external or internal harmony" and so concludes that Mustapha is flawed because his selflessness "is not sufficient to heal the suffering of his brother and rival" (p. 191). This notion of an "external flaw" does not seem to me very useful and I prefer to regard a character like Mustapha or Clorimun as exemplary.

13. "Letters of Mrs. Evelyn" (1671) in *Diary and Correspondence of John Evelyn*, ed. William Bray and John Forster, 4 vols. (London, 1854), 4: 25–26.

14. Kathleen Lynch, *Roger Boyle, First Earl of Orrery* (Knoxville, Tenn.: University of Tennessee Press, 1965), p. 67.

15. Ibid., p. 159.

16. Gilbert Burnet, *An Enquiry into the Measure of Submission to the Supream Authority* (London, 1688), p. [B3v].

17. E.g., "An act concerning the King's succession," 25 Hen. 8, c. 22, viii (1533); "An act concerning the succession of the crown," 28 Hen. 8, c. 7 (1536); "An act for the establishment of the King's succession," 35 Hen. 8, c. 1 (1543); "An act for the repeal of certain statutes concerning treasons and felonies," 1 Edw. 6, c. 12 (1547); "An act to restore to the crown the antient jurisdiction," 1 Eliz. 1, c. 1, xxvii–xxx (1558); "Certain offences made treason," 1 Eliz. 1, c. 5 (1558); "An act for the assurance of the Queen's royal power," 5 Eliz. 1, c. 1 (1562). 25 Edw. 3, stat. 5, c. 2 is a more complex statute than my summary would indicate, including also such crimes as violating the queen and counterfeiting. John G. Bellamy in *The Law of Treason in England in the Later Middle Ages* (Cambridge: Cambridge University Press, 1970) explains its complexities and also discusses its relation to developing ideas of sovereignty. Here I am only interested in it as necessary background to the Restoration law of treason.

18. "None that shall attend upon the King . . . shall be attainted," 11 Hen. 7, c. 1, and see A. M. Honoré, "Allegiance and the Usurper," *Cambridge Law Journal* (1967), p. 217, who argues that in spite of later interpretations the original framers did not mean king *de facto* by "king for the time being."

19. J. T. Tanner, *English Constitutional Conflicts of the Seventeenth Century* (1928; Cambridge: Cambridge University Press, 1961), pp. 161–62.

20. 3 *Acts & Ords. Interregnum* xxxiv–xxxvi.

21. Kel. J. 15.

22. Robert Howard, *The Great Favourite, Or, the Duke of Lerma* (London, 1688), p. 24; Howard notes in his preface that he was prompted to write his play when a gentleman, whom he does not name, brought a play called *The Duke of Lerma* to the King's Company. He advised the players to reject the script, but Hart persuaded him to rework the material himself. I see no reason to doubt Howard's statement that he made very substantial alterations or his statement that he changed the character of Maria into a virtuous one. Maria is a chief agent of the moral he wishes to draw from Lerma's story. (Subsequent citations in the text are to this edition.)

23. Barbeau, *The Intellectual Design*, pp. 105-26, also considers this play to have political interest, though she argues its purpose is to establish the following pious moral: "that justice is restored on earth through the instrumentality of lawless, ambitious men who act unwittingly to bring on their own destruction and the success of the virtuous" (p. 106).

24. Louis Teeter, "The Dramatic Uses of Hobbes's Political Ideas," *ELH* 3 (1936): 140-69; John A. Winterbottom, "The Place of Hobbesian Ideas in Dryden's Tragedies," *Journal of English and Germanic Philology* 57 (1958): 665-83; Quentin Skinner, "The Ideological Context of Hobbes's Political Thought," *Historical Journal* 9 (1966): 286-317.

25. George Villiers, Duke of Buckingham, et al., *The Rehearsal*, in *The Rehearsal . . . and the Critic*, ed. A. G. Barnes (London: Methuen and Co., 1927), p. 40. Subsequent citations in the text are to this edition.

26. George McFadden, "Political Satire in 'The Rehearsal,'" *Yearbook of English Studies* 4 (1974): 120-28, has recently argued for more topical political satire, identifying Bayes with Arlington and the two kings with Charles and James. The 1704 *Key* does suggest that the two kings were supposed by some to be the king and the Duke. It is conceivable to me—though certainly not obvious—that Buckingham and his collaborators may have had this in mind. However, to argue, as McFadden seems to, that the final descent of the two right kings from the clouds was intended to show the audience of 1671 that Charles had not regained his throne because of his divine right to it but because parliament "acting as an independent body" had given it to him as "a free gift" seems to me pressing things too far.

27. Edward Howard. *The Usurper: A Tragedy* (London, 1688), p. 70.

28. Clayton Roberts, *The Growth of Responsible Government in Stuart England* (Cambridge: Cambridge University Press, 1966), chap. 6.

29. C. H. Firth, *Dictionary of National Biography*, s.v. "Villiers, George."

30. John Neville Figgis, *The Divine Right of Kings* (1896; New York: Harper and Row, 1965), p. 45 and passim.

31. John William Allen, *A History of Political Thought in the Sixteenth Century* (1928; London: Methuen, 1960), p. 268.

32. Robert Sybthorpe, *Apostolike Obedience* (London, 1627), p. 13; Roger Maynwaring, *Religion and Allegiance: In Two Sermons* (London, 1627), pp. 13, 26.

33. Figgis, *Divine Right of Kings*, p. 137; Roberts, *Responsible Government*, p. 68.

34. George Hickes, *A Discourse of the Soveraign Power. In a Sermon Preached at St. Mary le Bow, Nov. 28. 1682* . . . (London, 1682), p. 20.

35. O. W. Furley, "The Whig Exclusionists: Pamphlet Literature in the Exclusion Campaign, 1679–81," *Cambridge Historical Journal* 13 (1957): 35.

36. See Wallace, *Destiny His Choice*, pp. 207–31, for a discussion of this pamphlet.

37. B. Behrens, "The Whig Theory of the Constitution in the Reign of Charles II," *Cambridge Historical Journal* 7 (1941–43): 51.

38. Lois G. Schwoerer, *"No Standing Armies!": The Antiarmy Ideology in Seventeenth-Century England* (Baltimore, Md.: Johns Hopkins University Press, 1974), chap. 6.

39. George Whiting, "The Condition of the London Theaters, 1679–1683: A Reflection of the Political Situation," *Modern Philology* 25 (1927): 195–206, and "Political Satire in London Stage Plays, 1680–83," *Modern Philology* 28 (1930): 29–43.

40. Teeter, "Political Themes," p. 428.

41. John Bancroft, *The Tragedy of Sertorius* (London, 1679), pp. 2, 4.

42. John Banks, *The Innocent Usurper; or, The Death of the Lady Jane Gray. A Tragedy* (London, 1694), p. 29.

43. Teeter, "Political Themes," p. 428.

44. There may possibly have been an anonymous *Augustus Caesare* in 1687.

45. James Rees Jones, *The Revolution of 1688 in England* (London: Weidenfeld and Nicolson, 1972), p. 122.

46. Sources of this account are in J. R. Bloxam, *Magdalen College and King James II, 1686–1688: A Series of Documents* (Oxford: Oxford Historical Society, 1886).

47. Jones, *Revolution of 1688*, p. 122; Brice Harris, *Charles Sackville, Sxith Earl of Dorset, Patron and Poet of the Restoration, University of Illinois Studies in Language and Literature*, vol. 26 (1940), p. 113.

48. D. T. Whitcombe, *Charles II and the Cavalier House of Commons, 1663–1674* (Manchester: Manchester University Press, 1966).

49. Donald Benson, "Halifax and the Trimmers," *Huntington Library Quarterly* 27 (1964): 119.

50. John Miller, *Popery and Politics in England, 1660–1688* (Cambridge: Cambridge University Press, 1973), p. 161; Miller offers an interesting account, though I believe he too much discounts the seriousness of the threat Catholicism posed to protestant Englishmen.

51. J. H. Plumb, *The Growth of Political Stability in England, 1675–1725* (1967; Harmondsworth: Penguin Books, 1973), pp. 73–74.

52. Quoted and discussed by Gerald Straka, "The Final Phase of Divine Right Theory in England, 1688–1702," *English Historical Review* 77 (1962): 647.

53. "Some Memorials of the Reverend Mr. Samuel Johnson . . . Communicated in a Letter to a Friend, by one of his Intimate Acquaintance" in *The Works of the Late Reverend Mr. Samuel Johnson* (London, 1710); J. Wickham Legg, "The Degredation in 1686 of the Rev. Samuel Johnson," *English Historical Review* 29 (1914): 723–42. (Legg takes an unnecessarily harsh view of Johnson in my opinion.)

54. William Hawkins, *A Treatise of the Pleas of the Crown*, 2 vols. (London, 1716–21), bk. 1, chap. 17, sec. 16.

55. 6 *S.T.* 74.

56. 6 *S.T.* 513–64.

57. 6 *S.T.* 564.

58. 6 *S.T.* 1508–9.

59. John Brydall, *Decus et Tutamen: Or, a Prospect of the Laws of England, Purposely framed for the Safe-guard of the King's Majesty, His Sacred Person, Crown and Dignity, against all Traiterous Speeches, Designs, and Conspiracies, to which are added, Peculiar Notes upon the Judgement in High Treason* (London, 1679), p. 20. Cf. Sir Edmund Saunders's *Summus Angliae Seneschallus* (London, 1680).

60. 2 *S.T.* 359.

61. Hawkins, *Treatise*, bk 1, chap 17, sec. 35.

62. *Works of Samuel Johnson*, p. ix.

63. Kel. J. 71.

64. 5 *Parl. Hist.* 965 (1695).

65. Samuel Reznek, "The Statute of 1696: A Pioneer Measure in the Reform of Judicial Procedure in England," *Journal of Modern History* 2 (1930): 26.

66. William Congreve, *Complete Plays*, ed. Herbert Davis (Chicago:

University of Chicago Press, 1967), p. 351; cf. Maximilian E. Novak, *William Congreve* (New York: Twayne Publishers, Inc. 1971), pp. 122–28.

67. John Bancroft, *King Edward III, With the Fall of Mortimer* (London, 1691), dedication. Subsequent citations in the text are to this edition. Cf. *The London Stage, 1660–1800*, 5 vols. in 11, ed. William Van Lennep, et al. (Carbondale, Ill.: Southern Illinois University Press, 1960–68), 1: 390–91, for comments on authorship.

68. De la Mere [Henry Booth, 2nd Baron], *The Late Lord Russel's Case, With Observations Upon it* (London, 1689), p. 4.

69. N. N. [signed at end], *A Letter from Oxford, concerning Mr. Samuel Johnson's late book* (Oxford, 1693), pp. 17–18.

70. Thomas Hobbes, *Behemoth*, ed. William Molesworth (reprint ed.; New York: Franklin, 1962), pp. 30–31.

71. Charles Ward, *The Life of John Dryden* (Chapel Hill, N.C.: University of North Carolina Press, 1961), p. 196.

72. *Timoleon: or, The Revolution. A Tragi-Comedy* (London, 1697), "Preface." Subsequent citations in the text are to this edition.

73. Nicholas Rowe, *Three Plays*, ed. J. R. Sutherland (London: Scholartis Press, 1929), dedication "To the Right Honourable William, Lord Marquis of Hartington" (subsequent citations are to this edition). See also Willard Thorp, "A Key to Rowe's *Tamerlane*," *Journal of English and Germanic Philology* 39 (1940): 124–27.

74. Eugene Waith, *The Herculean Hero* (London: Chatto and Windus, 1962).

75. Donald B. Clark, "The Source and Characterization of Nicholas Rowe's Tamerlane," *Modern Language Notes* 45 (1950): 145–52.

Notes to Chapter 3

1. "The Husband's Instruction to his Family; or, Household Observations, Fit to be observed by Wife, Children, and Servants" (London, 1685).

2. *An account of marriage, or the interests of marriage considered and Defended, against the unjust attaques of this Age* (London, 1672), p. 17; see also *Marriage Promoted. In a discourse of its Ancient and Modern Practice, Both under Heathen and Christian Common-Wealths. Together with Their Laws and Encouragements for its Observance* . . . (London, 1690), pp. 46–47.

3. Manby v. Scott, 1 Mod. 129.

4. John Newton, *The Penitent Recognition of Joseph's Brethren: A Sermon Occasion'd by Elizabeth Ridgeway. Who for the Petit Treason of Poysoning Her Husband, was, on March 24, 1683/4 . . . Burnt at Leicester* (London, 1684); Elkanah Settle, "An Epilogue to the French Midwives' Tragedy" (London, 1688), Mrs. Hobry was apparently French by birth, but was burned at Leicester fields; cf. another broadside, "A Warning-Piece to all Married Men and Women, Being the full Confession of Mary Hobry," 28 *Parl. Hist.* 782 (10 May 1790).

5. *Reflections upon Marriage*, originally published 1697, quotation from the preface to the 3rd. ed. (London, 1706).

6. Lawrence Stone, *The Crisis of the Aristocracy, 1558–1641* (Oxford: Clarendon Press, 1965), p. 669; Stone, *The Family, Sex, and Marriage in England, 1500–1800* (New York: Harper and Row, 1977).

7. Robert South, "The Virtuous Education of Youth, the Surest, if not Sole way to a happy old Age," in *Sermons Preached upon Several Occasions*, 4 vols. (Philadelphia, 1844), 2: 282.

8. David Ogg, *England in the Reigns of James II and William III* (Oxford: Clarendon Press, 1955), p. 78.

9. Gilbert Burnet, *An Exposition of the Thirty-nine Articles of the Church of England* (London, 1699), p. 288.

10. George Hickes, *A Discourse of the Soveraign Power. In a Sermon . . .* (London, 1682), p. 21.

11. *Lady Alimony; or, The Alimony Lady* (London, 1659), p. [A2v].

12. John Harrington Smith, *The Gay Couple in Restoration Comedy* (Cambridge, Mass: Harvard University Press, 1948), pp. 74, 84; the comedy of 1675–87 he discusses as "cynical comedy."

13. Sir William Killigrew, *Four New Plays* (Oxford, 1666), p. 2.

14. Thomas St. Serfe, *Tarugo's Wiles; or, the Coffee-House* (London, 1668), p. 5. Subsequent citations in the text are from this edition.

15. See Charlotte Bradford Hughes's introduction to *John Crowne's Sir Courtly Nice* (The Hague: Mouton, 1966), pp. 38–39, for comparison of this passage with the Spanish source.

16. Stone, *The Aristocracy*, p. 598.

17. Colley Cibber, *An Apology for the Life of Colley Cibber*, ed. B. R. S. Fone (Ann Arbor, Mich.: University of Michigan Press, 1968), p. 84.

18. Sir Walter Scott, *The Life of John Dryden* (Lincoln, Nebr.: University of Nebraska Press, 1963), p. 90; and cf. my "Studies in the Comedy of John Dryden" (Ph.D. diss., University of Virginia, 1967), chap. 2.

19. Vivian de Sola Pinto, *Sir Charles Sedley, 1639–1710: A Study in the Life and Literature of the Restoration* (London: Constable and Company, 1927), pp. 252–55, 266.

20. Sir Charles Sedley, *The Poetical and Dramatic Works of Sir Charles Sedley*, ed. Vivian de Sola Pinto, 2 vols. (London: Constable and Company, 1928), 1: 113. Subsequent citations in the text are to this edition.

21. See my "Studies in the Comedy of John Dryden," chap. 7, for discussion of these double plots.

22. Thomas Dekker, *The Dramatic Works of Thomas Dekker*, ed. Fredson Bowers, 4 vols. (Cambridge: Cambridge University Press, 1953–61), 1: 30.

23. Chilton Latham Powell, *English Domestic Relations, 1487–1663* (1917; reprint ed., New York: Russell and Russell, 1972), pp. 200–1.

24. William Shakespeare, *The Complete Works of Shakespeare*, ed. George Lyman Kittredge (Boston: Ginn and Company, 1926), p. 359.

25. Hazelton Spencer, *Shakespeare Improved* (Cambridge, Mass.: Harvard University Press, 1927), pp. 45, 276–81; Arthur Colby Sprague, *Beaumont and Fletcher on the Restoration Stage* (1926; reprint ed., New York: B. Blom, 1965), pp. 8–10, 12, 20, 22, 45–46, 53.

26. John Lacy, *The Dramatic Works of John Lacy, Comedian*, ed. James Maidment and W. H. Logan (1894; reprint ed., New York: B. Blom, 1967), p. 384.

27. William Cavendish, Duke of Newcastle, *The Triumphant Widow, or the Medley of Humours* (London, 1677), p. 98.

28. Joseph Arrowsmith, *The Reformation* (London, 1673), p. 17.

29. John Crowne, *City Politiques*, ed. John Harold Wilson (Lincoln, Nebr.: University of Nebraska Press, 1967), p. 134.

30. *An Account of Marriage* (London, 1672), p. 53. This tract seems to be one of a group published in the early seventies: cf. *Reflections on Marriage and the Poetical Discipline* (1673), *Animadversions on Two Late Books* (1673), *Conjugium Conjurgium* (1673), and *Marriage Asserted* (1674).

31. *Remarques on the Humours and Conversations of the Town* (London, 1673), pp. 39–40, 75–76, 80–81.

32. Joseph Fisher, *The Honour of Marriage* (London, 1695), dedication and p. 1; J. Turner, *Discourse on Fornication* (London, 1698), p. 1; Tom Brown, *A Collection of Several Late Petitions, &c. to the Honourable House, viz., I. The Ladies Petition. II. The Batchellors Remonstrance . . .* (London, 1693), p. 1.

33. P. F. Vernon, "Marriage of Convenience and the Moral Code of Restoration Comedy," *Essays in Criticism* 12 (1962): 370–87.

34. *Sylvia's Revenge, Or, a Satyr Against Man, in Answer to the Satyr Against Women* (London, 1688), pp. 19, 10; cf. *Sylvia's Complaint, or her*

Sexes Unhappiness. A Poem, Being the Second Part of Sylvia's Revenge, or, A Satyr against Man (London, 1692).

35. Humphrey Prideaux, *The Case of Clandestine Marriages Stated, wherein are shown the Causes from whence this Corruption ariseth* (London, 1691).

36. George Elliot Howard, *A History of Matrimonial Institutions,* 3 vols. (1904; reprint ed., New York Humanities Press, 1964), 1: 446.

37. William Wynne, *The Life of Sir Leoline Jenkins,* 2 vols. (London, 1724), 1: lii–liii.

38. 3 Lev. 411 (1693/4) and see Charles Viner, *A General Abridgement of Law and Equity,* 23 vols. (London, 1742–53), 15: 264–65; 11 & 12 Will. 3, c. 4 (1700).

39. Stone, *The Aristocracy,* p. 642.

40. *Marriage Promoted.*

41. Sir Robert Filmer, *Observations concerning the original of Government, Upon Mr. Hobs Leviathan, Mr. Milton against Salmaisius, H. Grotius De Jure Belli* (London, 1652) in *Patriarcha and Other Political Works of Sir Robert Filmer,* ed. Peter Laslett (Oxford: Oxford University Press, 1949), p. 59. Cf. Gordon J. Schochet, *Patriarchalism in Political Thought: The Authoritarian Family and Political Speculation and Attitudes, Especially in Seventeenth-Century England* (New York: Basic Books, 1975), chapters 7 and 8 on Filmer, 10 and 11 on minor Restoration controversialists, and 12 on Hobbes. Schochet argues that when he wrote "Hobbes was unique in attempting to derive the father's power over his children from their consents" (p. 241).

42. Locke's distinctions between patriarchal and political authority are discussed by Gordon J. Schochet, "The family and the origins of the state in Locke's political philosophy," in John W. Yolton, ed. *John Locke: Problems and Perspectives* (London: Cambridge University Press, 1969), pp. 81–98. The same essay appears as chapter 3 in Schochet's *Patriarchalism in Political Thought.*

43. 3 Keb. 433.

44. 1 Mod. 127.

45. Bridg. O. 235.

46. 1 Keb. 363–66.

47. "It hath been urged that the practice for these last twenty years hath been that the mercer shall recover in such cases; and that they, before whom it was adjudged, got their knowledge in the best of times, though unhappily they came to be Judges in the worst," said Bridgeman. Cf. Stone v. Walters (1649) where the court decided a wife "was enabled to make a

contract for things needful to her, and that such contract should bind her husband."

48. 1 Keb. 383; cf. Henry Conset, *The Practice of the Spiritual or Ecclesiastical Courts* (London, 1685), who says from the time of citation the judge may tax the husband with the cost of litigation and alimony for the wife (p. 277). John Godolphin, *Repertorium Canonicum* (London, 1678), p. 509, agrees with this.

49. For detailed discussion of earlier seventeenth-century opposition to the ecclesiastical courts see Ronald A. Marchant, *The Puritans and the Church Courts in the Diocese of York, 1560–1642* (London: Longmans, 1960), and Christopher Hill, *Society and Puritanism* (New York: Schocken Books, 1967), chaps. 8–10.

50. Henry Cary, *The Law of England* (London, 1666), p. 59; Edward Hickeringill, *News from Drs. Commons: Or a True Narrative of Mr. Hickeringill's Appearances there, June 8, 1681 . . . with a Protestation v. their Spiritual Court* (London, 1681).

51. William S. Holdsworth, *A History of English Law* (London: Methuen, 1942), 3: 530.

52. Gellert Spencer Alleman, *Matrimonial Law and the Materials of Restoration Comedy* (Philadelphia: n.p., 1942), p. 11.

53. 2 Vent. 14.

54. 3 Mod. 164.

55. 2 Keb. 554; cf. 1 Vent. 42, 146.

56. 1 Ld. Raym. 444; 12 Mod. 244; name spelled variously, "Lungworthy," "Longworth," etc.

57. Robinson v. Greinold (or Gosnold), 1 Salk. 112; 6 Mod. 171; and for summary see Strange in Bolton v. Prentice (1744), 2 Str. 1214.

58. 1 Eq. Ca. Abr. 61.

59. 1 Salk. 116; 1 Ld. Raym. 444 differs on the date.

60. 2 Str. 1214.

61. 1 Chan. Cas. 252. The significance of *Whorewood* v. *Whorewood* was debated in *Head* v. *Head* (1747), where a letter from Sir Leoline Jenkins to Bridgeman was alluded to as explaining the court's intention in the case, but Sir Leoline was a civil lawyer and official of the ecclesiastical courts whose advice Bridgeman does not seem to be following exactly when he invites Mrs. Whorewood to return to him if she is ill-used. The letter is to be found in Wynne, *Life of Sir Leoline Jenkins*, 2: 723.

62. Gilb. Rep. 1.

63. Preq. Ch. 498.

64. 1 Eq. Ca. Abr. 67.

65. 8 T. R. 546.

66. "An Admonition to all such as shall intend hereafter to enter the state of Matrimony Godly and Agreeably to Law" (London, 1671); text first issued by Matthew [Parker], Archbishop of Canterbury; Henry Swinburne, *A Treatise of Spousals or Matrimonial Contracts* (London, 1686), p. 15 (Swinburne was judge of the Prerogative Court at York; his *Treatise* was published posthumously and this is the first edition); Conset also warns against remarriages after divorce and notes that they are "a thing frequently done" (*Practice of the Spiritual*, p. 279).

67. John Cosin, "Bishop Cozen's Argument, Proving that Adultery Works a Dissolution of the Marriage. Being the Substance of Several of Bishop Cozen's Speeches in the House of Lords, Upon the Debate of the Lord Ross's Case," in *The Works of the Right Rev. Father in God, John Cosin, Lord Bishop of Durham*, 2 vols. (Oxford, 1843–55), 4: 492.

68. "The Roose Case: Third Reading," in F. R. Harris, *Life of Edward Montague*, 2 vols. (London, 1912), 2: 327, appendix 1.

69. *Practical Catechism*, quoted by Arthur Robert Winnett, *Divorce and Remarriage in Anglicanism* (London: Macmillan and Co., 1958), p. 89.

70. Harris, *Life of Edward Montague*, 2: 328.

71. Sir Charles Wolseley, *The Case of Divorce and Re-marriage thereupon Discussed, By a Reverend Prelate of the Church of England and a private Gentleman. Occasioned by the late Act of Parliament for the Divorce of the Lord Rosse* (London, 1673), pp. 46–47.

72. John Sprint, *The Bride-Woman's Counsellor. Being a Sermon Preach'd at a Wedding, May the 11th 1699, at Sherbourn, in Dorsetshire* (London, 1699), pp. 13–14; Sprint blames "disobedient wives" for bringing "so much Reproach and Disgrace" on matrimony, p. 4.

73. Alleman, *Matrimonial Law*, pp. 115–18, cites these examples and later ones.

74. *Tom Essence; or, the Modish Wife* (London, 1677), pp. 6–7.

75. Ghosh, ed., *The Works of Thomas Otway*, 1: 60–1.

76. Robert D. Hume, " 'The Myth of the Rake in "Restoration" Comedy,' " *Studies in the Literary Imagination* 10 (1977): 25–55.

77. Stone, *The Family*, p. 502.

78. Susan Staves, "*Mr. Limberham* and the 1677–78 Season," in "Studies in the Comedy of John Dryden," chap. 5.

79. Allardyce Nicoll, *A History of Restoration Drama* (Cambridge: Cambridge University Press, 1923), p. 211.

80. Ogg, *England in the Reigns of James II and William III*, pp. 321–23; *POAS* 5: 193, 439–40.

81. Bertha M. Stearns, "The First English Periodical for Women," *Modern Philology* 28 (1930): 45–59; A. H. Upham, "English 'Femme Savantes' at the End of the Seventeenth Century," *Journal of English and Germanic Philology* 12 (1913): 276.

82. Elkanah Settle, *Fatal Love: or, The Forc'd Inconstancy* (London, 1680), p. 18.

83. Robert Ornstein, *The Moral Vision of Jacobean Tragedy* (Madison, Wis.: University of Wisconsin Press, 1960), p. 171.

84. William Walsh, *A Dialogue Concerning Women, Being a Defense of the Sex* (London, 1691), pp. 66–67. Walsh was considered insufficiently committed to women's cause by the authors of *A Defence of the Female Sex* (cf. Upham, "English 'Femme Savantes'," p. 273) and "On the Author of a Dialogue Concerning Women," *POAS* 5: 7–11.

85. Charles Gildon, *Phaeton: or, The Fatal Divorce* (London, 1698), p. 15.

86. Kathleen Lynch, "Thomas D'Urfey's Contribution to Sentimental Comedy," *Philological Quarterly* 9 (1930): 250; Lynch also discusses *Love for Money* (1689), *The Richmond Heiress* (1689), and *The Campaigners* (1698).

87. Ernest Bernbaum, *The Drama of Sensibility* (Boston: Ginn and Company, 1915), pp. 4–5.

88. Keith Thomas, "The Double Standard," *Journal of the History of Ideas* 20 (1959): 195–216.

89. Anthony Kaufman, " 'The Hard Condition of a Woman's Fate': Southerne's The Wives' Excuse," *Modern Language Quarterly* 34 (1973): 44–45.

90. Sir John Vanbrugh, *The Provok'd Wife* (Lincoln, Nebr.: University of Nebraska Press, 1969), p. 7.

91. Mary Pix, *The Innocent Mistress* (London, 1697), pp. 24, 5.

92. Upham, "English 'Femme Savantes,' " p. 276; Rae Blanchard, "Richard Steele and the Status of Women," *Studies in Philology* 24 (1929): 325–55.

93. Georges Ascoli, "Essai sur l'histoire des idées feministes en France du xvi* siècle a la révolution," *Revue de synthèse historiques* 13 (1906): 50–51; cf. Michael Seidel, "Poulain de la Barre's *The Woman as Good as the Man*," *Journal of the History of Ideas* 35 (1974): 499–508, which offers a convenient summary of the argument, though adds nothing substantive to Ascoli, whom he does not cite.

94. Louis B. Wright, *Middle-class Culture in Elizabethan England* (Chapel Hill, N.C.: University of North Carolina Press, 1935), pp.

465-507; the same material is reviewed in Carroll Camden, *The Elizabethan Woman* (1951; rev. ed., Mamaroneck, N.Y.: P. P. Appel, 1975), pp. 239-271.

95. John Harrington Smith, "Shadwell, the Ladies, and the Change in Comedy," *Modern Philology* 46 (1948): 33.

96. 4 W. & M., c. 9; cf. 21 Jas. 1, c. 6; 5 Anne, c. 6 (1705) dropped the requirement of literacy.

97. Ascoli, "Essai sur l'histoire," p. 162n.

98. "An act to prevent malicious maiming and wounding," 22 & 23 Car. 2, c. 1 (1670); Irene Coltman, *Private Men and Public Causes: Philosophy and Politics in the English Civil War* (London: Faber, 1962); Marchamont Needham, *The Case of the Common-wealth of England, Stated; or, the Equity, Utility, and Necessity of Submission to the Present Government* (London, 1650), p. 5.

99. Conset, "Epistle to the Reader": "That our Ecclesiastical Laws professed in this Land, have lain, and at this instant, do lye under most unjust and severe Imputations, I am very sensible," and cf. *Practice of the Spiritual*, pp. 37, 39, 142, 167-68, 280.

Notes to Chapter 4

1. 13 & 14 Car. 2, c. 1.

2. Sir Edward Dering, *The Parliamentary Diary of Sir Edward Dering, 1670-73*, ed. Basil D. Henning (New Haven, Conn.: Yale University Press, 1940), p. 27 (January 1670/1.)

3. 13 Car. 2, stat. 2, c. 1, v & vi.

4. 13 & 14 Car. 2, c. 4, iii, iv, ix, x, xi.

5. 13 & 14 Car. 2, x, xi.

6. 15 Car. 2, c. 5.

7. Gilbert Burnet, *History of My Own Time* (London, 1838), p. 96.

8. Ibid., p. 126.

9. Dering, *Parliamentary Diary*, pp. 125-26.

10. "An act for preventing dangers which may appear from popish recusants," 15 Car. 2, c. 2, ix; officeholders also had to take the oaths of allegiance and supremacy and to receive the sacrament according to the usage of the Church of England.

11. Burnet, *History*, p. 255.

12. 30 Car. 2, stat. 2, c. 1, iii.

13. "An act for removing and preventing all questions and disputes concerning the assembling and sitting of this present parliament," 1 W. &

M., c. 1, vi, vii. My discussion of the revolution in the following
paragraphs is indebted to Gerald M. Straka, *Anglican Reaction to the
Revolution of 1688* (Madison, Wis.: State Historical Society of Wisconsin
for the Department of History, University of Wisconsin, 1962); otherwise
unidentified quotations are from Straka.

14. *The History and Proceedings of the House of Lords, From the
Restoration in 1660 to the Present Time*, 8 vols. (London, 1742–43) 1:
351–52.

15. Sir George Etherege, *Letters of Sir George Etherege*, ed. Frederick
Bracher (Berkeley, Calif.: University of California Press, 1974), 3 January
1689, p. 264.

16. Straka, *Anglican Reaction*, p. 54.

17. J. P. Kenyon, *The Stuart Constitution, 1603–1688: Documents and
Commentary* (Cambridge: Cambridge University Press, 1966), p. 472.

18. "On the Late Metamorphosis of an Old Picture of Oliver Cromwell's
into a New Picture of King William," *POAS* 5: 149–51.

19. "A Weasel Uncased or the In and Outside of a Priest Drawn to the
Life," *POAS* 5: 250.

20. Quoted in Quentin Skinner, "The Context of Hobbes' Theory of
Political Obligation," in *Hobbes and Rousseau*, ed. Maurice Cranston and
Richard S. Peters (New York: Anchor, Modern Studies in Philosophy,
1972), p. 122; and see also *POAS* 5: 238–56, and Charles F. Mullet, "A
Case of Allegiance: William Sherlock and the Revolution of 1688,"
Huntington Library Quarterly 10 (1946): 83–103.

21. 5 *Parl. Hist.* 756.

22. Quoted in Straka, *Anglican Reaction*, p. 53.

23. Quoted from MS diary in G. W. Keeton, *Lord Chancellor Jeffreys
and the Stuart Cause* (London: Macdonald, 1965), pp. 173–74.

24. Another pamphleteer quoted but not identified in *The Plain-
Meaning Protestant* (Oxford, 1644), pp. 12–13.

25. John Gauden, *A Discourse Concerning Publick Oaths* (London,
1662), p. 9.

26. Sir Robert Howard, *Four New Plays* (London, 1665), p. 77.

27. Harold James Oliver, *Sir Robert Howard* (Durham, N.C.: Duke
University Press, 1963), pp. 6–12, 39.

28. Samuel Johnson, *The Lives of the English Poets*, ed. George Birkbeck
Hill, 3 vols. (Oxford: Clarendon Press, 1905) 1: 214.

29. William Hazlitt, *Lectures on the English Comic Writers*, in *The
Complete Works of William Hazlitt*, ed. P. P. Howe, 21 vols (London: J. M.
Dent, 1930–34), 6: 63.

30. Ian Jack, *Augustan Satire: Intention and Idiom in English Poetry,
1660–1750* (Oxford: Clarendon Press, 1952), pp. 17–18; Michael C.

Seidel, "Patterns of Anarchy and Oppression in Samuel Butler's *Hudibras,*" *Eighteenth-Century Studies* 5 (1971-72): 294-314.

31. Ruth Nevo in *The Dial of Virtue* (Princeton, N.J.: Princeton University Press, 1963), shares this view.

32. Samuel Butler, *Hudibras,* ed. John Wilders (Oxford: Clarendon Press, 1967), 2, 2, 141-42; references are to part, canto, and line. My discussion depends not only on Wilders's notes, but also the more copious notes of the older Zachary Grey ed., first pub. 1744.

33. Various detailed historical allegories have been suggested, especially for the first canto, though Butler denied any particular "Persons of Quality" were meant (letter to Sir George Oxenden, Appendix A in Wilders) and Wilders remains skeptical (pp. xxxvii-xxxix). See Hardin Craig, "*Hudibras,* Part I and the Politics of 1647," *Manly Anniversary Studies* (Chicago: University of Chicago Press, 1923), pp. 144-55; Ellen Douglas Leybrun, "*Hudibras* Considered as Satiric Allegory," *Huntington Library Quarterly* 16 (1953): 141-60; Ward Miller, "The Allegory in Part I of *Hudibras,*" *Huntington Library Quarterly* 21 (1958): 323-43.

34. Nevo, *Dial of Virtue,* pp. 226-27.

35. John Tombes, *Sephersheba; or the Oath-book. Being a Treatise Concerning Swearing* (London, 1662), p. 59 (second sequence of p. nos.); the book is a revised version of lectures originally given in 1636.

36. Christopher Hill, *Society and Puritanism* (New York: Schocken, 1967), chap. 11.

37. Felix Makower, *The Constitutional History and Constitution of the Church of England* (New York, 1895), pp. 434-45; Brian L. Woodcock, *Medieval Ecclesiastical Courts in the Diocese of Canterbury* (London: Oxford University Press, 1952); Carson I. A. Ritchie, *The Ecclesiastical Courts of York* (Arbroath: Herald Press, 1956); Ronald A. Marchant, *The Church under the Law: Justice, Administration, and Discipline in the Diocese of York, 1560-1640* (Cambridge: Cambridge University Press, 1969), pp. 4-5; Elizabeth Mellinger, *Kentish Sources: VI Crime and Punishment* (Maidstone: Kent County Council, 1969), pp. 182-85.

38. My discussion of oaths and perjury is indebted to Sir James Fitzjames Stephen, *A History of the Criminal Law of England* (London, 1883); Sir William S. Holdsworth, *A History of English Law,* 7th ed. (London: Methuen, 1956-66); Sir Frederick Pollock and Frederick William Maitland, *History of English Law Before the Time of Edward I,* 2nd ed. (Cambridge: Cambridge University Press, 1968); and Helen Silving, "The Oath," *Yale Law Journal* 168 (1959): 1329-90.

39. Cf. Peter Hunter Blair, *An Introduction to Anglo-Saxon England* (Cambridge: Cambridge University Press, 1960), pp. 228-35.

40. 3 *S.T.* 1315, 1320-21.

41. 2 Salk. 682.

42. "The ability of every man that shall be impanelled in any inquest or ataint in *London*," 11 Hen. 7, c. 21 (1494).

43. "Perjury committed by unlawful maintenance, embracing, or corruption of officers, or in the chancery, or before the King's council," 11 Hen. 7, c. 25 (1494).

44. "An act for the Punishment of such as shall procure or commit any wilful perjury"; see also 32 Hen. 8, c. 9.

45. 2 Dy. 242b (1564–65).

46. Cro. Eliz. 521.

47. John C. Hogan, "Murder by Perjury," *Fordham Law Review* 30 (1961): 288. Hogan also discusses King v. Macdaniel (1754), in which a group of conspirators falsely accused one Joshua Kidder of being a highwayman in order to get a forty pound government reward; they were convicted of wilful murder, but the judgment was arrested.

48. 10 *S.T.* 1311.

49. Cf. Pollock and Maitland, *History of English Law*, p. 195.

50. 7 *S.T.* 1041.

51. 10 *S.T.* 238 (1684).

52. 8 *S.T.* 550–746 (1681).

53. 8 *S.T.* 681, and cf. 625.

54. 8 *S.T.* 628.

55. 8 *S.T.* 633.

56. 8 *S.T.* 706.

57. Quoted in Silving, "The Oath," p. 1350.

58. Skin. 79; cf. Dayrell v. Glascock, Skin. 413.

59. Pollock and Maitland, *History of English Law*, p. 206.

60. H. L. McClintock, "What Happens to Perjurers," *Minnesota Law Review* 24 (1940): 749.

61. William Hawkins, *A Treatise of the Pleas of the Crown* (London, 1716–21), 2: 46, 29.

62. 7 *S.T.* 1082–90.

63. 10 *S.T.* 1185.

64. 2 Salk. 691; cf. Rex v. Crosby (1693), Holt K. B. 753 and Rex v. Davis and Carter (1694), Holt K. B. 754–55. Emphasis was first placed on witnesses' having been discredited by the punishment of the pillory, rather than by the nature of the crime.

65. Thomas Comber, *The Nature and Usefulness of Solemn Judicial Swearing, in a Sermon Preached July 14th, 1681* (York, 1682), pp. 14–15; this is an assize sermon.

66. Macaulay attacked the justices in great detail; modern scholars

whose special field is not seventeenth-century British history continue to give them a very bad press, for instance, Rauol Berger in his book on *Impeachment*. George W. Keeton, *Lord Chancellor Jeffreys*, is a devoted but not entirely convincing attempt to defend Jeffreys against his many attackers.

67. Alfred F. Havighurst, "The Judiciary and Politics in the Reign of Charles II," *Law Quarterly Review* 66 (1950): 242 (a two-part article, 62-78, 229-52); Holdsworth and Stephen take basically the same attitude. See also Havighurst's "James II and the Twelve Men in Scarlet," *Law Quarterly Review* 69 (1953): 522-46.

68. 10 *S.T.* 1298.

69. 10 *S.T.* 1315.

70. John Crowne, *City Politiques*, ed. John Harold Wilson (Lincoln, Nebr.: University of Nebraska Press, 1967), p. 72.

71. Ibid., p. xviii.

72. Nathaniel Lee, *Lucius Junius Brutus*, ed. John Loftis (Lincoln, Nebr.: University of Nebraska Press, 1967), p. 53.

73. John Robert Moore, "Otway's *Venice Preserved*," *PMLA* 43 (1928): 170-71.

74. William McBurney, "Otway's Tragic Muse Debauch'd: Sensuality in *Venice Preserved*," *Journal of English and Germanic Philology* 58 (1959): 380-99.

75. Lee, *Lucius Junius Brutus*, p. 4, referring to *Discorsi sopra la Deca di Tito Livio*, bk. 1, chap. 16, and bk. 3, chap. 3, where Machiavelli emphasizes the necessity of the deaths to the establishment of the republic.

76. G. Wilson Knight, *The Golden Labyrinth* (London: Phoenix House, 1962), p. 166.

77. Aphra Behn, *The Works of Aphra Behn*, ed. Montague Summers (London: Heinemann, 1915) 5: 72, 74.

78. George Woodcock, *The Incomparable Aphra* (London: T. V. Boardman and Company, 1948), p. 207.

79. Frederick Link, *Aphra Behn* (New York: Twayne, 1968), p. 144.

80. John Wendell Dodds, *Thomas Southerne, Dramatist* (New Haven, Conn.: Yale University Press, 1933), p. 111.

81. *The London Stage, 1660-1800*, 5 vols. in 11, ed. W. Van Lennep, et al. (Carbondale, Ill.: Southern Illinois University Press, 1960-68), 1: 434.

82. J. F. Molloy, quoted in Dodds, *Thomas Southerne*, p. 125.

83. "An act that the solemn affirmation and declaration of the people called *Quakers*, shall be accepted instead of an oath in the usual form," 7 & 8 W. 3, c. 34 (1696).

Notes to Chapter 5

1. Robert Boyle, *A Free Inquiry Into the Vulgarly Receiv'd Notion of Nature* (London, 1685/86), p. 49.

2. Leo Strauss, *Natural Right and History* (Chicago: University of Chicago Press, 1953), p. 82.

3. *Plato V* 483E, trans. W. R. M. Lamb (New York: Heinemann, Loeb Classical Library, 1925).

4. Noted in W. K. C. Gutherie, *A History of Greek Philosophy*, vol. 3 (Cambridge University Press, 1962), p. 114; I am indebted to Gutherie and Strauss thoughout this discussion of the origin of natural law theory.

5. Thucydides *History of the Peloponnesian War* 5. 105, trans. Hobbes, in *The English Works of Thomas Hobbes of Malmesbury*, 11 vols., ed. Sir William Molesworth (London: J. Bohn, 1839-45), 9: 104.

6. Cicero *Laws* 1. 12; trans. Clinton Walker Keyes (London: Heinemann, Loeb Classical Library, 1928).

7. Nathanael Culverwel, *Of the Light of Nature: A Discourse*, ed. John Brown (Edinburgh, 1857), p. 61.

8. Gilbert Burnet, *Some Passages of the Life and Death of the Right Honourable John, Earl of Rochester, Who Died the 26th of July, 1680* (London, 1680), pp. 38-39.

9. Aristophanes *Clouds* 1430, trans. William Arrowsmith (Ann Arbor, Mich.: University of Michigan Press, 1962).

10. Cf. on libertinism, René Pintard, *Le libertinage érudit dan la première moitié du xviiͤ siècle* (Paris: Boivin et cie, 1943); J. S. Spink, *French Free Thought from Gassendi to Voltaire* (London: Athlone Press, 1960); Dale Underwood, *Etherege and the Seventeenth-Century Comedy of Manners* (New Haven: Yale University Press, 1957), pp. 11-39; Maximilian E. Novak, *William Congreve* (New York: Twayne Publishers, Inc., 1971), pp. 42-51.

11. Samuel Parker, *A Demonstration of the Divine Authority of the Law of Nature* (London, 1681), pp. i-iii; James Tyrrell, *A Brief Disquisition of the Law of Nature, According to the Principles and Method laid down in the Reverend Dr. Cumberland's ... Latin Treatise on that Subject* (London, 1692), pp. [b7v], 2.

12. Michel de Montaigne, *Montaigne's Essays*, trans. Charles Cotten, 3 vols. (London, 1738), 1: 115-17.

13. See Louis Bredvold, "The Naturalism of Donne in Relation to Some Renaissance Traditions," *Journal of English and Germanic Philology* 22 (1923): 491-502; Margaret Wiley, *The Subtle Knot: Creative Scepticism*

in Seventeenth-Century England (orig. 1952, New York: Greenwood Press, 1968).

14. 25 Hen. 8, c. 6 (1533). This statute was repealed in the first year of Mary's reign by general words repealing all statutes that had created new felonies in Henry's reign, but it was revived by "An Act for the Punishment of the Vice of Sodomy," 5 Eliz. 1, c. 17 (1562).

15. John Locke, *Essays on the Law of Nature*, ed. W. von Leyden (Oxford: Clarendon Press, 1954), pp. 181–82; Locke's final position is more complicated than this, as we shall see below.

16. Parker, *A Demonstration*, p. 2.

17. Benjamin Whichcote, *Moral and Religious Aphorisms*, ed. Samuel Salter (London, 1753), Century 4, 349; Century 11, 1006; Ralph Cudworth, *A Sermon Preached before the Honourable House of Commons, At Westminster, March 31, 1647* (Cambridge, 1647), preface "To the Honourable House of Commons"; Culverwel, *Light of Nature*, p. 18.

18. Simon Patrick, *A Brief Account of the New Sect of Latitude-Men*, The Augustan Reprint Society no. 100 (1662; Los Angeles, 1963), p. 24.

19. Henry More, *A Collection of Several Philosophical Writings of Dr. Henry More* (London, 1662), pp. 22, xxi, 12.

20. Howard Warrender, *The Political Philosophy of Hobbes* (Oxford: Clarendon Press, 1957), pp. 46–47, 64–71, and passim, makes a persuasive case on this point, though I do not agree with his interpretation generally.

21. *Sodom: or the Quintessence of Debauchery* (Paris: Olympia Press, 1957), pp. 54, 67. *English Works* 2: 9, 214–15.

22. Cudworth, *A Sermon Preached*, p. 26.

23. Hugo Grotius, *Prolegomena to the Law of War and Peace*, trans. Francis W. Kelsey (New York: Liberal Arts Press, 1957), prol. 11, and cf. 39–40; *The Rights of War and Peace*, trans. A. C. Campbell (Washington: M. Walter Dunne, 1901), bk. 1, chap. 1, sec. 10, p. 22.

24. Anton-Herman Chroust, "Hugo Grotius and the Scholastic Natural Law Tradition," *The New Scholasticism* 17 (1943): 101–33; James St. Leger, M. M., The *"Etiasmi Daremus" of Hugo Grotius: A Study in the Origins of International Law* (Rome: Herder, 1962), pp. 45–57.

25. Culverwel, *Light of Nature*, pp. 33, 67; Samuelis Pufendorfi, *De Jure Naturae et Gentium. Libri Octo* (Lund, Sweden, 1672), book 2, chapter 3; Samuel Pufendorf, *De Jure Naturae et Gentium. Libri Octo*, trans. C. H. Oldfather and W. A. Oldfather, 2 vols. (Oxford: Clarendon Press, 1934), book 2, chapter 3; Tyrrell, *Brief Disquisition*, pp. [b5v-b7].

26. Hobbes, *Leviathan* 1, 15, 104; cf. 1, 14, 84, and 2, 26, 174.

27. Cudworth, *The True Intellectual System of the Universe*, 3 vols. (London, 1845), 3:501.

28. See Brian Barrey, "Warrender and His Critics," *Philosophy* 43 (1968): 117-37.

29. Cudworth, *Intellectual System* 3:499-500, 501.

30. Patrick, *Brief Account*, p. 90; cf. also Strauss, *Natural Right and History*, p. 194.

31. David Hume, *A Treatise of Human Nature*, ed. L. A. Selby-Bigge (Oxford: Clarendon Press, 1949), bk. 3, pt. 1, sec. 1, p. 469.

32. G. E. M. Anscombe, "Modern Moral Philosophy," in *The Is-Ought Question: A Collection of Papers on the Central Problems in Moral Philosophy*, ed. W. D. Hudson (London: Macmillan and Co., 1969), pp. 175, 180.

33. Cudworth, *Intellectual System* 3: 514.

34. John Arthur Passmore, *Ralph Cudworth: An Interpretation* (Cambridge: Cambridge University Press, 1951), p. 49.

35. Tyrrell, quoted by von Leyden in "Introduction" to *Essays*, p. 61.

36. Locke, *Essays*, p. 171; and cf. *Essay* 1, 3, 9. Some churchmen like Parker continued to cling to universal consent as evidence for natural law.

37. Locke, *The Reasonableness of Christianity, as Delivered in the Scriptures*, in *Works*, 7: 139.

38. Locke is consistent in his natural law theory throughout his career, though the emphases do change and though the hedonism is more fully developed in the *Essay* and later works than in the earlier *Essays on the Law of Nature*. See Richard Aaron, *John Locke* (Oxford: Clarendon Press, 1965), pp. 31-35, for comments on the influence of Gassendi's hedonism on Locke in midcareer, and also E. A. Driscoll, "The Influence of Gassendi on Locke's hedonism," *Philosophical Quarterly* 12 (1972): 87-110.

39. See John William Yolton, "Locke on the Law of Nature," *Philosophical Review* 67 (1958): 477-78, and John W. Lenz, "Locke's Essays on the Law of Nature," *Philosophy and Phenomenological Research* 17 (1956-57): 105-14.

40. Tyrrell, *Brief Disquisition*, on More, pp. [b2v], 85-90, on Locke, pp. [e6v], 16-17, 209-10, 216, passim.

41. Shaftesbury, *Characteristicks*, 3 vols. (n. p., 1737), 2: 54.

42. Ernest Tuveson, "The Importance of Shaftesbury," *ELH* 20 (1953): 267-99.

43. John Arthur Passmore, "Richard Cumberland," *Encyclopedia of Philosophy* (New York: Macmillan Co. and Free Press, 1967), and see

Frank Chapman Sharp, "The Ethical System of Richard Cumberland and Its Place in the History of British Ethics," *Mind* 21 (1912): 371–98.

44. Patrick, *Brief Account*, p. 11.

45. William Hawkins, *A Treatise of the Pleas of the Crown*, 3rd ed. (London, 1739), chaps. 2–5.

46. 1 Keb. 620.

47. 1 Sid. 169.

48. 3 Keb. 608, and cf. 1 Vent. 293. More detail and discussion of additional cases may be found in G. D. Nokes, *A History of the Crime of Blasphemy* (London: Sweet and Maxwell, 1928), especially pp. 42–52.

49. Fort. 98; in Rex v. Hill a man was indicted for printing poems by Rochester "tending to the corruption of Youth," but Hill went abroad and was outlawed before the case could be decided. David F. Foxon in *Libertine Literature in England, 1660–1745* (London: Shenval Press, 1964) alludes to a 1660 imprisonment of John Garfield for writing *The Wandering Whore* and a 1688 conviction for the sale of *The School of Venus*. The legal grounds of these proceedings are unclear; they are not considered in the law reports as precedents in the later cases I am discussing.

50. 2 Str. 788.

51. 2 Str. 834.

52. Henry Neville, *The Isle of Pines*, in *Shorter Novels: Seventeenth Century*, ed. Philip Henderson (New York: Everyman, 1930), p. 233; as first published the story was supposed to be "A True Relation" by "Henry Cornelius Van Sloetten."

53. Edward Howard, *The Six Days Adventure, or the New Utopia* (London, 1671), p. [A3v].

54. Hazelton Spencer, *Shakespeare Improved* (Cambridge, Mass.: Harvard University Press, 1927), pp. 192–210; Arthur Colby Sprague, *Beaumont and Fletcher on the Restoration Stage* (1926; reprint ed., New York: B. Blom, 1965), pp. 232–38; Jean Gagen, *The New Woman: Her Emergence in English Drama, 1600–1730* (New York: Twayne, 1954), p. 166.

55. Allardyce Nicoll, *A History of Restoration Drama* (Cambridge: Cambridge University Press, 1923), p. 117.

56. William Davenant, *The Dramatic Works of Sir William Davenant*, ed. James Maidment and W. H. Logan, 5 vols. (Edinburgh, 1872–74), 3: 262.

57. Elkanah Settle, *The Empress of Morocco and Its Critics* (Los Angeles: Augustan Reprint Series, 1968), p. 52.

58. Elkanah Settle, *Cambyses, King of Persia: A Tragedy* (London, 1672), p. 59.

59. Cf. Maximillian E. Novak, "Margery Pinchwife's 'London Disease': Restoration Comedy and the Libertine Offensive of the 1670s," *Studies in the Literary Imagination* 10 (1977): 1–23.

60. Sir George Etherege, *The Man of Mode*, ed. W. B. Carnochan (Lincoln, Nebr.: University of Nebraska Press, 1966), p. 44.

61. John Dryden, *Works*, 8: 240.

62. John Banks, *Vertue Betray'd; or, Anna Bullen* (London, 1682), p. 6; subsequent citations are to this edition.

63. William Congreve, *Complete Plays*, ed. Herbert Davis (Chicago: University of Chicago Press, 1967), p. 202.

INDEX